James C. Malin (1893–1979) was a pioneering historian of the Midwest, trained in ecology, agronomy, and social science methodology. His holistic view of human and natural history produced brilliant and still controversial interpretations. This collection makes accessible a broad selection from among his eighteen books and nearly one hundred articles.

Malin's focus was the grassland, Kansas, and local history, which he approached eclectically, "from the bottom up." He drew on plant and soil science studies, state and national census reports, manuscript records, old newspapers, and field research to arrive at historical, scientific, and statistical explanations for human phenomena. Yet he stressed individuality and man's "contriving brain and skillful hand"; his keynote was human ingenuity in adaptation to the limits of the natural habitat. Paralleling the French *Annales* historians, Malin helped rewrite the history of the plains. His fearless mind and methodology influenced a generation of historians, geographers, and agronomists.

A major introductory essay by Robert P. Swierenga, professor of history at Kent State University, assesses Malin's significance for American historiography, locates each of the nineteen selections in Malin's thought, and specifies its relevance.

JAMES C. MALIN

# HISTORY
# &
# ECOLOGY

## Studies of the Grassland

Edited by Robert P. Swierenga

University of Nebraska Press

Lincoln and London

Library of Congress Cataloging
in Publication Data

Malin, James Claude, 1893–
History and ecology.

"List of works by
James Claude Malin": p. 353
Bibliography: p. 356
Includes index.
1. Man – Influence of
environment – West (U.S.)
2. Grasslands – West (U.S.)
3. West (U.S.) – Description
and travel.
4. West (U.S.) – History.
5. Kansas – Rural conditions.
6. Agriculture – Kansas – History.
I. Swierenga, Robert P.
II. Title.
GF504.W35M34    1984
333.74'0978    83-16951
ISBN 0-8032-4144-5
ISBN 0-8032-8125-0
(alk. paper)

# Contents

# Preface

In his lifelong studies of the North American grassland, James Claude Malin integrated the study of history and natural ecology as no other modern scholar has done. Malin conceived of human history as one infinitesimal segment of the time continuum stretching from prehuman geologic time to prehistorical human time and, in the last few thousand years, to historical time. Given this long-term perspective, the historian's task is to reconstruct human history as part of the whole of natural history, past and present. The historian is obliged to tell the story of particular past peoples in particular places at particular times, with the primary focus on the myriad ways in which people interacted, successfully or not, with their natural environment, both changing it and being changed by it. Thus, for Malin, humans always exist with other living things in a truly symbiotic relationship, and it is the historian's role to recount past human events in those holistic terms.

Malin's ecological interpretation of history is as imaginative and theoretically robust as the work of his better-known predecessors Frederick Jackson Turner, who tied the disciplines of history and cultural geography, and Walter Prescott Webb, who wedded technology and history. Turner stressed spatial relationships in human history, and Webb underscored human mechanical ingenuity. But Malin alone included the history of the natural habitat, as well as geographical and cultural artifacts. If "land makes a people," then Malin was correct to study the natural history of that "land." His signal contribution was to show, on the basis of the developing soil science research of the period 1900–1945, that the physical environment of each region of the earth had set parameters within which humans had to learn to live. But within these boundaries, people had considerable freedom of choice. Human ingenuity surmounted the limitations of any physical environment within the wide natural givens. The frontier, or "unoccupied space" in advance of white settlement, shaped human behavior, but man, not land, was the primary determinant. This was true because every ecologic region, in Malin's view, was "complete in itself, a relatively stabilized product of nature" that contained all the necessary resources for successful human occupancy and that was largely impervious to human destructiveness by tillage, cropping, or grazing.

The study of history has been enriched by Malin's ecological perspective. Scholars studying man-land relations can ignore Malin only at the peril of limiting the impact of their work. With the increasing ecological awareness of modern society, Malin's original research provides a theoretical basis for integrating human history and earth history in order for humankind to realize the goal of earth-keeping.

This book provides a convenient entrée for historians, geographers, rural sociologists, ecologists, and all those who desire to familiarize themselves with the essential work of a pioneer social science historian. I have surveyed James Malin's eighteen books and more than eighty articles, and from that huge corpus I have selected nineteen exemplars that illustrate Malin's path-breaking ideas, findings, and methods for studying the Great Plains grassland. Malin hammered away at some of his unorthodox themes year after year, trying to win for them greater acceptance. Some repetition was thus unavoidable, but I have tried to keep it to a minimum.

Part I focuses on Malin's exciting ecological theories and concepts of grassland history, on his critique of Turner and Webb, and on his efforts to develop a value-free geographical terminology. Part II provides a number of case studies of environmental adaptation by pioneer Kansas wheat farmers that portray in microcosm the great interpretive power of Malin's concepts and methods. Part III offers examples of Malin's innovative quantitative methods to chart grassland demographic and agricultural patterns. The social statistical research methods that the Kansas scholar first originated in the 1930s have guided several generations of social science historians and were a foundation for the new social history and new rural history that emerged in the 1960s. The book concludes in Part IV with a bibliography of all of Malin's books and a selection of his major articles on the subject of ecological history.

Malin's unique style is presented here at its finest, largely untouched, with original documentation, tables, and illustrations. A few deletions are indicated by ellipses or, with longer ones, asterisks. Several photographic illustrations were omitted from Chapter 7. Minor cosmetic revisions were made in the text, tables, and illustrations to correct obvious errors and inconsistencies. Malin's cross-references are adjusted to the present book. Annotation follows the form of original presentation. In his books Malin customarily followed author-date scientific form; citations for the selections from those books are here grouped at the end under References. Notes for the other, individually published, chapters appear at the end of each selection.

This collection of James C. Malin's major works was made possible by the enthusiastic encouragement of Pearl E. Malin. Although I did not have the privilege, enjoyed by more than one hundred other scholars, of writing a thesis or dissertation under Professor Malin's direction, or to join one of his famous summer seminars for postgraduates, Malin yet encouraged and taught me through his voluminous writings and by correspondence. Mastering Malin's published works may indeed be more beneficial and challenging, if not as envigorating, as attending his demanding seminars. Thankfully, his inimitable style and verve are imbedded in all his writings. None need miss his insightful ideas, pungent criticisms, and wry wit.

For one's work to be judged useful by colleagues is the ultimate compliment to a scholar. James Malin deserves such accolades, for his writings continue to instruct us.

ROBERT P. SWIERENGA

# Editor's Introduction

*James C. Malin's Ecological
Interpretation of the Grassland*

Research in any field of knowledge depends on clear theoretical concepts and adequate data. In the study of the settlement of the American West, three scholars have provided the basic theoretical constructs on which rests virtually this entire field of knowledge. The triumvirate is Frederick Jackson Turner, Walter Prescott Webb, and James Claude Malin. Turner proposed his frontier hypothesis in the famous paper of 1893, "The Significance of the Frontier in American History." Webb a generation later formulated his environmental thesis in *The Great Plains* (1931), and Malin presented his ecological concepts in *The Grassland of North America* (1947).

All three scholars were natives of particular regions of the West and steeped in its culture and geography. Thus, inevitably, they confronted the questions of regionalism and environmentalism: What is a region? How can one delimit it? What is the significance of man-land relationships? Did one affect the other and, if so, to what extent? As ardent regionalists, their fresh conceptual insights emerged as by osmosis from their particular physical and cultural milieu. For Turner, a native of rural Wisconsin, the Upper Mississippi Valley was the prototypical frontier. The native Texan, Webb, considered the southern, semiarid plains to be such a region, whereas the grassland of the central plains was the locus of the frontier for the Kansan, Malin.

Of these seminal scholars of the trans-Mississippi West, Malin's work for a variety of reasons is least understood and appreciated. Yet he surpassed

his predecessors in perceiving the interrelatedness of physical environment and human occupancy, in the interdisciplinary breadth of his
scholarship, in his innovative research methods, and in his voluminous
publications. Malin devoted his entire career of nearly sixty years to the
study of the low-rainfall central plains of Kansas. As a lifelong plainsman
and a professor of history at the University of Kansas for forty-two years
(1921–63), he tramped and photographed the grassland landscape of the
Jayhawk State, imbibed its folk culture, studied the history of its farms and
cities, and taught its young. Having worked as a youth on the family farm
and as a teenager in his father's hardware and farm implement business in
Lewis, Kansas, Malin learned at first hand the slow folk process of cumulative innovation by which local farmers experimented with new machines,
methods, and crops for dry-land agriculture. "There was no plan before-
hand for these things," he realized later, "but they just fit together. That is,
after they've happened you can see how they fit together. As a historian, I
became interested in writing the history of that area of Kansas."[1] The entire
state of Kansas later became Malin's laboratory. In addition, he sampled
extensively the federal and state manuscript population censuses in the
archives of the Kansas State Historical Society. No one else has mastered
the state's historical literature and research materials as Malin did.

While Turner and Webb readily acknowledged the interdisciplinary
nature of historical study, Malin alone immersed himself in the literature of
the natural and physical sciences as they related to the ecological history of
the western grassland. In six books and several dozen articles, Malin
sought to define the grassland as a unique ecological environment and to
describe the social processes by which man and nature coexisted in a state
of tension. Trained under a biologist, Charles Sylvester Parmenter (1860–
1922) of Baker University, and a historian, Frank Heywood Hodder (1860–
1935) of the University of Kansas, the free-spirited Malin adopted his
mentors' eclectic and unconventional methods. In his own words, Malin
explained that the ecological approach to history included "all the elements that enter into a situation as historical activity, especially facts and
thoughts formulated by the sciences in areas not traditionally recognized
by historians."[2]

Some of the esoteric nontraditional histories that Malin synthesized into
regional human history were land topography, rocks and substrata,
climate, flora and fauna, fire, insects, and even soil microorganisms. In the
words of an anonymous reviewer of the *Grassland* volume, Malin "summarized a whole new galaxy of auxiliary sciences represented by the plant
sciences, climatology, animal and insect ecology, geology, social physics,

genetics, and agronomy." Malin's purpose in integrating the natural sciences with history was to gain greater insights into human life itself, which he believed could not be distinguished sharply from nonhuman history. Ecology, said Malin, "deals with groups or assemblages of living organisms in all their relations, living together, the difference between plant, animals and human ecology or history, being primarily a matter of emphasis."[3]

This wide-ranging capability enabled Malin to view the grassland over long durations of time as a total ecological system. Bison, jackrabbits, grasshoppers, cactus, wild and tame grasses, cattle, and rainfall all contribute to the unstable equilibrium of the region and are significant variables in the endless harmonization process between human cultures and physical environment. In brief, Malin rejected fragmentation and illustrated how to study the complete history of a region, including its prehistory, by drawing upon knowledge from all relevant academic disciplines.

James Malin's ecological interpretation of the grassland provided a foundation for the new rural history that developed in North America in the 1950s.[4] He broke free from the traditional methodologies and concepts that had often limited history to the study of past politics and elites, as derived from written records. Malin studied past human behavior systematically and comprehensively, by going to the field along with the botanist and soil scientist. He sought to understand past human experience as it was actually lived, the style of life and activities of farmers and villagers, their demographic behavior, farming practices, social structures, and community institutions. He considered the effects of economic, political, social, and environmental forces on human behavior as part of the larger picture. Malin's goal was a unified conception of regional history, a holistic history, in which human behavior is the key factor.

Malin's unique historical concepts closely resembled those of his contemporary, Marc Bloch, a founding father of the famous French *Annales* tradition.[5] Bloch did pioneering studies in French rural history in the 1920s and 1930s. Rather than limiting himself to the traditional institutional and legal aspects, he sought to understand the totality of French rural history. No Paris armchair scholar, he roamed over rural France to penetrate the peasant mentality, learn the daily routine of farming, and capture the smell of hogs, hay, and manure. His ideal was to unite historical perspective with local knowledge and experience. He immersed himself in the literature of all disciplines relating to land and agrarian communities—agronomy, cartography, economics, geography, philology, psychology, sociology, and folklore—and he asked "why" questions. Why did hamlets develop in one place and nucleated villages in another? Why were some farmers innovators? Why did crop patterns differ from one area to another? Bloch's innovative approach revolutionized the study of agrarian history in Europe and captivated countless young scholars who continued his work when World War II cut short his brilliant career.

Malin was cut from the same cloth as Bloch, although he had no acquaintance with Bloch's work or that of others of the *Annales* school of scholarship.[6] Like Bloch, Malin urged colleagues to study history "as a whole" and to examine each topic "in relation to the cultural totality to which it belongs."[7] Malin likewise raised the broad issues. Was the grassland a natural environment? Was it a finished product? Or was it ever-changing and never completed? Was the grassland adequate in resources for sustaining human life? What was the process of human adaptation? To what extent did human occupancy change this environment, and reciprocally, to what extent did the environment change the settlers? In answering these questions, Malin turned to the natural sciences, as Bloch had done a decade earlier. Malin's model integrated the human actors into the total cultural setting and especially stressed the adjustments forced upon farmers by the grassland environment. The natural landscape, cultural artifacts, and individual behavior all came under his range of vision, although the environmental forces received more attention than the social forces.

Malin's amazing reach into the technical scientific literature of ecology was not his only accomplishment. Like the French scholars, he also pioneered in the quantitative, local-community approach to studying population changes over time. There are at least two roots of this methodological innovation. Most important is the influence of his teacher, Frank Hodder, who stressed the significance of local history for understanding change in its broader context. A lesser factor, which is discussed below, was Malin's negative reaction to the historical relativism that was rampant in the profession in the 1930s. Like other founders of social scientific methods in history, such as William O. Aydelotte, Malin imbibed from his mentor a spirit of deep dissatisfaction with the unsupported and impressionistic generalizations found in writings on Kansas history. The careful counting of relevant populations on the basis of individual-level data, he became convinced, would show the actual facts and serve to correct mistaken notions and assumptions. Mass figures such as the United States census reports were inadequate. They were based on arbitrary boundaries and masked local differences either by canceling out the behavior of smaller groups in the population or overemphasizing the role of a dominant group. The writing of survey history from "the top down," Malin insisted, "partakes too much of the fitting of generalizations to particular cases rather than arriving at a generalization from the study of the underlying detail." American history in general and population studies in particular, Malin contended in 1940, must "be written from the bottom up. . . . The mass statistics tell only part of the story, and it is necessary to balance one type of procedure against the other, recognizing that both are essential to a complete and balanced treatment of population problems."[8]

Another asset of local-community history, in Malin's view, is that it recognizes the fact that people do not live compartmentalized lives. The units of analysis are small enough that all aspects of human population behavior can be "envisioned as a whole."[9] The problem of statistical validity can then be solved by comparative studies of a number of selected sample communities. Malin's remarkable insights regarding the potential of local-community studies and his call for history written from the bottom up became the guiding principles of the new behavioral historians such as Allan G. Bogue, Lee Benson, Peter Knights, and Stephan Thernstrom.

To provide material grist for his scholarly mill in local studies, Malin exploited a plethora of local serial records that few scholars of his generation deemed worthy of attention. These included land records, probates of wills, church and school records, and "most important of all," in Malin's words, the original census schedules of population and agriculture at both the state and federal level. Based on these sources and particularly the manuscript censuses of Kansas from 1860 to 1925, Malin in the early 1930s inaugurated the first individual-level studies of geographical mobility and interstate migration among Kansas farmers. His key technique was nominal record linkage, which permitted him to follow thousands of specific farm operators from one census to the next.

Malin's research results differentiated between five Kansas farming zones (see fig. 10.1) and overturned prevailing assumptions based on published census statistics. Instead of a pattern of increasing farm turnover, which was the conventional wisdom, Malin discovered a reverse trend: Kansas farmers were highly mobile only during the frontier period; subsequently they became less fluid, and after World War I they achieved a high level of stability. Moreover, the turnover rates in the eastern semi-humid zones and in the western semiarid zones were similar for any given community age. Thus Malin's fresh approach of studying communities in historical perspective by using local records and standardizing for time and place provided striking insights in population studies and laid the methodological base for all future geographical mobility research.

The Kansas historian's innovative techniques also yielded fresh conclusions about interstate migration. To measure the volume and direction of interstate population movement, Malin exploited the rich Kansas state census enumerations of 1875 to 1925, which listed each resident's state of birth and state of last residence. This enabled him to determine rates of direct and indirect, or multiple, migration and also, in the case of large families, to chart the migration routes based on the state of birth of successive children. Again, the Kansas historian was the first to employ the technique of birth-state data in the censuses to construct residential mobility indices. His findings show that the proportion of Kansans who migrated directly to the Sunflower State increased to 60 percent by 1875 and then declined sharply. Moreover, movement into Kansas until 1915 was mainly long-distance, that is, from noncontiguous states. Furthermore, foreign-born residents increasingly displaced the native-born on Kansas farms. Both conclusions, in Malin's view, ran counter to the Turner thesis of successive frontiers and Americanization of the soil.[10] Thus Malin happily contributed to the revisionist critique of the Turner frontier thesis.

A second decisive influence on Malin's work was his strong reaction against the legacy of rank subjectivism that he found among the "new historians"—James Harvey Robinson, Carl Becker, and Charles Beard. If "everyman is his own historian," as Becker claimed in his presidential address to the American Historical Association in 1931, and if written history "is an act of faith," as Beard asserted in a similar setting in 1933, then each historian's reconstruction of the past was a figment of the imagination and thus as valid as any other view.[11] Malin openly rejected such subjectivist thinking and firmly held to the possibility of objective history, within the limits of human knowledge. Systematic sampling, counting, aggregation of individual-level data, and replicable research designs, Malin believed, would restore the necessary degree of objectivity to historical study.

To prove his point, Malin turned to primary manuscript sources, as noted earlier, and quantified the migration, settlement, and cropping practices of the early residents of Kansas. He also immersed himself in the vast local newspaper collection and proceedings of agricultural societies in the archives of the Kansas State Historical Society as has no scholar before or since. From these sources, he documented the folk wisdom by which the pioneer settlers by trial and error learned to farm in harmony with the ecological givens of the plains region.

Despite his methodological boldness, however, Malin refused to accept the logical outcome of quantitative analysis, that of generalizing and theorizing on the basis of aggregate data in order to establish laws of human behavior. The Kansas historian insisted on the uniqueness of each historical situation in space and time and on the distinct individuality of each person as a free moral agent within that particular historical reality. A person "does not follow laws in his behavior," Malin argued, "because within limits, he possesses the power of choice." This freedom to choose leads to unique behavior.[12]

Malin, it is clear, adopted the inductive method of science, but on philosophical grounds he rejected the scientist's goal of classification according to likeness and difference, in order to derive laws of behavior of matter or living things. Man's "contriving brain and skillful hand," said Malin, is an elemental creative force not bound by environmental or cultural determinants. So opposed was Malin to any general theory that might encourage a closed system of thought that he rejected all theories and labels. He even objected when a sympathetic historian described his work, appropriately enough, as an "ecological" interpretation of history. One suspects that the Kansas scholar overly enjoyed his lonely crusade against the reigning historical orthodoxy of relativism in the twenties and thirties. As he admitted in a characteristic understatement: "Being an individualist and a bit stubborn about freedom of scholarship as against abject compliance with groupthink," he insisted that no label could adequately encapsulate his scholarship.[13]

Malin's grassland trilogy, more than his other work, exemplifies his unique scholarship and view of history. Published during a four-year span in the late 1940s, the trilogy included *Essays on Historiography* (1946), *The Grassland of North America: Prolegomena to Its History* (1947), and *Grassland Historical Studies: Natural Resource Utilization in a Background of Science and Technology,* volume 1, *Geology and Geography* (1950). In studying any earth area such as the western grassland, Malin insisted (in the preface to the third volume) that "it is essential to avoid . . . any form of geographical determinism, of holism, or gestalt dicta about the whole being greater than the sum of its parts." The historian should freely pursue his topic in all its aspects: "He has no thesis to prove, or problem to solve, and no necessity of formal organization."[14]

Despite his many disclaimers, Malin's grassland studies did prove a thesis and establish major new interpretations of the midwestern frontier experience. The central thesis of his work was that the agricultural adaptation by European forest-culture people to the treeless grassland environment was a painfully slow and disorganized folk process that succeeded only because of the ingenuity and resourcefulness of individual settlers.

Not geographical space, but the human mind and skills are the cardinal factors in human progress, Malin believed. The physical environment is absolutely determinative only within fairly wide limits of tolerance. Geographical givens set the outer boundaries within which people have freedom to adapt in optimum ways. "The individual is the ultimate creative force in civilization," was Malin's dictum. He lamented the fact that historians and geographers placed "too much emphasis . . . upon space and not enough upon people in time and in the capacity of man to unfold the potentialities of the mind in discovery of new properties of the earth."[15]

Malin's treatment thus enlarged the concept of space to include multitudinous space-time units of limited duration—"partitioned space"—which were the result of ever-changing technological "discoveries." There is no end to the world "frontier," no closed space, because "man's capacity to discover new relations has no known limit." In the essay "Ecology and History," Malin gave the classic formulation of his main thesis:

The earth possesses all known, and yet to be known resources, but they are available as natural resources only to a culture that is technically capable of utilizing them. There is no such thing as the exhaustion of the natural resources of any area of the earth unless positive proof can be adduced that no possible technological "discovery" can ever bring into the horizon of utilization any remaining property of the area. . . . Historical experience points to an indeterminate release to man of such "new resources" as he becomes technologically capable of their utilization.[16]

In short, land *use,* not its *availability,* was the crucial factor. The frontier was, and remains, an open-ended, perpetual process of intelligent use of resources.[17]

A theme related to the openness of history and geography is that the time-space segments are interrelated. All ecological activity comprises a seamless web of past, present, and future. Malin perceived each chronological segment of space-time as part of a whole. Therefore, every vegetation map must be dated, Malin insisted, because plant growth varies, depending on prevailing conditions that are always in flux. Never was there a time, even before human occupancy, when natural processes had produced a final "climax succession," such as the grassland-buffalo matrix in the presettlement prairie-plains, which many scientists believed was a finished product of nature best suited to the climate of the region. Such a concept of a pristine, stable "state of nature" is a myth, Malin believed, and he urged grassland soil scientists to posit a pattern of instability rather than "equilibrium" in the ecology of the plains. Malin coined the phrase "unstable equilibrium" to express this concept of indeterminacy.[18]

With his revisionist view, Malin took issue with the founding school of American plant ecology, that of the University of Nebraska Professor Frederic E. Clements and his foremost disciple, John E. Weaver.[19] The Clements School taught that the grassland had reached its climax after countless natural successions, or adaptations by living species to soil and climate. Human occupation disrupted this steady state and threatened irreparable harm to the grassland equilibrium. Malin rejected this notion of a "permanent climax" and the assumption derived from it that the prairies must be saved from the plow. Rather, he espoused the alternative theory of Henry Chandler Cowles of the University of Chicago, leader of the Chicago School, who held that the grassland was an open ecological system in which vegetation continually changed, depending on climate, microorganisms in the soil, and the activity of plants and animals.[20] No vegetation could ever be stable, and any appearance of stability was deceptive.

When the United States Department of Agriculture in the dust-bowl era of the 1930s adopted the Clements-Weaver interpretation and propagated it in the highly effective film "The Plow That Broke the Plains," Malin wrote a scathing denunciation. He demonstrated from the writings of early explorers that floods, muddy rivers, and dust storms on the plains predated man's arrival and tillage. "There was no such thing as an undisturbed grassland in the conventional sense," Malin argued. "Man's turning over of the sod with the plow is only a more complete process of cultivation of the soil that took place continuously in nature" from the burrowings of prairie dogs, the cutting hooves of buffalo herds, and even the heaving of the ground during freezing and thawing.[21] Likewise, the Missouri River carried heavy silt long before the first plow broke the plains. The erstwhile "clean river" image was a myth. In short, "disturbance is not only the normal condition in nature," according to Malin, but it was "a positive contribution to the well-being of vegetation and soil." For the emotionally charged terminology of "virgin land" and "rape of the land," Malin substituted the sterile historical terms *native grassland* to designate the prehuman era, *domesticated native grassland* for the era of food-gathering habitation, and *plowed native grassland* after 1850 when European agriculture began.[22]

Another key point of Malin's historical perspective on the grassland is that throughout geological and historical time all regions of the earth— whether grassland or forestland, deserts, tropics, polar circles, or oceans— are adequate for all native vegetation and higher life forms within their limits. Human occupants must fit their culture into the natural givens of their environment. Each area is "biologically complete," deficient in nothing; and successful human habitation depends on utilizing the available natural resources to the best advantage.[23] As Malin aptly stated: "The plains country is normal for hard spring and hard winter wheats, the bread wheats, and they do grow successfully where the rainfall is greater than about thirty inches. Western Kansas has a normal climate for the grain sorghums, but it is subhumid for corn. Likewise, white-faced cattle (Herefords) will thrive on the plains where buffaloes were most numerous but cannot compete with Shorthorns in the Bluegrass region of Kentucky." Thus, "an area is never super or sub anything for its native fauna or flora, and it is not deficient in anything that constitutes its natural condition." Malin, therefore, rejected the pejorative words *superhumid, humid, subhumid, semihumid* or *semiarid,* and *arid* in favor of the descriptive words *wet, high-rainfall, mid-rainfall, low-rainfall,* and *dry.*[24]

It is notable that Malin shifted his thinking over the years on several major points. In his early work in the 1930s, when Webb's influence was strong, Malin stressed the need for human adaptation to fixed, stable environments.[25] But later, after reading the geographer Carl Sauer's *Agricultural Origins and Dispersals* (1952) he came to believe that the stress on adaptation smacked of geographical determinism. Malin consciously tried to reorient his assumptions; he allowed that creative human beings enjoyed a considerable measure of freedom in learning to live with their environment, and perhaps to modify it.[26] Even the "natural resources" of a given region are culturally defined by the inhabitants rather than determined by climate, fire, or any "climax formations." Consequently, said Malin, "new skills acquired by man create new natural resources and new opportunities. The process is indeterminate." Thus, in geography as in history, the human mind is the crucial variable. Each landscape in every place and time is unique and subject to continuous, irreversible change, due to the interaction of numerous independent variables—climate, minerals, living species, even human cultural artifacts such as revolutions in transportation and communication. In his essay "Ecology and History," Malin stated his major proposition succinctly: "Each and every place and time is unique and change is continuous, irreversible, and indeterminate.[27]"

Although Malin's major contribution was to meld the methods of geography and history as a way of organizing regional history, his primary interest, as Thomas Le Duc perceptively noted in a review essay on the grassland trilogy in 1950, was "really the relation of ideas to action; studies of grassland adaptation afforded the medium."[28] The primary intellectual issue for Malin was the presuppositions about the nature of the universe that had guided scientists since the Enlightenment. Is this a "Finished World," as the eighteenth-century rationalists believed, or an "Open World," as the nineteenth- and twentieth-century evolutionists assumed? If finished, civilized man must learn to live in harmony with the state of nature and restore equilibrium wherever it has been destroyed. If evolutionary, man must learn to live with "endless transformations within an open system."

Most American scientists, including soil scientists, as well as political and social reformers, whether progressives or liberals, based their thinking on the finished world, according to Malin. He, of course, espoused an open world, although without believing that mankind was the end-product. For if the universe was truly an open system, Malin reasoned, then even humans are not necessarily the terminal product.

Malin made all finished-world advocates his intellectual enemies. He attacked none more vociferously than Progressive and New Deal adherents of the "Turner cult," whose closed-space doctrines dominated American historiography from the 1890s until the 1930s. Turner, in his dramatic analysis of the closing of the American frontier, presented at the 1893 World's Fair in Chicago and in subsequent writings, suggested that people would have to turn increasingly to government planning to preserve the pioneer democracy traditionally safeguarded by the free-land frontier environment.[29] It was Malin's firm belief that adherents of the Progressive movement before World War I and New Dealers in the 1930s seized upon Turner's ideas of closed space as ideological justification for totalitarian planning. Even though they distorted Turner's teachings and created a false Turner legend, they yet used his prestige as a "peg of respectability" upon which to hang their own misguided ideas.[30]

Since Malin's grassland research began in the early 1930s just at the outset, coincidentally, of the New Deal, his strident charges against Turnerian geographical determinism were considered by many historians to be "motivated by political prejudices."[31] It is true that Malin, in the belief that ideas have consequences, linked Turnerian historiography with public policy decisions. Nevertheless, it was his initial research findings based on hard data in the Kansas manuscript censuses that led him to reject Turner's ideas concerning social and demographic patterns of frontier settlement.

Only gradually over a ten-year period (1933–43) did Malin develop his full-scale assault on the Turner hypothesis. He began, innocently enough, with a census study of his home community of Lewis in eastern Kansas

(Wayne Township, Edwards County). Malin presented these initial findings in an innocuous local high school commencement address in May 1933. The community newspaper subsequently published his conclusions serially. Since the "experience of this community did not conform with the traditions of the Turner school," Malin selected a second sample township in western Kansas (Kanwaka Township, Douglas County). The second study confirmed the first, and, as Malin later recalled, this "led to the addition of new samples and finally to the generalized study of 1935 on population turnover." In this piecemeal manner, as the scope of his research expanded and early findings were confirmed, Malin came to realize the larger significance of his work for revising Turnerian historiography. Malin's presidential address to the Agricultural History Society in 1944, "Space and History," represented his attempt to explain that larger significance.[32]

Malin's innovative methods of conducting individual-level research in regional social history, not political prejudices, led him to revise Turner at major points. Happily for Malin, his research findings conformed to his understanding of history as an open world. Robert Galen Bell, a former student of Malin, who in 1965 interviewed him at length, shares the same opinion:

> That Malin has been a trenchant critic of the use of the famous frontier thesis to justify value judgements in favor of a planned society is an understatement. That he has been motivated by his own political prejudices to attack the frontier thesis seems untrue. Believing as he does that an understanding of history must be based upon a recognition of the complex interplay of multiple factors, each operating as an independent variable, he naturally opposes any interpretation which singles out one factor like the geographical determinism of Turnerian theory.[33]

In short, Malin consistently held to his philosophy of history from beginning to end.

This is not to assert that Malin's ideas are above criticism.[34] With seeming inconsistency, he held that historians should assume human uniqueness whereas social scientists properly study aggregates of individuals in order to derive behavioral laws. Nevertheless, Malin himself showed a perennial interest in aggregate analyses and in cause-and-effect relationships. His extensive census research on population mobility uncovered common patterns of group behavior that, if not governed by social laws, revealed highly predictable patterns. Malin never reconciled this lawlike behavior with his conviction that human behavior is unpredictable. He also understood the natural sciences better than his contemporary scientists understood history; yet he unduly denigrated the contribution of the agricultural scientists to the success of farmers and ranchers in settling the grassland.

Malin's statistical analyses of quantitative data were generally unsophisticated, and sometimes he misread his own evidence, as for example in his conclusion that frontier farmers were older than their counterparts in the East, when in fact they were somewhat younger. Malin's Kansans were not portrayed in their ethnoreligious diversity, nor did he follow leads in comparing the behavior of native-born and foreign-born farmers. Indeed, as Bogue observed, Malin's treatment of the evolving agricultural history of the grassland was selective at best, despite his commitment to a holistic history. The process of land-taking, capital formation and taxation, mechanization productivity, and even animal husbandry are largely ignored.

Malin's idiosyncracies were also well known and conspired to limit his influence on the profession. He was a prolific writer, the author of eighteen books and more than eighty articles, but his pedantic writing style and (self-admitted) disjointed organization daunted even his most sympathetic readers.[35] He privately printed by offset lithography, from typewriter composition, many of his most significant books. In the case of his later historiographical books, this practice resulted in part, as he once explained, from the fact that his books "were denied publication through conventional channels." But the earlier *Grassland* book would surely have found a publisher's acceptance, if Malin had persisted after an initial rejection. Whatever the cause, Malin's writings suffer from the absence of a sharp editorial pencil, and their restricted marketing kept them from a wider readership. Malin's place within the historical profession was also affected by his tough-minded disposition. As Bell aptly noted: "Malin was never a man easy to know, understand, or appreciate. . . . A serious scholar, burdened by his times and embittered in his later years, he was willing to forego friendship for research."[36]

This picture may be too harsh. Malin maintained a wide correspondence during his long career, and his letters could be gracious and helpful to younger scholars, as this writer can testify. Allan Bogue, who did postgraduate work with Malin, acknowledged that he "owes much" to the Kansas historian for "his ingenious search for new lines of approach to the history of the grassland of North America." Indeed, said Bogue, "if historians had fully followed his leads, the agricultural history of the grassland could justifiably be labelled today as 'pre-Malin' and 'post-Malin.'"[37] Out of respect for his scholarship and influence on the profession, Malin's colleagues in agricultural history honored him with the presidency of their society in 1943. The Kansas State Historical Society had accorded him the same status in 1941. Evidence that younger specialists also recognized the important contributions of the Kansas curmudgeon is the fact that an entire session of the Western History Association Conference of 1972 was devoted to the "Historiography of James C. Malin," and a number of eminent scholars published a festschrift in his honor in 1973.[38]

Malin enlarged the scope of the discipline of history by including the findings of the natural sciences in the story of human occupation of the plains. To this day, his is one of the few efforts to integrate geography and geology as part of historical analysis. Malin transformed prehistory into history by incorporating events prior to man on the historical time-line of the Midwest. In addition to this vertical extension, Malin expanded history horizontally by bringing into each chronological segment the simultaneous interplay of all forces, natural as well as social. His was truly an interdisciplinary approach. And with the emergence of the new rural history, for which Malin's work provided the foundation, he may eclipse Turner and Webb in scholarly esteem.

Quite properly, Malin is respected as an ecological historian. He first brought the findings of the natural and physical sciences into the purview of the historian, and, conversely, he introduced to natural scientists the historical aspects of their disciplines and the role of ideas in shaping interpretations of their data. It is this synthesis of science, technology, and history—applied in a significant regional setting—that Malin deemed to be his primary contribution. He wrote: "Few scientists are trained in history and social science, and likewise, few historians and social scientists have training in science."[39] This statement is unfortunately almost as true today as when Malin first wrote it in the mid-1940s.

## Notes

1. Interview, Gould P. Colman with James C. Malin, 29–31 March, 1972, p. 4, transcript, Cornell Program in Oral History, Cornell University Libraries, Ithaca, N.Y.

2. James C. Malin, *On the Nature of History* (Ann Arbor, Mich: J. W. Edwards, 1954), p. 27. In college, Malin earned "three equal majors" in history, biology, and psychology-philosophy, and a minor in mathematics (Colman interview, p. 2).

3. Review of *The Grassland of North America, American Historical Review* 52 (1948): 410; James C. Malin, *The Grassland of North America: Prolegomena to Its History, with*

*Addenda and Postscript,* rev. ed. (Gloucester, Mass.: Peter Smith, 1967), pp. 156, 407; Malin, "Ecology and History," in *Grassland,* p. 408.

4. See Robert P. Swierenga, "The New Rural History: Defining the Parameters," *Great Plains Quarterly* 1 (1981): 211–23.

5. Marc Bloch, *French Rural History: An Essay on Its Basic Characteristics,* trans. Janet Sondheimer (Berkeley: University of California Press, 1966); G. Debien, "Marc Bloch and Rural History," trans. Helen E. Hart, *Agricultural History* 21 (1947): 187–89.

6. James C. Malin to the author, 15 September 1973: "I am not familiar with the work of Marc Bloch as a model for agricultural history, although I am familiar with the French geographer's emphasis on regional and other local studies in geography." Malin briefly mentioned the theory of possibilism of Lucien Febvre, another founder of *Annales* (*Grassland,* pp. 44, 265), but there is no evidence that Malin read this important French-language journal.

7. I am indebted to Robert Johannsen for pointing out this quote from Malin's *Essays on Historiography,* in "James C. Malin: An Appreciation," *Kansas Historical Quarterly* 38 (1972): 460.

8. James C. Malin, "Local Historical Studies and Population Problems," in *The Cultural Approach to History,* ed. Carolyn F. Ware (New York: Columbia University Press, 1940), p. 300.

9. Ibid.

10. Ibid., pp. 304–5.

11. Carl Becker, "Everyman His Own Historian," *American Historical Review* 36 (1931): 233–55; *Everyman His Own Historian* (New York: F. S. Crofts & Co., 1935). Charles A. Beard, "Written History as an Act of Faith," *American Historical Review* 39 (1934): 219–27. See Beard's yet stronger statement in "That Noble Dream," *American Historical Review* 41 (1935): 74–87.

12. James C. Malin, "Writing of General Histories," *Kansas Historical Quarterly* 21 (1955): 375. Malin's stress on the larger social whole, while insisting on the uniqueness of free-willed individuals, bears striking resemblance to the human ecology theories of Robert E. Park, founder of the Chicago school of sociology. See J. Nicholas Entrikin, "Robert Park's Human Ecology and Human Geography," *Annals of the Association of American Geographers* 70 (1980): 43–58.

13. On "ecological" interpretation, Malin, *Grassland,* p. 324. Malin's reference was to the article of Thomas Le Duc, "An Ecological Interpretation of Grasslands History: The Work of James C. Malin as Historian and Critic of Historians," *Nebraska History* 31 (1950): 226–33.

On relativisim, Robert Galen Bell, "James C. Malin and the Grasslands of North America," *Agricultural History* 46 (1972), 414–24. Once Malin revealingly observed, "Man is not happy unless he is worrying about something." Malin's major concern in the interwar period was the rise of totalitarianism in Germany and its companion, the "atheistic-existential" social theories and metaphilosophies implicit in modern science.

On individualism, James C. Malin, *The Contriving Brain and Skillful Hand in the United States* (Lawrence, Kans.: Author, 1955), p. 338.

14. Malin, *Grassland Historical Studies,* p. v.

15. Malin, *Contriving Brain,* pp. 403–4.

16. Malin, *Grassland,* pp. 410–11; rpt., in *Contriving Brain,* p. 404.

17. Le Duc, "Ecological Interpretation," pp. 232–33.

18. James C. Malin, "Soil, Animal, and Plant Relations of the Grassland, Historically Considered," in *Grassland,* pp. 441, 466–67.

19. Ronald C. Tobey, *Saving the Prairies: The Life Cycle of the Founding School of American Plant Ecology, 1895–1955* (Berkeley: University of California Press, 1981), esp. pp. 76–154, 191–221.

20. Malin, *Grassland,* pp. 7–8.

21. Malin, *Grassland,* pp. 131–32, 139–40.

22. Colman interview transcript, pp. 108–9, 119, 152.

23. Ibid., 154–55.

24. Malin, "Grassland, 'Treeless,' and 'Subhumid,'" *Geographical Review* 37 (1947): 242.

25. Early in his career, however, Malin had already emphasized group behavior as more important than the physical environment in explaining why settlers left pioneer Kansas communities ("The Turnover of Farm Population in Kansas," *Kansas Historical Quarterly* 4 [1935]: 339–72.)

26. This intriguing insight comes from Bell, "Malin and the Grasslands," p. 418, and is based on a four-day interview with Malin in 1965. In the final edition of *The Grassland of North America* (1967), Malin also noted that he had done some "fresh thinking" and was "prepared to go much further in revision of traditional views than was practicable at the earlier date" (p. 399). The clearest brief statement of Malin's later position is in his very positive review of Sauer's *Agricultural Origins and Dispersals* (1952) in *Agricultural History,* which is reprinted in *On the Nature of History,* pp. 122–25.

27. Malin, *On the Nature of History,* pp. 124–25; *Grassland,* p. 404.

28. Le Duc, "Ecological Interpretation," p. 230.

29. Malin, *On the Nature of History,* p. iii. See "Space and History," *Agricultural History* 18 (1944): 65–74, 107–26.

Turner expressed these ideas in his 1910 presidential address to the American Historical Association, "Social Forces in American History," published in *The*

*Frontier in American History* (1920; reprint, New York: Holt, Rinehart and Winston, 1950), pp. 311–34, esp. pp. 320–21.

30. Malin, "Space and History," p. 73.

31. Bell, "Malin and the Grasslands," p. 423.

32. *Lewis* (Kans.) *Press,* 1 June–6 July 1933; Malin, *Grassland,* p. 323; "Space and History," pp. 65–74, 107–26.

33. Bell, "Malin and the Grasslands," p. 423.

34. For some of the views on this paragraph and the next, I am indebted to Allan G. Bogue, "The Heirs of James C. Malin: A Grassland Historiography," *Great Plains Quarterly* 1 (1980): 105–31, esp. 109–11; and "Farmer Debtors in Pioneer Kinsley," *Kansas Historical Quarterly* 20 (February 1952): 87.

35. The admission is in the preface of *Grassland Historical Studies,* p. v. See the comments of Bell, "Malin and the Grasslands," pp. 424; Le Duc, "Ecological Interpretation," pp. 227–28.

36. Bell, "Malin and the Grasslands," p. 424.

37. Bogue, "Heirs of James C. Malin," p. 111; "Farmer Debtors in Pioneer Kinsley," p. 82. Cf. Bogue's eulogy to Malin, *American Historical Review* 84 (July 1979): 915. Bogue's positive reappraisal of farm mortgage debt instruments was one example of Malin's influence. Malin had earlier reached similar conclusions; see his "Mobility and History: Reflections on the Agricultural Policies of the United States in Relation to a Mechanized World," *Agricultural History* 17 (1943): 177–91. Bogue's emphasis on farmers' behavior, as revealed in the manuscript censuses and other individual-level sources, also owes much to Malin's influence.

38. One of three papers presented to the Western History Association is published: Robert W. Johannsen, "James C. Malin: An Appreciation," *Kansas Historical Quarterly* 38 (Winter 1972): 457–66. The festschrift is Burton J. Williams, ed., *Essays in American History in Honor of James C. Malin* (Lawrence, Kans.: Coronado Press, 1973). See also Robert Galen Bell, "James C. Malin: A Study in American Historiography" (Ph.D. diss., University of California, Los Angeles, 1968).

39. Malin, *Grassland,* p. 326.

PART I

# Ecological Theory
# &
# the Grassland

Ecology is history writ large in James C. Malin's thought. Ecology is the
study of organisms—plant, animal, and human—living together in all
their relationships. History is thus primarily "a matter of emphasis," of
focusing on man's changing role in and impact on his natural environment. The emphasis on human influence in nature is more than incidental
for Malin; it is crucial to a proper scientific interpretation of any geographic
region. Natural scientists of all stripes, Malin insisted, must build into their
theories an historical dimension of long duration that would allow them to
measure precisely the changing impact of human occupance on a
particular earth region from the earliest aborigines to the latest tech-
nocrats. Unless they take account of historical, archeological, and anthropological evidence, natural scientists are prone to suffer from presentism
and to err in their theoretical work.

This problem of cultural relativity plagues not only modern scientists
but also the original white settlers of the grassland. When eastern "forest
man" met the prairie-plains region, his first questions were, "Why is the
prairie treeless, and what can I do to change it?" But the question should
have been, "How can I learn to live advantageously and comfortably in this
environment?" In simple terms, this is Malin's ecological approach to
grassland history. No geographical region of the earth, he believed, is
inferior or superior to any other. Each is completely sufficient in itself and
contains adequate natural resources for human habitation, provided the

people have the necessary technological tools and skills to exploit them. "Natural resources can not be exhausted until man's contriving brain and skillful hand are exhausted" (*Grassland of North America,* p. 474).

In any geographical region, Malin held, there is ecological competition over time between two or more human cultures, in the same way that plants and animals compete, with the ecologically stronger (or more technologically advanced) invading the earth area of the weaker. Each cultural invasion brings new technologies that release resources that were latent under the displaced culture. But, whether superior or not, every occupant of society depends upon nature and natural forces and must learn to live in relation with plants, animals, and fellow humans.

Historically, Malin portrayed the cultural invasions as aboriginal and then civilized. The civilized invasions began with the Mediterranean-centered culture shifting to northwestern Europe during the medieval era, and then moving to an Atlantic-centered pivot of world power in the sixteenth century. Under the influence of mechanized power in the nineteenth century, the invasion shifted to the interior grassland of North America—the breadbasket of the world. Although Malin believed the advent of the air age would cause power to shift to a polar axis, he underestimated the significance of American grain in world affairs. Grain from the American grassland has become more central to modern civilization than oil. When the Kansas pioneers struggled to perfect suitable wheat varieties in the 1870s and 1880s, little could they imagine a future time when their efforts would be so crucial to global survival.

CHAPTER 1

# The Grassland
# of North America:

*Its Occupance and the Challenge*
*of Continuous Reappraisals*

[In this chapter, written in the mid-1950s, James Malin offers his mature conclusions about the nature of the grassland, its economic development, and the use of its strategic geopolitical importance in the twentieth century. He considers problems of definition and conceptualization as well. Ecologists in the early twentieth century differed sharply in their attempts to draw the boundaries of the grassland and to explain its unique vegetational cover and semiaridity. Malin pointedly rejects the view that human occupance has been destructive of a perfected and completed environment. He calls on scholars to consider geological, anthropological, and historical evidence before and after European settlers occupied it. Only such a before-and-after analysis will provide a clear picture of the impact of human occupance.]

## The Problem of Definition

Any attempt at regional definition of a portion of earth space involves time as one of the determining criteria. Also, in view of the fact that the term *grassland* has been designated as the term descriptive of the region proposed for study, that selection implies that the definition is in terms of vegetational cover. As plant growth varies with total prevailing conditions, both temporary and long term, every vegetational map has to be dated. For some areas conditions have been so decisive that over long periods of time no major variation has occurred. In transition zones between such relatively stabilized nuclear areas, the vegetational cover has fluctuated to a greater or lesser degree with the prevailing variability of environment. Extremes of moisture and temperature operated differently upon each type of vegetation as well as upon particular species. As between trees and grass, trees may expand their coverage over a period favorable to their growth and then suffer a severe setback, or even destruction, by an extreme of drought and heat or extreme cold; such weakened woody growth as may have survived may be finished off by disease or insect enemies. In addition, we know that destruction from fire caused by lightning took its toll.[1] Added to these hazards were those introduced by man, primitive and modern, particularly the use of fire. The factor of fire has been little understood and has been subject to much exaggeration as well as lack of discrimination. Generalization is always dangerous and nowhere more so than on the matter of fire and vegetation. The variables are too numerous: time and method of using fire, hot or cold, variations in response to fire of different types of vegetation, the several species of grasses and of woody growth.

These matters are not merely theoretical, although they strike at the very foundations of the ecologists' concepts of succession and climax. They raise an honest doubt as to whether the idea of climax vegetation is even legitimate or of practical value. At any rate, the idea needs restatement based upon fresh thinking. Possibly the term *steady state* recently introduced into soil-science literature might be open to less objection because it is not yet freighted with so many unwarranted overtones, implications, and inferences.

Gilpin (1860) compared the European and the North American continents to a bowl: Europe, a bowl turned upside down, therefore high in the middle and sloping to the sea in all directions; North America, a bowl turned right side up, a rim around the outside and great valleys in the interior, closed off from free atmospheric circulation from the seas. North America had in fact a double rim on the west and on the south of 49° north latitude. This double rim encompassed the Great Basin area, mostly moist desert; at the north the Palouse prairie, in the middle the sagebrush desert, and at the south the Larrea Desert. The moist desert permitted some grasses, and this, therefore, in a limited sense made it a grassland.

The Rocky Mountains continental divide, however, was the major physical feature of the interior. It formed a barrier separating all west of it from the great interior valleys whose rivers emptied northward into the Arctic waters, eastward into the Atlantic through the St. Lawrence gap in the eastern rim, and southward into the Gulf of Mexico. The high point of the three watersheds was the nearly level plain of the Dakotas and Minnesota, modified by the glaciation of the Pleistocene.

Geologically speaking, all this was the work of comparatively recent time. The Appalachian Revolution formed the mountains of that name, the eastern rim of the American bowl, during Permian time. The Rocky Mountains were formed by the Laramide Revolution of late and post-Cretaceous time, but the Cascadian Revolution of Pleistocene time completed the Pacific coastal rim. The Mississippi Valley proper was largely Pennsylvanian (Later Carboniferous); parts of east-central Kansas, much of Oklahoma, and northern Texas were Permian; and the northwest of these areas were Cretaceous and Tertiary formations. However, much of the entire surface was reworked during the Pleistocene by glaciation, combined with winds and water.[2] Cut off from ocean moisture on the west by the double rim of mountains, the moisture of this area east of the continental divide is derived from warm, moist air masses moving northward from the Gulf of Mexico to meet cold, dry air masses from the Canadian plain; the whole moves eastward. Thus, close to the mountain barrier the annual rainfall is scanty, increasing somewhat to the eastward, but highly variable within the unique continental interior (Borchert, 1950).

The geologists who dealt with the rocks of later geological time represented in the central part of this grassland commented upon their relative softness, which meant that, where exposed, they were subject to rapid erosion; most of them were covered by unconsolidated Pleistocene deposits. Few of the streams but were turbid. Hayden recorded that water in the several tributaries of the Missouri River began to clear only above the meridian of the mouth of the Musselshell (1863, chap. xii). The high country received an annual average rainfall of 10–25 inches. A rhetorical question that may be worth pondering is what would happen in the way of erosion if the Great Plains area should be visited with an annual average rainfall of 40–50 inches. The fact is that the scanty rainfall of the area constitutes its major value to the occupying human culture.

The "natural" properties of the vegetation of the Mississippi Valley east of the river itself were long a subject of disagreement mixed with a degree of mystery (Adams, 1902a, 1902b; Transeau, 1935). Shaler (1889a, 1889b, 1891a, 1891b) considered the prairie condition of much of the country to be the consequence of fire used after about A.D. 1000. Interested particularly in Kentucky history, he suggested that, if European intervention had been delayed another five hundred years, the prairie might have extended as far east as the Appalachian Mountains. He had been impressed particularly by the excavations he had made around the salt springs at Big Bone Lick, Boone County, Kentucky, which revealed a succession of deposits from glacial times to the date of his work. In Mississippi, Hilgard (1860, pp. 349, 361–62) contrasted the vegetational status of parts of that area as the white man had received it from the hands of the Indians with its condition in 1860: a well-grassed, longleaf-pine savanna versus a country denuded of both trees and grass.

In the northern Ozark country west of the Mississippi River, Beilman and Brenner (1951) emphasized "the recent intrusion of forests in the Ozarks" during historic time. The invasion of trees dated from the time that the use of fire by the natives was curtailed and virtually eliminated. The rapid spread of woody growth in eastern Kansas and Nebraska during the first decade under white settlement was the subject of particular comment in 1867 by Bayard Taylor. So far as he described what he saw of the spread of woody growth at the expense of grass, his account was a significant document. A syllogistic conclusion from these last two examples is to be avoided, however. Only in some of the terrain most favorable to trees could timber have grown to maturity for marketable lumber, especially in eastern Kansas and Nebraska. Even in the stream bottoms, the oak-hickory-walnut combination disappeared west of 97° west longitude (Fort Riley and Council Grove), or at about the western boundary of the tall-grass country.

In the mid-latitudes west of the hundredth meridian the short grasses, the buffalo *(Buchloë dactyloides)* and the blue grama *(Bouteloua gracilis)*, were characteristic. Between 97° and 100° west longitude in this area the vegetation was conspicuously mixed and represented species from both the tall-grass and the short-grass areas. There was wide variation in accord with topography and soil. Two strips of sandy outcrops in Oklahoma and northern Texas produced the Cross Timbers which ran generally north and south. Sand-dune country along the Cimarron, south of the Arkansas and north of the Platte rivers, grew bunch grasses. At the extreme north the needle grasses *(Stipa)* predominated, and at the south the mesquite grasses *(Hilaria)* were characteristic. Variety was more conspicuous than were the uniformities emphasized by some of the plant ecologists.

The soils formed in the tall-grass area were mostly on the acid side, while those west of about 97° or 98° west longitude were alkaline, a characteristic of so-called "arid soils" first explained by Hilgard (1892). The scanty rainfall and the absence of leaching, which accounted for alkalinity, also contributed to the explanation of the phenomenal fertility of these grassland and desert soils.

## On the Nature of Grassland Instability:
## Problem of Conceptual Orientation

Whenever and wherever a discussion is proposed of man-earth relations, or of man-food relations, certain fundamental conceptual barriers usually tend to block a free and effectual meeting of minds about even the nature of the problem. One of these is the assumption, tacit or explicit, that, as differentiated from plants and other animals, man's relations with the earth and all its properties are always destructive. A second barrier, which is really a corollary of the first, is that the imperative responsibility of any student of these matters is to provide the bases for restoring what man, especially "civilized" man, has supposedly destroyed. The overtones, if not the explicit assumption, are those of urgency of decision and of action to forestall disaster. The time scale of the geologist and the anthropologist is essential to maintain perspective on the area in question which has been "destroyed" repeatedly, both before and since the appearance of man, and is now the abode of man. The grassland of North America is conspicuously the product of destruction, and, as applied to this problem, destruction and creation are merely different aspects of the same thing. All areas of the earth's surface present a similar process to challenge the curiosity and understanding of men, but possibly a grassland reveals to the observation of contemporary men a more direct opportunity to study certain of the forces actively at work than do some other areas.

As the first draft of this paper was being written, March 11, 1955, a thermonuclear bomb had just been exploded in the Nevada desert. Afterward, red dust, falling over Baltimore, Maryland, some 2,200 miles eastward, aroused fear of radioactive fall-out from the explosion. In undertaking to allay that alarm by assuring the public that the red particles were nothing more dangerous than red dust blown from the Texas range country, the Weather Bureau inadvertently created another alarm about the destruction of the Great Plains by dust storms, supposedly caused by overgrazing and by plowing up the grass for wheat, cotton, and sorghum. Man is not happy unless he is worrying about something.

The Great Plains dust storms are a case in point that illustrate the problem and its overtones—the immediate push-button reaction in terms of a supposed solution to dust storms—to restore the Great Plains to their "original" grassland equilibrium as supposedly enjoyed in the state of nature. According to this stereotype, aboriginal man was a superior being, endowed with the wisdom of nature and of nature's God of the so-called "Enlightenment" of the eighteenth century—only civilized man was evil.

Of course, not everyone reacted to the Weather Bureau's explanation in this manner, but this generalized response was more inclusive than it should have been, even among people in possession of some specialized knowledge about the subject.

The red dust that fell over Baltimore had its determinable origin in Permian time, hot and dry, during which beds of gypsum and salt were deposited, along with the materials from which the red soils of northern Texas and western Oklahoma were derived. The restoration philosophy does not propose to restore Permian conditions or those more favorable to prolific growth of vegetation which laid down the Pennsylvanian, Cretaceous, or Tertiary coal fields. There is no intent here merely to be facetious. If some past condition must be restored, why not choose that most favorable to present desires? Is it any more possible to restore less remote than more remote time conditions? Are not all such changes in space and time irreversible? Each space-time situation is the product of a unique combination of factors which never can be brought together again.

Early interpretations of the geological history of Pleistocene time as applied to the area east of the Rocky Mountains were oversimplified generalizations. Johnson's monographs (1901, 1902) were the most influential and, from the standpoint of geological history, represented the Great Plains as having been formed from debris washed out from the Rocky Mountains and thereafter undisturbed, except as it was eroded on either side and cut through from west to east at its northern end by such rivers as the Platte, the Republican, the Arkansas, the Canadian, and the Red. But that oversimplified view of the stability of the area has been disproved conclusively by Pleistocene research and archeological excavation, separately and in cooperation, during the second quarter of the present century. Instead of having been cut once, it was found that a large part of the Great Plains had been eroded and redeposited several times. Aboriginal village sites were excavated which revealed a succession of occupations of identical spots, separated by varying thicknesses of wind-blown material. Also, even on the high ridges of eastern Kansas south of the glaciated area, a large portion of the current soils are derived from loessal materials.

The stereotyped formula for soil formation pictured by Marbut (1936), in the Department of Agriculture's *Atlas of American Agriculture,* divided the soil body into four horizons: A, B, C, and D—the D horizon being unweathered rock. A stabilized, soil-forming process was represented as being found in the weathering of rock at the bottom as fast as erosion removed top soil. Thus, soil was supposedly formed normally from the bottom up. Whatever the degree of validity of that formula as a generalization, it has comparatively little applicability to the grassland, where the soils are derived so extensively from material transported by wind, water, and glacier. The soil material is added at the top as well as being eroded from the top. More often than is realized, the additions are in excess of the subtractions. The red dust that worried Baltimore in March, 1955, was only a demonstration of the continuance of Pleistocene geological and soil-forming processes actively at work in unbroken sequence. Mature soils in the sense of Marbut's soil stereotype can scarcely be expected. The same observations apply to the plant ecologists' stereotype of plant succession and climax. They are constructs of the mind, not realities, and never have been realities.

A further emphasis upon the absence of a stabilized condition in the grassland must be focused upon the period of about three centuries between the first arrival of Europeans into the interior of America and the middle of the nineteenth century, when the actual displacement of the Indians by white men began. Two changes of conditions occurred during that interval that were revolutionary in their effects upon Indian culture: the introduction of the horse and the change of location of many tribes. The Sioux, in part at least a forest people, were pushed southwestward into the northern grassland, the last stage in that process being completed after the New Ulm, Minnesota, massacre of 1862. Both of these revolutionary changes in the cultural pattern of what are usually called "Plains" Indians were too recent and too sudden to represent a stabilized culture in equilibrium with environment.

The question does not appear to occur to historians that the Indian culture might have been headed for a major crisis, possibly disaster, even if displacement by white culture had not intervened to give disaster a different form as well as to provide the Indian with a good alibi. In fact, there is reason to assert that these Indian cultures were already off-balance and were running into trouble prior to any definite "pressure" being placed upon them by the actual invasion of the area and their displacement by white men. Proof of such an assertion would be difficult, and, in a strict sense, possibly it is not subject to proof. But at the same time the opposite, which is the orthodox assumption upon which most history has been written, presents even greater difficulties. A mere unquestioned acceptance of an unproved assumption does not constitute proof, regardless of the penalties imposed upon those who refuse to conform to the requirements of orthodoxy. In any case, the conditions prevailing in the grassland interior during the century from 1750 to 1850 were anything but the eighteenth-century ideal "state of nature."

Proof is yet forthcoming that imitation of the Indian culture would have been a safe course. But under no circumstances could such a course have prevented dust storms in this grassland. No more vivid description of a dust storm has been recorded than that of Isaac McCoy, written on the spot in what is now north-central Kansas during the fall of 1830 (not 1930),[3] when the so-called "native Plains Indians" were still in full possession. And dust storms in Kansas (1850–1900) have been described from contemporary records by the present writer. No more brazen falsehood was ever perpetrated upon a gullible public than the allegation that the dust storms of the 1930s were *caused* by "the plow that broke the Plains."

### Railroads and Land-Mass Power

The United States completed legal possession of the mid-latitude grassland of North America (between the forty-ninth parallel and the Rio Grande) during the late 1840s. This made of the United States a two-front nation, facing both the Atlantic and the Pacific oceans, and laid the basis for a claim of right to a voice in the affairs of both the Atlantic and the Pacific systems. At that particular time in modern history the possession of the mid-latitude portion of the land mass of North America was fraught with a peculiar significance and one that has not been adequately interpreted. The power lent to this geographical position, and to the United States as its possessor, was for a duration of but one hundred years, since which the whole situation has changed. The greater part of that century was the century of world peace (1814–1914) and a century in which steam railroads virtually monopolized the communication systems of land-mass interiors.

The new series of world wars since 1914, air communication, and atomic bombs have changed basic relationships. The point is stressed here that the power vested in geographical position is held only on temporary loan and is not inherent in geographical position per se. The power wielded by a geographical site changes with the cultural technology that uses it. It is not the purpose of this chapter to explore the ramifications of these facts from the standpoint of world history, but what is said here about the grassland of North America must be envisioned in such a world perspective in order to have any particular meaning.

Down through the centuries, when the Western world faced the Mediterranean Sea and, after 1492, the North Atlantic Ocean, power was wielded through water communications. So long as land communications were dependent upon the muscle power of men and animals, costs of interior transport of heavy commodities were prohibitive. Economies of water transport did not extend to upstream navigation of the great rivers that drained continental interiors. The steam locomotive operating on iron railroads changed all this, because even the steamboat operating against the current of great rivers could reach only limited interior parts.

Prior to the steam railroad, penetration of the interior of the North American continent had followed water-communication systems. Penetration of the interior country from any water-based point was limited by the prohibitive costs of muscle power. The exceptions only tend to highlight the rule. Large areas not served by water were bypassed in the settlement process. Conspicuously, there was no connected frontier line in the Turner tradition; instead, scattered water-based diffusion centers served the land-mass interior areas. This applied particularly to the country east of the Mississippi River. West of that stream the diminished rainfall and the number and navigability of streams rendered water-based penetration of the grassland relatively unimportant for the area as a whole. By the early 1850s, in the state of Missouri, the argument was made that the available land accessible by water was already virtually taken up. To occupy and to develop the remainder of Missouri, railroads would have to be built. In Kansas, where there were no navigable rivers, and which was organized and opened to settlement in 1854, the issue was explained explicitly by Robinson (1859). Without railroads, corn at Lawrence, thirty to forty miles from the Missouri River, was worth nothing for sale on the Missouri River markets, because the cost of carriage by animal power equaled the normal market price. The steam railroad not only made the grassland a grain-growing area but also provided a structure for its livestock economy. It made possible also the marketing of the Pacific Coast fruits of California and the Northwest at the population centers of the East. So much for the grassland and its occupance in its own right. Comparatively, however, during the period of nearly a century of steam-railroad dominance of communication in continental interiors, by coincidence, the United States was the only great land-mass state that was in a position to capitalize fully upon this unique advantage.

## Commercial Economies

In approaching the study of the history of the commercial economies of the grassland, certain prerequisites are imperative. Because the grassland possessed environmental peculiarities quite unlike the conditions of the forest, European-American culture with its forest background approached it with an unconscious ecological outlook quite foreign to the require-

ments of life under the strange conditions that had produced a grassland.
Regardless of what the origin of the grassland may have been, the fact
remained that conditions had produced grass there and not forest. Again,
regardless of origins, occupance must be effected in terms of grass, not of
forest. Still again, regardless of origins, the potential capacities of the grassland had to be tested by the new occupants to determine what they were.
There were no precedents for European-American culture, which was
derived predominantly from the British Isles and northern Europe. The
first obligation of the historian in studying this particular state of occupance is to determine the total body of knowledge and the ecological
outlook these people possessed at the outset of the invasion of the grassland, regardless of whether it be called "science" or "folk thought." Next
on this theme of knowledge and attitudes must be traced the growth and
accumulation of the total fund of information and the transformation of
attitudes. The record is not in the nature of a straight-line growth but is one
of highly irregular pattern, if pattern there be, and of many false starts and
bypaths. Only in large perspective can it appear to represent anything like a
consistent and reasoned structure of thought about man and the earth. Too
often the tendency appeared to insist upon simple answers and to create
stereotypes, and nowhere more conspicuously than in the sciences, theoretical and applied; and stereotypes interfere with understanding.

An approach to the grassland from the standpoint of the history of
agricultural economies must necessarily emphasize the range-livestock
industry and field-crop production. The tall-grass area to the eastward presented relatively little difficulty to the westward extension of traditional
forest man's livestock and crops: cattle, hogs, sheep, corn, oats, and soft
wheats. West of the strictly tall-grass area the issues were increasingly challenging. Westward toward the Rocky Mountains, rainfall diminished and
elevation increased. Also, the north-south latitudinal range was greater and
imposed wider variability in temperature and photoperiodicity. Domesticated livestock and field crops introduced into the area could scarcely be
expected to possess equally the capacity to exhibit their full potentials, or
even to survive, in all parts of so extended a geographical space. Livestock
presented lesser difficulties in these matters than field crops, but, with
more extensive and sounder scientific information, greater emphasis was
being placed upon specialized breeds of livestock for each area and
purpose.

The history of the livestock industry in the North American grassland
has never been told in a comprehensive manner or with objectivity and
perspective. Besides the bias of a particular frame of reference which viti-

ates the standard accounts, the basic research for much, if not most, of a comprehensive history is yet to be done. The past of the livestock industry in all its aspects needs to be written as a whole without pretense of telling the whole of the past.

The particular frame of reference which distorts the history of the range-livestock industry is the result of undue emphasis upon the Texas influence and upon cattle. Of course, Texas has never been noted for modesty. According to United States history, the United States annexed Texas, but, according to Texas history, Texas annexed the United States. That is the Texas contribution to the generalized theory of relativity.

When Texas "brags," of course it is done facetiously, and each "brag," bigger than its predecessor, is expected to bring a hearty laugh. Nevertheless, there is a serious side to the Texas exaggeration that has left an indelible impress upon the writing of the history of the whole western area of the United States and especially upon the history of the livestock industry and upon land-utilization policies. Webb's *The Great Plains* (1931) brought those elements together within the covers of one book in such a form as to give them a wide currency, if not influence. It incorporated the Johnson geological interpretations of the High Plains (see pp. 10–17, 419–22) with the combined views of the Powell report on arid lands and the Johnson High Plains report on land utilization. All this fitted neatly into the "big cattleman's" view of the type of society that should monopolize the area and keep it in grass. The erroneous view of Johnson on Pleistocene geological history of the Plains is no longer a matter of doubt. Unfortunately for accurate thinking, the social philosophies of both Powell and Johnson, especially the former, have gained an acceptance that is remarkably uncritical of geographical determinism and its consequential regimentation of society.

Among the merits of the Powell report on arid lands was the fact that he did recognize that the limited area with which he dealt possessed a unique character that justified a special treatment. Yet, in spite of the fact that he was both a geologist and an ethnologist, his social philosophy for the area was essentially a prescription of social statics. Landholding in large lots, except for limited irrigation communities, would have afforded opportunity for only a favored few; and this view committed him to a social structure so rigid and static as to be without capacity to absorb even a normal population increase. At the same time, by creating a powerful vested interest, the plan would not necessarily have insured constructive, long-term utilization policies. Quite certainly it could not have prevented either the physical or the economic disasters of the 1930s.

Powell was notably blind to soil science and was in no sense abreast of the status of the subject even in his own day and in the environment for which his system was designed. At the time of the arid lands report in 1878, Hilgard had not yet published much of his basic ideas leading to a new soil science; but, as those contributions were issued, Powell failed to understand their significance. He never realized what the soil problem was that needed to be understood.

This emphasis upon Powell, Johnson, and Webb is not intended to leave the impression that the Powell plan was adopted as the policy for the original occupation of the arid region for which it was designed. But it did have some bearing upon more recent policies and still possesses an unfortunate propaganda influence.

Besides cattle from Texas, the northern ranges were stocked from the Pacific Coast as well as from the farms of the eastern states. The most important influence of all, however, for reconstruction of the history of the cattle industry as a whole has been the contribution of pure-bred animals from Great Britain, the European continent, and India and the creation of new hybrid breeds. The story of sheep likewise is in the process of being reconstructed on a more meaningful basis.

The first English colonists to settle in what is now the United States brought with them the seed for traditional English crops: wheat, oats, barley, rye, etc., and the tillage methods of the homeland. For various reasons, their labor achieved no great success. The Indians taught them the culture and uses of the maize, the Indian staple. One of the most remarkable aspects of European adaptation to America was the manner in which corn (Indian maize), especially the dent type, became an integral part of American culture. When Americans reached the western extent of the tall-grass prairie where corn could not be depended upon because of the hazards of climate, they stubbornly persisted in growing corn because they could not, or would not, adjust to an agricultural system without it. A large part of the excessive hardships in the grass country of the late nineteenth century was the result of this failure in adjustment. The soft wheats, spring and winter types, according to latitude, were likewise subject to a high casualty rate. The belated introduction to and reluctant schooling in the uses of hard wheat provided a remarkably reliable grain crop for bread. After the opening of the twentieth century came durum, a spring wheat suitable for macaroni flour. The hard spring wheats dominate the northern grassland and the hard winter wheats the central portion.

For the central part of the grassland the sorghums became a major crop, affording a reliable substitute for corn. Introduced first, after the middle of the nineteenth century, were the saccharine varieties, used for syrup, but which became more widely grown as a forage substitute for corn. Kaffir and milo, etc., were introduced near the end of the century. In their mid-twentieth-century forms, as developed by plant-breeders, the grain sorghums afford a reliable feed for livestock as a substitute for corn and thus have become an integral part of the range-livestock economy where corn could not be grown. This facet of the whole situation must be stressed as one of several which demonstrate that the range-livestock industry could not survive on grass alone.

Fibers, both cotton and wool, were produced extensively. Texas and Oklahoma were the leading short-staple cotton states but were challenged after World War II by California, which developed the growth of irrigated, long-staple cotton under a highly mechanized regime. Historically, the range-sheep industry was identified almost exclusively with wool production, using the fine-wool breeds, especially the Merino. The shift to the dual-purpose English breeds for meat and wool came late. The inter-regional aspects of lamb production will be noted later.

## Regional Interrelations

No summary of commercial economies of the grassland, however sketchy, can forego reference to the mineral resources of the region and their peculiar relation to the necessities of such an area. Without forests, the grassland was dependent largely upon outside areas for the building materials and fuel traditional to American culture. The search for substitutes for wood was persistent and not immediately or fully successful. This introduces one of the most conspicuous aspects of the occupance of the grassland–regional interdependence. Not only the steam railroad but industrialization in all its aspects contributed what were essentials to the grassland economy. Capital and consumption goods furnished by the industrialized regions had to be paid for in money derived from cash crops. A degree of subsistence economy, such as had been the resort of the pioneer in the forest, was virtually impossible on natural grounds, and this imperative demand for money emphasized the necessity of specialized cash crops. Railroads made possible the import of sawed lumber, which was put together with machine-made nails. The grassland was characteristically a "sawed house," not a "sod house," country and still remains so. Coal for fuel was shipped in largely to supplement the lower-grade bituminous or lignite coals produced in some parts of the region. The opening of the mid-continent oil and gas fields on a large scale after the beginning of the twentieth century afforded for the first time an efficient fuel, not only for use in the grassland, but eventually for large-scale export to other regions. The industrial minerals existed only in the mountain areas, but the accent on uranium during the last decade opened unknown possibilities.

Regional interdependency of another sort evolved out of the Texas cattle drives of song and story. First driven northward to market, the animals were found to fatten on the way, or were held on northern range to fatten on grass, before shipment by rail to Corn Belt feed lots or to market for slaughter. In 1887 the Santa Fe Railroad built southward into the Texas range country, and others followed. Soon afterward the controls for Texas fever were worked out. On the basis of these developments a stabilized procedure evolved to ship southwestern cattle to the Kansas-Oklahoma bluestem pastures to be grass-fattened for slaughter or to be fattened and matured for Corn Belt feed lots. Out of these practices a favorable rail-rate structure emerged: billing, with pasture stopover privileges, and standard pasture contracts from April 1 to October 1. According to the estimates of the United States Department of Agriculture's Agricultural Marketing Service, an annual average of 360,000 head of cattle was received in these pastures over the period 1943–52. Not only was this a larger number of animals but it represented a far larger potential of high-quality beef than was ever marketed from the southwestern range during the most fabulous days of the notorious Texas cattle drives, when grass, cattle, and Texans were supposed to be close to a "state of nature." This simple statement of facts suggests many more challenging questions about grass, soil, conservation, and cattle than can be considered here.

The chain of established services just described, that is, breeding on the range, maturing, and grass-fattening in transit on the bluestem pastures, full-feed finishing in the Corn Belt feed lots, and slaughter at the packing centers of Kansas City, St. Louis, and Chicago, represented, among other things, the pull of the great population centers of northeastern United States and Europe. It was an intricately woven pattern stretching diagonally across the United States, virtually from one corner to the other, and was the product of a complex of forces operating through a century of time. Like Topsy, it "just growed" and was not planned, although, after it had taken shape, interested parties at various points and times did consciously perfect details. In the sheep industry, although on a less permanent basis and in less volume, a somewhat comparable procedure also operated to move Idaho and Arizona lambs to feed lots near the major packing centers for finishing or to the winter-wheat pastures of the hard winter-wheat belt for maturing and fattening.

The first challenge to these systems came from the Pacific Coast, especially from southern California, which was sustaining a phenomenal population growth. The bid of the Pacific Coast for food supplies became conspicuous during the depression decade of the 1930s and mounted to all but revolutionary proportions during and after the World War II boom. The economic continental divide had been located some distance west of the physical continental divide. Before the end of World War II the economic divide had moved eastward to such an extent as to draw much business to the southern Pacific Coast from western Nebraska, Kansas, Oklahoma, and a large part of Texas. Thus far, the Pacific Northwest has not generated a comparable drawing power from the northern end of the grassland. Great oil and gas developments and hydroelectric power may operate similarly in that area, but on the eve of atomic industrial power the historian must refrain from prophecy.

The interrelationships that have become effective between or among regions have not been the consequence of any preconceived plan, but that does not mean that no planning was undertaken. During the winter of 1876–77, and while the controversy was pending over the outcome of the disputed presidential election of 1876, a conciliation program was proposed. According to this plan, a through railroad was to be assembled and/or constructed from Philadelphia through the southern states to connect with the Texas and Pacific Railroad and southern California. Had this over-all project been executed together with a favorable rate structure, the effects upon the Old South and upon the southern grassland would have been momentous. Possibly the Texas–Kansas–bluestem pasture–Corn Belt–Chicago system previously described might not have emerged.

At the outbreak of World War II a similar plan was before the Interstate Commerce Commission, with a view of making Richmond, Virginia, a packing center and of diverting southwestern livestock through the Gulf states to be fed on their way east. World War II blocked the plan, but it was fought by all the interests in the Texas–Kansas–Corn Belt–Chicago system already in being, as well as by southern California, just then drawing heavily upon the same source for supplies of meat. One observation at least about the proposed Richmond plan is in order. Like much social planning of such magnitude, there was little, if anything, that was positive in the system for the country as a whole; its conspicuous characteristic was a proposal to benefit one region at the expense of others without any certainty of benefiting anybody on a long-term basis.

## Strategic Status

The regional interdependence just described was the product of railroads, supplemented by internal combustion engines on land wheels, whether tractors, trucks, or automobiles. New forces of air communications were at work on a reorientation and a redistribution of power. Already the fact has been pointed out that, for the first time in history, the potential of land-mass power had been implemented by steam railroads, dating from the mid-nineteenth century. The internal combustion engine in its several applications to surface movement in space supplemented and extended what steam railroads had begun. The effect of air power was not necessarily to withdraw the loan of power from geographical positions intrusted with power under the rail regime. But the strategic significance of every site underwent a re-evaluation in terms of air power. Significantly, in a north circumpolar system, the North American grassland interior again rated a new loan of power, but subject to a substantial reassessment of relationships—among them a north-south orientation in addition to, rather than instead of, the exclusive east-west orientation of surface communication systems. Besides being called upon to provide bread, meat, fibers, coal, oil, gas, and uranium, the North American grassland served other functions at the mid-point of the twentieth century.

At the center of the North American continental land mass, this grassland contained the nerve centers of the military communication systems that defend or strike in its behalf. In such a perspective would anyone be so naïve as to insist that the problem of the grassland could be solved by turning it back to the Indian or to the cattleman? Instead of a return to the simplicity of a grazing country, the challenges of atomic power indicate a further incorporation into the complex network of areal and cultural interdependence. Much more, indeed, has become involved than the exclusive interests of the United States as an individual nation. This grassland region of North America, the interior of the United States and Canada, occupies one of the key geographical positions in the north circumpolar system of political power actually in being. Intrusted with such a loan of power, a heavy responsibility rests upon its holders for the use that is made of the opportunities committed to its charge.

## Notes

1. Two examples of reported lightning-ignited prairie fires in the High Plains are cited. The location was Cheyenne County, Kansas, near the intersection of 40° north latitude and 102° west longitude at an altitude of nearly 4,000 feet. The number of such examples might be multiplied indefinitely. In using newspaper sources as evidence, not all references to lightning as a cause of fires would be acceptable. These particular instances possess characteristics that contribute to credibility: the specific location is given; the community turned out to fight the fire; the area burned was specified; and the record was printed within the week. The point to be emphasized is that such discriminative details would seem to differentiate these reports from the rumor category and, in making the record specific, would justify the use of these cases and many other similar ones that might be cited in the High Plains newspapers and would constitute proof of lightning as a cause of prairie fires. *St. Francis* (Kans.) *Herald,* July 13, 1911: Bird City Department: "Not every year will the prairie grass burn in July, but such is the case now. During one of our electrical storms last week lightning struck a little ways southwest of W. D. Kyle's place burning over quite a territory before the flames were extinguished." *St. Francis* (Kans.) *Herald,* August 3, 1911: "Last Thursday a bad prairie fire destroyed the winter range of Henry Weaver. Sunday another big fire raged off southwest of Asa Cress's place. It burned a place 2½ miles long and 1½ miles wide. It was set by lightning and required the most heroic efforts on the part of the settlers to extinguish it and save some winter pasture. This year when feed is scarce the loss of the grass will be sorely felt."

2. Any clear realization of the role of glaciation dates from slightly more than a century ago. An intensive investigation of Pleistocene times, especially accompanied by a realization of the interplay of geological processes and primitive man, dates particularly from the Folsom discoveries of the second quarter of the twentieth century.

3. "Had a little rain last night—the country is exceedingly parched with drought. When we got on to the prairies, the ashes from the recently burned prairies, and the dust and sand raised so by the wind that it annoyed us much, the wind raising, I found that the dust was so scattered that it became impossible to perceive the trail of the surveyors, who had gone a few hours ahead of the horses. While conversing with Calvin about the course we should go, we discovered the atmosphere ahead darkening, and as it had become cloudy, we fancied that a misting rain was coming upon us, and made some inquiry respecting the security of our packs. A few minutes taught us that what we had fancied to be rain, was an increase of the rising dust, sand, and ashes of the burnt grass, rising so much and so generally that the air was much darkened, and it appeared on the open prairies as though the clouds had

united with the earth. Our eyes were so distressed that we could scarcely see to proceed. . . . The wind blew incessantly and excessively severe. . . . Was about to select a camping ground, when we met a man whom the Doctor [sent] to inform me that he could not proceed with his work, and that they waited for us in a wood a mile ahead. It being very difficult for me to look at my pocket compass I told the soldier . . . to lead us back. He set off with great confidence that he could find his way back and in a few minutes was leading us north instead of west. . . . On finding the surveyors, we encamped for the residue of the day. Even in this wood, and after the wind had somewhat abated, the black ashes fell on us considerably" (Barnes, 1936, p. 365).

Wind and dust accompanied the expedition farther west, and on October 26 the Republican Valley was reached: "Wind very high, scarcely allowing us to pass" (*ibid.,* p. 368). October 27: "Today we reached the Republican, . . . and to our great disappointment we found it more destitute of grass than any place we had seen where wood was to be found. The river runs over a bed of sand—the banks low, and all the bottom lands are a bed of sand white and fine, and now as dry as powder ought to be. I never saw a river along which we might not find some rich alluvial moist bottoms, on which, at this season of the year, could not be found green grass. But here there is in a manner none.

"We examined along the river for grass until satisfied that none could be found and then turned back to a creek we had passed five miles back. . . . The scarcity of wood on the river and the sandiness and poverty of the bottoms, greatly discourage me as to the country—While the great scarcity of food for our horses made us fear that we should not be able to proceed much further" (*ibid.,* pp. 368–69).

The entry of November 5 represents the country about the ninety-eighth meridian and reads: "Completed the line of the outlet to 150 miles, and stopped. For some days we have discovered that our horses were failing so fast, that we must soon return, or lose them all. . . . We are beyond all Indian villages, and 50 miles, or more, into the country of Buffaloes. . . .

"After we completed our survey, we turned on to a creek, and were looking for an encampment—the day calm and fair—when suddenly the atmosphere became darkened by a cloud of dust and ashes from the recently burnt Prairies occasioned by a sudden wind from the north! It was not three minutes after I had discovered its approach, before the sun was concealed, and the darkness so great, that I could not distinguish objects more than three or four times the length of my horse. The dust, sand, and ashes, were so dense that one appeared in danger of suffocation. The wind driving into one's eyes seemed like destroying them. . . .

"The storm commenced, sun three quarters of an hour high in the evening, and blew tremendously all night. It had abated a little by morning. The dust was most annoying at the commencement. There was no clouds over us" (*ibid.,* pp. 371–72).

# CHAPTER 2

# Grassland, "Treeless," & "Subhumid"

## A Discussion of Some Problems
## of the Terminology of Geography

[In this essay of definition, James C. Malin urges scholars to choose positive rather than negative terms to describe the grassland region. He suggests quantitative concepts instead of subjective symbol words derived from noncomparable regions. Just as immigrant "forest man" had to accept the natural adequacy of the grassland, so scholars must master the ecological sciences in order to understand the natural history of the region.]

Geographers and historians seem to be unaware of the extent to which they are committed to subjective rather than quantitative terminology. One region is described in terms of another, the one with which the writer of the description happens to be familiar. Because the civilization of western Europe and eastern America developed in a predominantly forest environment, the prevailing geographical terminology is that of the forest or high-rainfall climate. As forest man moved into the prairie of Indiana, Illinois, Kentucky, and the country farther west, he called it "treeless" and "subhumid." These negative terms measured the new region by the characteristics of the accustomed forest enviornment and found it deficient. If a grassland man had been entering a forest region, by the same principle he would have been justified in calling the forest "grassless" and "super-humid." The point to be emphasized is that a geographical area should be described in positive terms that delineate its characteristics in quantitative language, and by independent standards or units of measurement.

The interior of North America is a grassland, and, according to the definitions of plant ecology, grass is the normal or climax vegetation. If the grass is plowed up and the land abandoned, it tends to return to grass through a process of succession of plants, beginning with weeds and ending, after many years, in substantially the original species of grasses, together with their associated forbs. In a forest country the corresponding succession tends to restore the original forest.

As regards the terms designating the volume of moisture available in any region, the accepted nomenclature is based on forest man's standards of western Europe and eastern America, taking the normal of those regions as humid. Variations from this subjective concept of normal are subhumid or superhumid. But Illinois is humid for corn, the South Carolina coast is humid for rice, Cuba is humid for sugar cane, the plains country west of the 100th meridian is humid for blue grama grass, the Arizona desert is humid for cacti and creosote bush, and the southern Idaho desert is humid for sagebrush. If the term *humid* or *subhumid* is used, then the question arises, "Humid or subhumid for what?" For each of the plants just listed as illustrations, the volume of rainfall is normal in its proper region. A rainfall of about five inches is a normal amount for the moist desert where creosote bush and cacti are native, and a rainfall of 15 inches is normal for blue-grama-grass areas.

## Natural Regional Adequacy

To approach the problem from a somewhat different angle, any area of the earth's surface should be treated in terms of its adequacy for all native vegetation and animal life within its limits. An area is never super or sub anything for its native fauna or flora, and it is not deficient in anything that constitutes its natural condition. When man introduces his so-called "civilization" from one area into another, he cannot expect to be successful unless he utilizes plants and animals for which the new area is normal. His transplanted civilization becomes successful to the degree to which he is able to harmonize it with the principles of natural regional adequacy. The plains country is normal for hard spring and hard winter wheats, the bread wheats, and they do not grow successfully where the rainfall is greater than about thirty inches. Western Kansas has a normal climate for the grain sorghums, but is subhumid for corn. Likewise, white-faced cattle (Herefords) will thrive on the plains where buffaloes were most numerous but cannot compete with Shorthorns in the Bluegrass region of Kentucky.

In order to avoid the concept of adequacy or deficiency, a set of terms is suggested here that are quantitative. For the traditional terms, *superhumid, humid, subhumid, semihumid* or *semiarid,* and *arid,* substitute the terms *wet, high-rainfall, mid-rainfall, low-rainfall,* and *dry.* These would express the purpose of classification with reference to precipitation in simple, common language. If these particular terms meet objection, then let someone bring forward others that are strictly quantitative. Likewise, the terms descriptive of the vegetation of a geographical area should specify what is present, not what is absent—*forest, grass, desert shrub,* and so on. Forrest Shreve provided a model approach to desert vegetational nomenclature on a quantitative basis in his terms "simple stands" (1–3 species in combination), "mixed stands" (4–12 species), and "rich stands" (more than 12 species) (Shreve, 1942, p. 202).

## A Forest Man's Reaction to Grassland

A conspicuous example of a forest man's reaction to the grassland is to be found in the report of Captain R. B. Marcy on his expedition up the Canadian River in 1849. The trail on the south side of the Canadian River led him across the north end of the Llano Estacado near the present Texas–New Mexico boundary line:

When we were upon the high table land, a view presented itself as boundless as the ocean. Not a tree, shrub, or any other object, either animate or inanimate, relieved the dreary monotony of the prospect; it was a vast, illimitable expanse of desert prairie—the dreaded "Llano Estacado" of New Mexico; or, in other words, the great Zahara of North America. It is a region almost as vast and trackless as the ocean—a land where no man, either savage or civilized, permanently abides; it spreads forth into a treeless, desolate waste of uninhabited solitude, which always has been, and must continue, uninhabited forever; even the savages dare not venture to cross it except at two or three places, where they know water can be found. The only herbage upon these barren plains is a very short buffalo grass, and, on account of the scarcity of water, all animals appear to shun it. [Marcy, 1849, p. 42]

Marcy calls the grassland a "desert prairie," "the great Zahara," "a treeless, desolate waste," and "barren plains" but at the end describes it as covered with buffalo grass. Two features seem to have controlled his thinking about the country he was describing: it was treeless, and it was waterless. It had moisture as well as buffalo grass, because moisture was necessary in order to have buffalo grass, but Marcy apparently wanted the evidence of running water that he could see—streams or springs.

## A Practical Example of Regional Understanding

An outstanding example of practical understanding of the significance of
regional differences is furnished in the address of T. C. Henry of Abilene,
Kansas, before the county fair of 1870 (*Abilene* [Kans.] *Chronicle,* Nov. 10,
1870). Henry was not a scientist; he was a real-estate promoter with a farming background in New York State. He had gone to Alabama after the Civil
War to raise cotton with freedman labor but found it impossible to make a
profit on seven-cent cotton that cost 20 cents to produce. He then turned to
Kansas, in 1867, and by 1870, at the age of twenty-nine, was a leading citizen
in a frontier community. His ideas of regional differences were born, therefore, of practical experience in New York, Alabama, and Kansas, and probably no scientist has ever stated the fundamentals more effectively. The
thing about Kansas that seems to have impressed Henry most was the presence of native grass, and it provided him with his central theme for the
comparison of the three regions. In the East it was necessary to cut the trees
of the forest to let in light, and to dig drainage ditches "in order that the
earth might bring forth grass." The first task of the forest pioneer was to
prepare grass, and he might spend the greater part of a lifetime "before he
could possess himself of a meadow" comparable with native Kansas grass.
In the East he must cultivate and renew his field of tame grass, but in Kansas
grass was the natural vegetation, which perpetuated itself.

The South was faced with the fact, "startling in its importance, that no
valuable variety of grass has ever been grown there," and to this, even more
than to political and social factors, he thought, were to be ascribed "the
present prostration and comparative poverty of those states." Furthermore, he was convinced that until an adequate remedy for this grassless
condition had been provided, even the corrections and reforms resulting
from the Civil War could not assure any degree of prosperity. The immediate effect of the war had been to make matters worse rather than better
throughout the South in general, and "today the happiest and most flourishing section in the entire south is eastern Tennessee. The single fact that
clover *is* grown there, and cotton *cannot* be, accounts for the great difference." The only other grass-growing section of the South, he pointed
out, was in Texas:

The culture and growth of grass insures a diversity of agricultural employment and
occupation that otherwise cannot exist. . . . Then the greatest means of fertilizing
and recuperating the soil is withheld and instead of the beautiful system of rotating
crops . . . the entire attention is directed to the simplest cultivation of some one or
two staples.

Henry argued that the people of Kansas must recognize that there was less rainfall in Kansas than in Ohio or New York and that Kansas could not grow rice like Carolina or corn like Illinois. He challenged the right of those states "to set up a standard of superiority." But, he continued, Kansas did grow grass and wheat and livestock better than those states, and the smaller amount of rainfall was the factor that assured this Kansas superiority; Kansas farmers should capitalize on their advantages, study nature, "adapt the crop to the soil," or "prepare the soil for the crop." He was convinced that eastern methods of farming were not suitable in Kansas, and "the sooner we recognize and acquaint ourselves with these differences and place ourselves in harmony with them, the sooner may we avail ourselves of the unequalled and exclusive opportunities our country affords." In another place he said: "Then let us stop claiming foreign advantages, and advantages too that are diametrically opposed to the real and essential ones that we do possess, and proceed in our own independent manner 'to work out our own salvation.'" And once again he restated his theme that the Kansas system of agriculture should be "distinct and apart—as our necessities are distinct and apart": in the differences lay the advantages that Kansas, a grassland, possessed over the eastern forest land.

## Ecological Factors

No geographer or historian is adequately equipped to discuss regionalism who does not possess a fair competency in the field of ecology—either plant or animal ecology, but preferably general ecology, which includes both. And the term *ecology* itself ought to be sufficiently inclusive to embrace soil science. The ecology of soil microorganisms is as much a part of the discipline as the ecology of forest, grass, or desert plants, and of invertebrates, mammals, or other kinds of large animals. Some microbiologists hold that microorganisms show as distinctive a geographical distribution pattern as the large plants and animals. It is in connection with the study of geographical areas from the standpoint of ecology that the conventional subjective or relativistic regional terminology becomes particularly irritating.

Three of the factors that determine climate for a geographical area are moisture, temperature, and light. Additional factors of environment, for purposes of ecology, are topography and soil. The first three must be considered, not only in terms of annual quantity, but in terms of seasonal distribution and variability within each calendar year and over a series of years. Obviously, any attempt to combine all these elements into an ecological efficiency formula would become complicated, even if it were scientifically possible. A number of attempts have been made to combine some of them, but all such systems have been open to adverse criticism. Stephen B. Jones (1932) has given a competent evaluation of the Köppen system of climatic classification and others derived from it or similar to it.

The simplest form of precipitation-efficiency index attempted to make allowance for evaporation (Transeau, 1905). Although this was an attractive and superficially reasonable procedure, it was illusory even with respect to soil moisture in a quantitative sense. Evaporation is linked with too many factors to be subjected to measurement as a practical procedure—temperature, topography, soil texture, wind, character of the vegetational cover, and water requirements of plants. From the ecological point of view, precipitation efficiency becomes even more complicated because of differences among plants in seasonal water requirements and in physiological water requirements and variations in the availability to roots of soil moisture in relation to soil texture (20 per cent moisture in sand may be wet, whereas 20 per cent moisture in fine clay may be dry). Much the same kinds of questions can be asked under the head of precipitation efficiency as were asked under the head of rainfall: efficiency of what plant, topography, soil, seasonal distribution, and so on. Similar series of problems arise in the consideration of the factors of temperature, light, topography, and soil. Such efficiency and distributional indices are inaccurate, subjective, and arbitrary—fictions and illusions that are particularly deceptive because they are derived from complicated systems of mathematical calculations and scientific data that seem to invest them with a scientific certainty. Light has received too little attention. Topography and soils are often ecological determinants where rainfall, temperature, and light are uniform. Shantz's pioneer study of the ecology of the Colorado grassland pointed out the soil differences under grama, wire, and bluestem bunch grass where the other factors were constant (Shantz, 1911).

Of greater value, probably, than any approach by way of precipitation- and temperature-efficiency indices is the emphasis placed on variability and frequency of extremes in the systems of Russell (1934), Kendall (1935), Crowe (1936), Lackey (1937), and Thornthwaite (1941). The value of some of these systems is impaired, however, by the degree to which they are based on climatic determination in the tradition of Köppen. Too many aspects of such systems are subjective and arbitrary. The independent approaches of Crowe and Lackey are the most original, and the climatic-year concepts of Russell, Kendall, and Thornthwaite would gain immeasurably in significance if they were based on purely quantitative data.

## Factors of Survival in the Desert

The greater severity of the struggle for survival in the desert as compared with areas of higher rainfall has become an accepted assumption, almost axiomatic, though there is no clear scientific reason for such a conclusion. The limiting factors may be different in nature, but not necessarily more severe. In the desert and in low-rainfall climates, where variability is present in exaggerated form, environment may operate more directly than in higher-rainfall climates, where competition between plants becomes more decisive. The severity of the struggle for existence is different, but apparently not greater in the one than in the other, because in either place, over a long series of years, the so-called "climax formation" allows only one new plant to survive to replace each dying plant of a species, irrespective of the increase potential of the several species (Sumner, 1925; Shreve, 1934b, 1942).

The problem of survival of vegetation in the desert and in low-rainfall environments was approached in another manner by Kearney and Shantz (1911), and later by Shantz (1927) and by Maximov (1929). Vegetation was placed in four classes: drought-escaping, drought-evading, drought-enduring, and drought-resisting. Each class, and even the individual species within each class, meets the water requirements differently. Drought-escaping plants include the ephemerals, which grow quickly when moisture is available and mature seed, and thus survive the long droughts as seed awaiting the next rainy season. Drought-evading plants restrict growth or otherwise delay exhaustion of the water supply. This group includes native plants that restrict the amount of growth above ground and are widely spaced. Among the agricultural plants, it includes most of the cereals that are suited to the lower-rainfall areas, including the sorghums. Drought-enduring plants include desert shrubs that endure long periods without moisture by shedding leaves, even some twigs, make no new growth until water is again available, and then grow rapidly. The drought-resisting plants are those that store water in roots or stems to tide them over dry periods. Shantz classed the cacti in this group, but Maximov objected because succulents avoid severe internal water deficit through "storage and slow expenditure of water" and do not possess xerophytic features such as high osmotic pressure. The conclusion that is significant is the

wide variation in the physiological as well as in the structural characteristics of the kinds of plants that become adapted to the lowest-rainfall
environments. Most popular preconceptions about the nature of desert
plants had best be scrapped.

Maximov's work became a turning point in botanical concepts of how
plants meet their water requirements. He dismissed the traditional theories of structural defense against water losses and focused attention on the
properties of protoplasm and the ability to endure wilting. Ecological
thought has not been fully reoriented to the new point of view, and little
impression seems to have been made on the other disciplines in which
these views and their modifications should be fully appreciated and
integrated.

### Understanding Water Requirements

To the agronomist an understanding of the water requirements of plants is
essential. The morphology of the plant is not the essential mark of its adaptability as a crop for a low-rainfall region, and neither is the transpiration
rate. Ability to endure wilting is important. Also, crucial to successful agriculture are the seasonal water and temperature requirements. Assurance
of a winter-wheat crop has been found to depend primarily on the amount
of moisture stored in the soil at planting time in the fall—in other words,
the rainfall of the season preceding the harvesting of the crop. Unless
extremely severe, a shortage of rainfall in the spring of the harvest year has
little effect on yield (Hallsted and Mathews, 1936). But even when all moisture requirements are fully met, let one day of hot winds occur in June at
pollen time or in the early stages of the formation of the kernel in the head,
and the crop may be destroyed. Early maturity permits escape from, not
endurance of, temperature extremes. Corn requires both moisture and
high temperatures during the growing season of spring and summer. A
climate of summer drought and heat destroys the corn crop. Only the sorghums can provide a grain substitute for corn in the low-rainfall grassland.
They seem to possess in some degree an ability both to evade and to endure
drought. A good season for winter wheat is a bad season for corn, and the
reverse. Of what value is any general standard of precipitation or temperature efficiency or distribution as applied to whole geographical areas? In an
ecological sense too diverse a range of vegetation grows in each area for
such designations to possess much meaning.

## Marginal and Submarginal

A discussion of one term suggests inclusion of others that are related in the subjective sense as reflecting the idea of deficiency. The words *marginal* and *submarginal* have been adopted into the language of land use from an economic point of view, and to them the same challenge is issued—"Marginal or submarginal for what?" Instead of measuring everything in terms of a deficiency according to the measurer's standards, a more valid hypothesis would assume that every part of the earth's surface possesses utility. Nothing is marginal or submarginal except when measured by a standard that does not fit its natural characteristics, and the mere fact of the choice of an unnatural standard predetermines that the area to which it is applied must appear as deficient.

These considerations are not a digression from the central theme of this chapter. The power of custom is so strong that only by a better understanding of these ecological factors can an appreciation of the principal issues be attained. Each factor that enters as a component into the concept of climate, or into the concept of vegetation, or into the concept of region, should be treated as an independent variable. The quantity of rain that falls constitutes the moisture factor. The independent variables interact, and all together constitute the "circle of facts" for the study of any particular area of the earth's surface.

## Relation to Regional Psychology

In addition to the arguments for quantitative and positively descriptive terminology as a matter of good scientific methodology, the subject possesses a practical importance as a matter of regional psychology. This is illustrated conspicuously in the Great Plains region and its transitional borderlands. The propaganda of the drought decade of the 1930s and the argument that the territory was becoming a desert branded it as a deficiency region. Many extremists even argued that the Great Plains should be abandoned, except for livestock. The widespread reaction of the younger generation, thoroughly indoctrinated in the idea of deficiency, was a feeling of frustration and defeatism. These young people became convinced that there was no future for the region, that they were victims of a ruthless geographical determinism, and that their only hope was to leave. In the intensity of the urge to escape at any cost, they generally repudiated any suggestion of possibilities of adjustment. Obviously, there can be no normal cultural stabilization in an area dominated by such a complex of psychological frustration.

It may be justly argued that nothing in this chapter is new, that geographers and ecologists have repeatedly rejected subjective terminology. Yet as long as they continue to indulge in the condemned practices, the subject will call for discussion. An examination of the standard textbooks, and also of monographic literature, reveals clearly that an independent quantitative and positively descriptive terminology is not employed consistently. Much could be said also about the abuses that are associated with the social interpretations allegedly derived from geography. The issues are real, whether or not they are recognized. There is no intention here of magnifying verbalism—quite the contrary. The mere fact of giving a thing a name does not invest it with magical qualities. The British-American geologist G. W. Featherstonhaugh wrote of the concept of classification that he had no disposition "to assign any value to it beyond the facility it gives me of making myself understood" (1895, p. 12). To fulfill this function, however, a terminology must be founded on principles that convey accurate meanings to every reader.

## The Broad Application

The focus of this chapter is the terminology of forest, grassland, and desert, but everything said on those areas applies in principle to other geographical areas—to the Arctic, to the tropics, and to the ocean. All possess fauna and flora normal to their characteristic conditions. As the truly global era becomes a reality, these areas and their differences acquire a new importance. They should be described according to independent standards of measurement, their fauna and flora treated as normal, and each recognized as serving a significant function in a regionally interdependent world.

CHAPTER 3

# Factors in
# Grassland Equilibrium

[After studying the ecology of the grassland for a decade and reading all of
the early explorers' reports on its flora and fauna, Malin in 1947 prepared
his tour de force, *The Grassland of North America,* which he rightly considered
his most original and significant work because, as he observed later, "it
opened up so many things." Chapter 10, which is included here, offers a
synthesis of his findings on the true natural state of the grassland. From his
perspective, the grassland was superior to the forest lands in pasturage,
hay, and grain crop productivity. Malin thus felt compelled to defend the
region from its supposed friends, the soil scientists and government conservationists of the 1930s, who he believed had unjustly maligned it. Malin
demonstrated the need for natural scientists to test their theories with hard
historical and archeological evidence, with facts "that every schoolboy
knew," as he stated. Such a historical perspective would enable scientists
correctly to deal with the fundamentals of drought, dust storms, river sedimentation, and lightning fires and to shape appropriate conservation
policies.]

## Plant Relations

A land of uniformity and monotony was the first reaction of forest men to
the grassland, and to many it was not only their first but their lasting
impression. Nothing could have been more erroneous. The deficiency was

in the mind of the forest man and not in the grassland. Because of the absence of trees, the grassland possessed in its structure fewer vegetational layers and a lesser range of height of the layers and lesser spread between them. The composition of the vegetation presented, nevertheless, a wide range of variety of grasses, forbs, and woody plants. All were in intense competition with each other and with invader plants. The tall-grass prairie possessed more layers and height than the mixed prairie; and that in turn than the short-grass plains, but the desert-grass transition again introduced increased numbers of layers, height, and spread. Not only were there more layers and greater height at the two extremities of the grassland, the forest borders and the desert borders, but the proportion of woody plants was likewise greater in those borderlands.

The layering of vegetation was an aspect of biological equilibrium in the competition of nature; some plants thrived on light, others were destroyed by it; some thrived on shade and others were destroyed by it. In the long periods of time involved in the evolution of the grassland formation, the equilibriums were worked out which established vigorous plants in each category in the places in which they possessed the qualities of survival. Invader plants could not survive unless they possessed characteristics and vigor which fit them into a niche in the complex system. In few places were there pure stands of any one species. In fact, under most circumstances, pure stands of any vegetation were signs of weakness rather than strength. The fullest equilibrium in nature was attained over long periods of time and stresses where species of varied characteristics provided the most complete interchange of compensations with each other, with animals, and with soil. In cultivated fields of controlled pure stands, the farmer provided those compensations artificially and periodically, by rotation of crops, addition of fertilizers, and machine tillage. In nature, these processes operated simultaneously and continually as a consequence of the variety in the forms of plant and animal life. The grasses constituted the principal portion of the vegetation, the forbs of the composite family were usually second, and the legumes third in rank. The literature has not made clear the role of the composites and was not sufficiently specific about the contribution of the legumes to the fertility of the grasslands. The popular opinion was to call them all weeds, and as they had little or no forage value, to wish to kill out all such weeds. The presence of the legumes was vital, however, as nitrogen fixers of varying efficiency, and there is need of studies describing exactly and quantitatively the place of each of the major legumes, the varying combinations of them, and their over-all significance.

In collecting plants in the grasslands, the earliest explorers seemed more interested in what they called plants rather than grasses. These forbs were a conspicuous feature of the landscape and appeared prominently in the herbaria even though many of the collectors lost large parts of their findings as the result of accidents of travel. Nicollet's area of collecting was between the Mississippi and the Missouri rivers, partly forest, partly grass (1836–1840), and he listed 82 composites and 33 legumes, as well as species of other families, and 42 grasses. He lost about half of his specimens. Frémont (1843) lost part of his collection, but the catalogue of those preserved included 93 composites, 33 legumes, and 18 grasses. Abert's (1846) list included 19 composites, 18 legumes, and 5 grasses. Emory's (1846) southwestern desert collection included 11 specimens of grasses which were sufficiently complete for identification, and 9 not identified as to species, at least 2 legumes, and 4 composites. Marcy's (1852) Red River expedition yielded 27 each of composites and legumes, and 29 grasses. John Torrey was the principal authority who made the classification for most of these collectors.

Within the unstable equilibrium of plant competition for light, water, and nutrients, seasonal distribution was an important factor. Many small annuals matured and seeded in the early spring before the grasses and other perennial plants made their growth. The characteristic grasses tended to make their growth in the late spring and early summer, becoming dry by mid-summer, but even among them there was a seasonal succession. Many prominent tall forbs made their principal growth during the summer and fall.

Below the ground surface there was competition in many respects more significant (if one aspect of biology could be more significant than another) to the problems peculiar to the survival of vegetation in the grassland climate than above the surface. That the most of the grassland vegetation was under the ground was no mere figure of speech. The roots of the grassland plants presented a wide variety of forms and habits. The roots of the grasses were fibrous, and of the short grasses finely fibrous. Those of the forbs mostly were either branched or tap roots. As pictured diagrammatically by Weaver and Fitzpatrick (1934, p. 123) for the tall-grass prairie of eastern Nebraska, there were roughly three levels of roots: prairie June grass *(Koeleria cristata)* in the first fifteen inches, little bluestem *(Andropogon scoparius)* extending to five feet, and the *Psoralea floribunda,* a forb, more than five feet. By individual species, the depths were more varied so that the idea of three levels tended to be minimized, except for the basic fact that different species tended to occupy different levels of the soil and thus did not compete with each other for water and nutrients so much as the individual plants of a species competed with each other. The big bluestem

*(Andropogon furcatus)* roots reached depths of five to seven feet and the *Amorpha canescens,* a nitrogen fixer, as much as twelve to sixteen feet. Roots of different species responded differently to the drouth of the 1930s in the vicinity of Hays, Kansas (Weaver and Albertson, 1943). The depths of buffalo grass roots before and after the eight-year drouth were four and one-half feet and two feet respectively; blue grama five and two feet. On a different plot in the same vicinity growing the taller grasses, big bluestem prior to the drouth reached five feet, and seven years later, six feet; blue-stem wheat grass *(Agropyron smithii)* depths were six to seven and seven to eight feet respectively for the two periods, and sideoats grama *(Bouteloua curtipendula)* five and six respectively.

The plant that captured Frémont's imagination from the start of his expedition in 1842 as characteristic of the tall-grass prairie was the *Amorpha canescens* (lead or tea plant or false indigo). His interest in it was excited by its outward appearance, but by unforseen coincidence the emphasis the plant received in his journal contributed in an important manner to better understanding of the mechanism of biological equilibrium. Science was later to establish the role of certain legumes as nitrogen fixers, and this one fell into that class (Weaver and Fitzpatrick, 1934). In his journal describing the natural history between Fort Leavenworth and Bent's Fort in 1846, Abert mentioned the same plant and also the prairie indigo *(Baptista leucan-tha),* as conspicuous. Wislizenus (1912) and Frémont (1843) commented on the *Psoralea esculenta* (various common names, Pomme Blanche, Pomme de prairie, and prairie potato), and all travelers in the southern grassland wrote of the mesquite trees, both legumes. Marcy (1854) commented that settlers recognized mesquite land as particularly valuable and competed for its possession. It seems possible that there was more reason for this choice than just the tradition, usually unfounded, that forest land was more fertile than land without trees. It is an error to assert, as has been done (Shelford, 1944), that it was cattle that spread the mesquite tree from south central Texas northward to Oklahoma. All the explorers reviewed, who covered the grassland from the Canadian River southward between 1845 and 1854, testified to the presence of the mesquite prior to any cattle drives through that region.

Among the various means by which the grassland plants survived the severe fluctuations of climate, not the least were those below ground. The several varieties of *Ipomea* and of *Psoralea* presented in exaggerated form, in their large roots, a reservoir for storage of water and food. The plant food reserves served also as food for rodents and for Indians. Few of the grasses most characteristic of the drier portions of the grassland produced any substantial crop of viable seed. Severe drouth, heat, and periodic overgrazing tended to reduce the probabilities of seed production, and prairie fires the possibilities of seed survival. In the age-long process of evolution of grassland plants, those had survived and established dominance that could most successfully propagate themselves, and except for the buffalo grass which spread by stolons (runners), the most of them depended primarily upon underground parts, rhizomes for the most part, but some upon corms, bulbs, or tubers. It should be emphasized also that such underground parts were particularly important as defenses against the temperature extremes of heat and cold. The plant tops died down each year and might be burned off, the seeds might not mature or might be destroyed, but the underground protection made survival possible. Thus in the ecology of the grassland, the vegetation had attained a stability against the hazards of light, water, and temperature.

## Animal Relations

Animal ecologists were behind the plant ecologists in their study of the grasslands, and plant ecologists ignored largely the animal factor, yet scientific information on the influence of animals upon soil formation and upon plant succession and climax was essential to the understanding of the grassland as a natural region. Grinnell's (1923) study of California rodents is one of the most significant American works available. He estimated the burrowing rodent population as constituting one-half of the whole number of mammals in the state. These burrowing rodents extended east to about the 100th meridian, beyond which they began to disappear. The rodent relations to soil and vegetation were summarized under nine heads: the substratum was weathered by the opening up of deep holes; substratum material was brought to the surface, scattered, and subjected to weathering; wind and water distributed this loose soil; rainfall was absorbed through the rodent runways, run-off minimized and evaporation retarded; a more vigorous vegetational cover was promoted by this conservation of moisture; soil fertility was improved; buried vegetation was incorporated into the soil; runways, galleries, and holes counteracted the packing effect of hoofed animals; and the rodents as grass eaters competed with grazing animals in consuming and converting vegetation which contributed to soil fertility, and to restriction on growth, the extent depending on varying numbers. Ants, which were characteristic also of grasslands, made important and similar contributions as had been elaborately explained years earlier by Charles Darwin.

Formosov (1928) summarized his own and the research of other Russian scientists on the subject of the grasslands of central Eurasia, regions little disturbed by the activities of modern civilization. He tied his paper directly into that of Grinnell by restating the latter's conclusion that "on wild land the burrowing rodent is one of the necessary factors in the system of natural well being." The Russian observations confirmed fully all that Grinnell had said and elaborated and emphasized it, but there were important respects in which Formosov went further. Among the former points was the conclusion confirming the importance of loess formation by wind-transported dust from rodent mounds. Of the additional conclusions, a most significant one was the effect of raw soil thrown out upon the surface in retarding vegetational succession. Until such soil materials had been subjected to the long-term soil forming process, they promoted the growth of a vegetation different from that prevailing upon fully formed soil. The final effect, therefore, of such animal influences was to "contribute towards maintaining a more stable existence for the dominant vegetation."

The role of the hoofed animals, antelope, mountain sheep, and wild asses, was explained by Formosov. In ungrazed areas, excessive growth of grasses, especially the taller and bulkier type, the feathergrass *(Stipa capillata),* suppressed partially or wholly the weaker plants such as *Festuca ovina, Koeleria gracilis,* and *Poa bulbosa.* Furthermore, the excess of dead cover smothered the dominant grass itself, resulting in replacement by weeds and a new succession sequence before reestablishment of the original dominant. Where hoofed animals grazed, however, they removed excess leafage, and by tramping broke loose dead stalks, preparing the way for new growth of grass. Grazing and tramping down of grass also reduced water losses through transpiration and evaporation during dry periods, and tramping promoted the natural reseeding process. In extended spaces the grass was sometimes tramped out altogether, especially at resting places and around lakes and watering places. The whole complex of activities contributed to the well-being of the animals and promoted the equilibrium of soil-vegetation relationships through the process of natural tillage. As a conclusion to this summary of Formosov's study, the fact should be pointed out that some of the dominant grasses involved were species of the same genera that occupied so largely the northern portion of the North American grassland, and the animal population had performed in North America a similar function. With settlement the original large wild animals were largely exterminated, but many of the small ones still occupied the grasslands where agricultural operations did not interfere. Probably the insect population remained more completely, but in somewhat changed proportions, and some new ones had been introduced. One tentative reservation should be made to this generalization, however, until more is known of the regional distribution of microorganisms of the soil.

The role of insects was an important component in natural processes. Hayes (1927) demonstrated that in Riley County, Kansas, a large part of the insect population burrowed into the top thirty inches of soil for the winter. If they died there, their remains enriched the soil, but as most of them emerged the next season they channelled and areated the soil both in entering and in leaving. It is important further that grasshoppers and other insects were sensitive to heat. As pointed out by Ball (1937), among the effective means of controlling grasshoppers in the grasslands was to graze off the grass in an infested area, another example of the relative stabilization of equilibrium through natural biological controls.

The Clements (1916a, 1916b; Weaver and Clements, 1929, 1938) theory of climax and disclimax as applied to the different subdivisions of the North American grassland was based on the contention (1936) that in the natural state, before the coming of the white man, the influence of wild animals, fires, and Indians on the vegetation was negligible. Thus he denied that in the true prairie the bluestems were real dominants, that on the plains the gramas and buffalo grasses were real dominants, and that on the desert the mesquite shrubs, creosote bush, and sagebrush were real dominants. In all cases they were apparent dominants because of overgrazing, fires, rodents, and human influences, and by protection could be restored to nature. One of the strangest aspects of Clements's (Clements and Clements, 1933, 1937) argument was in attributing greater vigor and capacity of resistance to these plants, which he called false dominants, than to the real dominants. Obviously, his definition of dominant capacity was one that recognized as true dominants only those grasses that thrived under perpetual optimum conditions. Even under Clements's climate definition of the grassland, this seemed inconsistent, because climate analysis revealed the grasslands as areas of fluctuating climatic extremes rather than uniform climatic optimum. It seemed inconsistent also with his whole theory of dynamic ecology to base the concept of dominants upon requirement of an optimum which must necessarily be substantially static. In this as well as later, in declaring (Clements and Clements, 1940) that at their maximum, the wild animals exerted "only a transient effect upon the [grass] climax," his views seem to conflict with those expressed elsewhere (Clements and Shelford, 1939) insisting that plant and animal relations should always be studied together as bio-ecology.

A field experiment with a buffalo herd in the Wichita National Forest,

Oklahoma, was carried out in the summer of 1933 (Clements and Clements, 1933). The contention of Clements was that this proved that a buffalo herd straggled like cattle when grazing on the open range; that buffalo did not graze grass clean and uniformly; that a grazed area recovered its growth of mid-grasses when fully protected; that the mid-grasses were the true dominants; and that it was demonstrated conclusively that the buffalo herds did not produce the short-grass plains disclimax. Irrespective of whether or not his conclusions might be correct, his summer's experiment proved nothing. It is an example of the too-frequent assumption that a laboratory experiment is proof of what would happen in nature. A small herd of semi-domesticated, fence-broke buffalo would not necessarily graze in the same manner as the mass -herds of wild animals in their annual migration in open space, and their effect upon grass would not necessarily be in any manner comparable. Furthermore, the influence upon grass and soil would not be determined by one season, but would have to be considered on the long-term basis which would allow for climate fluctuations, frequent prairie fires, prolonged drouths, and the pulverizing of denuded soil by thousands of hoofs.

In his dicta concerning the buffalo experiment, Clements did not consider the problem of population numbers, increase potential, die-ups resulting from drouth, overgrazing, severe winters, and disease. In fact, elsewhere, he (Clements and Shelford, 1939) denied the relevance of these factors, attributing control of numbers of wild animals in general to sunspot cycles.

The most effective statement of the historical point of view as opposed to the theoretical hypothesis of Clements, and of Weaver and Clements (1929, 1938), was a brilliant paper by Larson (1940) applying particularly to the northern plains. He contended that the short-grass plains was a true climax and that the survival influence was a natural and integral part of it. The argument was directed particularly at Weaver's and Clements's three types of evidence: the reappearance of the taller grasses under protection, the reestablishment of the taller grasses during wet years, and the photographs taken by the Hayden expedition of 1870. The first point was met by quotations from historical records indicating that buffalo were probably as numerous as cattle and that the overgrazed grassland was a natural condition. The second point was answered by appeal to Taylor's restatement of the Liebig law of minimum as the test, not the maximum (in this case rainfall) as the test of plant behavior. The issue of the photographs was met by pointing out the location of the sites photographed as non-typical plains and that the interference with the buffalo herds provided unnatural conditions. A final point was Larson's insistence that the "marked ability of the short grass dominants to withstand overgrazing" indicated an adaptation of long duration.

Vestal (1931), in a review, likewise challenged the Weaver and Clements (1929) theory of the true short-grass climax of the southwestern desert. Agreeing that overgrazing existed and caused to some extent the results described in the prominence of desert shrubs, he pointed out that in this region as in South Africa there was reason to assume that overgrazing took place under natural conditions and that the characteristics of desert shrub–short grass had prevailed for many thousand years. Carpenter (1940) recognized also the validity of the animal relations, and although he cited little specific historical evidence, he quoted an early description by J. Hildreth of the country near the 98th meridian in Oklahoma, between the site of Oklahoma City and the Wichita mountains, in which taller grasses, short grasses cropped close by buffalo, bushes, and cactus all appeared.

Irrespective of the controversial questions of cause, there were fluctuations in the numbers of wild animals in nature. At the minimum extreme in numbers there would tend to be more food than the animals would consume, and at the maximum end there would not be enough. Over a term of years that would span a series of such fluctuations there seems to be good reason to believe that a relatively stabilized equilibrium would be maintained and that regardless of increase potential, one plant and one animal of each of the component climax species would survive. Of course, if that were to be interpreted literally, it would mean a static end-product condition, which is not valid. The ideas of change and succession mean that there would be a long-term drift or tendency for the composition of the life forms to change. Except for intervention of some unusual disturbing factor, however, such change would be slow. As respects the numbers and food supply for both plants and animals, the numbers would tend to approach the danger zone of survival. The biological principle has become so generally recognized as a fact that the burden of proof lies against anyone challenging its validity. As a matter of adequate scientific proof, as applying to Clements's theories of climax and disclimax in the grasslands, the verdict for the present must be rendered, not proven.

Buffalo numbers, in what is usually called the state of nature, would carry the story back to the jurisdiction of the anthropologist or at least as far as the historical geographer as outlined by Sauer (1941), but within the time-span of written records they were subject to disturbance from two directions, from the Spanish with their horse culture from the south, and from the English and their appropriation of the land which drove the Indians west.

The direct pressure of the Spanish upon the buffalo range was relatively slight, but indirectly their northward march through Mexico as far as Santa Fé in the sixteenth and seventeenth centuries influenced all animal relations, and also introduced domesticated stock, sheep, cattle, and horses, to graze the grass of the occupied land. More fundamental to the buffalo problem, however, was the acquisition by the Indian of the grassland of the horse culture. The traditional dates and explanation of the acquisition by the Indian of horses were the escape of horses from either the Coronado or De Soto expeditions, or both, after about 1540. The discovery by Aiton (1939) of the Coronado muster-roll destroyed completely this convenient hypothesis when it was revealed that, of the horses on that expedition, there was only one mare and there was no record of her escape. Furthermore, the chances of survival of a few horses and their progeny in a wild country were virtually zero, even if there were proof that one or more pairs of stallions and mares escaped. The spread of the horse culture among the plains Indians, from the centers of Spanish influence in New Mexico, must not have occurred until late in the seventeenth and early eighteenth centuries as a relatively slow process. The Indian on horseback undoubtedly became a major disturbance factor to all animal life of the areas affected, because it gave to the Indian for the first time a mobility that revolutionized his culture, including his methods of hunting, particularly the hunting of the buffalo, and the following of buffalo migrations. Supplies of meat for food, and skins for clothing and shelter, must have modified the Indian population in relation to the buffalo population, and to the population of all animals directly or indirectly affected by hunting on horseback, or made accessible by the new potentials of Indian migration in horse pursuit of sources of food supplies. In the long run the whole biological equilibrium was affected by the introduction of the horse factor.

In the English advance from the east, the forest game was first affected by settlement, which eventually displaced both game and Indians in the regions actually occupied, as well as by systematic commercial trapping for furs by the French and by the English in the early seventeenth century. The buffalo in the interior were disturbed directly by the encroachment of white settlement west of the Appalachian Mountains in the last quarter of the eighteenth century. By the time of the first Wislizenus (1912) and Frémont (1843) expeditions, it was a well-established conviction among mountain men such as Fitzpatrick, Bridger, and Carson that the buffalo numbers had been already rapidly depleted. Plains Indian raids into Mexico were attributed (Report of Secretary of War, T. S. Jesup, 1850) to the driving pressure of this increasing scarcity of game. The progressive change in Indian-buffalo relations reached other Indian-game relations, and in turn was reflected in the animal-grass relations. Clements (1928) advanced the theory of a buffalo concentration zone resulting from the pressure of the advancing white frontier upon the buffalo range. There does not appear to be any historical basis for such a theory, however, as the problem of diminishing buffalo numbers had become a serious Indian food supply issue before the middle of the nineteenth century and was forcing rapidly, prior to 1850, a new Indian policy of reservations and government annuities to the disturbed Indians (Malin, 1921). Incidentally, also, all this occurred prior to the invention and use of the revolver, the breech-loading Sharps rifle, and the repeating rifles usually associated with the wholesale slaughter of the buffalo.

Any discussion of the problem of buffalo numbers in the pre-horse culture era, or the changes in numbers of buffalo and Indians during the century or so of the horse culture prior to the Anglo-American contacts, must necessarily be primarily theoretical. Attempts to reduce the problem of buffalo numbers to a mathematical basis become somewhat absurd when subjected to analysis. Within the period of Anglo-American records some evidence can be assembled tending to show a relation of buffalo numbers to grass, water, and winter storms which resembles closely the experience of the domestic range cattle industry. The Abert and Emory reports of 1846 represented relatively good moisture and grass conditions of the plains and the buffalo migration route was well to the west, Emory said, between 98° and 101°. His report was focused on the matter of subsisting troops sent across the plains, and he warned that "their [the buffalo] range is very uncertain." He pointed out that "the buffaloes are sometime driven by the severity of the winter, which is here intense for the latitude, to . . . feed upon the cottonwood." Kansas newspapers reported that during the drouth period of the 1860s spring flood water of the Kansas River carried masses of carcasses of buffalo that had died on the plains during the severe winter of scarce grass and storms. Charles Goodnight (Haley, 1936) reported large scale die-ups in the Texas Panhandle, and in 1872 the T. P. Roberts upper Missouri River report mentioned that "dead buffaloes were quite numerous on the plains about the falls." As a result of the severe drouth of 1860 Kansas newspapers reported that one effect had been to drive the buffalo eastward earlier than usual, and many were then east of the Republican River. That meant east of 98°. At this time the encroachment of settlement upon the buffalo range was reducing the buffalo to a limited space which interfered with free movement in the natural adjustment of their range to fluctuating climatic and grass conditions. This deals with freedom of range, rather than concentration of numbers, but it is only in this sense that there could be any validity to Clements's theory of concentration, and that is not his version of it.

The study of the natural history of the buffalo has important bearings on contemporary great plains policies. It was a part of the cattleman's propaganda to argue that there would have been no great plains problem if the farmer had been excluded and the area left to the cattle. The behavior of the buffalo disproves that propaganda conclusively, as their survival depended upon freedom in dry years to vary their migration range as far east as the tall-grass prairie. The buffalo, in open space, did what the government was called upon to do as emergency relief in the 1930s in shipping great plains cattle east to the tall-grass country for feed.

Furthermore, as a normal system of conducting the cattle business, the great plains and the desert southwest were not independent regions. After the cattle tick controls were inaugurated, it became standard procedure to breed cattle on the range, then ship them east to pasture and feed lot for maturing and finishing for slaughter. The Kansas-Oklahoma Bluestem Pastures, east of 97°, became the largest single eastern pasture area in this livestock economy of regional interdependence (Malin, 1942a).

The influence of animals in the grassland was in many respects in the nature of a natural tillage. Abert (1846) described the old buffalo wallows east of 98° that had become covered over with vegetation, and farther west, some in which that process apparently had not been completed. On the former he said that the plants "grow more luxuriantly than on other portions of the prairie," and on the latter that "only in the buffalo wallows one meets the silver margined *euphorbia.*" The prairie dog towns also received the comment that there appeared "a species of *esclepias,* with truncated leaves." The influence of the pocket gopher was multiple as indicated by the fact that the horses' feet sank fetlock deep in the loose earth, and the earth from the subsoil was scattered over the vegetational cover. From the standpoint of the immediate effect on plants alone, the wallowing of the buffalo, and the digging of holes by the gophers, prairie dogs, badgers, kit foxes, etc., as well as the Indian digging roots for food, was disturbance. From the standpoint of succession and climax theory, the disturbance set back the plant succession causing a repetition of greater or lesser extent of plant succession to reestablish the climax. The processes were not occasional, but continuous. A third aspect of the action of these animals was that they contributed to the penetration of rainfall into the loosened soil and into the holes, diminished or prevented run-off into the streams, and conserved that moisture against rapid evaporation from the loosened soil. The digging of the soil and the subsequent mixing by rain, wind, and animals of that soil with vegetation and animal droppings was the final stage in the process of natural tillage performed by these animals as a part of the natural processes of perpetuating the long-term vigor of the vegetation of the grasslands. In this long-time sense, and as a completed operation, the actions of the wild animals were not plant disturbance in a negative or destructive sense, but rather a positive process of natural renewal.

## Climate Relations: Wind, Water, and Soil

In undertaking the description of climatic relations of the grassland from the standpoint of biological equilibrium, the historian is embarrassed by the volume of ill-advised propaganda of the conservation movement. Much of this is in the form of publications of private organizations, interested in some manner in the problem; much has been written by government officials, and issued by commercial publishers; but the greatest volume of this material is governmental publications. Nothing in this discussion is to be interpreted as opposition to conservation, but it is intended as a protest against misinformation and misuse of information in an excess of zeal to sell conservation policies to the public. Some of these policies were themselves unsound. Furthermore, all policies, sound or unsound, should be subjected to the test of full public discussion. The leading book in its field, *Soil Conservation* (1939), by H. H. Bennett, an official in the federal soil service, opened with a discussion of the "virgin land" in which he pictured a nearly perfect biotic balance and removal of soil no faster than new soil was formed in nature. The water in the rivers was clear, he maintained, except under flood conditions which sometimes muddied the Mississippi and the Missouri. Another example is found in a governmental publication, *Little Waters: Their Use and Relation to the Land* (1935, revised 1936), by H. S. Person, in which was presented a diagram, (figure 29) representing erosion: for 1492 the surface lines were horizontal denoting complete absence of erosion, and for 1935 the lines showed differing degrees of denudation and gullying. This diagram and diagrams from other sources of similar validity were used in school books, fixing in the minds of students visually such totally false impressions. It should be recorded, however, that Person's text was carefully written, for the most part, the figure being the offending aspect of the publication.

  Among the standard forest conservation arguments, dating from the early stages of that movement, was the contention that cutting forests caused floods and erosion. A challenge to this is found in Person, *Little*

*Waters,* which questioned whether cutting timber modified much the run-off of water, as undergrowth sprung up which might possess greater density. The point of emphasis was that erosion was promoted only when the land was cleared off, and kept clear of new growth, but not by cutting the commercial timber. Another kind of argument was that floods were caused by careless farming which had caused the loss of the top-soil (Sears, 1936; and Meyerhoff reply, 1936). Similar charges were made with respect to plowing or grazing the grassland.

The cause of floods could not be attributed to such origins, as every school boy knew who read the spectacular story of the capture, during a flood, of Fort Vincennes by George Rogers Clark in the American Revolution, when neither the trees nor the top soil of the Ohio Valley had been disturbed. In the history of Missouri River floods, that of 1844 seems to have set the all-time record at Boonville, Missouri, of 32.8 feet. Even the flood of June 1947 reached a crest at only 32 feet. Although several qualifying factors should be considered in interpreting these records of over a century, the simple fact presented by the figures is sufficient challenge to the propaganda that severe floods are man-made and of recent origin.

The Lewis and Clark expedition found the Missouri muddy in 1804 (Coues, 1893), and the geologist G. Swallow, in his Kansas report of 1866, reviewed the deposits of varying thickness in the Kansas and Missouri river bottoms, with emphasis on 1844:

That from the flood of 1844 is very conspicuous throughout the length of the Missouri and Kansas bottoms in this state. It is sometimes six or eight feet thick, particularly in low bottoms, so heavily timbered as to obstruct the current.

In 1854 an observer said of Missouri River water that "a common drinking glass full of it, allowed to settle, deposits a sediment at least half an inch thick" (*New York Tribune,* June 22, 1854). The Roberts engineering report of 1872 declared that "the water of the Missouri River, from the mouth of the Muscleshell down, never, even in the lowest stage, becomes clear."

In the accounts of the Texas explorations of 1849 only a few clear streams were mentioned, and in plains geography the occasional appearance on the maps of a stream named Clear Creek is a matter of significance in emphasizing that a clear stream was the exception. The clear headwaters streams were mostly limited to the limestone outcrop along the escarpment of east-central Texas, or similar outcrops in other parts of the grassland, but such clear beginnings did not flow much distance until they became muddy. Abert (1845) noted the muddy waters of the Canadian, on occasion too muddy for a bath. He described how the violent rainstorms eroded the ravines. Similar descriptions were recorded by Frémont and by Cross. The last named related also how he gathered fuel in the upper Platte Valley from the drift on the upland washed down by the floods.

The character of the streams of the drier grassland has been insufficiently emphasized and appreciated in connection with the history of the area. Except for the beds of the Missouri, Canadian, and Pecos, few rivers of the plains lie below the ground water level (Webb, 1931). The typical plains streams lie above the ground water level and often the beds are higher than the surrounding country. This was noted by some early travelers, Frémont (1843) in particular, describing the Platte tributaries. Geologists did not notice and describe this peculiarity until later, Warren (1859) describing the Niobrara as running along a ridge and having few tributaries. Merrill (1924) excused Warren's lack of understanding of the explanation, because Warren was not a geologist.

A second characteristic of the streams of the grassland, and this applies to those of most of the region, is the one stressed by Cross (1849) that they were merely "drains of the prairies" carrying off the local precipitation. To put it in the negative; they were not fed in volume by deep-seated perpetual springs or glaciers. Cross made the point also that the Platte was really only a drain of the mountain snows which melted into spring floods, and a drain of the prairies. When the melting of the snows and the spring rains synchronized, the floods were frequently disastrous. Both the rains and the melting of the snows were highly seasonal, so after the spring floods, the stream beds were dry, or nearly so, most of the remainder of the year.

The muddy character of the Mississippi River in 1834 so impressed the geologist G. W. Featherstonhaugh, while on an expedition to the Ozark Mountain region, that he suggested experiments to determine the annual load of sediment carried by the river. By this procedure he proposed to calculate the age of the river and the rate of the retreat of the ocean as the result of silt deposits. Merrill (1924) credited him with being the first American geologist to make such a suggestion for estimating geological time.

The excesses of political agitation, the sensationalism of various types of social agitators, and the lack of historical perspective of the 1930s planted in the public mind erroneous ideas of causes of wind erosion and dust storms. The film, *The Plow That Broke the Plains,* distributed by the federal government, was only the most conspicuous of the devices around which was crystallized the idea that the plow was the cause of dust storms, and second only to the plow, allegedly, was overgrazing. The legend was built up assiduously that the western country was becoming a desert. Rexford Tugwell, undersecretary of agriculture, delivered an address May 15, 1935, in which he pictured the doom of the trans-Mississippi West as of 2235 A.D., 300 years hence, unless something like the Tennessee Valley Authority was adopted for that area. It was presented in the form of a journal of an exploring expedition investigating the Great Desert:

This week we have crossed the Mississippi River and have journeyed in our high-wheel motors deep into the great desert. Our dust masks have been useful, for without them we should be unable to travel for more than an hour or two after dawn. The Mississippi was nearly dry so that our pontoons sufficed for the crossing.

Our records show that at the junction of this with another river, the Missouri, there was once a considerable city and that this was a country devoted to the cultivation of grain. There now are only moving pieces of dust for hundreds of miles. Of the city little remains except some skeletons of twisted steel. It is not recommended that excavations be carried out at this point, since everything of historical value was moved to the eastward as the desert encroached.

The cause of these desert conditions is different from that which ruined the civilization to the east. Here it was the exposure of the plains to the wind. There it was the destruction of trees and the washing away of hills by the characteristic torrential rains of summer. Today we are camped on the bank of a river which falls over an escarpment evidently built of masonry. We think it must have been intended to dam up a canyon and form a lake to furnish continuous power. We assume that the lake filled with silt and that the power or irrigation venture failed because the river runs only during the spring floods.

We have seen no living thing since leaving the Tennessee Valley. We expect to return soon for the study of the records which have concentrated there as civilization has disappeared elsewhere on the continent. We expect to spend a few more weeks analyzing the soil of this desert, measuring, as well as we can, the climatic changes since vegetation disappeared, and collecting specimens of various remains.

Of course this address was not representative of the serious work of the regular staff of the department of agriculture, but unfortunately the political influence of such extremes left its mark upon the myth built up about the great plains.

In a spirit similar to Tugwell's desert speech, Paul B. Sears, a well-known botanist, published a book, *Deserts on the March* (1935). The latter part of the book contained much information on sound soil conservation practices, but it was set in a historical framework indicated by the title. In reviewing the history of civilization, the destiny of different peoples was represented as being determined by soil destruction—man-made deserts were pictured as marking the seats of once-great empires. From the standpoint of historical methodology, Sears did not state his question in a form that was subject to proof—it was a meaningless question. From the standpoint of historical evidence, he did not present documented facts that could be shown to possess the alleged cause-and-effect relationship between civilizations and deserts. In any case, this supposititious historical introduction did not prove that the plains, or any other part of the United States, was undergoing a man-made change into a desert.

In 1935 the Tugwell-directed Resettlement Administration began production of the documentary film, *The Plow That Broke the Plains* (3 reels, 30 minutes). As the *Literary Digest* (May 16, 1936) described it, they entered Montana in September, "worked into Wyoming, on the wings of a blizzard, shot scenes in Colorado, Western Kansas, and the Texas Panhandle, from which they were blown by high winds and choking dusts." There were only 700 words in the story, the remainder being told by the camera, with music "as an explanation and emotional accompaniment." The picture sequence was grass, cattle, the plow, drouth, dust storms, and desert, supposedly representing fifty years of change. At the close, some of the projects of the Resettlement Administration were shown by which some of the human damage might be repaired, but it was said that damage to forty million acres could never be undone.

In May 1936, when the film was given the first public showings, much was made of the fact that the film was not taken by the regular distributors. A few candid observers pointed out that the film length of thirty minutes was too long for a short, and too short for a regular feature, and therefore it could not be programmed without disrupting theatre schedules. Also, it put city theatre audiences to sleep. Some theatres in New York tried the device of advertising it as "the picture no one dared to show," but without significant results. Of course, that was fraudulent advertising! The *Survey Graphic* predicted that the film would be in great demand among educational institutions, and that was correct.

As history the film was indefensible. To be sure, each separate photograph, of which the 2,700 feet of film was composed, was an authentic picture as of the year 1935, but the film as a whole was not photographic history. The sequence of the photographs and the cause-and-effect relationships were not a camera record of historical change; they were arrangements of photographs of a single date pieced together to produce the illusion of a time sequence. The historical effect of change from grass to man-made desert was solely the result of the artificial design or purpose in the minds of the producers. In other words, if run in reverse order, the same pictures could be made to show the transition in fifty years from desert to grassland. It was all a matter of arrangement.

After three years of protests from the plains states, an Associated Press dispatch of April 19, 1939, quoted Representative Mundt of South Dakota as saying that the National Emergency Council had agreed to make no additional commitments to exhibit the film until it could be changed to meet the criticisms of the residents of the plains. The changes were not made, and the film was withdrawn from circulation. Copies of it, already in educational film libraries, however, were still available.

Photography is a medium of communication particularly adaptable to the uses of propaganda, or of mere sensationalism in the news. Faked drouth pictures, or photographs with misleading captions, became an issue during the latter part of 1936. The historian is indebted particularly to the *Fargo* (North Dakota) *Forum* for its aggressive attack upon such practices. This campaign succeeded in attracting national attention, was reported in August and September 1936 by the Associated Press and other news services, and thus became a matter of public record in the newspapers served by those news agencies.

One example was that of a bleached bovine skull which appeared in photographs, in different settings, designed to depict drouth damage. According to the evidence brought out in the controversy, the pictures were taken in May 1936 in Pennington County, South Dakota. At that time of the year there was no drouth damage. Obviously, as the skull was conspicuously weathered, it was from an animal that had been dead a long time and from causes quite unknown to the photographer. According to the Associated Press report, August 29, 1936, the official photographer admitted moving the skull from place to place, but he denied that such a procedure was faking a drouth damage photograph. Another example, apparently merely sensationalism, was pointed out by the *Fargo Forum,* and involved a newsreel agency which was charged with taking pictures of a farm family in Stutsman County, near Jamestown, North Dakota, supposedly fleeing from the drouth. The whole episode was said to have been "staged" for the moving picture camera, and the family in question was paid for services rendered, after which they returned to their home.

John Steinbeck's novel, *Grapes of Wrath,* a best-seller of 1939 (film version 1940), exploited the drouth in the great plains as well as the migratory labor question in California. As applied to the plains, its theme was the effect of drouth in the "Dust Bowl" and of tractor farming, as the causes of human degradation. As a literary work, undoubtedly it was an effective piece of writing. It was not the first time that fiction had been used for social propaganda purposes. As a piece of reporting of the contemporary scene, it was grossly inaccurate. The location selected, Sequoyah County, borders on Arkansas. It is on the western flank of the Ozark region, a hill country, not the plains. Its climate is of the high-rainfall type, and climate and soil make it an area suitable for highly diversified farming, not mechanized wheat, cotton, or corn farming. The most effective criticism of the book is to be found in Elmer T. Peterson, *Forward to the Land* (1942). Even so far as Steinbeck's argument could have been applied to the plains country, it misrepresented the factor of mechanization in agriculture, which was a constructive step in the agricultural revolution—significant to the agriculture everywhere in the twentieth century and nowhere else more so than to the plains.

A large part of the surface of the plains region had been formed by soil materials transported from the mountains and deposited over the parent rock. Water sorted the materials in the process of depositing them, and winds blew the finer particles up and down the plains area. A substantial portion of the plains soils, developed from transported materials, were classified and mapped by the federal and state soil agencies as wind-blown soils long prior to the dust storms controversies of the 1930s. Possibly part of that dust storm process of soil material distribution occurred prior to the establishment of the general grass cover, but it is certain to the historian that much of it continued throughout the whole span of time since the country was known to the white man. To be crystal clear, it is true that dust storms did not arise from a soil covered with vegetation, but the point at issue is that always some parts of the plains were bare or relatively so as a result of the activities of animals, especially rodents, and large portions were exposed to the wind from time to time through the action of fire, drouth, and wild animals. As Grinnell and Formosov pointed out, these · influences were continually disturbing some part of the grasslands, delaying or destroying a theoretically normal succession series and forestalling any achievement of a uniform theoretical climax. It was only in periods of prolonged climatic fluctuations on the drouth side that these conditions became general and serious. The review of the exploring expeditions affords a conspicuous and reliable documentation of the soundness of this point of view.

Archeologists have shown from evidence that seems all but conclusive that during archeological time there were recurring periods of extensive soil blowing (Seltzer, 1940; Steward, 1940; W. D. Strong, 1940; Van Royan, 1937; Wedel, 1940, 1941, 1947). Excavations of Indian village sites show successive occupations of the same location, sometimes three or more, separated by thick deposits of wind-blown material. There would seem to be little room for difference of opinion relative to this basic situation, although views may vary as to the length of the periods of soil blowing, as to why the sites were abandoned from time to time, and as to what became of the Indians during the intervals.

An explicit example of dust storms on the plains during historical time is afforded by the journal of Isaac McCoy, October–November 1830, recording an expedition engaged in surveying the boundary of an Indian reservation north of the Kansas River. The entry for October 18 was written near the southern boundary of the present Nemaha County, Kansas, about 96° west longitude:

Had a little rain last night—the country is exceedingly parched with drought. When we got on to the prairies, the ashes from the recently burned prairies, and the dust and sand raised so by the wind that it annoyed us much, the wind raising, I found that the dust was so scattered that it became impossible to perceive the trail of the surveyors, who had gone a few hours ahead of the horses. While conversing with Calvin about the course we should go, we discovered the atmosphere ahead darkening, and as it had become cloudy, we fancied that a misting rain was coming upon us, and made some inquiry respecting the security of our packs. A few minutes taught us that what we had fancied to be rain, was an increase of the rising dust, sand, and ashes of the burnt grass, rising so much and so generally that the air was much darkened, and it appeared on the open prairies as though the clouds had united with the earth. Our eyes were so distressed that we could scarcely see to proceed. . . . The wind blew incessantly and excessively severe. . . . Was about to select a camping ground, when we met a man whom the Doctor [sent] to inform me that he could not proceed with his work, and that they waited for us in a wood a mile ahead. It being very difficult for me to look at my pocket compass I told the soldier . . . to lead us back. He set off with great confidence that he could find his way back and in a few minutes was leading us north instead of west. . . . On finding the surveyors, we encamped for the residue of the day. Even in this wood, and after the wind had somewhat abated, the black ashes fell on us considerably.

Wind and dust accompanied the expedition farther west and on October 26 the Republican Valley was reached: "Wind very high, scarcely allowing us to pass." October 27:

Today we reached the Republican, . . . and to our great disappointment we found it more destitute of grass than any place we had seen where wood was to be found. The river runs over a bed of sand—the banks low, and all the bottom lands are a bed of sand white and fine, and now as dry as powder ought to be. I never saw a river along which we might not find some rich alluvial moist bottoms, on which, at this season of the year, could not be found green grass. But here there is, in a manner none.

We examined along the river for grass until satisfied that none could be found and then turned back to a creek we had passed five miles back. . . . The scarcity of wood on the river and the sandiness and poverty of the bottoms, greatly discourage me as to the country—While the great scarcity of food for our horses made us fear that we should not be able to proceed much further.

The entry of November 5 represents the country about the 98th meridian and read:

Completed the line of the outlet to 150 miles, and stopped. For some days we have discovered that our horses were failing so fast, that we must soon return, or lose them all. . . . We are beyond all Indian villages, and 50 miles, or more, into the country of Buffaloes. . . .

After we completed our survey, we turned on to a creek, and were looking for an encampment—the day calm and fair—when suddenly the atmosphere became darkened by a cloud of dust and ashes from the recently burnt Prairies occasioned by a sudden wind from the north. It was not three minutes after I had discovered its approach, before the sun was concealed, and the darkness so great, that I could not distinguish objects more than three or four times the length of my horse. The dust, sand, and ashes, were so dense that one appeared in danger of suffocation. The wind driving into one's eyes seemed like destroying them. . . .

The storm commenced, sun three quarters of an hour high in the evening, and blew tremendously all night. It had abated a little by morning. The dust was most annoying at the commencement. There was no clouds over us.

Another early example illustrates the conditions in the east central part of the present state of South Dakota, east of the Missouri River. I. N. Nicollet described his experience of July 1839: "As the growth [of grass] is too scant to prevent the dust from being raised by the almost incessant winds that blow over them [the plains], the traveller is very much inconvenienced." This entry was for the mid-summer when the winds were least severe and the summer growth of grass would have provided the fullest cover. It would be still more informative if continuous records were available on both of the preceding localities for the windy spring months of March, and April of the next year when the country was most barren of vegetation; when drouth, grazing, the tramping of hoofed animals, and prairie fires had most completely exposed the soil to the action of these winds. Furthermore, these deal with the country east of the 99th meridian, not the more critical high plains. Another example of a dust storm was related for the Snake River sagebrush country in connection with Major Osborne Cross's expedition to Oregon in 1849.

During the early years of Kansas settlement, the dust storms in 1855 evoked the comment that "this annoyance, however, will not be so great when the surrounding country is brought under cultivation, and the prairies cease to be burned" (Malin, 1946). During the 1930s the argument was just the opposite, that dust storms were caused by "the plow that broke the plains."

In the very nature of the case, the records are too incomplete to determine either the extent or the intensity of early dust storms as compared with the 1930s, but they are sufficiently comprehensive to establish the fact that on repeated occasions dust storms were extensive, and severe. These samples are only a few from the present author's collection of the records of a century of dust storms (Malin, 1946). To complete the record, attention is called to the fact that the National Archives has collected and organized for research purposes all the weather records of agencies of the federal government. They are described in a National Archives Special List No. 1, "List of climatological records in the National Archives" (1942). These materials have not yet been examined for information on dust storms. Sand and dust storm reporting was inaugurated during the 1870s, and these manuscript reports should contain a revealing story which would expand the one told by the present author from the printed sources (1946).

On the basis of experience in plains agriculture, farmers came to the conclusion that the blowing of the soil, of the water, or of the wind transported types did not necessarily damage the productivity of the fields concerned. On occasion it was pointed out that a field blown to the depth of plowing might produce better crops than formerly. To the eastern soil conservationist such views were not only incomprehensible, they were vicious. These views of the practical plainsman received the endorsement of scientific men in a "Symposium on Loess" (Elias, 1945) in which Elias said the same thing with respect to Nebraska loess and explained that the chemical breakdown of the constituent rock released supplies of necessary plant nutrients in a form available for roots. Of course, such an explanation on the part of the farmer or of the scientist was not to be interpreted as opposition to soil conservation, but it did call attention forcibly to the prevailing misinformation and misconceptions with respect to the soil problems of the plains.

A large part of the western soils of mid and low-rainfall areas have been formed from parent materials transported either by glacier, by water, by wind, or by combinations of them. They had been deposited to various depths over earlier geological formations. In some places the underlying rock protruded through the covering of transported material, or erosion had removed the covering material in part, exposing the underlying rock. In any case, the problems presented by transported soils were quite different from those of residual soils of high-rainfall areas. It was the latter that presented the critical problem in equilibrium—the formation of new soil underneath by decomposition of parent rock as fast as erosion removed the top soil. If top soil were removed more rapidly than new soil formation replaced it, then the bare rock would eventually be exposed. It was this fact that made erosion, of even a small amount of the normal soil profile, a matter of serious concern, and any large proportion a major disaster. The problem of western transported soils was different, except for those spots where the apron of soil materials was thin or the underlying rock formations were exposed, and even there the fact of lesser rainfall resulted in differences.

The theory of soil maturity as held by the Russian-American school seems open to question as applied to the transported soils of the mid and low-rainfall region. Agricultural experience has already called attention to the fact that some sandy and some loessal soils could be blown from a field as deep as it had been plowed and the fertility and productivity remain unimpaired, or nearly so. Or possibly the picture would be kept more accurately in focus by bearing in mind the quips of western newspapers that sometimes admonished readers not to worry if their belongings were seen going north today, because when the wind changed they would be blown back. It is clear from practical experience that soil fertility and productivity are not necessarily related to the development, or to the preservation, of the theoretically mature profile. Even Marbut's Plate 6, *Atlas of American Agriculture,* shows much of the most productive land of the grassland area as having soils without profiles, or with only imperfect profiles.

The perspective of agricultural experience affords a demonstration of the difficulties in which the soil scientists became involved in their soil erosion report and map (1935), in Part V of the Supplementary Report of the Land Planning Committee of the National Resources Board. The reconnaissance survey of soil erosion for the entire United States was made by the Soil Conservation Service, using the services of "115 trained soil-erosion specialists, who visited every county in the United States and prepared an erosion map on the basis of actual reconnaissance. . . . Since the survey was made in 2 months, ending October 15, 1934, it was impossible to indicate more than generalized or predominant conditions." In defining the different erosion classes and mapping their distribution, reference was made frequently to the percentage of the top soil removed by erosive action of wind and water. No standards of measurement were presented. How was top soil defined, and how was its original depth determined? What date was used as a basing point for original depth? According to the dust storm and water erosion record, such a date would be important and would have to be established, along with the record of the soil profile at that time. It is essential to an understanding of the unsatisfactory character of the report to make clear that there were no fixed markers against which top soil could be measured, nor "original" profile records that could be used for comparison. There is no indication of the extent of the acquaintance of the soil scientists mentioned with the counties which they surveyed, but it is obvious that they could not have possessed intimate knowledge of the physiographic history of those counties because no such historical records exist. Their estimates were necessarily guesswork of the most superficial kind, and based upon a soil theory that did not recognize adequately the fundamentals of the particular environment and its relation to soils.

The best test of the validity of this soil erosion survey is the production record of the following years. With the return of favorable weather conditions, 1942–1946, the hard winter wheat region experienced an unbroken succession of five good crops over most of the area, for some counties six, 1941–1946, a record not equalled by any other period since the country was settled.

For reporting purposes the state of Kansas is divided into nine divisions, by thirds in both directions. The eastern third, three divisions north to south, is traditionally a soft winter wheat area (wheat is not the leading crop), and is omitted from this discussion. It extends west to about 97°, the western limit of the tall grass-oak-hickory-walnut native vegetation. The middle third, three divisions north to south, extends approximately from 97° to 100°, the native mixed grass region, and a hard winter wheat region. The western third, three divisions north to south, is the short grass high plains, a hard winter wheat region. Table 3.1 gives comparative yields for the six hard winter wheat divisions, 1945, 1946, and estimated for 1947.

In each erosion class over 25 per cent of the land of an area was said to have been affected, and on the map each class was colored separately and numbered. A large part of the western third of Kansas was marked with the symbols 4 and 5. This meant that for areas marked as erosion class 4, over 25 per cent of the land had been subject to "slight soil drifting" and that "small amounts of surface soil are removed." This class of land constituted

**Table 3.1:** Hard Winter Wheat Yields: Kansas

| Division | 1945 Final (Bu. per Acre) | 1946 Final (Bu. per Acre) | 1947 June 1 Estimate (Bu. per Acre) |
|---|---|---|---|
| *Central third* | | | |
| North central | 13.3 | 15.0 | 17.0 |
| Central | 11.3 | 16.4 | 18.0 |
| South central | 14.1 | 17.1 | 17.0 |
| *Western third* | | | |
| Northwestern | 22.3 | 21.3 | 21.5 |
| Central | 19.1 | 15.3 | 20.5 |
| Southwestern (Dust Bowl) | 17.4 | 13.1 | 22.0 |
| *State average* | 15.5 | 16.2 | 19.0 |

a large part of the west central division of Kansas. Class 5 was similar to class 4, only more severely eroded, "where the soils have been blown off to depths ranging from 1 to 6 inches. The productive use of the land has been materially lessened, and the tendency is for its condition to become increasingly worse." Most of the southwestern division (the so-called Dust Bowl) was marked class 5.

In 1945, nineteen of the twenty highest-yielding counties were in the western third of the state, west of 100°. Stanton County, in the southwestern corner, led with an average yield of 31 bushels; Hamilton County, in the western central division, was second with 30.4; Cheyenne County, in the northwestern corner, was third with 30.1; and Wallace and Kearney counties, in the central western division, tied for fourth place with 28 bushels each.

The eight counties in the northwestern corner of Kansas were marked with the map symbols 4, 27, 37, and 38 for the erosion classes and their distribution. Erosion class 4 indicated "slight soil drifting" and the removal of "small amounts of surface soil." Under the explanation of class 27 appears the statement: "Twenty-five to seventy-five percent of the surface soil removed," and "crop yields and farm efficiency have been reduced by soil losses." Number 37 represents a situation of "over 75 percent of all surface soil removed. . . . Loss of surface soil is severe and generally complete." For class 38, the statement is that "over 75 percent of the surface was lost. . . .

Large areas of these lands are essentially ruined for cultivated crops. These conditions have resulted in abandonment of large areas."

The wheat crops of 1945 and 1946 were the climax of the period for the eight northwestern counties described in the preceding paragraph. The yield of wheat in 1946 was less than in 1945 but was 21.3 bushels per acre from 1,401,000 acres harvested, and was the highest yield for any similar area in the state. The state average yield was 16.2 bushels per acre. Of the ten highest county yields in the state, five are found in this group of eight northwestern counties. Only one county, Graham, fell below the state average. The three top yielding counties of the state were the three extreme northwestern corner counties, Cheyenne (24.7 bu.), Sherman (24.3 bu.), and Rawlins (23.5 bu.) lying in the area colored on the soil erosion map as of classes 4, 27, 37, and 38. In conclusion, these figures are all above the long-term averages for either the state as a whole or for the particular counties named. If averages for the term of years 1942–1946 were used, a similar general result would be obtained. If other groups of counties were used, conclusions in the same general direction would be obtained, the details varying with the area and the year. Obviously the soil was still highly productive, regardless of the soil erosion report of 1934.

The phenomenal hard winter wheat crop of 1947 accents further the soil problem in relation to erosion history, fertility, and productivity. At planting time in September 1946, there was a moisture deficiency, remedied by rains in the southwestern division of Kansas in early October, and in other divisions later. With the coming of rains, the wheat made a good growth affording wheat pasture for large numbers of cattle and sheep until heavy snows and severe winter weather forced some curtailments. On January 1, 1947, over a million sheep and lambs were on feed in Kansas, mostly on wheat pasture. Soil moisture tests, October 14–20, 1946, revealed moisture to a depth of 44.3 inches over the western two-thirds of the state—the hard winter wheat belt—summer-fallowed land having only a slight advantage over continuously cropped land. In April 1947 soil moisture conditions in the western third of the state were the most favorable on record, 47.4 inches. A moist, cool, late spring provided the background for the unprecedented June 1 winter wheat yield estimate of 19 bushels per acre for the state, second only to 1942, (includes soft winter wheat of eastern third), or a total production of 277,761,000 bushels, 25,995,000 bushels above the previous record established in 1931. The 14,619,000 acres for harvest in 1947 was the largest of record.

The 1947 crop prospects were too good to be true. The crop season was abnormal on the favorable side, and before the season ended, on the unfavorable side, a long overdue fluctuation in weather to redress the averages. In April, tornadoes appeared in the grassland from the Mississippi River states westward, the climax occurring in the Panhandles of Texas and Oklahoma, destroying a large part of Woodward, Oklahoma, April 9–10. They continued into June. Violent electrical storms occurred also, with driving winds and rain which tangled the rank, heavy-headed wheat. Hail beat paths through many counties, one to three times. On May 29, occurred a freeze in the northwestern counties, and in Colorado and Nebraska; and again, June 11, snow and freezing weather hit the last-named states. In the southwestern counties of Kansas hot winds came in June, especially on June 9, which blasted many fields. Other hazards were orange leaf rust, green bugs, Hessian fly, and root rot in scattered areas. And finally, in harvest time, a shortage of combines to harvest the grain, and a shortage of gasoline for combines and trucks, caused heavy losses, and there were some fires in ripened fields. Even weevils appeared in some grain as it came from the combines. The crop estimate of June 1 discounted only a part of these final hazards, but the most serious damage was revealed after June 1, or occurred after that date. With this fabulous crop made, and almost harvested, and a price of almost two dollars per bushel assured, the hard winter wheat region almost lived wheat twenty-four hours of the day. The July 1 estimate revised downward somewhat the figures of June 1, but the lateness of the harvest left uncertain the actual quantity of grain saved.

The *Kingman* (Kansas) *Journal,* July 11, 1947, reported that four hail storms had hit the county:

The harvest this year has been a headache for wheat farmers, caused by excessive rain, hail, and a shortage of machines. . . . With all the difficulties which have beset this harvest, farmers are not discouraged and are making arrangements to put in another crop and will gamble that "next year may be better." It is characteristic of the traditional spirit of the wheat farmer, if officers ever decide to enforce the anti-gambling law, the wheat farmer will be put out of business.

In Rush, Lane, and Wichita counties, reports of 30 bushel wheat were common and some fields made 40 and 50 bushels per acre. In Rooks County, yields of 45 bushels per acre were reported in the southern part of the county, while frost-damaged fields in the northern part of the county were reduced to 5 to 10 bushels per acre. Phillips County had much the same story, 5 to 30 bushel yields: "The five bushel fields look just as good as the 30 bushel fields—from the road," lamented the *Phillips County Review,* July 10, 1947, but, "with yields vastly reduced by the freezing weather, and by a long path of hail, Phillips County appears to have almost a normal wheat crop anyway." The *Norton County Champion,* July 3, 1947 reported:

Estimates of the 1947 wheat crop in Norton county have been drastically reduced the past week or two by bad hail storms, and increasingly more evident frost damage, plus other factors, until it is now estimated that somewhere near 30,000 acres will not be harvested. What looked like a two million bushel crop—or better— a few weeks ago, now appears to be closer the million mark—with a resulting loss to Norton county of around two million dollars, a severe blow. [A million bushel loss at two dollars per bushel was the basis for this estimate.]

There are some farmers who will harvest no wheat whatever, and others will harvest a bumper crop. In between lie the vast majority with a lot of 10 to 15 bushel wheat. . . .

It has been one of those years that just naturally can't be classed as a good crop year from any angle. Everything in the book happened to the 1947 crop—but still there will be a lot of wheat harvested, compared with what we used to consider a "normal" year in the 1930s.

Decatur County, adjoining Norton on the west, started off the harvest with a report, according to the *Oberlin Herald,* July 10, of wheat on the Bremer estate yielding 50 bushels per acre: "That is mighty good wheat in any language, and it comes as a quieting note after the many reports during recent weeks of damage from green bugs, freeze, etc." The following week a 60 acre field made 61 bushels per acre of 63 pound wheat, and the price at the local elevator was $2.05 per bushel.

These particulars have been presented in some detail to insure beyond the shadow of a doubt a record of the main issues. Wheat buyers reported the 1947 crop as showing one of the lowest protein averages on record. At Dodge City and Garden City percentages of 9.8 to 10 were recorded. These samples were lower than the great 1931 crop. In other respects, the 1947 grain was of the finest quality, testing up to 65 pounds per bushel. Agronomists had experimented, and debated the factors determining protein content, the most recent conclusions listing soil as the deter- minant, except climate in some instances, and variety. As a matter of historical record, high protein percentages were associated with unfavorable crop years such as the middle 1930s, and low percentages with favorable crop years such as 1931 and 1947. The claim that soil was the limiting factor did not meet the issue of why the same variety in the same field varied from year to year. What is meant by a favorable crop year? A crop year that is usually considered favorable for wheat in terms of weather conditions producing high bushel yields of grain is not necessarily favorable for high protein content. Which weather factor, moisture, sunshine, or temperature, or combination of them with soil and variety, is necessary to insure any particularly desired quantity or quality of product?

Nitrogen deficiency in the winter wheat region was a menace to the continued production of crops, according to some agronomists. The argument was advanced that in the higher-rainfall areas nitrogen could be restored by legumes, manure, and crop residues as well as by commercial fertilizers, but that in the low-rainfall areas these factors were deficient, especially varieties of legumes suitable for crop rotation programs. Experimentation revealed that in low-rainfall climates commercial nitrogen fertilizers gave unsatisfactory results. Again it is in order to raise the question whether the soil scientists have arrived at a satisfactory theory of soil fertility and productivity for low-rainfall climates. In the native vegetation the numbers of legumes, both of varieties and individuals, had been large in the tall-grass country, but diminished to the westward in the mixed-grass and short-grass country. Descriptions by early explorers suggest that some of the heavily sodded grama-buffalo grass areas approached the status of simple stands, with very few legumes. How did the short-grass country maintain its nitrogen supply? Studies of nitrogen supply under strictly native grass conditions are needed and might provide some perspective on the nitrogen question, and on the larger issues of soil fertility and productivity, and on the problems of soil conservation in low-rainfall climates.

Evidence may be piled up without end to demonstrate that the soil erosion survey of 1934 did not deal with fundamentals. In total production, the crop of 1947 exceeded the record production of 1931, which preceded the drouth and dust storm years of the 1930s. The protein factor in the drouth years ran high and in 1947 low, as in 1931. In yields per acre, the crops of 1945, 1946, and 1947 exceeded those of 1931 and earlier. The Stanton County record yield of 31 bushels in 1945 was topped again by the estimates for 1947. When the final figures are available on the 1947 crop, they may fall below those given in table 3.1 as estimated for June 1, but those reduced yields are not to be charged against nitrogen deficiency, loss of fertility, or of productivity, nor against wind erosion of soil. They were clearly the result of hazards intervening on the eve of harvest and after the record-yielding crop was virtually made.

The crop of 1947 and two dollar wheat was a curse to the hard winter wheat region, in providing the final fillip to the wheat boom: high-priced land, and large-scale speculative wheat production, which had already gone beyond reasonable proportions. The largest production reported under one management was 78 square miles in some seven counties in Kansas and Colorado. Many other instances of large acreage were on record. With the fluctuation in the weather to the unfavorable side, long overdue, such speculative mass-production operations create situations where it is a physical impossibility to supervise adequately such acreages under drouth and wind—dust storm—conditions. Unnoticed during the high tension over saving the fabulous wheat crop of 1947 was the announcement that after thirteen years the receivers for the Wheat Farming Corporation were closing the books on that unfortunate large-scale venture of the earlier wheat boom era. A 25 to 60 bushel yield, with wheat at two dollars per bushel, meant fifty to one hundred twenty dollars per acre gross income from a single acre and a single crop. What was such land worth, land that could not have been sold at ten dollars per acre, or possibly at any price, only ten years earlier?

## Desert Equilibrium

In dealing with the desert it is traditional to assume that there the struggle for existence was more intense than in other regions. This point of view has been challenged and needs revaluation, especially in a background of the recent findings in the field of developmental physiology. It would probably be valid to maintain that the problem of survival is different, for the several regions, but not necessarily more severe. On a long-term basis, stabilized plant and animal life appears to have been limited to replacement plant for plant and animal for animal. Thus in each region, irrespective of climate factors, the increase potential was offset by resistance factors of some kind which eliminated all but one survivor on the long-term average. In a temperate climate these adverse factors may be intense competition between plants, or insects versus plants, or animals versus plants, or combinations of them, rather than drouth or heat. There would seem to be no difference as respects severity of the struggle so long as all increase is eliminated except replacement of individual for individual.

A second tradition about the desert placed the emphasis almost exclusively upon the water relation of plants and animals, with little or no attention to temperature, light, and soil. Possibly this second proposition possessed more validity than the first, but even at that, there is doubt whether the assumption should be made without more complete information. The most comprehensive studies made thus far have been those under the sponsorship of the Carnegie Institution of Washington, and they have dealt mostly with water relations of plants, and less intensively with temperature, but the photosynthesis studies sponsored by the Smithsonian Institution may prove even more important as explaining plant and animal life irrespective of climatic regions. The inadequacy of the studies of animal relations on the desert makes an attempt at a general summary of the factors of desert equilibrium peculiarly unsatisfactory.

Observations carried out on completely protected plots in the Arizona desert near Tucson have provided some interesting data on the problem of the composition of desert vegetation (Shreve, 1929; Shreve and Hinckley, 1937). The oldest plots were brought under protection in 1906, and others in 1910 and 1928. In thirty years the large perennials scarcely changed in number, but the small woody perennials and the grasses increased greatly. The grasses which were negligible in 1906 covered 2.7 percent of the area in 1903, but the large perennial plants determined the appearance of the desert. In conclusion, Shreve and Hinckley emphasized that there was no common trend discoverable other than the increase in population of the small plants.

The limitations of the above experiment must be stressed in order not to leave erroneous impressions of its bearing on the controverted question of the nature of the desert climax. The areas were completely protected from grazing, and the relations of other animals to soil and plants were not considered in the report. The results can have, therefore, but a restricted bearing on the question of what the original wild state might have been. The limited area covered by grasses at the end of thirty years is worthy of note, but even more interesting is the fact that one large woody scrub, and no more, replaced each one that died during the thirty-year interval. Although not constituting proof, these experiments tended to cast doubt upon, rather than support, the theory that the shrubs constituted a disclimax.

The sagebrush problem appears clearer, from the records of the early explorers, than the southern desert brush problem. Spanish influence had not extended much into the sagebrush country except at its southern extension, but the clear dominance of the sage was so conspicuous as to induce nearly every early traveler to comment explicitly upon it. Abert's (1845) description of the dominance of sagebrush, with its accompaniment of cacti, was a conspicuous feature of his account of the country south of Bent's Fort, the present southeastern Colorado. Simpson's (1849a, 1849b) description of northwestern New Mexico and northeastern Arizona, the northern Spanish pueblo and Navajo country, deserves special attention. Unacclimated to the desert, Simpson was hypersensitive to its peculiarities and wrote with feeling of his trip westward from Santa Fé:

And, commensurate with this section, *arroyas,* cañons, *Mesas,* with their well-defined crests and escarpments; plateau and hemispherical mounds, intermitting dirty, clay-colored rills, dignified by the name of *rios,* (rivers) and an all-pervading dull, yellow, dirty, buff-colored soil,—have, in their respective magnitudes and relations, characterized the face of the landscape. . . .

In regard to the fertility or productive qualities of the soil for the whole area traversed this side [west] of Santa Fé, saving the inconsiderable exceptions which have from time to time been noted in my journal, the country is one extended *naked,* barren waste, sparsely covered with cedar and pine of a scrub growth, and thickly sprinkled with the wild sage, or artemisia, the color of domestic sage, suggesting very appropriately the dead, lifeless color of the wild.

In the western part of the country explored, Simpson stressed, September 5, that "the artemisia, as usual, has been the chief, and almost the only, plant, especially upon the uplands," and again September 6, "The artemisia has been the chief *flores.* The cactus which has been seen but seldom, today was more prevalent." The return route eastward was by way of the pueblos of Zuni, and Laguna along which the vegetation was more plentiful.

Frémont's . . . letter to the botanist John Torrey relative to the first expedition of 1842 emphasized more sharply what he thought of as characteristic plants of each subregion (Rodgers, 1942). For the Kansas River valley uplands, it was Amorphia; for the lower Platte Valley to the forks, it was Aster; for the return trip in September these valleys were yellow with Sunflowers; but from the Laramie fork to the continental divide at the South Pass, it was Artemisia which occupied "the place of the grasses." Frémont's second expedition, following a different route to South Pass and into the interior basin, emphasized artemisia again as the characteristic vegetation. For the country west of the South Pass, Frémont, in 1843, found sagebrush, and the account of Major Osborn Cross agreed with Frémont in emphasizing the sagebrush.

These records emphasize so strongly and in so many ways the prominence of the sagebrush for this period prior to white occupation, except in the Spanish section where white occupation reached further back in time, that there seems little ground for the theory that the modern sagebrush characteristic was a disclimax resulting from overgrazing by domestic animals. In order not to be misunderstood, there is no denial here that there had been overgrazing and abuse of the grazing value of the sagebrush country. The purpose is simply to emphasize that the historical descriptions do not seem to justify the contention that the brush dominance and the scarcity of grass was of recent origin.

## Conservation

The study of range management made great advances during the twentieth century (Malin, 1944a). Among the influences not sufficiently appreciated were the operations of rodents in the grassed areas as differentiated from the cultivated fields. The farmer tilled his land with machines and made war on rodents in his fields, but he carried this policy of exterminating rodents to the grassland without the accompaniment of artificial tillage. One or the other of these policies was a mistake. Range management experiments were carried out with contour furrowing using different widths, depths, and spacings for the conservation of moisture and control of erosion. This was artificial tillage and disturbance of the grasses which influenced succession and composition of the vegetation. This procedure was commended by Clements (Carnegie *Yearbooks* nos. 37, 39, 40, 1938, 1940, 1941). Others advocated permitting rodents to operate, by keeping them under biological controls, thus permitting the burrowing animals to engage in natural tillage (Shelford, 1944). It is not the purpose of this discussion to pass judgment on the merits of the policies involved, only to call attention explicitly to the issues. If adequately administered natural biological controls can accomplish the desired end, why resort to the elaborate and expensive system of artificial range conservation; or would a combination of the two accomplish more effective results than either one separately? From the standpoint of conservation as a whole, the issues are broader by far than matters of soil, of grazing, or of forestry, and should include wildlife resources and protection of fur-bearing animals as an integral part of a sound approach to conservation policies based upon an application of ecological principles. Programs for extermination of any particular species of wild animals should recognize the complexity of biological controls, and the fact that more damage than good may result from unsound policies (Hall, 1930a, 1930b).

One of the broadest and most significant discussions of nature and public policy was that of Shantz (1940), and one of his several points was the significance of wild land to man—roughly half of the world's land area or nearly the same proportion of the United States was wild land, which he predicted "will probably continue to be the back-log of civilization." Much had been done for conservation of forests, but not for wild land. What were the essentials of a policy for wild land? It was from a different approach, but in a similar broad spirit, that Shreve (1934b) recommended the revival of the viewpoint of the old-fashioned naturalist in seeing nature as a whole. Such approaches challenged a reconsideration of that much-abused term *submarginal land*—submarginal for what?

From the study of the ecology of the grassland in its natural state some important conclusions may be drawn, and one of the most important is that there was no such thing as an undisturbed grassland in the conventional sense. Man's turning over of the sod with the plow is only a more complete process of cultivation of the soil than took place continuously in nature. To say that a piece of grassland had never been plowed is a misstatement of the facts. It can mean only that the area had never been plowed artificially with man's agricultural tools.

New terminology might clarify much of the discussion of so-called native vegetation, because much of the disagreement relative to such questions stems from inaccurately or inadequately stated questions. Custom of long standing has settled upon the term *virgin* as applied to forests, or grassland, or soil, that has not been disturbed by civilized man. The term is a misnomer in the first place, because it is a sex term that has no proper applicability to vegetation, or to soil. In the hands of conservation propagandists, the term *rape* of the virgin continent, or *rape* of the earth, has often been introduced, carrying over into the discussion of nature the idea of sex crime. Nature does not offer any such parallel or analogy, and all such terms should be eliminated.

A new set of terms is offered here as a basis of discussion. As applied to the grassland, for instance, the term *native grassland* may be restricted to the condition prior to invasion by the white man's civilization. The term *domesticated native grassland* may be applied to areas after the white man's civilization has modified the vegetational cover somewhat and destroyed many or most of the native animals, especially burrowing animals, that influence vegetation and soil. The term *plowed native grassland* may be applied to land growing native grass species, but which has once been plowed, or artificially disturbed to an equivalent degree.

According to such a set of terms, it is clear that there exists in the United States little, if any, *native grassland,* because the original animal populations have been largely destroyed, and because the composition of the vegetation has been modified substantially. In overgrazed areas, the grass composition has not only been modified, but weeds (forbs) have greatly increased; often new species have been introduced. In carefully conserved areas, such as those reserved regularly for prairie hay, or in which systematic "weed" killing campaigns have been followed, the original forbs, both composites and legumes, have been largely or altogether eliminated, and burrowing animals destroyed. These are "domesticated" areas because the native grasses and other vegetation found there are growing under a greater or lesser degree of artificial environment. The use of the term *plowed native grassland* is necessary to distinguish regrassed areas from those not so disturbed, although the actual composition of the vegetation may not be substantially different from the other. The major difference may be only in the history of the treatment to which it has been subjected.

The importance of such considerations is emphasized by the conservation practiced by some landowners in the Bluestem Pasture Region of Kansas. Long years of use or misuse or ill-advised conservation measures, destroyed the legumes, and to compensate for this loss, lespedeza has been planted. This legume attains its greatest growth during the mid-summer after the bluestems have passed their prime, thus affording a longer pasturing period, but the lespedeza is also an efficient nitrogen fixer, which rapidly contributes to the reconditioning of the grassland soil. In part, man is doing, artificially, with this introduced plant, what nature once did in the original "native grassland."

## Idea of Regional Adequacy

Western civilization, which developed during the later medieval and the modern periods, was in some measure the product of its environment, a temperate and humid climate, a region mostly forested, and a soil more or less acid. The ideologies of this culture were fitted into this framework as a product of the historical process of adjustment. The region came to be accepted as right, adequate, and complete, and served as the standard of values by which all other regions were measured. Out of this background to both Europe and to eastern North America, among other things, grew the dogma of a geographical determinism that identified superiority in civilization with this particular set of standards. Closely allied with it was the idea of closed space resulting from the occupation of the temperate zone by the expanding westernized civilization and the consequent corollary of the struggle for control of the most valuable space.

In its relations with other regions, the tendency has been for this deciduous forestman to attempt to impose his particular culture upon them irrespective of its adaptability and to expect a uniformity of results in all parts of the world. Anything that resisted that pattern was assumed to be inadequate, inferior, or deficient: even nature had blundered. The invasion of the grasslands of the world by this machine civilization began during the early nineteenth century, but the major phase of that occupation came only in the later part of the century. The grassland was described in terms of deficiency: treeless, subhumid, and sterile. The assumption, that soil that did not grow trees was worthless for agriculture, proved to be not only false, but it turned out that forest soils were less productive. The natural neutral or alkaline reaction of the soil of the grasslands also proved its versatility in crop production over the acid forest soil which required constant treatments of lime for some crops. The forest region that grew trees, not grass, did not possess grass for livestock except as it was sown as a field crop—tame grass meadow and hay. On invading the grasslands, forest man refused to recognize native grass as the vegetation best adapted to the region, plowed up the native grass, and attempted to grow eastern tame grasses. When these grasses did not grow, he condemned the country. It took many years to learn that native grasses would perpetuate themselves and provide pasturage and hay for an unlimited time if only man would give nature a fair chance—which consisted mostly in just letting it alone (Malin, 1942a, 1944b). The grass man, if he took his region as the standard of values, could point the finger of scorn at the deficiencies of the forest land: grassless, wet, with an acid, leached, infertile soil. This study concentrates on the North American grassland, but study of an individual grassland is only the introduction to a comparative study of all.

It is not the intention of this statement of the case for the grasslands to imply that the forest lands were deficient. That would be to fall into the same error that afflicted forest man. There were differences as among the world's several natural regions and not a question of superiority of one over the other. The main purpose of this discussion is to reorient the prevailing point of view, and to insist that not only the grasslands and the forest lands, but also the other regions such as the Arctic, the desert, the tropics, and the oceans, were biologically complete products of nature, each expressed in its own manner and in terms of normal factors of equilibrium. The degree of success in the occupation by man of any of these land regions could be measured in terms of his ability to fit his culture into conformity with the requirements of maintaining rather than disrupting environmental equilibrium. The differences among the several regions did not represent deficiencies, rather, each difference represented an advantage useful to other regions by which they supplemented each other, and by which each made its own unique contribution to the world. There was no major land region to which some branch of the human race, together with plants and animals, had not proven adaptable and developed cultures as diverse and distinctive as the environment. If man found himself unable to cope with more than one of these several kinds of environment, it was man and not nature in that region that was deficient.

Other than the grassland, probably the Arctic has been more maligned than any other region, although possibly Vilhjalmur Stefansson might challenge the assumption that the grassland has received the worst treatment at the hands of the deciduous forest man. The Arctic land is not a wasteland nor the Arctic Sea a barren sea, and his emphasis on the capacity of plant growth under the influence of the light of the 24-hour day pointed to the importance of systematic and intensive research in the biological problems of the Arctic. Raup (1941) emphasized also the lack of biological knowledge of the Arctic and urged a program of research. The advent of air communications thrust both the grasslands and the Arctic, and especially the latter, into the orbit of the new twentieth-century struggle for power. With the challenge of the sea power theory of history, the grasslands became of greater world significance because of the land-mass concept of power that was coming so largely to dominate twentieth-century thinking, but also because of the agricultural productivity of their soils. The Arctic gained significance because of the reorientation of outlook in political geography in terms of air power which follows great circle routes between the circumpolar land masses. The people who most effectively meet the problems of these two regions may lead the world in the next era.

# CHAPTER 4

# Space & History

*Reflections on the Closed-Space Doctrines*
*of Turner and Mackinder*

[In the 1940s, Malin increasingly turned his attention to questions of philosophy of history, historical writing, and public-policy issues. He attacked no theory more vigorously than the "closed-space" ideas of Frederick Jackson Turner and Halford J. Mackinder, the British geographer who believed that the ending of the American frontier also marked the end of the four-hundred-year world frontier, the so-called Columbian Age. Malin used the opportunity of his presidential address to the Agricultural History Society in 1944 to offer a reasoned critique of this pessimistic interpretation of American history and American institutions. The apparent negative affects of such closed-space ideas on government policymakers in the 1930s greatly disturbed Malin, who believed that the advent of the air age opened a new world of rapid transport and instant telecommunications. The twentieth-century frontier was as real as the Columbian frontier for Malin. If the prescient Kansas historian could update this essay today, he surely could argue that the dawning of the space age belies any closed-space doctrines.]

## The Idea of Closed Space

The idea of closed space is derived from the fact that all unoccupied lands, or lands occupied by undeveloped peoples, have been appropriated—that no wholly new lands are available. The simple geographical fact is one thing, but its significance to man, to his past and future, became the subject of speculation which has had, and still has, a profound effect upon the policies of nations. As applied to the United States, the idea is associated particularly with the influence of Frederick Jackson Turner, who, in 1893, at the world exposition celebrating the four-hundredth anniversary of the Columbian discovery, called attention dramatically to the passing of the American frontier. In Europe, as applied to the world scene, the idea stems most conspicuously from the writing of the British geographer, Sir Halford J. Mackinder. The purpose of this paper is to examine the ideas of these two men and their influence in particular, and along with them the somewhat different views of Josiah Strong, Alfred T. Mahan, and Sir William Crookes, and finally to raise the issue of the implications of the air age in relation to the idea of closed space.

## Frederick Jackson Turner

For half a century the school of historians who professed to follow the teachings of Frederick Jackson Turner (1861–1932) dominated the writing of American history, and only in the last of the five decades has there been any substantial challenge to the adequacy of their version of the frontier formula. The ideas basic to Turner's own statement of the significance of the frontier in American history may be pieced together in a brief and simple form—it was too simple—a fact that violated the fundamental principles of social causation as the complex product of the unique interaction of multiple causes (Turner, 1920). It was undoubtedly this simplicity, however, which explains its powerful appeal to those who are satisfied only with simple certainties. "American social development," he said, "has been continually beginning over again on the frontier," and "this fluidity . . . furnish[es] the forces dominating American character." Also, he insisted that "the settlement of . . . questions for one frontier served as a guide for the next." Among the forces stressed first was that "the frontier is the line of most rapid and effective Americanization. . . . a steady movement away from the influence of Europe, a steady growth of independence on American lines." Furthermore, it exerted a "nationalizing tendency"; it was "productive of individualism"; but "the most important effect of the frontier has been in the promotion of democracy here and in Europe."

Two ideas in Turner's original essay that are fundamental, although not quoted widely, are found in its concluding paragraph. The first is the escape idea, or a form of the safety-valve doctrine so carelessly exploited by some of his students: "In spite of environment, and in spite of custom, each frontier did indeed furnish a new field of opportunity, a gate of escape from the bondage of the past." The second gives a final flashback to the world setting in contrast with the American and the suggestion that the end of the nineteenth century marked the end of European expansion ushered in by the Columbian discovery of America as well as the passing of the American frontier. Although speaking at the Columbian Exposition, apparently he did not intend to imply a parallel, and certainly not to stress it, as his reference was only by way of emphasis upon his American theme. In conclusion he remarked:

He would be a rash prophet who should assert that the expansive character of American life has now entirely ceased. Movement has been its dominant fact, and, unless this training has no effect upon a people, the American energy will continually demand a wider field for its exercise. . . . the frontier has gone, and with its going has closed the first period of American history.

In emphasizing the frontier aspect of Turner's thinking, the present author is well aware that Turner laid much stress upon the problem of sections, that he wrote an essay on this significance in American history, and that some of his disciples insist that the interpretation of sections, not the frontier, was his principal contribution (Turner, 1932). Irrespective of such suggestions, however, Turner has been remembered by his students, and his influence has been measured primarily by the famous essay on "The Significance of the Frontier in American History," and no dressing up will change the basic message of the sentence: "The existence of an area of free land, its continuous recession, and the advance of American settlement westward, explain American development." It was the conclusion that the frontier in this sense had come to an end that crystallized the interpretation and gave to it the peculiar force which impressed his readers.

The development of Turner as a historian and of the school that followed him parallels fairly closely a similar development in the biological sciences and to some degree probably is a product of the doctrine of the origin of species. The post-Darwinian scientific world accepted evolution but disagreed on how it took place. The war was waged between the geneticists and the environmentalists. A similar conflict was in progress in the field of the social sciences. Herbert Baxter Adams and the school of thought against which Turner protested were geneticists so far as social institutions were concerned, stressing continuity and the transit of European culture across the Atlantic. Turner and his school were environmentalists and stressed differences rather than continuing similarities.

In an earlier article the present author has pointed out that, "among other things, the frontier hypothesis is an agricultural interpretation of American history which is being applied during an industrial-urban age, an isolationist interpretation in an international age, and a geographical interpretation stressing the passing of the frontier and raising the question of the consequences of this closed system upon the character of American institutions. In many respects it is this third implication, the doctrine of closed space, which was the most revolutionary consequence of Turnerism" (Malin, 1943). In only one of his major essays did Turner indicate explicitly the nature of the changes in the social order which he thought resulted from the passing of the frontier. This is found in his presidential address before the American Historical Association in 1910 under the indefinite title "Social Forces in American History" (Turner, 1920). It is evident from this title that he had no special theory to announce as he had done in spotlighting the significance of the frontier and the sections in his earlier interpretative essays. "Two ideals were fundamental in traditional American thought," he said, individual freedom, with its corollary that "government was an evil," and democracy—" 'government of the people, by the people and for the people.' " Whether he approved or disapproved, he did not say, but he pointed out:

The present finds itself engaged in the task of readjusting its old ideals to new conditions and is turning increasingly to government to preserve its traditional democracy. It is not surprising that socialism shows noteworthy gains as elections continue; that parties are forming on new lines; that the demand for primary elections, for popular choice of senators, initiative, referendum, and recall, is spreading, and that the regions once the center of pioneer democracy exhibit these tendencies in the most marked degree. They are efforts to find substitutes for that former safeguard of democracy, the disappearing free lands. They are the sequence to the extinction of the frontier.

Turner was a historian and not a prophet; he had pointed out how government was being used to protect the common man against the misuse of economic power in the hands of a few; his discussion of the interventions of government had been in terms of preserving the freedom of the individual and democracy, and not of destroying them, and he was not predicting whether such interventions would prove adequate to the task.

In the United States in the 1890s the American people responded enthusiastically to the Turner idea of history. It seemed to be an explanation and a justification of the leading national characteristics of the final third of the nineteenth century: nationalism, which became a reality to this generation following the Civil War; individualism, of which they were acutely aware because it was being challenged by the public interest theory of governmental regulation; and democracy, of which there was a new consciousness growing out of the cycle of reform agitation culminating in the early nineties. It seemed to confirm Americans in their continental isolationism. Was not their United States a unique civilization; was it not superior to that of Europe and Asia? Culture-conscious Americans had been preaching for some time that they were a God-chosen people whose mission was to carry these ideas and institutions to the backward peoples of the world. Only in a limited degree, however, did the United States participate in the final end-of-the-century scramble for the last unattached islands of the Pacific, getting only the Phillipines, the Hawaiian Islands, and part of the Samoan group. Continentalism and individualism were too strong and left the United States mentally unprepared at that stage to compete seriously for a share of world space.

### *Halford J. Mackinder*

Traditionally, considerations of Turner have been cast on the provincial stage of American history. About the same time, however, that Turner was enunciating for historical purposes the doctrine of closed space as applied to the United States, Halford J. Mackinder (1861–1947) was propounding a similar doctrine as applied to the globe. In a paper before the Royal Geographical Society on January 25, 1904, he presented the view that the Columbian world as a period of geographical expansion lasting about four hundred years came to an end about the opening of the twentieth century. The same basic idea appeared in his book, *Democratic Ideals and Reality* (1919). Mackinder stressed the point that mankind, with no new lands to discover, explore, and exploit, faced a future within a closed globe and his activities were limited to the ordering of his living within this known available closed space.

In 1905 Mackinder formulated his concept of "manpower as a measure of national and imperial strength." As he restated it in 1919, "In that term is implicit not only the idea of fighting strength but also that of productivity, rather than wealth, as the focus of economic reasoning." This is a revolutionary idea. It became the heart of his concept of "Social Momentum" and imparted a special significance to his idea of society as a "Going Concern." When he set off the Columbian world as a unified period of history terminating at the twentieth century, more was involved than the idea of closed space. In the transition from the Medieval to the Columbian world, the principle of the use of land in exchange for services gave way to the accumulation and ownership of cash capital as the instrument of power. In the passing of the Columbian world, the Columbian form of capitalism was represented as being transformed by the introduction of the concept of the productivity of the Going Concern. In other words the capacity to produce economic goods became the central idea of the social system. The character of any civilization is determined by the nature of the factor through which power is wielded in society. The power derived from the Medieval use of land had yielded to the power derived from accumulated wealth, and it in turn was displaced by the power implicit in the capacity to produce. The Medieval social system had been based on group organization, the Columbian on the individual, and the Going Concern on a mechanized totalitarian society. In such a system there was no room for individual rights—for individual non-conformity. The state as a Going Concern was paramount, or it lacked the distinguishing characteristic of efficiency in social organization and could not survive the rivalry of competing Going Concerns. The individual became merely an impersonal unit of manpower in the service of the state. Whether or not Mackinder intended it in that way is immaterial; the logic of the sequences seems unavoidable.

So far as the present author is aware, the parallel between Turner and Mackinder has never been pointed out, and to reconsider Turner in this relationship imparts to the frontier hypothesis a new meaning. It would be a mistake to assume that the idea of closed space was original with either Turner or Mackinder. It was "in the air" during the last two decades of the nineteenth century and appears in many forms in the literature of the period. The Turner and Mackinder expressions of the idea gained recognition over other versions only because of the influence they came to wield in their respective fields. Their originality lay primarily in the synthesis and the application they made of ideas already rather generally available. This statement should not be taken as minimizing either man, because what are usually called new ideas are almost always of that character. The idea of closed space has been implicit in the writing of many who probably were not thinking of it consciously in such terms. Often it was present explicitly, but reader interest did not register it because attention was focused on something else. Once the idea is brought to conscious attention, however, it seems to appear everywhere.

In tracing the history of ideas there is a tendency to identify exact sequences in thought from one man to another and to say the second man got his idea from the first, citing title and page. Sometimes this direct influence is a fact that can be proven, but probably more often such procedures are fundamentally false. In any age certain characteristic ideas are in the air, and the second man may never have heard of the work of the first although the historian of ideas places them in sequence. Even the formulation of abstract ideas by the great philosophers is understandable only as a folk process in which many were saying much the same thing without knowing of each other. The great thinkers of the age were probably only the more successful synthesizers or perhaps merely publicizers of the common fund of ideas fermenting in their age. Therefore, the attempt to identify man-to-man transmission of specific ideas as it appears in the histories is frequently, if not usually, essentially false as a historical procedure. An understanding of the evolution of thought must be grounded in a comprehensive assimilation of the whole content of the age, the expression of the little people as well as the great, because the great are the beneficiaries of folk process and are probably seldom so much true creators as channels through which the folk process finds its fullest expression in explicit language which makes it a matter of record.

## Josiah Strong

In 1884, the year Turner was graduated at the University of Wisconsin, and therefore several years prior to the formulation of his frontier hypothesis, the Reverend Josiah Strong (1847–1916) was writing a book which had as its thesis the significance, both to the United States and to the world, of the exhaustion of public lands (1885). He argued that "the closing years of the nineteenth century are one of the great focal points in history. It is proposed to show that the progress of Christ's kingdom in the world for centuries to come depends on the next few years in the United States." The trans-Mississippi West was to dominate the United States, and in his opinion there were seven perils to be overcome if the United States was to fulfill its destiny. They were the dangers associated with immigration, Romanism, Mormonism, intemperance, socialism, wealth, and, most threatening of all, the city, because all the other perils, except Mormonism, appeared in the most aggravated form in the city. He pointed out that the "meaning of cheap public lands, and significance of their occupation. . . . and, hence, the future of the nation [was] to be determined by 1900." He argued that "the race [was being] schooled for the competition with other races, which will begin as soon as the pressure of population on the means of support is felt in the United States."

Emphasizing acceleration in the rate of change in civilization, Strong viewed the nineteenth century as the significant culminating period under the influence of steam and electricity. The nineteenth was the century of inventions, of modern science, and of "the *great ideas* which have become the fixed possession of men within the past hundred years"—particularly, individual liberty—"the idea that the government exists for the individual." Strong did not claim for the nineteenth century the origin of these things, only that during that period they became an effective part of the human heritage.

With respect to the trans-Mississippi West as the seat of power, he declared:

Twenty years of this century may outmeasure a millennium of olden time. . . . [and] ten years of the New West are . . . fully equal to half a century east of the Mississippi. . . . The West is characterized by largeness. Western stories are on the same large scale, so large, indeed, that it often takes a dozen eastern men to believe one of them. . . . The West is to dominate the East.

Strong's discussion of the exhaustion of the public lands was introduced by quotations from Thomas Carlyle and Lord Macaulay. Carlyle had said that American boasts of democracy were rubbish and that the laboring people were happy because of land. Macaulay had pointed to unoccupied lands and predicted that, when the American population was as dense as the British, American institutions would be brought to the test. "What is the extent of these public lands whose occupation means so much?" queried Strong, and his answer was, "Even if the increase [in rate] should cease, the demand for 1884, steadily continued, would exhaust the supply in *twenty years.*"

In world history, Strong held that each race was representative of a great idea and that the Anglo-Saxon race stood for two related ideas, civil liberty and "pure *spiritual* Christianity"—Protestantism—and that it was the mission of the Anglo-Saxons, with the western United States as the seat of power, to evangelize the world.

God, with infinite wisdom and skill, is training the Anglo-Saxon race for an hour sure to come in the world's future. Heretofore there has always been . . . a comparatively unoccupied land westward. . . . There are no more new worlds. The unoccupied arable lands of the earth are limited, and will soon be taken. . . . Then will the world enter upon a new stage of its history—*the final competition of races, for which the Anglo-Saxon is being schooled.* . . . Then this race . . . will spread itself over the earth. . . . Nothing can save the inferior race but a ready and pliant assimilation. . . . To this result no war of extermination is needful; the contest is not one of arms, but of vitality and of civilization.

For Strong, the idea of closed space, both American and world space, was not a calamity, but a process of completion, a fulfillment of destiny. Not only was God preparing the United States for this mission, but he argued that the backward races were being prepared to receive the impress of the civilization of the United States—also, to want it. For Strong, civilization was _"the creating of more and higher wants,"_ and opportunity would not vanish from the earth so long as higher wants were in store for humanity.

Fifteen years later Strong wrote another book using the same theme, but oriented in the perspective of the Spanish-American War (1900). Again he opened his argument with the land question:

Among the new conditions which confront the new century is the exhaustion of our arable public lands—a fact of both national and world significance.... The nation's energy has been chiefly concentrated on the industrial conquest of the continent, and the exhaustion of the arable public lands marks the practical completion of that conquest and constitutes the beginning of a new era in our industrial history.... Now a limit has been fixed, and our ever-increasing energy and wealth will find an ever-decreasing field for investment at home. This of course means that henceforth they will increasingly go abroad.

To the world it meant that civilization had circled the globe "and on the Pacific coast the European met the Asiatic. There are no more New Worlds; further west is the East." Furthermore, it meant increasing competition in the temperate zone, or "a movement toward the tropics; indeed, it means both, and both have already begun." As manufacturing productiveness increased, the home market was supplied, and it was necessary to find markets abroad.

Industrial expansion is an absolute necessity to competitive manufactures. It is not the ultimate way out, of course, for it cannot continue always; there are limits to this earth of ours, and we shall not establish an interstellar commerce. But the "ultimate" is a long way off, and does not concern us in this discussion. Industrial expansion is a present necessity, and will continue to be until the nations learn to substitute industrial co-operation for industrial competition....

In some directions there are no limits to possible progress. We can see no end to the changes which will come from new conquests of natural forces, but we easily foresee the end of the great movements which have sprung from geographical discoveries. There are no more undiscovered countries. . . . The commercial supremacy of the Pacific will be final.

By 1900 Strong was not optimistic about the future competition among nations in closed space, without resort to force. He quoted with approval

Professor Franklin H. Giddings's estimate of the battle of Manila Bay: " 'In my judgment it was the most important historical event since Charles Martel turned back the Moslems [732 A.D.], . . . because the great question of the twentieth century is whether the Anglo-Saxon or the Slav is to impress his civilization on the world.' "

Another quotation was taken from Émile de Laveleye: "A hundred years hence, leaving China out of the question, there will be two colossal powers in the world, beside which Germany, England, France, and Italy will be as pigmies—the United States and Russia." Strong added that these two nations face each other across the Pacific Ocean and that Sir Walter Raleigh had said: "Whosoever . . . commands the trade of the world commands the riches of the world and consequently the world itself."

The similarities between the Slav and the Anglo-Saxon were listed: equal numbers, rapidity of geographical and numerical growth, powers of racial assimilation, genius for organization and government, and lastly, the unoccupied lands of "the North Temperate Zone, which is the zone of power, are divided between these two races."

In contrasting the two races, Strong asserted:

The Anglo-Saxon is the supreme representative of civil and religious liberty; the Slav is the supreme representative of absolutism, both in state and church. Anglo-Saxon civilization is the one civilization in the history of the world based on the development of the individual. Russian civilization depends for its very existence on the suppression of the individual. . . .

In fundamental principles, in spirit, in ideals, and in methods they are diametrically opposed. They do not represent two different stages of development along the same lines. They spring from radically different conceptions, they aim at radically different ends; and the more fully they are developed, the more utter will be their unlikeness and the more inevitable their conflict.

The stupendous struggle of the future will be not simply between two Titanic races, but between Eastern and Western civilizations. For the Russian (a unique type) is an Asiatic who by long contact with the West has been thoroughly vitalized, has absorbed Western learning, has mastered Western military science, and who now, without loosening his hold on Europe, is returning to Asia, there to work out his destiny. . . .

Russia has a religious mission to control Asia; and the genius of the race and its geographical position unite to stimulate its purpose of eastward and southward expansion. Russia can wait, but never vacillates in her supreme purpose. That purpose runs through the generations as a thread runs through a string of beads. Her advance on China is a new ice age—a slow, resistless, paralyzing movement from the north. Already has she gained Manchuria, and now controls nearly one-half of the Asiatic coast-line of the Pacific, the whole of which is her aim. . . .

Is the Anglo-Saxon or the Slav to command the Pacific and therefore the world's future? . . . .

Unless prevented by Russia, England and America will give to China the blessings of European civilization, the triumph of which represents the liberation of the individual, not only politically, but religiously and intellectually. Bring the East thoroughly under the influence of the West, and it would be impregnated with a new life. Asia would gain political and religious regeneration; while the world would gain a new literature, a new art, and a new member of the sisterhood of nations.

If Russia gains control, Asia will remain Asiatic for centuries to come, China's vast resources will become the resources of the Slav, her millions his millions, with their power multiplied many fold by his military skill and his genius for organization. . . .

. . . Surely [the Pacific ocean] this New Mediterranean, which in the twentieth century is to be the center of the world's population and the seat of its power, is to be an Anglo-Saxon sea, provided only we place on it an adequate navy. . . . [A sea] wall of defense . . . cannot be mined or breached, and . . . never becomes antiquated. . . .

Now it is a significant fact that the sea stands guard over all six of the Anglo-Saxon families; and this sea-wall exempts them from the necessity of keeping great standing armies, thus saving them from the vampire of militarism, which curses the great Continental powers. . . .

. . . armies have often proved dangerous to liberty, navies have never fallen under that suspicion. In all the world's history . . . no admiral has ever seized civil power. Navies may defend a land; they cannot conquer it. . . . The Anglo-Saxon families [four of the six face the Pacific] are so placed in the world that they can defend themselves, command the Pacific, and accomplish their mission in behalf of civilization by means of sea power. . . .

. . . seeing its [world's] best hopes for liberty at stake in the far Pacific, [God] planned a colonization scheme for the ages which should place that ocean under the control of the race which is the special guardian of liberty.

Strong was conscious of the world revolution in communications and evaluated discriminatingly the significance of the outlook induced by these technological changes:

When communication beyond the edge of the village was only semi-occasional, the village was the little world of its inhabitants. . . .

With the advent of the railway, the telegraph, and the press, the narrow horizon was enlarged; national happenings became the subject of daily thought. . . .

. . . But the submarine cable and the triple-expansion marine engine have reduced the world to a neighborhood. . . . Thus our horizon has been enlarged to the measure of a great circle of the earth. . . .

. . . Life loves harmonies and resemblances, but these imply differences. Uniformity means stagnation. . . .

Life produces variety; and it can rise to higher forms only as it develops differences. . . .

A world life, then, as it is time's last offspring, ought to be the noblest, and therefore the most complex, possible only when the greatest differentiation has taken place.

The new status of the individual was stressed in the last chapter. A distinction between independence and freedom was explained as Strong saw the problem—a significant consequence of the closed geographical system and the higher civilization:

To be independent is to be exempt from reliance on others and from the rule of others. To be free is not to be exempt from law, but from arbitrary or despotic law. . . .

The progress of civilization involves the increase of organization, industrial, social, and political, and, therefore, necessitates an ever-decreasing independence, while it makes possible an ever-increasing freedom.

## Alfred T. Mahan

The name of Alfred T. Mahan (1840–1914) is associated primarily with the idea, announced in 1890, of the influence of sea power as a determinant in history (1890a). Because his contribution was founded on the concept of sea power as distinguished from the narrower one of naval power, its implications were much broader than mere military policy. The naval aspect included the concentration of power, command of the sea, fleet organization, and action as a single fighting unit. Such naval organization required overseas bases with the whole supported by production, shipping, and colonies. The effectiveness of sea power was further dependent upon geographical position and, as applied to the United States, required the possession of outlying positions off the Pacific and Gulf coasts as a first line of defense and a canal across the Isthmus to connect the Caribbean Sea with the Pacific Ocean. When sea power was dependent upon sails, the problems had been less difficult. A ship was relatively self-sufficient for long periods of time. But in the age when steam, steel, and science were being applied fully to naval warfare for the first time, all this was changed. Fleets became dependent upon bases for fuel, supplies, and repairs—all of which emphasized the need for overseas bases and communication to service the fleets in order to maintain the command of the sea. Of the essentials of sea power in 1890, the United States possessed only productive capacity based upon the development of the interior during the nineteenth century. Attempts to create shipping and colonies were already in evidence. The United States was looking outward but had not yet gone far toward translating ideas into action and concrete results (1890b).

By 1895 Mahan was stressing the point:

More and more civilized man is needing and seeking ground to occupy, room over which to expand and in which to live. Like all natural forces, the impulse takes the direction of least resistance, . . . the incompetent race or system will go down. . . . Because so much of the world still remains in the possession of [backward peoples] . . . [and the] energies of civilized states . . . are finding lack of openings and scantness of livelihood at home, . . . there now obtains a condition of aggressive restlessness with which all have to reckon. [1895]

Two years later Mahan was making a highly significant interpretation of the meaning of the nineteenth century to the modern world. He observed that practically all the world was occupied politically by the early nineteenth century.

The great work of the nineteenth century, . . . has been in the recognition and study of the forces of nature, and the application of them to the purposes of mechanical and physical advance. The means thus placed in men's hands, . . . were devoted necessarily, first, to the development of the resources of each country. Everywhere there was a fresh field; for hitherto it had been nowhere possible for man fully to utilize the gifts of nature. Energies everywhere turned inward, for there, in every region, was more than enough to do. Naturally, therefore, such a period has been in the main one of peace. . . . during which men have been occupied in revolutionizing the face of their own countries by means of the new powers at their disposal.

All such phases pass, however, as does every human thing. Increase of production—the idol of the economist—sought fresh markets, as might have been predicted.

To Mahan the twentieth century would settle the issue of "whether Eastern [China, India and Japan] or Western civilization is to dominate throughout the earth and to control its future." He held that American civilization was only an extension of European and "on the Pacific coast . . . are found the outposts, the exposed pioneers of European civilization." The Caribbean area, the Isthmian canal, and the Hawaiian Islands were the vital strategic nerve centers of the European civilization (1897).

In the main, Mahan's early ideas, political and economic, were reflections of the the current trends of neomercantilism and imperialism, but his later views contained much that was more peculiarly his own. The essay of 1895 developed the concept of closed space, the necessity for "room over which to expand and in which to live," and the idea of competition between higher and backward civilizations. These were the conventional views although the language was an anticipation of the phrasing of twentieth-century geopolitics. The essay of 1897 went further and stressed the ultimate struggle for survival and supremacy as between the Oriental culture of Eastern Asia and Christian civilization based upon Christianity. Mahan's interpretation of the nineteenth century was more original, however, and is of particular interest in contrast with Turner's. It was more comprehensive in scope, and for him the key that unlocked opportunity was science and its application to the full utilization for the first time of the gifts of nature. He insisted that "everywhere there was a fresh field." In the oldest countries of Europe the new mechanization provided "more than enough to do" for men in "revolutionizing the face of their own countries." For him it was not the closing of space in the conventional sense of space geography that precipitated the imperialistic impulse, or the struggle for survival of European over Oriental civilization as Mahan saw it, but surplus production in the Old World and the expansion of Old World energies into a similar development of the "gifts of nature," elsewhere. To Mahan closed-surface geography did not mean a closed world, because the nineteenth-century science and its application through machines was being transferred in the twentieth century to new regions for a continuation of the process there. It is evident, however, that as a military man, Mahan's preoccupation was more with the state than with the freedom of the individual as such.

## Sir William Crookes

The historian, the geographer, the clergyman, and the naval historian and strategist have passed in review, and each in turn has speculated on the different aspects of the phenomenon of closed space. Not even the laboratory scientist was immune to the influence of the idea. In his presidential address before the British Association for the Advancement of Science in September 1898, Sir William Crookes (1832–1919) warned that the end of new wheat land meant a shortage of bread for the world early in the twentieth century unless new sources of nitrogen could be devised.

Although stressing the end of new land available for wheat, a closed-surface geography, Crookes was not thinking in terms of a closed world. He sought in science a substitute for new land. With respect to the nitrogen supply, his confidence in the chemical profession was not misplaced. In the Crookes sense it is evident that a closed world order could exist only to those who were thinking in terms of space geography.

## Evaluation

In evaluating the influence of significant thinkers of any period, it is not enough to study their writings; it is equally important to examine the problem of how others used or misused their inspiration. The case of Josiah Strong is an example of how quickly and completely one of the important molders of public opinion of his generation could be forgotten as a personality. Possibly his interest was scattered over too many subjects instead of being concentrated sharply upon one simple idea. In many respects, nevertheless, his influence continues without specific identification with his name. Crookes, the chemist, as a prophet of opportunity through science, has had many rivals for popular favor, and in the multiplicity of voices neither he nor any other single spokesman for science has come to occupy a commanding position. The point of view, however, is widely held. Mahan is remembered primarily for his idea of sea power, and in that his work was too well done. Artificially deprived of a chance at sea power, Germany, between the two world wars, arrived first at a measure of understanding of the obsolescence of that form of military might and turned to air power. Once the world appreciated the significance of air power in warfare, the Mahan maxim of command of the sea was transferred to command of the air. Mackinder was thinking primarily in terms of future policy, using history and geography as the basis of planning for a world operating in closed space. In Great Britain, where his ideas were intended as a warning to his own people, he was largely ignored, and instead it was the enemy that recognized his ideas and in ruthless reinterpretation used them in the attempt to overthrow the very democratic ideals Mackinder was hoping to protect. The Germans had done much the same thing a generation earlier with Mahan's idea of sea power.

Turner himself gave little attention directly to planning the future, but during the second quarter of the twentieth century, the Turner idea was seized upon by others to an increasing extent for that purpose, especially by the adherents of the New Deal after 1932. Turner's essay of 1910 had asserted that the national government was being used as a substitute for the frontier, but that essay must be considered in relation to its background, which was the Progressive movement prior to World War I. In that perspective it cannot be interpreted as an endorsement of such totalitarian tendencies as the New Deal. He was not thinking of changing or discarding democracy and individualism but only of discovering the ways and means of preserving their traditional forms as practiced in an era associated with his idea of the frontier as a historical determinant. Turner died on March 14, 1932. What he would have said about the New Deal or about the issue of totalitarianism is speculation, but there is nothing in his published writings to indicate that he had lost faith in nationalism, democracy, and the individual. Those who have used the Turner tradition as a justification for totalitarian planning were not faithful to his teachings as history but were generalizing freely upon them, creating a Turner legend to suit their particular purpose. In different language, they were using the Turner prestige as a peg of respectability upon which to hang their own ideas, foreign to the American system, hoping that thereby those ideas might be made acceptable in the reflected light of Turner, the American historical scholar and the idol of his generation.

Some historians have come to challenge the validity of many of the tenets of the Turner school of historical interpretation, and the present author is one of them. As a product of his time and of the Middle Western environment, Turner was expressing both himself and his generation; he was teaching history in terms of unconscious propaganda. His themes were nationalism, democracy, and individualism, with the frontier as his instrument of instruction. Acceptance by his contemporaries, plus fifty years of worship at the shrine of the significance of the frontier in American history, are irrefutable evidence that he had given a full and accurate expression of the genius of his own generation of Americans, but it is not proof of the soundness and adequacy of his interpretation of American history. His was the first generation to grow up after the American Civil War, and it was their task to write into American history the results of that second American revolution in terms of a war of national unification (Malin, 1921).

Irrespective of the validity of Turner's interpretation of the significance of the frontier, or of idealization on the part of his erstwhile followers, the Turner tradition wielded a tremendous influence and as such continues as a major historical force to be reckoned with in contemporary American life. Only in the case of George Bancroft has an American historian exercised an influence at all comparable in importance with that of Turner, and his was of a different sort. As in the case of Mahan, Turner had done his work more thoroughly than he knew, and his frontier hypothesis, like a heroic legend, instead of serving as a stimulus to originality, became a closed circle of imitative routine, a voice of authority, in the persons of his disciples, to confound all non-conformists. This general statement is not to be applied to all of Turner's followers, however, as there was a virile minority whose personal loyalty is unquestioned, who deprecate the misuse of the Turner tradition, who appreciate the creative spirit it once inspired in Turner's hands, but who realize its limitations and inadequacy as a generalized interpretation of American history. It represented both a stage in the development of Turner's thought and in the evolution of American historiography.

CHAPTER 5

# Webb & Regionalism

[Every American historian of Malin's generation grappled with the implications of Walter Prescott Webb's *The Great Plains* (1931). Several scholarly conferences were devoted to evaluating this prize-winning book, most notably the Sky Top Conference of 1937 in Pennsylvania, sponsored by the Social Science Research Council. As a junior scholar and little published on the subject as yet, Malin was not invited to participate in the conference, but Webb's book made a very favorable impression on Malin. This chapter contains his critique, and, more importantly, Malin offers his holistic ecological approach to the problem of regional definition, a problem the Sky Top Conference ignored to its detriment. Malin called for a comparative analysis in other environments of the importance of technological breakthroughs—fencing, windmills, weapons, cattle-ranching, and the like—that enabled plainsmen to settle successfully in a hostile environment. Different technological applications in the same plains environment should also be studied. Such a comparative framework, Malin believed, would prove the idea of possibilism, as opposed to the environmental determinism implicit in Webb's book.]

The publication, in 1931, of Walter Prescott Webb's (1888–1963) *The Great Plains,* was a landmark in the regional approach by historians to the trans-Mississippi West, and it sychronized closely with the rising tide of criticism of the Turner frontier school of American history. Webb explained that he did not use the term *great plains* in the sense usually employed by geographers and historians. It was an area described in terms of topography (level), vegetation (treeless), and rainfall (subhumid), but all three did not apply to the whole area embraced in the great plains environment. The eastern part was treeless and level; the western part (interior basin) was treeless and arid; the middle part was the great plains proper, because it possessed all three characteristics. He placed the dividing line between east and west at 98°, and contended that early in the nineteenth century, upon coming out of the timber area in western Missouri, the frontier halted for about a generation. The line of this halt was near the dividing line, where it was necessary to await a preparatory period before a further advance took place. West of this line the environment differed so materially as to impose a new formula of living, the line constituting an institutional fault similar to a geological fault. The east failed to recognize the difference and to modify legislation accordingly or to permit western men to follow the dictates of the new region. The differences between the East and the West were defined further upon the basis of climatic characteristics, and geographical distribution of grasses and animals. The physiographical description was based primarily upon Johnson's monograph on the high plains, without a clear distinction of his differentiation between the high plains remnant and the idealized great plains.

In contrasting the pioneering process, Webb emphasized the dependence of forest man upon available wood, water, and natural water transportation, while in the treeless West the pioneer found it necessary to buy substitutes with money and transport them to the West. A change in weapons and warfare was given particular notice. The availability of these substitutes depended upon the Industrial Revolution, with its mass production of standardized goods at prices within the reach of the pioneer. According to this line of analysis, most of the necessary items did not become available until the decade of the 1870s, the renewed settling-in movement gained initial momentum slowly and then closed in the 1880s with a rush. The cattle business was emphasized as the principal industry of the great plains and the leading example of regional influence on institutions. Irrigation, its limitations, and the reconstruction of institutions under its influence, was another major theme, while dry-land farming received minor attention. In closing the account, the geographical influence was presented in literature, in song, and in the intangible factors of regional psychology.

In 1937 the Social Science Research Council undertook a series of critiques of significant works in the social sciences. Webb's *The Great Plains* was chosen in the history field and was assigned to Fred Shannon. His appraisal was presented, and a conference with a committee of nine was held at Sky Top, Pennsylvania, in September, 1939. It is not the purpose of this chapter to summarize in detail Shannon's appraisal or the report of the conference, as it must be read in full in order to be adequately understood. Shannon seemed to challenge Webb's basic assumption of definition, of regional uniqueness, of the importance of differences, and of his particular form of geographical determinism. Other subjects of adverse criticism were Webb's handling of reasons for delayed settlement of the plains, the revolver, the origins of the cattle business, barbed wire, windmills, artesian wells, irrigation, dry-land farming, etc. Webb refused to accept Shannon's work as a fair and competent appraisal, and declined to make a formal reply. He did attend the Sky Top conference and made a statement there of his position. Omitted from the membership in the conference committee were persons competent in plant or animal ecology, general physiology, soils, microbiology, and climatology. Charles C. Colby, a geographer, participated, but his specialty lay elsewhere. Neither Webb nor Shannon, nor members of the committee, revealed any specialized knowledge of these fields. Colby made suggestions relative to geographical matters, especially the soil question, but did not arouse any significant response from the other members on these matters. Louis Wirth, a sociologist, made some important points on general methodology and interpretation. As a sort of footnote to the Sky Top conference, attention should be directed to Shannon's book, *The Farmers' Last Frontier* (1945, chapters 1–2), in which he continued in his denial of the regional distinctions of Webb's book.

In 1942 the Rockefeller Foundation sponsored two conferences on the great plains; one at New York, in April, and the other at Lincoln, Nebraska, in June. At these meetings the membership represented history, literature, the press; and at the Lincoln meeting, anthropology was added. Among those present there were no significant conflicts of opinion in evidence. All appeared to be essentially orthodox in accepting the Webb type of regionalism. Peculiarly enough the Lincoln session was held at the University of Nebraska, the institution that had given C. E. Bessey, Clements, Weaver, and Shantz their opportunity as ecologists, and who in turn had given the University of Nebraska world-wide fame, but at this conference there was not ecologist present, no physiologist, no soil scientist, no climatologist, no geographer.

At the opening of the session at the Sky Top conference, Arthur M. Schlesinger as chairman stated, and later restated, that "no difference of opinion exists between Mr. Webb and Mr. Shannon regarding the principal thesis of the book, namely, that human institutions and ways of life changed upon reaching the Great Plains"; the differences lay in Webb's vagueness of definition of the great plains and his inconsistency in application (pp. 141, 194). As the present author reads the record, and the same impression was evident in the minds of some of the participants, the difference included the problem of regionalism. Shannon's own remarks seem to repudiate regionalism by his insistence upon his view that the pioneering process was one of continuous and gradual adjustment from the eastern coast to the desert. At any rate he made no indication of what he considered an adequate definition of great plains regionalism, and did not explain whether or not he thought any definition of regionalism in general, or this one in particular, was even possible. Wirth, the sociologist, thought the concept of regionalism should be explored, and asked Colby, the geographer, to discuss it. Colby concluded that the use of the term great plains "should not be an issue" (p. 147). Thus Webb became the "whipping boy" between the different views in which his use of regionalism, or the term *great plains,* was defended and condemned without reference to the basic issues of whether or not any regionalism was valid, and if so, whether or not an acceptable single definition was possible upon which all or even a majority could agree. Having failed upon that question, the further deliberations of the conference were largely futile.

As the present author understands Percy Williams Bridgman's position on the problems of methodology in physics, most of the controversies arise out of failure to define adequately the problem to be studied, and then to prescribe a set of procedures by which impersonal and objective conclusions could be reached. The Sky Top conference is a good example of the failure to do everything that Bridgman's dictum would demand before a conference could even begin. No two participants appear to have had the same idea of what Webb intended, or of what Shannon intended, or of the purpose of holding a conference at all.

An idealized approach to such a problem might start with a survey of the literature of physiography, of climatology, of physiology, of genetics, of plant ecology, of animal ecology, of soils, of soil microbiology, of agronomy, of the geographers' attempts at regional definition, and the question raised by some, whether or not regionalism possesses any validity.

Powell (1895) declared that he repudiated the basin concept of physiographic regions in favor of the slope concept. The basin concept, as applied to the Mississippi, would exclude the rivers of southwestern Georgia, southern Alabama, and southwestern Mississippi, because they drain directly into the Gulf of Mexico. They are, however, a part of the Gulf slope. Likewise, in the West the divide between the Red River and the rivers of Texas would, for the same reason, exclude most of Texas and New Mexico from the basin. They, also, were included within the Gulf slope. If the subject of study was mountain formations, as done by Gilpin and Shaler, then the divides between drainage basins would not separate the physiographic region being studied, but would become the central feature of the area. Slopes diverging from the crest of the mountain peaks and divides run to sea level and below. At what point between these extremes of elevation would the mountain formation become something else? Gilpin and Shaler both discussed basins, slopes, plateaux, and mountain formations without quibbling over the obvious fact that they overlapped and that the same area was discussed as a part of two or more different regions. It was not a question of one treatment being right and the other being wrong; they merely emphasized different aspects of the same body of facts which possessed a particular interest when related in different patterns, both of which were valid. Some purists, who insist upon carrying the logic of verbalism to bitter-end extremes, arrive at a destination of nihilistic futility by denying that there can be any valid physiographic regionalism.

In the field of climatology, the traditional approach was to define characteristics of climatic regions on the basis of mean averages of rainfall, temperature, and other properties. This approach emphasized uniformities. The more recent studies, which were directed at the problems of the relations of climate to living things, place the emphasis upon the extremes and frequency of fluctuations. Of particular interest to the present considerations are the systems of Russell (1934), and Kendall (1935), although those of Crowe (1933), Lackey (1937), and Thornthwaite (1941), may be fully as significant.

The general physiologist is concerned with the problem of protoplasm, irrespective of whether it is organized in the form of cells in plants, or in animals, and in its behavior as living matter. The phase of the protoplasm problem that bears most directly upon the historian's problem of regionalism is to follow the physiologist's experiments under different conditions of moisture, heat, light, and photoperiodism, and the extent of his ability to determine the limits of tolerance for fluctuations as respects frequency and extremes. The literature of the physiologist demands attention so long as biologists are of the opinion that the secret of the relations of plants and animals to cold, drouth, or light is determined in part or largely by the properties of protoplasm.

The geneticist is concerned with problems of inheritance and the relations of speciation to environment. The theories have been discussed and make clear the bearing of such problems on the possible significance of geographical environment upon mutations, and the problem of isolation in the establishment of species and geographical races.

The literature of plant and animal ecology deals with communities and their relation to the occupied area, the problems of distribution, the relation of species and individuals to each other, and to all the factors of environment. If geographical regionalism is admitted to possess any validity, these findings of ecology become essential elements in any valid determinations of boundaries.

The literature of soils is less satisfactory in giving aid at present, but that is not because of any lack of importance. When soil science is more developed, it should possess a more important role, especially if some current assumptions are correct that microorganisms exhibit a regional distribution as definite as the higher forms of plant and animal life.

The literature of the agronomist deals with the problem of agricultural crops. Whittlesey's (1936) maps of agricultural regions did not coincide altogether with the assumptions that might be derived from native plant regions, and the same is true of some type-of-farming area studies and mapping. There are some broad similarities, but with conspicuous differences and peculiarities of detail. The distribution of crops, geographically, under controlled conditions of cultivation necessarily presents a changing map of regionalism, especially under the influence of plant and animal breeding and introduction of species from other areas.

When the geographer and the historian have canvassed all of these fields of specialized literature, as they bear upon the problems of regionalism, they are in a position to attempt synthesis, employing the whole circle of facts or independent variables. It is only within such a comprehensive framework that they have a right to discuss definition of regionalism and the validity of employing the regional approach in their disciplines. Obviously, the particular regional definition that is framed will depend upon the purpose for which it is to be used, and more than one good definition is possible, each emphasizing valid aspects of the area of the earth's surface being studied as the habitat of man. And as the first organizing principle of history is time, the historian must recognize that factor in his treatment of man and region. If all parties to the Sky Top conference had possessed such a background for their consideration of Webb's book, the outcome should have been different. A large part of this controversy turned on quibbles over verbalisms, much as had occurred in the Turner controversies, rather than upon constructive discussions of the obvious intent of the author.

On some points, Shannon was disconcertingly candid. He admitted (p. 5) that he had never read Webb's book through until the previous year, presumably about the time he accepted the assignment to write the *Appraisal.* Furthermore, he confessed, "I was not employed as an expert on the history of the West" (p. 194). It is not in the least remarkable that Webb refused to recognize Shannon's critique as a competent *Appraisal.* In both the Sky Top conference and the Rockefeller Foundation Great Plains conference, the backlog of available scientific information and basic thinking which might be given a significant application to the study of history was not used. The members of the conferences did not appear to be acquainted with it, and the conferences were too narrowly organized to bring that kind of material into the discussions by specialists in these fields. Webb had not utilized all the backlog of available material as of 1930 when he was writing his book, but in a pioneer work, in which he was feeling his way, it would have been most unusual had he, or anyone, done so. The more important point is that in relation to the rank and file of the historical profession, or to the recognized leaders in the profession, he was much in advance, and even by 1942 in the great plains conferences, there was little evidence that other historians had gone beyond him. The really disturbing aspect of the matter was that there was little advance by either Webb or the others beyond the position of 1930, a sort of great plains orthodoxy seemed to have crystallized, and in the meantime the backlog of basic scientific thinking had been accumulating at an unusual rate. In these conferences there is no evidence that there was any recognition of the essential incompatibility of the Turner frontier and sectional tradition with the Webb regional approach. Had these conferences examined adequately the bases of regionalism as a historical method, the contrast should have become clear, as well as the more important conclusion that the study of history by this method brings out relationships in a significant manner that cannot be brought out by any other method. But, emphatically, no one method is so complete in itself that it should be adopted to the exclusion of all others.

Webb, Shannon, and most of the members of the Sky Top conference appear to have been thinking of regionalism in terms of geographical determinism. Wirth (p. 181) challenged the principle of determinism, calling attention to Lucien Febvre's theory of possibilism, and showed how Webb's treatment was inadequate to permit its application. He should have been more inclusive by applying his remarks to Shannon and to the other members of the conference. The omission, by Webb and Shannon, of the soil question, was pointed out by Colby as one of the most serious defects in the work of both men. Webb was excused because the works of Marbut and Kellogg had appeared after his book was published. Webb might well be excused for the omission, but not on that ground. Hilgard had distinguished between eastern and western soils some forty years earlier. Marbut had presented his treatment of western soils, together with a map, as early as 1923, and had published his views on soil classification in 1922 and 1928. Scarcely any historians were dealing with the new soil literature in 1931 or in 1939. Shannon made an effort to remedy the defect in his book of 1945, devoting a part of the first chapter to soils. In this, as in the case of others doing pioneering work, Shannon's handling of the new field was only partially satisfactory. He was not acquainted with soil literature as a whole, and depended for guidance too largely on the official version of the United States Department of Agriculture according to Marbut and Kellogg.

The idea of possibilism might be applied profitably to the issue of adaptations to regionalism, and contribute toward clarification of some of the matters at issue in the Sky Top conference—railroads, fencing, windmills, revolvers, and cattle industry—as well as others of a similar sort—housing and fuel, tillage and crops. In suggesting this approach to a better understanding there is no intent to make commitments to any philosophical system—only to state the problems in a form that is adaptable to objective treatment. The idea of possibilism might be considered in two different applications: the same technique applied to more than one kind of environment where it possessed a different cultural value in each; and more than one technique applicable in the same environment. In other words, it is often if not always probable that there is more than one way of doing things to achieve the same or similar ends. In the first instance it was possible for a new technique to be invented, developed, or utilized in several different environments, and in each serve a somewhat different purpose, sometimes highly significant and important, but not always, and yet combine into the cultural complex in a manner that would not serve an equal or equivalent function. It is those techniques that possess an unusual role that become both significant and important in imparting a regional peculiarity to the manner in which they are combined in the cultural complex. To the extent that more than one possibility exists, the element of determinism is eliminated. The particular method in vogue may be the outcome of tradition in which the trend is explainable only on the basis of historical development, but in other instances, a choice from the list of possible methods may be exercised consciously by individuals, groups, or communities. In either case, the understanding of the fact of alternatives discredits not only geographical determinism, but also discredits attempts to rationalize the imposition by compulsion of one particular formula chosen by arbitrary decision of authoritarian procedures. In modern history the two points of view have often been placed in sharp contrast; the English method of "muddling through" as it has often been called, permitted a high degree of flexibility in meeting difficult situations, in contrast with authoritarian methods so often imposed upon the continent of Europe.

A windmill might be used in any country, but in a country in which wind of any substantial velocity was a rarity it would never be of much importance. In the central North American grassland, however, where absence of wind was the exception, the windmill was both significant and important. Within a few months after the first settlers arrived and set up newspapers in Kansas, they began to discuss the wind and the opportunity afforded to put it to work cheaply, in a country short of fuel, for power purposes. It is beside the point to ignore this fact of immediate recognition of both importance and significance, and to argue merely that windmills did not come in quantity until the 1880s. To place windmills within the financial reach of the average pioneer farmer awaited cheap steel, mass production methods, as well as mechanical refinements of machine design. It is essential to distinguish the existence of a certain device or invention as fact, and the difference in circumstances of utilization and diversity of uses as fact.

The importance and significance of communication were quite properly emphasized by Webb in connection with the grassland culture. He was concerned most conspicuously with horse culture in connection with the primitive Indian occupation, the pioneering period of the white invasion, and the organization of the cattle industry. It was a man-on-a-horse relationship. The railroad came in for a share of attention, but Shannon challenged its regional significance. The statement of the problem might be broadened with profit to the discussion.

In terms of so-called transcontinental communications, from the Mississippi Valley, or country eastward, to the Pacific Coast, 1849–1869, the most important medium and route, in terms of volume of business, was the water route around Cape Horn; secondly, the interrupted water route by way of the Isthmus of Panama; and of least importance, the animal-powered land routes. Of the animal-powered forms of communications, if the emigrant wagon and its household freight are considered, the wagon was the most important, with the stage coach second. In terms of strictly commercial business and operations as a common carrier, the stage coach must be given first place as the carrier of messengers, mail, baggage, express, and other light freight; the freight wagon makes a poor second, and the pony express rates mostly for its spectacular value. By such tests, how were animal-powered communications a medium of major importance? They were vital, of course, but only under a particular set of circumstances, as a means of communications from water-served bases (later rail-served bases) to the interior where there was no water (or later rail) competition. Animal-powered communications were too expensive to be used except as a last resort, and the extent to which the stage coach and the wagon train came to symbolize the West is a conclusive demonstration of the fact that, except the Missouri River, there were virtually no water communications available, in the interior, west of the Mississippi River.

The heart of the grassland communications problem, in a regional sense, was more largely centered on the transportation of bulk commodities in and out of the region than in the matter of personal movement, but the modes of transportation that combined both were still more important. If a single symbol of the grassland was to be chosen it should be the wheel; in the case of the freight wagon, the stage coach, the farm wagon, and buggy, drawn by animal power; and the railroad, automobile, truck, and tractor, driven by mechanical power. Thus the wheel acquired a peculiar regional significance because of the virtual absence of water communications, because of the importance of bulk commodities in its essentially commercial as distinguished from its self-sufficiency economy, because of the extent of regional interdependence, and because of the possibilities of application of mechanical power. All together these constitute an aspect of culture that is peculiarly regional. Water was the primary dependence of man for communications, on a world basis, until the mid-nineteenth century when the advent of mechanically powered wheel communications superseded it for most inland services. In the second quarter of the twentieth century, both water and wheels are being superseded, in part, by air communications. The occupation of the grasslands of the world by modern civilization during the late nineteenth century was associated particularly with mechanically powered wheel communications, and the Arctic is being brought into the orbit of modern civilization by air communications. In North America the wheel pointed the advance westward, while air power points it northward.

In the case of fuel for the grassland, it was early realized that coal was essential. The preparatory period before the actual invasion began was one in which coal was displacing wood, in the forest country, in industry, in transportation, and in city heating, and developed there the coal-burning stoves and locomotives. The attitude of the grassland man toward coal was quite different from that of the forest man, who had used both coal and wood and to a substantial degree, outside of cities, still might make a choice.

The housing problem presented much the same situation. The use of sawed lumber, shipped from some distance, was quite general in the forest region, and in the grassland the same tradition prevailed, the difference being the shipping from longer distances and the consciousness that there was limited choice. In most respects the exceptions only tend to emphasize the prevalence of the rule. The sod house frontier myth (Dick, 1937, and Hafen and Rister, 1941) must be rejected because there was no frontier line beyond which sod houses prevailed, and the extent to which sod houses were used at any time or place was limited. After World War I, there was an interest in reviving in America the pisé, or rammed earth, method of utilizing earth as building material on the spot, and during the depression stabilized earth houses were built, using either oil emulsion or cement as the stabilizer. All three of these methods of constructing earth houses were used only in a limited degree. With few exceptions, the prevailing house type would be more accurately described as the sawed house, rather than the sod house.

In restating the fencing problem, much that has been said of the problem of fuel and housing applies. New research by Danhof (1944) and Hayter (1939) superseded or supplemented much of what Webb had to say. Danhof pointed to the fencing problem as insistent in some places, during the late colonial era, in the forest region. Experiments with substitutes occurred in several environments and with different materials. Wire was an early competitor, even barbed-wire was not at first a satisfactory adjustment, and Danhof concluded that Bessemer steel was the technological essential in providing a cheap, tough wire for both barbed and woven fencing, and that there were no regional implications in its origins. This was correct. The regional significance of barbed wire lay in its use, and the manner in which it fitted into the cultural pattern of the grassland economy.

The point made by Danhof, relative to Bessemer steel and fencing, is the same one the present author has made with a broader application. There could be no true machine age until steel had displaced iron. In other words it was not sufficient for iron to compete with wood, because wood was superior for so many uses. It required cheap steel to effect the real transition in substantial degree from wood to metal.

One word more, however, about the origin of barbed wire. Like so many innovations claimed by America, and by the West, the first barbed wire patents were probably not even American. According to A. M. Tanner (1892 and earlier), the first barbed wire patent was that of Leonce Eugene Grassin-Baledans, in France, July 7, 1860, and the second was that of Louis François Jannin, another Frenchman, in 1865, both of which antedated the first American patent, that of Hunt and Smith, in 1867. The third French patent was that of Gilbert Gavillard, August 27, 1867, which was similar to the second American patent, that of Michael Kelly, February 11, 1868.

The problem of weapons and the grassland would profit by a restatement. Webb's attention given to the Colt revolver was a significant attempt to study historically the impact of technology upon society. The particular aspect of that impact which he chose to examine was the interrelation of the revolver and the great plains, but in so delimiting his subject, he was not claiming that this was the only impact this weapon had made upon society, nor was he denying that the use made of it by the city underworld was not important, or was less important. It may appear pretentiously pedantic to elaborate upon such distinctions in defining the problem, but as the present author reads the record, most of the argument that has been aroused by Webb's revolver thesis has arisen out of disagreement upon the scope and limits of the problem.

In his book, *The Sharps Rifle* (1943), Smith chose three firearms as the significant ones in American history, because of major development in design and relation to history: the Kentucky rifle, the Colt revolver, and the Sharps rifle. Webb chose to deal with the second of these in contrast with the first, and in relation to Indians, horse culture, and open country. Incidentally, the research of Haven and Belden (1940) superseded much of Webb's historical details, identifying the Walker-Colt episode as 1846–1847 and delivery of the model during 1847, and they designate the period 1846–1860 as that of the establishment of the supremacy of the Colt revolver.

Contemporary recognition of the problems as just defined is available, the present author having collected several valuable items as a by-product of other research. Boynton and Mason (1855) visited Kansas during the summer of 1854 in the interests of immigration promotion and reported on their experience at Fort Riley:

We were surprised, incredulous, almost offended, when a young officer. . . . deliberately asserted, that our mounted men, though armed with revolvers, were in general not a match in close combat, for the mounted Indians, with their bows and arrows. But his explanations [of Indian methods of warfare] were satisfactory, and I shall henceforth regard these wild warriors as a formidable foe, even for those who are armed with the most effective weapons of modern times.

The army officer's explanation emphasized that few of the dragoons were trained horsemen, and that the horses were raw recruits as well, while the Indians and their horses were perfectly coordinated leaving both hands free, the arrows were effective at thirty yards, the Indians rode outside their horses, shooting from under the neck, they were almost invisible, and by circling tactics, yelling and frightening cavalry horses, rendered "any certain aim with the revolver impossible, while his arrows are discharged at horse and man more rapidly than even a revolver can be fired."

As bearing upon the Webb-Shannon differences, several points are not settled by this account. The Colt repeating rifle or the Sharps breech-loading rifle was not considered. Apparently, neither was in general use in 1854. Of course, the Spencer, Henry, and Ballard repeating rifles had not yet been invented. The aim of the revolver was bad, but there was no comparison as to how much worse other weapons of 1854 would have been in fighting the same Indians. The implication was that the rifle was not the equal of the revolver as of 1854. Furthermore, there was no commitment on how effective an experienced frontiersman would have been with the same equipment. Some positive conclusions seem warranted. The revolver was recognized as one of the most effective, or as the most effective, weapon of modern times as of 1854. In this account, the revolver had displaced the rifle. The dragoons, as fighting men, were not the equals of the Indians, even with weapon advantage. The Indians did fight in relatively close combat, within thirty yards. The rapidity of arrow shots was greater than the revolver, the arrows were effective, and in horsemanship the Indian was superior to the dragoon. This episode emphasizes the importance of exact statement of the questions at issue. The exact date is essential because of the rapidity of change in the weapon situation. Much of the significance of the Boynton-Mason account turns on the issue of men rather than on the issue of weapons.

The Sharps rifle was based on the Hall rifle; its inventor, Christian Sharps, received his basic patent in 1848 and a second patent in 1853. Trained in the Harpers Ferry arsenal in the technology of interchangeable parts, the design of his mechanism reflected that fact. Equipped with a sliding breech-block and designed for handling self-contained paper cartridges, it proved the most successful rifle of the decade of the 1850s. A Kansas newspaper item of February 1856, probably a disguised advertisement, claimed ten shots per minute, and said that the first lot had been sent by the federal government to the troops on the Texas frontier. A story in a second paper said that "the small carbine [is] now in use by the U.S. Mounted men." In testifying before a federal grand jury in Kansas in 1856, Dr. A. J. Francis said that arrangements had been made to place in the hands of "every reliable Free-State man a Sharps rifle and a brace of Colt's revolvers." In criticism of the policies followed in the Territory of Kansas a resident declared that "one regiment of mounted men, with Sharps rifles, stationed in Kansas, would have kept the peace without any difficulty."

The Spencer repeating rifle was based on the Sharps, the inventor had been employed in the Sharps plant, and he had used as many Sharps parts as possible in his new gun. Thus the influence of the Sharps rifle carried over into the repeater age. In 1865 the Ballard repeating rifle was attracting attention, one instance being given from central Kansas, that one man, armed with a Ballard rifle and plenty of ammunition had defended himself, successfully, for three hours against a party of twenty Cheyenne and Sioux. During the same year a newspaper article claimed the Ballard would fire fifteen shots per minute, was "particularly adapted to the Plains," and quoted General Conner as saying "I consider them the best arm in the world for Indian fighting." Later references cited the virtues of the Henry repeating rifle, and still later the famous Winchester '73.

It is clear that these contemporaries were thinking of the weapons, among other purposes, in connection with fighting Indians, but the significance lies more largely on a broader basis. Whether used for Indians, for border warfare, or for hunting, these weapons provided adaptability to the requirement of rapid movement, horse culture, and open country, where firepower was determined by flexibility and rapidity of fire rather than deadrest accuracy.

The range cattle industry was one of the subjects of difference between Webb and Shannon, and it turned on two issues: a matter of verbalism in the wording, and a failure of both to define altogether clearly the problem. The second is the really important one. A range cattle industry in any proper sense was impossible in the East because it was a forest region, or stated in terms of regional deficiency, a grassless region. With a very few exceptions of limited areas, the maintenance of a grass cover for grazing purposes in that region was done artificially. In a natural grassland, grass was the native vegetation and did not have to be maintained by artificial methods or the cultivation of tame grasses. That was one of the most difficult lessons that forest man had to learn on entering the grassland (Malin, 1940b, pp. 23–26; 1944b, pp. 33–34, 80–82; 1947). The range livestock industry of the grassland was founded on relatively unlimited quantities of permanent, native grass. The grass was what made it a permanent industry, rather than a passing phase of a process of settlement as was true of the limited pastoral activities of the East. Native grass, and not chronological priority or the method of organization, was the determinant (within the meaning of the law of minimum) which made the range livestock industry (not just cattle) unique within the experience of Anglo-Americans. In 1857 William Gilpin had pointed out this fundamental distinction as related to native grass and livestock "spontaneously supported by nature as is the fish of the sea."

The experience of T. C. Henry, one-time resident of New York State, Alabama, and Kansas, provided a clear-cut example of contemporary appreciation of these basic facts as of the 1860s and 1870s. Henry was born and reared in New York, but went to Alabama after the Civil War to make his fortune by raising cotton with freedman labor. He decided in 1867 that that he could not prosper on seven-cent cotton that cost twenty cents, and transferred his operations to Abilene, Kansas. Speaking before the Dickinson County fair in 1870, he described the process of making a farm in the East: cutting the forest to let in light, digging ditches to provide drainage "in order that the earth might bring forth grass," and the constant renewal of grass for pasture and meadow. As to the South, he pointed out that "owing to the fact, startling in its importance, that no valuable variety of grass has ever been grown there," even more than to the political and social factors, was to be ascribed "the present prostration and comparative poverty of those states," and that so long as nothing adequate to remedy this defective feature was supplied, not even the corrections and reforms of the war could secure to them the degree of prosperity and welfare that was afforded the states of the north where grass could be cultivated successfully as a part of the agricultural system. Isolated exceptions were found by Henry in the South as: "Today the happiest and most flourishing section in the entire South is eastern Tennessee. The single fact that clover *is* grown there, and cotton *cannot* be, accounts for the great difference." In Kansas, Henry admonished his neighbors that day to quit talking about Kansas as deficient in terms of eastern forest standards, and turn attention to "our exclusive advantages," one of which was native grass (Cf. Malin, *Winter Wheat,* 1944, pp. 32–35).

Another aspect of the desirable broader approach to the history of the range livestock industry relates to the general subject of stocking the ranges. The Texas aspect of the matter had been greatly overemphasized in nearly all the literature, as well as the cattle factor, with the result that there are no satisfactory histories of the range sheep industry available that are at all comparable to those devoted to cattle. The story of the stocking of the range with both cattle and sheep may start chronologically with the Spanish approach to the area from the southward into the whole area from eastern Texas to the California coast. When Captain Cooke marched west through New Mexico and Arizona in 1846 and drew his map, he marked on the area south of the Gila River in southern Arizona and northern Mexico "numerous herds of wild cattle from San Bernadino to the point where the San Pedro river is left."

Irrespective of how the area is broken down into subdivisions for convenience of historical treatment, that broad and relatively unbroken Spanish front should be kept clearly in the picture—the separation from each other of Texas, New Mexico, Arizona, and southern California in the cattle and sheep histories is primarily a delimitation of convenience which is relatively artificial. From the hide, tallow, and horn trade, southern Texas developed limited beef outlets, including in the late 1840s some overland drives which became fairly substantial across eastern Kansas and western Missouri when interrupted by the Civil War. The resumption after the war and the enlargement of the drives north is an oft-told story, becoming a process of fattening and maturing as well as marketing. The cattle business began in extreme southeastern Texas and spread northwestward into the interior rather slowly; by 1870 to a diagonal line from about 98° at the Red River to a point somewhat west of 100° at the Rio Grande (R. N. Richardson, 1943); or about 101° 30' by 1880 (Gordon, 1884); and by 1883 the invasion of the high plains was under way (*Texas Live-Stock Journal*). The quarantine against Texas fever was begun prior to the Civil War, at the Kansas line, but by 1883 the first line of defense was in northern Texas led by the cattlemen's associations which closed the trails or at least brought them under restriction. In 1883 they took a stand to try to establish the line at the Texas and Pacific railroad. The filling-in of western Kansas by farmers was only a secondary factor in that decade. The discovery of the nature of the disease (1889), and establishment of federal-state inspection and eradication programs (1890), gradually brought order into the industry. Railroad-building into the cattle country changed the procedure, especially after 1887, from drives to rail shipments to northern grass such as the Kansas Bluestem Pastures or to market and corn belt feed lots. The shipments to the Kansas Bluestem Pastures began in April; lease contracts expired October 1. Movement out of the pastures to market, as grass fat beef or later to corn belt feed lots for full feeding, usually began late in July, or in some cases young cattle might be held a second year for maturing (Malin, 1942a).

The southern Pacific Coast cattle trade began also in terms of hides, tallow, and horns (Dana, 1840), and after American annexation came the cattle boom and the sheep boom. The Pacific Northwest developed its resources partly from emigrant livestock and partly from California, cattle and sheep being trailed on a large scale eastward to the northern plains after the Civil War, the Texas blood not being much in evidence in Montana herds in 1860. By the mid-eighties cattle were shipped by rail. The best study of this aspect of the northern grassland cattle movement is found in articles by Oliphant (1932a, 1932b, 1946). Wentworth (1942) gave a good presentation of sheep trails, and Towne and Wentworth (1945) present the sheep industry as a whole, but further similar work is needed to provide systematic treatment of the cattle trails. A newspaper item in the spring of 1879 estimated 100,000 head of cattle would be moved east, from Oregon and Idaho that season. The following year one firm that had been in the business seven years was trailing 23,000 head from Oregon to the Yellowstone country, divided into three herds moving one day apart, and starting about April 25. (Other data: Burlingame, 1942; Briggs, 1940; Osgood, 1929.)

The stocking of the range from the East is possibly the most important, certainly not less so than the Texas source. Chronologically first was the livestock that was moved with emigrants to Oregon and California. In the very nature of the situation, information as to the volume and natural increase from this source is quite vague. A second source is the border livestock business which supported the overland trade and powered the wagon trains over the Santa Fé Trail and other wagon trails into the interior, about 250–300 oxen or mules for a train of twenty-five wagons. In 1857 Kansas City claimed to be "the stock market for the territory west. There are more sold here than at any point west of the Mississippi river, and more work oxen than at any other single point in America." The plains trade made the Missouri mule famous. The cattle of the freighting firm of Russell, Majors, and Waddell wintered on grass in the season of 1855–1856 as far as one hundred miles southwest from Kansas City and Leavenworth. The breeding stock necessary to provide the volume of work oxen needs systematic attention. So long as the wagon train was the foundation of the transportation system, the advancing frontier of settlement carried this livestock industry deeper into the grassland.

The volume of cattle and sheep driven commercially to California or other points in the West is difficult to evaluate, but the frequency of local news items mentioning such herds and flocks makes certain of a substantial flow during the 1850s and later. A Fort Scott, Kansas, dealer in work and beef cattle advertised in 1857 mentioning that he was located on the California trail "where much emigration and stock pass every spring for California." With the establishment of ranches on the plains this source of stock was available, and was used. With the boom in the early eighties, stock dealers were reported in 1883 as canvassing the South below the Texas fever line, collecting cattle from states as far east as the Carolinas and Florida, moving them to the Arkansas frontier from which they were driven into the plains. The same year this movement by stock trains westward from the Mississippi Valley states into the plains was the subject of special comment; in part, these cattle were being taken to the plains to improve the quality of the range herds. The volume of such movements, the methods of collecting, and the routes of movement from year to year have not received systematic attention.

In the long run, the most important sources of range cattle were the pure-bred herds, some being shipped direct from Great Britain, but more from stock farms of the Mississippi Valley. The first shipments were Shorthorn bulls to cross on Texas and other range herds. The Shorthorn was typically a tall-grass or tame-grass animal, and upon the short-grass plains did not prove satisfactory. At the end of the seventies, Scotch black polled cattle, first Galloways, and later Aberdeen-Angus, were tried out and boomed in the early eighties, but did not hold their own. The Hereford, popularly called Whitefaces, gained ground rapidly after 1876 but were handicapped at first by deficiency in the hind quarters. In 1881, C. Gudgel and T. A. Simpson, breeders at Independence, Missouri, imported Anxiety IV, a Hereford bull of unusual conformation and potency. The Anxiety IV blood strain immediately gained recognition as one of the most significant of the breed. Herefords quickly became the dominant range breed because of their vitality, rustling abilities, early maturing, and fattening qualities, and over 75 per cent of the range cattle in the 1930s were Whitefaces. In this story is to be found one of the most important of all the adaptations to environment, yet the biologists have given no explanation wherein lies the secret. Also, the history of the pure-bred herds that have provided bulls for the range since the 1860s has never been written, and it is this phase of the industry that the present writer ventures as the most important of all the sources which stocked the range, not in numbers, but in quality which produced prime beef superior to, and more uniform than, that produced upon the farms of the corn belt. Captain W. J. Tod, of Maplehill, Kansas, Captain Dan Casement, of Juniata, and R. H. Hazlett, of Hazford Place, are other Hereford men of national reputation. Captain Tod began his operations with George A. Fowler, of the meat-packing family, which suggests the importance of that industry in promoting livestock improvement. The railroad, commission men, and banking interests all played a vital role in the range industry as here presented.

The story of sheep is different, but possesses many features of similarity. The early phase of the industry turned on wool production so the Merino breeders of New England in particular prospered in growing breeding stock. With the shift to meat production as well as to wool, the longer wool breeds, Shropshire, Hampshire, and Southdown were preferred. Arizona and Idaho lambs and sheep were shipped in large numbers to mature or finish in the region east of the Rocky Mountains, illustrating a significant regional interdependence, each region serving one stage in the process.

The feature of regional interdependence of the livestock industry in all its phases is so important that it warrants some repetition and special emphasis. The legend has been built up by livestock propaganda, especially by the cattle interest, that the plains should have been left to the cattle men and had that been done, drouth periods would not have brought disaster. The utilization of the high plains of Texas makes the issue particularly clear as the cattleman's invasion occurred during the boom of the eighties and very nearly simultaneously with the small farmer invasion farther north. Both soon met disaster. Adverse winters, especially the disastrous one of 1885–1886 in the central area and 1886–1887 on the northern plains crippled the industry, and in conjunction with the next decade of drouth and world depression, the recovery was slow. Lying in southern latitudes the grass dried up early in any case, but dry seasons caused shortage. Shipping cattle north for grass reduced the numbers to what the Texas grass would probably support. Unexpected drouth conditions always forced additional shipments, sometimes only after much damage was done, the cattle arriving in Kansas or other northern pastures in weakened condition and sometimes with heavy losses in transit. It should be clear that there are two aspects of adjustment involved; larger numbers could be bred on the plains ranges than could be matured, the maturing and fattening being done in regions more suitable; and the inter-regional economy provided flexibility in making adjustments to the unpredictability of climate.

The depression of the 1930s, and World War II, worked a number of changes in the livestock economy. One change was a sharp emphasis upon calves and young cattle in interstate movement. Another change was the tendency to ship Texas and southwestern cattle to California markets. A third was even more important. During the 1930s the South turned extensively to the growing of Kudzu, a legume which served for grazing and for hay and seemed to provide that section, for the first time, with a possible equivalent of native grass as the basis for a livestock industry. Richmond, Virginia, developed ambitions as an eastern cattle center. The net result was for the South and the Atlantic Coast states to initiate a move-ment for reconstruction of railway rates from the southern range livestock states eastward. Hearings were held before the Interstate Commerce Com-mission early in 1941. The Kansas Bluestem Pasture country and the packing cities of the North protested the rate changes. The intervention of World War II obscured the possible development of this interregional realignment, but should the South draw any substantial portion of the southwestern cattle trade from the North, it would disturb an important interregional relationship which began a hundred years earlier.

# CHAPTER 6

# Ecology & History

[In this short essay, which Malin presented at an interdisciplinary symposium, "The Orientation of Ecology," in 1948, he describes various
approaches to an ecological interpretation of history, including a behavioral analysis of the process of adaptation by settlers, a classified catalog of
the exploration reports by naturalists, and the use of regional "ecological
traverses" and field studies to compare sample geographical "slices" of the
grassland in successive time periods. The primary focus is on adaptative
behavior among settlers in the central grassland, where people of differing
abilities and cultures competed against an ever-changing environment.]

The present discussion of the relations of ecology and history is organized
around five points: A statement of premises incident to collaboration of the
several disciplines across the boundary lines; some implications of a
general ecological interpretation of history based upon variations in options made available by cultural changes; an ecological re-examination of
the history of the United States, with emphasis upon methods; a review of
the grassland problem as a concrete example to illustrate the meaning of
adaptation; and, finally, a consideration of the grassland in relation to
mechanically powered-minerals culture which provided the background
for its occupation after about 1850.

The premises upon which the discussion rests include the dependence
of society upon nature and natural forces, not upon a conquest of nature;
the unity of knowledge; and the existence of a body of methodology suffi-

ciently common to all disciplines to afford a working basis for collaboration in matters of interdisciplinary nature. Both history and ecology may be defined as the study of organisms in all their relations, living together, the differences between plant, animal, and human ecology or history being primarily a matter of emphasis. Therefore, all forms of single- or limited-factor interpretations are rejected as fragmentation of knowledge, with its resultant distortion of facts.

At any level, cultures afford man the opportunity to exercise options in ordering his relations with environment with himself, and as the culture changes the range of the options shifts. Since ecology has become a recognized discipline, it is appropriate to re-examine history with special reference to ecological relations and the significance of these shifting options; the Mediterranean-centered culture yielded to Western Europe, and then to an Atlantic-centered pivot of world power. Included in this selective competition is the transit of culture to the world outside Europe, and then, since about the middle of the nineteenth century, the invasion of the grassland of North America and elsewhere, together with the changing options under the influence of a mechanized-power culture. This article focuses attention primarily upon the meaning of ecological adaptation as applied to the United States.

## The Turner Frontier Hypothesis
## and Its Closed-Space Corollary

The validity of the Frederick Jackson Turner frontier interpretation of history has been challenged, and upon sound grounds within the traditional methods of writing history. But before leaving the problem of the frontier hypothesis, whether American or New World discovery and expansion of Europe, attention is called to another body of associated ideas, which may be challenged effectively by an ecological methodology applied to history. The term *geographical discovery* is, after all, a subjective term, purely relative in character, whereas scientific method presumes a definition of terminology in a form that is both objective and operational. The idea of discovery applied only to Europeans, not to the aborigines of the lands "discovered." The same is true of the concept of the "frontier"—the frontier of what? Obviously, the frontier of the culture of modern Europe. Again, what is the "new land" about which Turner and Halford J. Mackinder and others wrote so insistently? To whom was it new? Certainly not to the American Indian, to the aborigines of Australia, or of Africa, nor to the Chinese. Europe and European-peopled America considered their culture a superior, or master, culture, and themselves perhaps a master race, and thought of "discovery" and of "frontier of new land" in a subjective and egocentric sense. For the most part, the invading culture refused to recognize that the displaced cultures possessed any values, or that the peoples concerned possessed any rights which should be respected. Newness, however, implies the operation of the factor of time, subjective and relative, and time is a ruthless leveler of persons and things. Given a sufficient lapse of time, the tables might be turned upon these invaders by another invading culture.

A scientifically conceived ecological methodology applied to human history would emphasize ecological competition of two or more cultures for dominance in given earth areas, which could be made as objective and exacting as when applied to plants and animals—competition of cultures of differing degrees of complexity, the ecologically stronger invading the earth area occupied by another. But such a methodology would avoid value judgments and would recognize instead differences and similarities. The land involved would not be new land, but land that has been exploited for unknown generations, and that, in consequence of cultural invasion, became subject to a mode of exploitation different from that under a previous culture, and in that sense the cultural techniques might be called new to the land of the displaced culture. The land was not new; only the introduced technology of exploitation was new to the land. In further development of this line of thought, newness is involved because the more complex invading culture possessed technological tools and skills which made available different or wider ranges of options as applied to the exploitation of the area, bringing into the flow of utilization existent resources that were latent under the displaced culture. That point deserves special emphasis. The earth possessed all known, and yet to be known, resources, but they were available as natural resources only to a culture that was technically capable of utilizing them. There can be no such thing as the exhaustion of the natural resources of any area of the earth unless positive proof can be adduced that no possible technological "discovery" can ever bring to the horizon of utilization any remaining property of the area. An attempt to prove such an exhaustion is meaningless, because there is no possibility of implementing such a test. Historical experience points to an indeterminate release to man of such "new resources" as he becomes technologically capable of their utilization. At one stroke, such a concept renders the Turner-Mackinder doctrine of "closed space" meaningless, and correspondingly destroys the basis of the argument of the "closed space corollary to the Turner frontier hypothesis," which holds that a welfare state—a regimented social order—must be instituted to serve as a substitute for the "closed frontier" in order to preserve American democracy and opportunity.

## Ecological Re-examination of the Data of History:
## The Occupation of the United States by Europeans

There are several other possible methods of approach to an ecological re-examination of the history of the United States. Four are indicated here. One fruitful method would be to trace the occupation of the area by Northern Europeans, allowing for a contrasting occupation of the Middle Americas by Southern Europeans. These Northern Europeans were the product of a forest culture in a maritime climate. For present purposes of stating the problem in terms of ecological data, the issues may be brought out effectively by asking a series of questions, but without now attempting answers. What ecological concepts or impedimenta did these Europeans bring to America as a part of their cultural heritage? What did they expect to find? What did they find that they expected, and what did they find otherwise than expected? How did they react to what they found? To what extent did they recognize differences? How did they make adjustments to the differences they recognized, that they did not recognize, or were slow to evaluate? How did that adjustment, or lack of it, or lag, affect their cultural concepts and behavior?

As the occupation of the interior of North America advanced, the population, accustomed to a forest-maritime environment, found it necessary to readjust to a continental climate and to a grassland. The series of questions formulated to apply to the transit of culture across the Atlantic applies equally well to the advance into the interior, but where the emphasis as between Europe and the American seaboard was upon similarities, the emphasis as between the maritime seaboard and the continental interior would be placed more sharply upon differences, especially west of the forest-prairie boundary. In both areas there would be substantial emphasis upon differences, however, as between the southern and northern latitudes, which involve temperature differences and short- and long-day photoperiodism.

A second possible approach to this ecological re-examination would be the history of the exploration of North America by naturalists: the geologist, the botanist, and the zoologist. The story of the geographical exploration of the continent has been told frequently, but scientific exploration came relatively late, and the story has not been told adequately, if at all, for any field of science. Such historical writing as has been done in connection with science emphasized the most obvious aspect: collection of material, its classification and naming—the making of a classified catalogue. An ecological examination of this process would supplement and extend the record of what has thus far been primarily taxonomic.

A variant of the foregoing approach would be found in a series of biographical studies of leading naturalists who participated in the scientific cataloguing of North America. This would be done with a view to reconstructing their ecological outlook and reactions to the work upon which they were engaged.

The construction of ecological traverses of America, or of regions, is another fruitful procedure. The idea of the traverse is borrowed from the geographer, but the materials, procedure, and objectives would be ecological. The primary focus of ecological traverses would be historical. They would be run for several successive time periods and in several directions, especially east and west and north and south, through areas of different topography, altitudes, and rainfall patterns. The materials would be written documents descriptive of ecological facts which would be evaluated systematically. Such ecological traverses of chosen historical time periods could then be compared with current ecological traverses of identical routes based upon field studies of ecological survivals. I have presented sample studies for traverses, as of about 1849, in my book *The Grassland of North America*. These were undertaken experimentally, and the details of techniques and methodology need to be perfected as experience is gained in practice.

How much has man modified the ecological setting of history in America? No certain scientific answer can be given because the necessary historical-scientific investigations of an ecological character have not been made. The samples of ecological history completed indicate less fundamental change than is usually assumed by conservation propagandists. At present, answers must, perforce, be tentative, and largely a matter of personal opinion. This is peculiarly unfortunate when public attention is being bombarded by propaganda to authorize gigantic programs dealing with natural resources.

## The Grassland Problem: The Meaning of Adaptation

When forest man met the prairie in the Ohio Valley and Great Lakes regions as the American frontier of white settlement moved westward, he was puzzled about the fact that these earth areas were covered with grass. A voluminous literature grew up dealing with the question of why the prairies were treeless. Although there may be exceptions, forest man tended to avoid settlement in the open prairies. If he took prairie land, it was contiguous to forest land, which he made the base of his farm establishment. Several reasons have been assigned for the retarded settlement of the prairies, some of which are inconsistent and apply obviously to different kinds of grassland: wetness, difficulty in plowing grass sod, low degree of fertility, prevalence of disease, lack of water, of wood, of navigation, and of protection against the hazards of climate. Because the problem has not been adequately defined, there is much contradiction, misunderstanding, and some controversy. Sometimes trees and sometimes grass occupied soil inferior for the standard agricultural crops of the area. It is possible, however, to trace the major steps in the substantial reversal of forest man's concepts about the soils of the grassland, but soil scientists generally have not yet arrived at an adequate understanding of them. A long list of other problems needs examination and reorientation in order to clarify history as well as to afford perspective on the present, both the successful adjustments and the numerous ecological blunders, and to define the meaning of adaptation.

The British breeds of beef cattle were introduced into the plains. One of these breeds, the Hereford, possessed latent characteristics that were released so conspicuously by the new environment as to enable it to dominate the region from Mexico to Canada. The beef and dairy breeds of Brahman cattle from Asiatic India possessed desirable characteristics for the hot, dry, Southern plains. Among field crops, the competitive experimentation with wheat varieties proved that the hard spring and winter wheats from Russia possessed adaptive capacities; likewise, the sorghums from Africa and Asia, mostly imported by way of the higher-rainfall East, established themselves in favor in various parts of the grassland; and, in addition, alfalfa from the Mediterranean area, by way of Chile, was introduced into the economy of California and the plains. It is important to emphasize that all the animals and plants involved in these so-called adaptations to the plains were introduced without biological change from their original environments to the new, and that in the original environments they possessed all the qualities that they demonstrated under the new conditions. In their original environment, they possessed in some, and possibly in most, cases characteristics that were relatively unnoticed or latent, but which became conspicuous or even decisive under the options of the plains environment. The process was one of selective experiment with materials already in existence elsewhere, and no one understood the biological mechanism involved. Much is still not understood. Only in the second quarter of the twentieth century did the second, or creative, phase of biological adjustment emerge in effective form, based upon the genetics of mutation and hybridization and the correlation of breeding and agronomic programs with the principles of developmental physiology. This phase has only begun, its potential is unknown, but for the first time the ecologist and the historian gain a new insight into the meaning of adaptation, the mechanism of biological behavior of the past, and one which opens the door to future adaptive breeding programs with chosen objectives.

Soil physics, tillage methods, and the tools with which to operate a farm were the product of the forest-maritime environment. Here again concepts stood in the way, as well as the practices and the tools designed to meet traditional conditions. But there was much in this cultural accumulation, latent or relatively so, that possessed values that became significant and important in the grassland: in plowing technology, the steel plow, the lister, and disc machinery; methods of handling the soil to conserve moisture and to retard wind erosion; harvesting machinery, particularly the header; and the beginnings of horse-powered agriculture.

This approach to history makes no commitments about the validity of the concepts of civilization, about its rise and fall, and about progress. What are they, anyway, but philosophical speculations? What is envisioned here is an intermediate, selective, ecological competition of people occupying earth areas under the changing range of options afforded by cultures of differing degrees of complexity.

# CHAPTER 7

# Man,
# the State of Nature,
# & Climax

*As Illustrated by Some Problems of
the North American Grassland*

[James Malin considered this essay his most provocative statement on the interrelation of history and ecology. He warns botanists, zoologists, and soil scientists that their research findings will lack validity and power unless they measure quantitatively the ecological impact of human habitation, both aboriginal and civilized, on the North American grassland environment.]

The state of nature as it is commonly accepted is nonexistent. When man appeared upon the scene, he destroyed such a state, because he possessed the unique capacity to act with a purpose. No matter how primitive, he introduced the factor of planning, and the element of choice. The length of time man has occupied the North American continent has been variously estimated. Prior to about 1930, the maximum was set at about 3,000 years. After that approximate date, the Folsom man discoveries led a large segment of anthropologists to reach back 40,000–50,000 years. The new carbon-14 test, applied at the mid-twentieth century, affords a new measuring device, the application of which, not yet complete, is constructing a new calendar, with 10,000 years as the probable maximum and Folsom man possibly near half that figure.[1]

The contention of this paper is that the botanist, zoologist, and the soil scientist cannot expect any real success in many aspects of their own disciplines, in an ecological sense, until some tangible achievement is made in dealing with the problem of man's influence. Such a necessary recognition of the role of man affords a common ground between them and the geographer and the historian. First, the nature of the problem of man, as an ecological factor, must be discussed and defined, in order to appreciate the full range of the ramifications involved. Once the significance of the problem is fully recognized, then, possibly, methodology can be formulated and techniques and tools devised that may achieve some exactitude of measurement, and thereby place the study upon a quantitative basis. If success attends such efforts, then the accumulation of necessary data will follow. All that can be attempted here is to undertake the first step of definition and discussion of the nature and scope of the problem as applied to a particular area of concentration, and some of its implications to all the disciplines concerned.

The true state of nature existed only prior to the emergence of man. The disciplines most concerned in the study of that time are geology and paleontology in their several phases. If the study of the state of nature as modified by aboriginal man is the center of interest, then to the two disciplines already mentioned must be added archaeology and anthropology, plant and animal ecology, geography, and soil and other sciences. It is history based upon human remains, or documents, prior to the invention of writing. If the focus of study is upon the occupance of the continent since European man arrived in 1492, the conventional conception of history derived from written documents is added to all the others. Of the three stages, the first deals with the true state of nature, the second with aboriginal man's modification, and the third with European man's modification. The first two involve a dual culture conflict, the last two a triple culture conflict. How can either regime of human occupance be determined and measured?

The speculative or philosophical status of most of the approaches to the problem of the North American grasslands under man's influence may be illustrated by a brief reference to the work of a number of distinguished specialists. Carl Sauer, a geographer, took an extreme view of aboriginal man's influence upon nature, attributing the grassland and the extinction of certain Pleistocene animals to man's use of fire.[2] His views carry great weight west of the Rocky Mountains. C. W. Thornthwaite also took an extreme view of culture control of environment, applied more particularly to European man in America. As the extensive erosion in the West was attributed by him to the influence of man, he held that the remedy lay in the same hands, especially by means of government planning. Because of his being in government service, his influence was widely disseminated by high-pressure official propaganda.[3] The position of Kirk Bryan was near the opposite extreme from Sauer and Thornthwaite, holding to the dominance of impersonal natural forces effecting climate changes sufficient to shift the balance of equilibrium on the side of erosion or introduce such instability that man's role was only a minor factor in the larger complex setting.[4] Under this interpretation, remedial measures by either private or governmental action were of limited benefit. Ellsworth Huntington occupied the extreme position also in maintaining climate determinism.[5]

In the field of plant ecology, F. E. Clements formulated a doctrinaire concept of ecological succession, climax, and disclimax, the last phase being charged particularly to the work of European man.[6] This theoretical construction had little realistic relation to such historical evidence as was available.

In the field of soil theory, C. F. Marbut and his associates and successors in the USDA adapted the highly doctrinaire Russian soil theory to the United States: the idea of profile and maturity as soil climax.[7] This stereotype also possesses doubtful value, except in a few limited spots, in understanding the problems of the grassland, where the soils are largely derived from transported materials, and disturbance is the most conspicuous characteristic of the environment. There is little room for the idealized view of the conservationist literature, that soil was derived from the disintegration of underlying rock as rapidly as stabilized erosion in a state of nature removed it at the top—a state of mythical equilibrium—until that state was destroyed by modern man. H. H. Bennett declared that the Missouri and Mississippi rivers ran clear during this "state of nature."[8]

George F. Carter offered the suggestion, relative to California aborigines and grasses, that the gathering of edible seeds aided in the dissemination and reproduction of some species, creating an artifical climax. The passing of the Indians and the invasion of Mediterranean rye were approximately coincident in time, and the elimination of the native grasses may have been the result of a cause-effect relationship.[9] O. F. Cook made the suggestion, revived by Higbee, that the dominance of the chicle forest in Maya areas of Central America reflects the deliberate protection of that species for its edible nuts.[10] Likewise, Carter and Higbee make a similar suggestion for the dominance of the oak-hickory-chestnut deciduous hardwood forest in the eastern mid-latitudes of the United States.[11]

As stated, all these interpretations are, in the scientific sense, unproved. They are in the nature of speculation, hypotheses, theories, philosophical assumptions—or whatever term most appropriately designates propositions that are not subject to scientific proof in the broad, general form in which the question is stated. Of course, many scientific data have been brought to bear upon them, and the scholarly standing of the men mentioned is such that much of their work stands the test, within limits. Is it possible, then, to formulate the essential questions in meaningful forms subject to proof?

## The Problem of the Great Plains

Less broad than the propositions just stated is the problem of the so-called Great Plains portion of the North American grassland and immediately related areas. W. D. Johnson offered the first major interpretation of that area: that the Great Plains were the relatively undisturbed remnant of the apron of debris that had been washed down from the Rocky Mountains in the process of weathering. No rivers had cut through the Llano Estacado, but he viewed the mid-latitude section as having been dissected by such rivers as the Canadian, Arkansas, Smoky Hill, Republican, and Platte. Within the past two decades, however, the Johnson theory has had to be discarded as too simple. Geologists dealing with Nebraska and Kansas have arrived at the conclusion that the drainage system of these mid-latitudes has changed materially, possibly more than once, during the Pleistocene, and that the material has been eroded and redeposited accordingly. In other words, during Pleistocene time, the area was in a state of continuous disturbance under the influence of impersonal forces.[12]

Late in Pleistocene time man appeared, possibly 5,000–8,000 years ago, in the mid-latitudes (a more exact dating may emerge from the carbon-14 method of measuring time). From that point, the purposive influence of man was added to the impersonal forces contributing to continuous disturbance in the area. Archaeological work and its interpretation by anthropologists have only begun in the grass country east of the Rocky Mountains, and in some areas only sketchy preliminary surveys have been made for some subdivisions. Since Folsom and Yuma man, several successive cultures have occupied the country, the extent, density, and persistence of which are only beginning to be understood. Archaeological evidence is lacking as yet to construct satisfactory maps of distributions and historical sequences of occupance. Sites have been located upon which successive cultures have been recorded in archaeological remains, one above the other and separated by accumulations of wind-blown material.[13] These records are unmistakable evidence of continuous disturbance, both impersonal and human, upon the same site. Possibly a reasonably accurate dating, or calendar, of these occupations and of intervening abandonment may be constructed, and upon a sufficient number of sites, with a distribution wide enough to be really meaningful.

By narrowing down step by step in space and time, particular sites come into perspective, and the bridge can be built from the purely archaeological documentation to the written, the intervening transition involving both. The expedition of Coronado into the Great Plains in 1541 is such an instance, although for other spots dated events may be associated as accurately or more so. The route of Coronado and his terminus in Quivira have long been matters of dispute, but the most recent studies brought to bear upon the problem, utilizing both archaeological and written evidence, have agreed upon the Rice-McPherson County, Kansas, area as the most probable site of Quivira.[14] As these counties were settled by Americans during the 1870s, the period between Coronado and American settlement was about 330 years. The archaeological estimates of time indicate that the same culture that Coronado met persisted until the early eighteenth century, allowing a time span of about 150 years between the two occupations.

Since American contacts were established in the area, intermittent disturbances of considerable proportions have been conspicuous. For instance, dust storms were an integral element in the physical and ecological history of the country within the period of written record, and during the years that the only direct and tangible human influence was that of the nineteenth-century Plains Indians occupants. The missionary-surveyor Isaac McCoy described a typical dust storm, in what is now east-central Kansas, in the fall of 1830.[15] The printed record of dust storms, with particular reference to Kansas, has been compiled by the present author for 1850–1900.[16] These accounts do not describe the particular sites involved in the Quivira remains, but those village sites are within the area covered and were subject to the same general conditions that affected the region as a whole.

## Movement of Soil

The definition and delimitation of the problem under discussion may be facilitated by an approach from another direction, followed by the necessary narrowing of space and time to pin-point the essential issue at stake. Taking the Mississippi Valley drainage basin as a whole, the records of the U.S. Geological Survey indicate that no greater quantity of water or silt passed Baton Rouge into the Gulf of Mexico in 1951 than when records began, upwards of a century earlier. The high-water mark of the Missouri River flood of 1951 did not exceed the high-water mark of the flood of 1844 at Boonville, Missouri. Such facts run counter to the assumptions of most conservation propaganda, but they are vital in evaluating the influence of human action upon the area as a whole as well as upon any particular spot. In spite of great damage to man's improvements in the valley, especially urban development in flood bottoms (which never should have been made in the first place), the great flood of 1951 in the Kansas Valley was of great benefit, by and large, from the standpoint of agricultural resources as reflected in improved productivity of bottom land. Serious erosion occurred in some uplands, and the gains must be balanced against the losses for the valleys as wholes. For the Mississippi Valley as a whole, or for the Kansas Valley as a whole, natural resources in terms of water erosion meant, primarily, only a movement of soil from one place to another within the valley, and not a dead loss.

The problem of wind erosion must be approached in similar fashion. Sand and dust are moved by the wind from place to place, but the net loss is negligible, and probably not greater than formerly—that is, prior to occupation by Americans within the century. According to the archaeological evidence, the thickness of the wind-blown material that interlayers successive aboriginal village sites would indicate greater dust storms by far than occurred during the decade of the 1930s. The movement of dust by air currents is continuous, but the meterological service had not kept records and had not devised instruments and techniques for recording the phenomena. During the still part of the night, dry dust fall is usually most conspicuous. A partly enclosed patio floor of the author's residence has afforded opportunity to verify dust fall; red, yellow, or black dust collected in measurable quantities repeatedly during the night, the color giving some indication of the probable place of origin. Repeated checking with the local weather observer and with published reports of near-by weather stations on such occasions has not revealed any record by them of such occurrences. Likewise, during the summer of 1951, when rain fell nearly every day, measurable quantities of dust fell with the rain. Water erosion moves soil from a higher to a lower position topographically, but airborne dust is deposited everywhere. The question for which there is no present answer is, How much? And neither is there an answer in exact measurements to the question, What is the net gain or loss from combined movements of soil materials? A further question should be entered in the record: Does this soil lose in its capacity to produce vegetation by being moved from place to place either by water or by wind? If the answer is always in the affirmative, then why is land in flood bottoms often greatly benefited by floods? If it is not lost in that case, then the burden of proof would seem to lie against the claim that it is always lost.

## Aboriginal Cultures

It is a truism that archaeologists deal with excavations; one of their chief badges of office is a spade. But if all erosion carried soil to the ocean, they would have no remains of human culture to uncover. What are the sources of the cover, or overburden, under which the evidences of human occupation are buried? First is the accumulated matter derived from vegetation; second, if the site is on a slope, water erosion would wash material from higher points; third, dust fall derived from wind erosion would accumulate on high as well as on low spots, both dry and wet deposits.

One of the first men to publish descriptions of the Rice-McPherson County sites was John August Udden, a young Swedish teacher (later to become a distinguished geologist) at the Academy of Bethany College, Lindsborg, Kansas. In 1881, when he was twenty-two years of age, his students called his attention to the Paint Creek archaeological remains, and in his spare time he worked over a period of seven years at the site. His published report did not appear until 1900. He described two types of mounds, which he interpreted, respectively, as burial and dwelling sites. The burial mounds were "usually built on high bluffs or on upland hills." They were covered with earth and vegetation, and within them was "a pile or layer of rocks" under which were human remains. The mounds he called dwelling sites "do not occupy any conspicuously high places, but usually lie on or near some flat and fertile lowlands as on the border of an alluvial plain." They were really not mounds, he explained, "but merely flat surface of the ground where dwellings of an earlier race have once been standing. They would never be noticed, were it not for the relics of household art, chase, and warfare scattered about the place."[17] Wedel denied that they were building sites. His verdict was that they were village refuse dumps, but for present purposes the original use is not at issue.

There is no exact dating either of the time of first or last occupance of the Paint Creek site, or of its duration. The accepted minimum of time elapsed since aboriginal abandonment and Udden's observations is about 150 years. The significant part of Udden's description is that "they would not be noticed, were it not for the relics." This would seem to imply that so far as soil and grass composition were concerned there was no apparent difference between the low, flat mounds and the intervening prairie. Upon digging through the mounds, Udden noticed that upon reaching the prairie level, the ground was harder. Having lived in Kansas during a dry, dust-blown period of the later eighties, and as a geologist being professionally interested in wind-blown materials,[18] he attributed the mounds to dust accumulation around the houses. Even if we accept Wedel's interpretation of origin, the dust-and-sand accumulation thesis would apply equally well. Outwardly, at least, the marks of men (scars?), representing possibly 200 or 300 years of occupance, had been erased within 150 years, except for some unevenness of the surface. The present author checked one of these sites with some care at two different times during the summer of 1951 and could find no evidence of surface variations in soil or vegetation that could be attributed to aboriginal occupation. The same aboriginal culture covered at least five or six central Kansas counties and extended down the east side of the Arkansas River valley at least as far south as Arkansas City, where some excavating has been done. These people lived by agriculture, cultivating advanced varieties of corn, beans, and melons, they dug native roots from the prairie soil, and they hunted wild game. Yet this area was always described by the first white settlers as virgin prairie, and by the conservation enthusiasts as undisturbed by abuse at the hands of man until white Americans broke the sod and upset the perfect equilibrium of the state of nature.

One of the overriding facts that has been kept in the foreground throughout this paper is the virtually continuous character of disturbance to soil and to vegetation during the whole Pleistocene and Recent time. The disturbance was the consequence of impersonal forces alone, physical and animal, prior to the advent of man, and to both impersonal and human purposive forces since. Without going to the extremes of Sauer, we may say that aboriginal man, through occupance over long periods of time, through agricultural pursuits, use of fire, killing of selected game, utilization of selected plants, and digging in the earth for root plants, certainly destroyed vegetation altogether in some spots of considerable size again and again, and interrupted succession of vegetation over wide areas where he did not destroy it. His selected utilization of animals and plants undoubtedly exercised an important influence upon the relative dominance not only of those particular species, but upon the whole range of interrelations of equilibrium throughout the grassland as well as in particular spots. Even though the nature of these influences has not been, and probably cannot be, reconstructed with any degree of completeness, the fact of such human influence cannot be denied or ignored. Even the nineteenth-century Plains Indians exercised a similar influence, in spite of the fact that their culture was substantially different from the culture of the people found by Coronado. In spite of such a record of destruction and interruption of succession, there existed a wide range in succession stages in the grassland, associated with a variety of conditions resulting from disturbances derived from natural forces of water, wind, and animals, and from planned action of man. The fact should be clear also, that certain kinds of damage done to nature by the action of man are more easily repaired than is usually recognized—and especially than is alleged by conservation enthusiasts, whether private or official. In other words, there are influences of human action upon nature that are quickly, and largely, if not fully, reversible.

The Quivira sites are only one instance of many that might be studied in a similar manner throughout the grassland. The archaeological materials that are accumulating for interpretation are so numerous and so new that one hesitates to generalize about the possibilities of correlating the archaeological evidence with the written documents. The point that is certain is that the reappraisal of the role of man must modify substantially the prevailing views of the history of the grasslands.

## The Soil Question

What corollaries or conclusions are to be derived from these facts? What other aspects of the study of the grassland must be re-examined in a fundamental fashion in the perspective of such historical approach to the region? What is soil? How was it formed? And what span of time was involved? What of agriculture in the grassland under the long-term utilization essential to the support of the existing human culture? What of the proposed valley development of natural resources and conservation planning that has for some time occupied the spotlight of political controversy? Certainly some fundamental reconsiderations are in order. Why the haste to flood many of the sites of prior human culture before adequate investigations and interpretations of human occupance can be made? Why flood them at all, period? Once archaeological evidence is destroyed, whatever enlightenment might have been derived from it regarding the experience of man is irretrievably lost, and through the blunders of jockeying for current political advantage. Instead, it should be preserved in the interest of finding the most tenable solutions.

The limits of this article preclude any attempt to discuss the three major positions. Subjects two and three are offered only as suggestions, and the first, the soil question, is discussed only briefly and primarily in the spirit of inquiry to direct thought into fresh channels.

How can the idealized type of theoretical climax, either of soil or of vegetation, have culminated under the conditions of continuous disturbance established by history? The calendar of events does not allow the time necessary, 100,000 or even 10,000 years to produce five inches of topsoil as claimed by conservationists, or to complete succession and climax of vegetation for the area as a whole. Difference was more characteristic than uniformity. If this interpretation of facts is in error, then the concept of climax must be redefined, especially in its time requirement, both as respects soil maturity (climax) and vegetational climax. Furthermore, in that case, the implication that vegetational succession and climax are dependent upon progressive soil changes in the direction of maturity needs restatement or abandonment.

Does soil age have any relation to fertility or productivity? And, if so, what is meant by soil age? Is soil anything more than a medium, useful but not essential, to the growth of vegetation? How shall soil age be measured? To this last question there are three possible and quite different answers: First, by length of time in place sufficient to produce a well-defined profile according to the Russian-American school of pedology, with horizons A, B, C, D. Second, the length of time since initial weathering from rock, including the history of the weathered material as it may have been removed from place to place by action of water and wind. Does the weathered material gain or lose properties by such change of place? Third, the length of time involved in successive geological time periods—successive cycles of sedimentation, consolidation, and erosion down to the present. This last point is illustrated and emphasized sharply by inferences that the writer draws from studies of the selenium problem and of trace elements. In undertaking to explain the high concentrations of selenium in the soil at some points in South Dakota and Wyoming, Trelease and Beath advance the view that the selenium in the Cretaceous rocks was probably derived from the magma, or molten rock, exposed in Rocky Mountain formation; that Tertiary formations were derived from reworked Cretaceous strata, and thereby selenium became more highly concentrated; and that modern concentrations are a further development of the process, aided by certain plants that serve as selenium accumulators.[19] To what extent is selenium only an unusual example of the problem that is involved in all soil evolution, a problem that must be recognized in any attempt to explain the presence or absence of particular properties in any soil?

An evolutionary approach to soil theory is posed from another direction by the deficiency of some soils in trace elements. This problem appears to arise in connection with (but not exclusively) soils derived predominantly from shales and sandstones rather than from marine limestone deposits. After World War II, Kansas established an experimental substation in the southeastern part of the state to study the problem of such soils, of crop production upon them, and of feeding animals upon those crops. As with the selenium problem, which represents the presence of undesirable elements, the absence of desirable elements introduces questions of human nutrition.

In the low-rainfall areas of the grassland, the soils are derived largely from transported materials, largely wind-blown, and other parts from water-worked materials modified by the wind; the same is true of the bottom lands of the valleys in the higher rainfall areas. This fact is emphasized for Kansas by R. I. Throckmorton's soil map, constructed before the subject was confused by later theories of pedology.[20] In some limited areas of low rainfall in the west, and in larger areas in the higher-rainfall eastern portion of the grassland, the soil has been formed in place, and is the residual product of soil formation that seems to fit approximately into the diagrammatic formula of the Russian-American school of Marbut and his successors. Between the soils that shift rapidly under the influence of wind and water and the predominantly residual-type soils are all possible variants, with repeated disturbances under the influence of wind, water, and man, both aboriginal and contemporary, prominent in their history. Man's influence upon the total situation may easily be exaggerated; likewise, the influence of aboriginal man may be ignored under the influence of egocentric twentieth-century man. Both these perversions of history and science have occurred, and most of the literature available is vitiated by one or the other—or both—these errors.

In an area as varied as the grassland of North America, each spot must be evaluated in its own right. On soils derived from transported materials, which are of substantial thickness—and these occupy much of the low rainfall grassland—the topsoil may be eroded by wind or water down to plow depth, not merely once but several times, without impairing the productivity of the land. E. W. Hilgard, who did the most fundamental thinking about soils that has been done in America, pointed this out for arid soils of California in 1892.[21] Farmers in the grassland in question have learned this unimpaired capacity from long experience, and have compelled reluctant scientists to recognize it.

In the study of soil, why should there be exaggerated emphasis upon soil maturity in terms of profile? Has profile, per se, any necessary significance, and if so, under what limited circumstances of place and associated situation? An evolutionary or historical approach to soil formation reaches back in time beyond the range of such oversimplified stereotypes.

Obviously, the North American grassland has supported a succession of human cultures over a long period of time. You say the present one is different? Yes, but so were each of the others different from what had gone before. Beware of the egocentric present-mindedness of the dominant thought of the mid-twentieth century! Beware of its arrogance and intolerance! Not only of its arrogance, and intolerance of all contemporaries who differ with it, but of its attempt to escape from history by ignoring or ridiculing the past. Time is a ruthless judge and, in the end, Time has the last word.

A large part of American research funds and energy is expended upon technological research of a short-term character to achieve functional ends, often primarily for political advantage. In the past, the basic thinking of the modern world has been done almost exclusively by Europeans. Two world wars have destroyed Europe physically, but what is critical is that Europe offers no recognizable evidence that it has the vitality to revive its capacity to think creatively. And no Marshall Plan, or any other artificial stimulus, can perform that miracle. Neither is there any present recognizable evidence that either the United States or Russia has the capacity to assume the responsibility for the fundamental thinking they have helped to destroy. Government funds, foundation funds, university funds, poured out to any Johnny-come-lately for "quickie research," cannot meet the challenge. Fundamental results cannot be produced in a summer, a year, or two years, with progress reports semiannually, or annually, to be reviewed by administrative authority to determine whether results justify renewal of support for another term. Creative thinking may require the sacrifice of a lifetime, and expectations for the requisite basic thinking must be geared to the cumulative power of generations of untrammeled effort, a situation now virtually nonexistent. The intrinsic problems of grasslands everywhere await a more comprehensive body of thought of this order of potentiality and action.

## Notes

1. Since this was written, a further revision, involving a drastic reorientation, has been proposed by G. F. Carter (*Scientific Monthly* 73 [1951]: 297). The effect of his proposal is only to add emphasis to what is said here.

2. C. Sauer, *Geographical Review* 34 (1944): 529.

3. C. W. Thornthwaite, C. F. S. Sharpe, and E. F. Dasch, *Climate and Accelerated Erosion in the Arid and Semi-Arid Southwest, with Special Reference to the Polacca Wash Drainage Basin, Arizona,* USDA Technical Bulletin no. 808, May 1942 (Washington, D.C.: GPO); S. C. Happ, *Journal of Morphology* 5 (1942): 338.

4. K. Bryan, *Annals of the Association of American Geographers* 31 (1941): 219; *Science* 62 (1925): 338; *New Mexico Quarterly* 10 (1940): 227; D. Whittlesey, *Annals of the Association of American Geographers* 41 (1951): 88.

5. E. Huntington, *Civilization and Climate* (New Haven, Conn.: Yale University Press, 1915); *Mainsprings of Civilization* (New York: Wiley, 1945).

6. F. E. Clements, *Plant Succession: An Analysis of the Development of Vegetation,* Carnegie Institution Publication no. 242 (Washington, D.C.); F. E. Clements and V. E. Shelford, *Bio-ecology* (New York: Wiley, 1939).

7. C. F. Marbut, *Soils of the United States,* part 3, *Atlas of American Agriculture* (Washington, D.C.: GPO, 1935).

8. H. H. Bennett, *Soil Conservation* (New York: McGraw-Hill, 1939), pp. 1–3.

9. G. F. Carter, *Scientific Monthly* 70 (1950): 73.

10. O. F. Cook, *Annual Report of the Smithsonian Institution* (Washington. D.C.: GPO, 1903), pp. 481–97; E. Higbee, *Geographical Review* 38 (1948): 457.

11. E. Higbee, *op. cit.*; G. F. Carter, *op. cit.*

12. W. D. Johnson, *Twenty-first Annual Report of the U.S. Geological Survey,* part 4 (Washington, D.C.: GPO, 1899–1900): 609–741; *Twenty-second Annual Report of the U.S. Geological Survey,* part 4 (Washington. D.C.: GPO, 1900–1901), pp. 635–69; R. F. Flint, *Glacial Geology and the Pleistocene* (New York: Wiley, 1947); G. E. Condra and E. C. Reed, *The Geological Section of Nebraska,* 2d ed., Nebraska Geological Survey Bulletin no. 14 (Lincoln, 1943); *Correlation of the Pleistocene Deposits of Nebraska,* Nebraska Geological Survey Bulletin no. 15 (Lincoln, 1948); J. C. Frye, *Transactions of the Kansas Academy of Science* 49 (1946): 71; E. H. Colbert et al., *Bulletin of the Geological Society of America* 59 (1948): 541; R.F. Flint et al., *Bulletin of the Geological Society of America* 60 (1949): 9.

13. W. R. Wedel, *Transactions of the Kansas Academy of Science* 50 (1947): 16.

14. W. R. Wedel, *Explorations and Field-Work of the Smithsonian Institution in 1940* (Washington, D.C.: GPO, 1941), p. 71; Smithsonian Institution Miscellaneous Collection 101 (1942), p. 7; *Transactions of the Kansas Academy of Science* 50 (1947): 16;

H. E. Bolton, *Coronado, Knight of Pueblos and Plains* (Albuquerque: University of New Mexico Press, 1949).

15. L. Barnes, *Kansas Historical Quarterly* 5 (1936): 364.

16. J. C. Malin, *Kansas Historical Quarterly* 14 (1946): 129, 265, 391.

17. J. A. Udden, *An Old Indian Village*, Augustana Library Publication no. 2 (Rock Island, Ill., 1900), p. 10.

18. J. A. Udden, *The Mechanical Composition of Wind Deposits*, Augustana Library Publication no. 1 (Rock Island, Ill., 1898); *The Cyclonic Distribution of Rainfall*, Augustana Library Publication no. 4 (Rock Island, Ill., 1905). (Udden's later career was identified primarily with Texas and included the study of oil and gas geology.)

19. S. F. Trelease and O. A. Beath, *Selenium: Its Geological Occurrence and Its Biological Effects in Relation to Botany, Chemisty, Agriculture, Nutrition, and Medicine* (New York: Authors, 1949).

20. R. I. Throckmorton, *Twenty-eighth Biennial Report of the Kansas State Board of Agriculture* (1931–32), pp. 33, 91, 100–101.

21. E. W. Hilgard, *A Report on the Relations of Soil and Climate*, USDA Weather Bureau Bulletin no. 3 (Washington, D.C.: GPO, 1892), p. 19.

PART II

# Environmental Adaptations in the Grassland: Case Studies

In the early 1930s James Malin embarked on an ambitious research program of local and regional adaptation that guided his work for more than two decades. The research strategy was to sample representative areas of each of the major agricultural regions of the Jayhawk State and to undertake comparable case studies for each region that traced the "development of the whole community life." His goal was to write a general history of agricultural evolution in Kansas from 1850 to 1900 that illustrated the creative human adaptation to the agricultural frontier and subsequently the disintegration of a "unified community life" under the impact of urbanization and industrialization.

Malin's strategy was to construct fairly uniform and comparable data bases by using similar techniques and asking similar questions. Malin's holistic research design for the study of the Central Plains was unique and without precedent at the time, although it paralleled the grand designs of his contemporaries—Joseph Shafer's Domesday studies of Wisconsin frontier development and Frank Owsley's study of southern yeoman farmers.

The sample communities and regions that Malin selected were Edwards County in the central wheat belt (see map of Kansas, p. 167, showing type of farming areas), the bluestem pasture region in the east, a four-county transition zone between the bluestem grassland and central wheat belt, the "Elbow region" of mixed farming centered around Kansas City, and two cornbelt counties in the northeast. Only the western cattle-sorghum region beyond the 100th meridian was not studied in detail.

In each regional investigation, Malin discovered common themes. First, the ecological givens of a region established the broad natural parameters within which human adaptation, if successful, must occur. Second was the theme of regional adequacy. Each region possessed the natural resources necessary to enable its human inhabitants eventually to enjoy a "good living." Third, successful adaptation was an "incremental folk phenomenon" by which the "average practical farmer" followed his instincts, often against the advice of agricultural experts and scientists. The common man discovered the best wheat varieties and invented the necessary farm machinery by a process of selection. The successful ones passed on their marginal innovations "from person to person by precept and practice." Folk wisdom was superior to scientific theories, Malin concluded (*Winter Wheat in the Golden Belt of Kansas,* pp. 250–51). Fourth, the total culture of the Kansans influenced the ways in which they utilized the natural resources of their geographical area. Inert properties of the earth only become natural resources useful to humans by the application of intelligence and cultural technology. Natural resources are as limited or unlimited as the minds of the region's inhabitants. Thus the cultural composition of the population and its shaping by technological forces influence, to a great extent, the process of societal construction in a developing frontier such as Kansas. Finally, the Kansas grassland and its inhabitants, like all other geographical regions of the earth, were linked symbiotically to adjoining regions and to the larger world system. Goods, services, and information freely flowed to and from the interior North American grassland and Europe, Asia, and Africa.

# CHAPTER 8

# On the Nature of
# the History of
# Geographical Area

## *With Special Reference to*
## *the Western United States*

[This essay, which Malin presented to a biological sciences conference in 1960, summarizes the main features of his famous course at the University of Kansas, "The History of the Trans-Mississippi West." This may be taken to present Malin's mature reflections on the ecological approach to historical study and the nature of regionalism in general and the western grassland in particular. The "proper subjects of study" for a geographic region, Malin insisted, are "its geological history, its ecological history, and the history of human culture since the beginning of occupance by primitive men."]

## Introduction

In this chapter attention is focused upon geographical area as an object of study: upon the history of a chosen area and of the human cultures that have occupied it from the earliest primitive men to the present. Although applicable to any such area, for present purposes the emphasis is upon the western United States, and especially upon the southern Great Plains region. This procedure affords a number of innovations. Treated in its own right, the history of a geographical area includes a consideration of all that has been present or is present within the bounds chosen. Proper subjects of study, from this point of view of geographical area, are its geological history, its ecological history, and the history of human culture since the beginning of occupance by primitive men—in the case of the western

United States, some 10,000 years since men reached the Folsom cultural level. The term *culture,* as used here, is that of the archaeologist and anthropologist and denotes the sum total of a way of life.

This is in contrast with the traditional frontier formula, in the Frederick Jackson Turner tradition, which is concerned with little more than the beginning of European-American, especially Anglo-American displacement of Indians and the beginning of the exploitation of their lands according to a form of master-race colonialism. One of the most frustrating aspects of the frontier thesis is the lack of any agreed definition, without which scholarly application to historical study is impossible. According to the frontier thesis, the frontier came to an end in 1890, and with its passing the history of the West ended also. On this practice consult the several textbooks written according to the Turner Frontier Thesis, and where there are more than one edition, compare the several editions: Frederick Logan Paxson, Robert E. Riegel, Dan E. Clark, Ray A. Billington, Thomas D. Clark. The fact should be noted also, that the traditional historian does not deal with cultures, and the word *culture* if used by him is not given any logical or consistent definition or usage. And furthermore, the point is emphasized that culture as used here does not mean "civilization," with its invidious implications about the uncivilized, and the supposedly superior and inferior peoples. The term *culture* involves no value judgments.

The study of the history of the western United States as geographical area is not the study of 17, 20, or 22 separate states that lie within the area. To be sure, each state is a geographical area and has a history. Each was organized for political purposes, and the boundaries were defined according to the exigencies of politics of a particular time. Rarely were these boundaries defensible on the basis of facts and reasoning from facts. They were for the most part arbitrary and in many respects would seem to defeat the best interests of the inhabitants. Yet, as political entities the people of each state accumulated a body of traditions, loyalties, and prerogatives and would not consider mergers or transfer of territory. The study of state history is a legitimate subject, both in its own right, and on occasion, in relation to other partitions of space. But in dealing with the western United States as a geographical area, the emphasis is placed as largely as possible upon phenomena that concern the area as a whole and its major parts. Instead of dealing with individual states, therefore, when subdivision of the entire area is desirable, it can be done meaningfully on the basis of selected criteria suitable to the purpose.

Technology is among the aspects of human cultures that are involved in their competition anywhere, and by the term *technology* as used here is meant more than mere mechanical inventions. The term *technology* includes all manner of ideas and social inventions, and the relative efficiencies for particular purposes of differentiations in the ways of life of competing groups. This competition may occur along the boundaries of areas occupied by these groups, however precise or vague those boundaries may be; or competition may occur through the instrumentality of persons, institutions, or ideas, finding lodgment within the area occupied by competing groups. Peaceful penetration may occur effectively within a rival society, rather than by force applied along boundaries, or expended in control of the sea.[1] Such operations of culture competition occur unconsciously, as well as deliberately, among all societies that make contacts, directly or indirectly, with each other. Unquestionably, the effects of such competition of cultures are related to their capacity and success in occupance of geographical areas.

In this context, the discovery and occupance of the Americas by people of modern European culture since the fifteenth century is only one small segment of the whole history of the Americas as a geographical area, and of their occupance by human culture 400 against some 10,000 years plus. Cultural technology gave to the people of the invading European culture an overwhelming power to overrun, and to displace, or to annihilate the more primitive peoples. From the standpoint of the peoples occupying the Americas prior to the Columbian discovery, the following centuries were stark tragedy. The invading Europeans conquered or destroyed the Indians, fought each other for supremacy, and established their own cultures. For the victors, this was a glorious adventure. To possess any measure of validity, the so-called frontier thesis would have to be treated within the anthropologist's formula of competition of cultures, but historians do not deal with it in that manner.

The western United States is a geographical area, but is not a region within the meaning of geographers, or a section within the meaning of political historians. Some subareas within this larger space may lend themselves in a significant manner to recognition as regions when such treatment may appear to be desirable. Regions and sections, being related to particular selected and limited criteria, are not necessarily of long duration. Usually, they are used as terms applied to areas and periods of time within the quite brief duration of European culture in America. To the whole study of geographical area and to its succession of occupying cultures over some 10,000 years, they may be mostly irrelevant, but some regions may suggest significant conclusions.

The passion of scientific method and social science for classification and uniformities should not mislead the student of areas into the assumption that political boundaries that cut across, or include widely different geographical characters or regional unities are necessarily in error or that they should enlist the missionary zeal of the reformer to effect uniformities as a panacea for all ills. The balancing of divers forces may result, but not necessarily so, in a sounder adjustment to realities than would be probable under overwhelming majorities dominated by a single body of regional interests. On occasion, minorities may be more right than the majority. But what is right? New technology may change radically the character of the area or regional culture. Is right to be equated as belonging to obsolescence or innovation, or neither?

## Variety in Continental Landmasses Subject to Study as Geographical Areas

Every landmass of the earth of a size sufficient to be rated as a continent contains nearly the full range of possible physical variety except as to the greatest extremes of temperature, light, and moisture. This generalization, as is always the case with generalizations, must recognize exceptions. If the South Polar landmass is considered a continent, it is one exception, but nevertheless it exhibits variety within the limits of its temperature and light variables. Greenland would likewise rate as an exception.

But considering the generalization as applying to the conventionally accepted continents—and subject to the prevailing cultural technologies—Europe and Asia (or Eurasia), Africa, Australia, and the Americas, only Europe (separate from Asia) does not contain a dry desert or a rainforest. If Europe and Asia are classed as one continent, Eurasia, that exception disappears. All continents contain conifer and hardwood forests, grasslands, moist or shrub deserts, and dry deserts, together with all the transitional types, except Australia, which lacks the conifer and hardwood forests.

## Habitability by Man of Continental Landmasses

Habitability by man of any area of the earth depends, not upon the properties of the area per se, but upon man's capacity to utilize the properties that exist there, and turn them to his advantage. No other assumption about history is tenable, unless an outright geographical determinism is imposed. Of course, in terms of geological time, paleontology reveals the succession of genera and species that have come and gone, and man may pass from the scene in the course of this succession principle. But short of this kind of liquidation of the human race, the properties of man as an invéntive animal afford him science and technology for seemingly unlimited potentiality to convert the properties of the earth to his use. Natural resources cannot be exhausted until his contriving brain and skillful hand are exhausted. The first requisite of a natural resource is an idea. In consequence, as long as man is capable of new ideas he may continue to reappraise the properties of the earth, bringing new ones continuously into the horizon of his utilization. On the basis of this approach to history, no continental landmass can be denominated uninhabitable, sometime, not even the South Polar continent.

## The Problem of Time: Geological and Calendar Time; History and the Sciences

As time is the major organizing principle of history, the historian must consider the several concepts of time. The time elapsed since the Creation, according to Judaeo-Christian Biblical calculations, was about 6,000 years. For present purposes, omitting the philosophical problem of finite and infinite time, scholars of all disciplines have been confronted with the geological time of rock records, and calendar time of writing men. The acceptance of the theory of evolution by nineteenth-century men was delayed by the time barrier necessary to account for it. The duration of time attributed to Biblical authority was not sufficient. Geology was largely responsible for breaking down this time barrier, and for introducing Western culture to the conception of such immensity of time as made biological evolution appear as a feasible and reasonable explanation.

The task was too well done, however, and the geologist and his academic allies became victims of their own victory over Genesis. To them, geological and historical time of written documentation became irreconcilable. The very immensity of geological time tended to isolate modern historical man from all geological time. Man's written history was of so short a duration as to seem insignificant, even meaningless to the larger frame of reference. Men must learn not to be overwhelmed either by the immensity of geological time, or by the immensity of recorded detail of recent and present time. Geological processes still continue in the geological time scale, only in such multiplicity of detail that the mind fails to comprehend it all as a continuing whole. But, on the other hand, the records of anonymous men with whom the archaeologist deals left their imprint upon a period of geological time—the Pleistocene—with sufficient clarity to lead to an inescapable conclusion that this overlapping of geological and human calendar time is not merely a case of parallel records, but that they are of the same order of magnitude and are an integrated whole. The geologist can no longer ignore man and his capacity to change the face of the earth, nor the fact that he had done so within the range that the geologist has been accustomed to claim as his own monopoly. The realization is not impossible, by both the geologist and the historian, that the transition from impersonal, anonymous man of geological history to the named, individualized man of written history can be comprehended, and that it can be done without doing violence to either discipline. Archaeology and anthropology have already gone a long way toward building the bridge which renders attainable, at least among those scholars who have been working in these overlapping borderlands of knowledge and have been integrating them. To be sure, the rank and file of all the academic disciplines related to this complex task have been little affected, and are scarcely aware of what is taking place. Although slowly, it has been gaining in acceptance and in effectiveness.

### The Historian's Orientation among Specializations: General History (Synthesis) and Histories of Individual Sciences—Innovations in Science since About 1930

Of course, the historian could not be expected to master all the disciplines necessary to the study of history according to the comprehensive plan outlined here. Nevertheless, an orientation was possible in these disciplines, and sufficient to prepare him to cooperate effectively in larger syntheses of the whole of the history of a chosen geographical area. Within the range of the possible also was the comprehension of the full significance of this point of view, and that alone should work a revolution in thinking about history.

Something may be said in extenuation of traditional history and historians in their failure to respond to the opportunities available. The disciplines concerned with either new or the rethinking in the older ones necessary to the new point of view had been quite recent. Much of the intensive research, and the consequent revolution in thought in Pleistocene geology dated from about 1930. Even more revolutionary had been the thought about primitive man in North America, and especially in the Great Plains. Instead of a maximum of 3,000 years formerly allowed for man's occupance of North America, the discovery of Folsom level culture and subsequent findings, place man at that cultural level in the Great Plains area at least 10,000 years ago. This new point of view began to be accepted during the nineteen thirties, but its full impact only became adequately appreciated after World War II. Paralleling these re-orientations in knowledge about geology and anthropology, ecology made a partial adjustment in theory and in substance to the fact of primitive man and his capacity to change the face of the earth, including profound influences upon both plant and animal life. Older scholars, if they made their adjustments to all this new knowledge, were obliged to reeducate themselves. Few historians, indeed, knew what was going on. Much allowance must be made, however, for these older scholars who failed to recognize their opportunities. No such excuse was available to the generation trained after World War II, when the validity of these revolutions in thinking had already been proven out by specialists in their respective fields to a point where no competent scholarship could possibly ignore them. Graduate school training programs did not reflect any real understanding of the requirements and the opportunities.

The history of the western United States offered in perspective, and in a relatively abbreviated form, the full gamut of the human story. An unusual opportunity was available to trace a unique version of the old story of competition of widely different cultures running their full course. The relatively brief time-perspective on the history of the geographical area, in terms of human occupance, was an advantage in some respects, and one that should have been capitalized, not lamented or abused.

## Historical Orientation: Directional

When and how did the more complex primitive cultures reach the interior grassland of North America? Not enough is known as yet to justify much in the way of generalization, but some major outlines appear to be taking shape.[2] In terms of cultural development, Nuclear America extended from Peru to Southern Mexico. From that general area and by routes not clear, cultural patterns were diffused northward. North of the Rio Grande and of the Gulf of Mexico there was intermingling in various complex relationships within the main continental mass of North America. Seemingly, the great interior grassland received cultural contributions from all directions, but predominantly from the south, southwest, and southeast, but in any case, not from the advances of a single uniform front line of migration.

In this perspective, one of the main contentions of Herbert E. Bolton took on an added interest. Although dealing only with the traditional European occupance of North America, he insisted that that process should be studied as primarily a movement of European occupance from south to north, with some invasion from the Pacific Coast to the eastward, and from the Atlantic Coast westward, and from some relatively isolated points in the interior outward where a foothold was established. Bolton had challenged, and rightly, the manner in which historians treated the history of the United States almost exclusively from the British point of view—English colonies in America, and their expansion westward across the continent, thus defying the simplest facts of chronology and geography.[3] True, the striking similarities between the movement of primitive cultures and modern European occupance, south to north, together with the necessary qualifications, may be merely coincidence, yet even as coincidence, the phenomena are of interest.

If the situation was described in terms of cultures instead of political jurisdiction, thus going beyond the Bolton methodology and transforming the historical study into one of a history of competition of cultures, a wide scope of the traditions of political history would undergo revision. Spain had lost political jurisdiction to Mexico, and Mexico in turn to the United States in 1848, and for more than a century United States "Americanization" has been the order of the day. But with what success? The process of culture competition continued despite changes in political jurisdiction. The Spanish-Indian culture yielded but slowly and only in limited aspects. In others it gained adherents. The way of life possessed values that attracted some people from other cultures. It even expanded the influence of certain of its culture traits beyond the geographical limits of 1848.

## The Recent End of the Time-Scale

In revising attitudes toward the western United States and history of geographical area, the recent end of the time-scale was entitled to some fresh thinking. For frontier historians, the area had no history after 1890, the date of the miscalled "end of the frontier." Their interest ends with "frontier beginnings." This point of view violated the basic principle of continuity of history. On the contrary, whatever the shifts in culture occupying the given area, the history of the area continued.

Human cultures occupying the area were constantly subject to scientific and technological innovations. Men were engaged in reappraisals of the potentialities of the properties of the earth and of its culture. Indian, buffalo, and furs gave way to grass and cattle, and partially, grass and cattle gave way to field crop agriculture. During periods of adversity, some pessimists of an earlier day recommended that the Great Plains be given back to the Indians. Of more recent date, especially during the nineteen thirties, the recommendation was modified—give the country back to the cattleman and grass. But this proposal was just as absurd as the first and fully as impossible.

A single illustration must suffice: a look at the United States Census figures for selected areas of the Southern Great Plains, with emphasis upon those for 1940–1960. According to tables (8.1, 8.2), the areas associated with Odessa and Midland, Texas, which acquired Metropolitan area status for the first time in the census of 1960, experienced the most phenomenal gains in population. For the twenty-year period 1940–1960, Odessa's increase was 500 per cent, and Midland's was 474 per cent. The third largest gain for the same period came to the Lubbock Metropolitan area, 200 per cent, and among the strictly High Plains cities the Metropolitan area of Amarillo took fourth place in growth, 141 per cent. Among cities just

**Table 8.1:** Population Southern Plains Cities

|  | 1900 | 1910 | 1920 | 1930 | 1940 | 1950 | 1960 |
|---|---|---|---|---|---|---|---|
| *Oklahoma* | | | | | | | |
| Oklahoma City | 32,452 | 64,205 | 91,295 | 185,389 | 204,424 | 243,504 | 317,542 |
| Tulsa | 7,298 | 18,182 | 72,075 | 141,258 | 142,157 | 182,740 | 258,563 |
| *Texas* | | | | | | | |
| Abilene | 3,411 | 9,204 | 10,274 | 23,175 | 26,612 | 45,570 | 89,428 |
| Amarillo | 1,442 | 9,957 | 15,494 | 43,132 | 51,686 | 74,246 | 137,083 |
| Dallas | 42,638 | 92,104 | 158,976 | 260,475 | 294,734 | 434,462 | 672,029 |
| El Paso | 15,906 | 39,279 | 77,560 | 102,421 | 96,810 | 130,485 | 272,239 |
| Fort Worth | 26,688 | 73,312 | 106,482 | 163,447 | 177,662 | 278,778 | 393,388 |
| Lubbock Co. | 293 | 1,938 | 4,052 | 20,520 | 31,853 | 71,747 | 128,068 |
| Midland | 1,741 | 2,192 | 1,795 | 5,484 | 9,352 | 27,713 | 62,497 |
| Odessa | - | - | Inc. 1927 | 2,407 | 9,573 | 29,495 | 79,123 |
| San Angelo | - | 10,321 | 10,050 | 25,308 | 25,802 | 52,093 | 57,811 |
| San Antonio | 53,321 | 96,614 | 161,379 | 231,542 | 253,854 | 408,442 | 584,471 |
| Waco | 20,686 | 26,425 | 38,500 | 52,848 | 55,982 | 84,706 | 96,776 |
| Wichita Falls | 2,480 | 8,200 | 40,079 | 43,690 | 45,112 | 68,042 | 103,204 |
| *Colorado* | | | | | | | |
| Denver | 133,850 | 213,381 | 256,401 | 287,861 | 322,412 | 415,786 | 489,217 |
| *New Mexico* | | | | | | | |
| Albuquerque | 6,238 | 11,020 | 15,157 | 26,570 | 35,449 | 96,815 | 198,856 |

**Table 8.2:** Population Southern Plains Metropolitan Areas

|                | 1940    | 1950    | 1960      | 1950-1960 Increase % | 1940-1960 Increase % |
|----------------|---------|---------|-----------|----------------------|----------------------|
| *Oklahoma*     |         |         |           |                      |                      |
| Oklahoma City  | 244,159 | 392,439 | 502,707   | 28.1                 | 106                  |
| Tulsa          | 193,363 | 327,900 | 414,117   | 26.3                 | 114                  |
| *Texas*        |         |         |           |                      |                      |
| Abilene        | 67,525  | 85,517  | 120,377   | 47.6                 | 78                   |
| Amarillo       | 61,450  | 87,140  | 148,433   | 70.3                 | 141                  |
| Dallas         | 398,564 | 743,501 | 1,073,573 | 44.4                 | 169                  |
| El Paso        | 131,067 | 194,968 | 310,690   | 59.4                 | 137                  |
| Fort Worth     | 225,521 | 392,643 | 568,484   | 44.8                 | 152                  |
| Lubbock        | 51,782  | 101,048 | 155,485   | 53.9                 | 200                  |
| Midland        | 11,721  | 25,785  | 67,332    | 161.8                | 474                  |
| Odessa         | 15,051  | 42,102  | 90,298    | 114.4                | 500                  |
| San Angelo     | 39,302  | 58,929  | 63,415    | 7.0                  | 61                   |
| San Antonio    | 338,176 | 500,460 | 683,262   | 36.5                 | 102                  |
| Waco           | 101,898 | 130,194 | 148,336   | 13.9                 | 45                   |
| Wichita Falls  | 73,604  | 105,309 | 129,866   | 23.3                 | 76                   |
| *Colorado*     |         |         |           |                      |                      |
| Denver         | -       | 612,128 | 923,161   | 50.8                 |                      |
| *New Mexico*   |         |         |           |                      |                      |
| Albuquerque    | -       | 145,673 | 260,318   | 78.7                 |                      |

Note: The numbers for 1960 are the preliminary United States
Census reports, except Abilene, Texas, which are final.

eastward of the High Plains, the well-established Metropolitan areas of Dallas and Forth Worth continued their sensational pace, 169 per cent and 152 per cent.

Denver, Colorado, long a substantial commercial center generally looking eastward from near the continental divide, now divided its allegiance, if it did not actually look westward. But Albuquerque, New Mexico, was even more dazzling. From a town of 6,238 in 1900, the skyrocketing began during the nineteen forties into a city of nearly 200,000, the nucleus of an urbanized area of 260,318 in 1960. Conspicuously, it was a link along with Denver, between the Pacific Coast and the interior, tending to turn the orientation of the Southern and Middle Great Plains toward the West Coast. By 1960 the economic continental divide lay well to the eastward of the physiographic continental divide.

The outstanding fact population-wise was urbanization and population explosion in these areas of low rainfall. Obviously the explanation was not grass and cattle. At some points significant developments other than these were first evident in retrospect at fairly early dates: at San Antonio during the first decade of the twentieth century; at Tulsa, El Paso, and Wichita Falls in the second decade; and at Abilene, Amarillo, Lubbock, and San Angelo in the third decade. Lubbock had appeared in the census as an incorporated city in the enumeration of 1910, and Odessa in that of 1930 (incorporated, 1927). Even during the Great Depression and Drouth of the nineteen thirties only El Paso recorded a population loss. It would seem that these facts should have made clear something of what was involved, but if they did not, then the startling combination of circumstances that account for the population figures, 1940–1960, challenge all conventional interpretations of "the arid Great Plains" fit only for livestock. Technology afforded the realization of new potentials within the area, and in its relationships with other areas—oil and gas developments, irrigation-grown cotton, automobile and air communications, the beginning of the atomic age, rare minerals, and new commercial exchange relations between the Pacific Coast and the interior east of the continental divide. Science and technology and many innovations induced by the mechanization of society during the mid-twentieth century require new explanations related to the new resources brought into the horizon of utilization.

These are only suggestions. Other areas of the western United States may be analyzed in a similar manner to reveal their different and unique stories, some more than others less sensational during the last two decades.[4]

## The Historian Not a Prophet

To the historian, the future is out of bounds, but there is no reason to assume that the phenomenal developments of the twenty years, 1940–1960, will continue as straight-line cumulations. The unpredictability of particular events in history is an inexorable principle. If the particular cities or the area are to continue their growth, or even to hold their own, their populations must be alert to constant reappraisals of potentials, and to rivals who may exhibit more originality, judgment, and energy. In any case, it would be suicide to expect the current social structure to survive on grass and cattle alone. That simple solution has long since been outmoded. Thought about the future of the southern Great Plains must gamble on the unknown, not on the past that no longer exists and is beyond revival. Grass and cattle are and should continue to be indefinitely of importance, but only as one of several resources. The features which are most emphasized about the area as characterizing it to its disadvantage are not necessarily handicaps. Under new technologies those features may be turned into advantages.

The concept of conservation itself, both in theory and application, is in constant need of reexamination, especially to free it and keep it free from the naïve implication that natural resources are in imminent danger of exhaustion. If utilization of the natural resources of an area were limited to one or two or just a few possibilities, then exhaustion might be a danger. But there is no reason, even if it could be done, to impose such a restriction upon the area or upon its interrelations with other areas. The first requisite of a natural resource is an idea, and so long as men's minds are not exhausted of ideas the existent properties of the earth new to men may be brought into the horizon of utilization. In that perspective there is no threat of exhaustion except that men betray themselves. Conservation is extension of use of the properties of the earth, and the heart of any conservation program lies in the discovery of properties of the earth that can be utilized, thus expanding natural resources available to men. No valid reason exists for assuming that men will not be present in the area for at least another 10,000 years or indefinitely longer. Of course, there is. no magic in that particular number, but it so happens that human culture of at least Folsom level of complexity has existed in the area, supposedly, for that length of time, so if man has learned anything during this immediate past 10,000 years, what more may he learn in the next 10,000! The answer lies in ideas in men's minds, and only incidentally in the earth.

## Illustrative Resource Application: Interpretation

As a general proposition, a focus must be kept on the fact that throughout the history of the human race, a concentration of population always raised the question of scarcity of those resources most in demand at the particular time and place. The nature and extent of requirements depended upon the state of cultural technology. Quite understandably, among the resources most heavily drawn upon were water, food, and fuel. In England of the fifteenth century, during the reigns of Henry VIII and Elizabeth I, a wood fuel scarcity became a matter of concern, and coal as a substitute, or even as a more efficient source of heat, was the subject of legislation. Technology made available an abundance of a more efficient resource. This was prior to the opening of the New World to English exploitation, and it is important to historical perspective to appreciate fully, that present problems in this department are not new, nor peculiar to the era following this miscalled passing of the frontier, or to the low-rainfall areas of the earth.

Likewise, water supply was always a problem where large populations gathered, and regardless of the amount of the annual rainfall. Babylon, ancient Rome, Paris, London, and New York, as well as the interior valleys and cities of southern California, undertook to solve their water scarcity by drawing water from wider and wider geographical areas and carrying it through conduits. Some cities drew upon ground water supplies to such an extent as to result in threatened or actual seepage of seawater into the fresh ground water. Eventually, the next step must be to purify seawater, which is technologically possible, and when the pressure is sufficient, will be made economically feasible. The southern plains are only another step removed. It would be foolish to predict, especially when knowledge of present supplies and their possibilities is so inadequate.[5] When and if the need is sufficiently urgent, the way will be found.

The fact must be kept in mind also, that population concentrations are often mobile. Shifts in geographical location occur, and as already pointed out, are related to technology. Those concentrations of people that have persisted longest have been related over long periods to man's basic needs under the prevailing culture. The more specialized technologies and their resources are necessarily more ephemeral in their influences. The more fertile the mind of man in his inventive activities, the more risk must be assumed. That fact is one that technological man must learn to live with and take in stride.

Some conclusions to such lines of reasoning are clear. Solutions to resource problems that are technologically possible will be made economically feasible if and when the controlling society is convinced of the necessity. This means successive reappraisals of the values contributed by the culture of the limited geographical area to the controlling society, and decisions about whether or not the contribution of the area justified the cost. The issue cannot be evaded by falling back upon geographical determinism and defeatism.

A second conclusion is that, technologically, society has become so mechanized and the division of labor and skills so specialized that no longer does justification exist for talking about rural and urban society, and agriculture and industry, as separate, or rival, or competing systems in the nineteenth-century and earlier sense. Integration of society has occurred to such a degree in fact as to render those traditional concepts obsolete. No definite boundary exists where rural-agricultural social organization leaves off and suburban-urban-industrial structure begins. For the transitional state of society now existing at mid-twentieth century, the term *metropolitan society* may be pressed into service until a new and more accurate terminology is available.

In the study of the histories of ancient culture no one has proved that any culture declined because of water and/or fuel shortage, or of soil depletion. Many times such cause-effect sequences have been alleged, but never proven. So far as generalization in such matters is permissible, more plausible would be the contention that these alleged causes were results; that a rival culture appeared which exercised a more effective power over its geographical area. In consequence, the first culture was no longer able to compete successfully with its neighbors, and the relative inefficiency of its culture technology led to the neglect and to the deterioration of its natural resources, and finally to their substantial destruction. If such a model for the study of decline of a culture is valid, then the exhaustion of its natural resources was a result, a consequence, not a cause. In such a culture, man's contriving brain and skillful hand had failed to function with sufficient originality or creativity. The peoples of the twentieth-century world may well ponder these propositions. Already, for some of them, time may have run out.

## Notes

1. In a totally different but stimulating context, boundaries and related matters are discussed by Stephen B. Jones, "Boundary Concepts in the Setting of Place and Time," *Annals of the Association of American Geographers,* 49 (September 1959): 241–55.

2. Gordon R. Willey, "New World Prehistory: The Main Outlines of the Pre-Columbian Past Are Only Beginning to Emerge," *Science* 131 (8 January 1960): 73–86. Joseph R. Caldwell, "The New American Archaeology," *Science* 129 (6 February 1960): 303–7.

3. Herbert E. Bolton, "The Epic of Greater America," *American Historical Review* 38 (April 1933) 448–73; *The Spanish Borderlands,* Chronicle of America Series (New Haven, Conn., 1921); with Thomas W. Marshall, *Colonization of North America, 1492–1783,* (New York, 1921).

4. Since the present paper was written, a somewhat similar point of view was presented using the new population data of 1960 as applying to the southwestern United States west of the continental divide, Andres W. Wilson, "Urbanization of the Arid Lands," *Professional Geographer* 12 (November 1960): 4–7.

5. See R. L. Nace, (United States Geological Survey), "The Water Outlook for Texas," *Cattleman* (Fort Worth, Tex.) 45 (April 1959): 42–44, 80, 82, 84, 86. Nace emphasized, and quite properly, how little is known certainly about what constitutes water conservation, and how many interests are involved.

CHAPTER 9

# The Adaptation of
# the Agricultural System to
# Subhumid Environment

*Illustrated by the Activities*
*of the Wayne Township Farmers' Club*
*of Edwards County, Kansas, 1886–1893*

[Malin began his local and regional studies by investigating the original manuscript census records of Edwards County, Kansas, and the minutes of the farmers' club of his home town of Lewis in Wayne Township. Out of his research Malin developed his conception of regionalism. From the outset, his central focus was on the process by which local farmers learned to live in the grassland environment in the latter decades of the nineteenth century. This chapter contains the first published results of that seminal work, based on the minutes of the farmers' club. Here Malin documents the folk process of development in cropping and livestock decisions, by which the "sod buster" through thick and thin "had learned sufficiently how to adapt himself to the plains to enable him to stay and to maintain control."]

One of the most interesting problems in the history of the westward movement in the United States is the adaptation of the agricultural system to environment. The first and probably the most difficult stage in that process was met by the original colonists from Europe. After the first discoveries of basic crops and cultural methods suitable to the different latitudes of the Atlantic seaboard, the succeeding generations did not find it necessary to make a large number of basic changes at any one time, so long as settlement was moving through the humid and forested regions. The situation was different, however, on reaching the transition country between the well-watered areas and the plains country, relatively treeless and deficient in rainfall for the type of crops and cultural methods practiced during the advance from the seaboard. On the plains proper the difficulties were met with full force. Had the line of settlement moved as slowly through the transition belt into the plains as it had during the earlier stages of the frontier, it is possible that the adjustment might have been made without excessive hardship, but the railroads carried the rate of settlement much faster than the settlers could adapt the agricultural system to the new habitat.

There are several possible approaches in a historical study of the process of adjustment, and each affords a view of a different facet of the problem. Only when all these approaches have been utilized can the matter be seen in its entirety. In the present study the central interest is a farmers' club and its consideration of the intensely practical problem of making a living in west-central Kansas between 1886 and 1893. Failure to find at least a partial solution meant destitution, and for many individuals of the group that was the eventual outcome. They had to make their own agricultural experiments and bear the expense and losses entailed by failure. The agricultural colleges and the experiment stations had not yet become a practical factor in the situation.

The Santa Fe Railroad was built through Edwards County along the north side of the Arkansas River during the summer of 1872, and the first settlers arrived about the same time. Until 1877 settlement was limited to the north side of the river, partly because of the broad sandy river-bed and the ridge of shifting sand hills about three miles wide along the south bank. Possibly a few settlers ventured to the south side before 1877, but no definite record of occupation has been found prior to that year, when a considerable number moved eastward from Kinsley, the county seat, and southward from Larned in Pawnee County, to take possession of the sandy-loam land beyond the hills. Drouth and terrific heat during 1879 and 1880 drove out most of these pioneers, the first casualties in the advance attack on this sector of the plains. Resettlement followed during 1883–86, so the Census of 1885 presents a cross-section view of the population and the agricultural system of the recently occupied Wayne Township.[1]

There were 70 dwellings, many of them built of sod, which housed 77 families. The population consisted of 122 married persons, 4 widowers, 1 widow, 54 adult single persons, and 134 minors and children. There were 181 males and 134 females. Of the 315 people, 20 men and 6 women were foreign-born, mostly from England and Scotland. Classified according to birthplace, the farm operators and their wives, 107 in number, are credited as follows: New York, 28; Ohio 18, Illinois, 15; Pennsylvania, 10; Kentucky, 5; Iowa, 4; Wisconsin, 4; Michigan, 3; Virginia, 3; Massachusetts, 2;

Indiana, 2; and for several other states, 1 each. The thirteen original states contributed 43, and these, together with those from Michigan, Ohio, and Kentucky, totaled 69. Classified according to the state from which they came to Kansas, the sources were: New York, 24; Illinois 21; Ohio, 15; Pennsylvania, 9; Kentucky, 9; Iowa, 5; Virginia, 2; Michigan, 2; District of Columbia, 2; Indiana, 2; Nebraska, 2; and several others, 1 each. In this list the original states contributed 37, and this number, together with those from the first tier to the west, totaled 63. These figures bring out the highly significant fact that the farm operators for the most part migrated directly from the Old East to the semiarid plains, and furthermore, that the states immediately east of Kansas made almost no contribution to the population of Wayne Township.

There were 60 men who were farm operators and 47 women who were farmers' wives or land operators in their own right. The average age of the men was 40.83, and of the women 38 years, or a combined average of 39.6. The figures merely record in statistical language the fact that the average farm operator had arrived at about middle age. Stated negatively, they were not young people just starting out in life. Only 9 of the 60 men were between 21 and 29 years of age; 20 were in their thirties, 17 in their forties, 10 in their fifties, and 4 in their sixties. In this group 51.6 percent were 40 or above.

The farmers of the township may be divided into three groups—ranchers, large farmers, and small farmers. In the first group there were 12 men and 9 women. They were older than the average of the community by about 5 years, the average age of the men being 44.8 and of the women 42.3 years. Five of the 12 men were 50 years or older. If the sons associated with their parents in the business of ranching are excluded from the calculations, the average age of the ranch group is 50 years for the men and 48 for the women.

The large-farmer group included 20 men and 18 women. The average age of the men was 42.35 and of the women 39.66 years, the combined average being 41.6. Six of the 20 men were over 50, and 12, or 60 percent, were 40 or more. The eldest farmer of this group was 64 and the youngest 26. The eldest married woman was 61 and the youngest 23.

The small-farmer or 160-acre group included 28 men and 20 women. The average age of the men was 38 and of the women 34.1 years, the combined average being 36.4. These averages were about three years below those of the whole community and put them just barely under 40. The eldest man in this group was 60 and his wife 56, while the youngest married man was 24 and the youngest wife 18. The next youngest married woman, however, was 24. Twelve of the 28 men, or 42.8 percent, were 40 or more; 13 were in their thirties, and 3 in their twenties.

Of the 12 ranches, 2 produced sheep, and the rest cattle. Among the latter, one emphasized dairying while the others were almost exclusively beef producers. The 2 sheep ranches were unfenced, and the owners made little preparation for winter feed. The smaller of the ranches included 1,540 acres and carried 1,000 head of sheep during 1884. Two hundred and seventy-five tons of prairie hay were put up for the winter of 1884–85. Only 10 acres were planted to sorghum and 5 acres to millet in 1885. No other livestock or crops were grown. The larger sheep ranch embraced 1,760 acres, and carried 3,000 head of sheep in 1884. Although no prairie hay was cut that year, the planting program for 1885 included 75 acres of field crops, 20 acres of rye, 20 acres of sorghum, and 30 acres of millet. This ranch had 2 horses, 1 milch cow, and 2 other cattle. The wool clip of the 2 ranches in 1884 was 6,000 and 8,000 pounds, respectively. There is no indication that shelter was provided on either ranch. The winter of 1884–85 was severe, and in consequence the first ranch lost 400 and the second, 1,000 sheep from starvation and exposure.

The story of the cattle ranches in not so dismal. Their average size was 2,144 acres, but they ranged from 960 to 4,800 acres. A little later, the Inter-State Galloway Cattle Company, having acquired the Norton ranch, held some 10,000 acres, mostly in one unit. Of the 12 ranches totaling 25,730 acres, 7 had fenced land amounting to 10,760 acres. As there were wide variations in ranch management, it is difficult to state what might be called typical. Based on averages, the typical ranch had 2,144 acres, and was stocked with 5 or 6 horses, 4 mules, 8 or 9 milch cows, and 193 other cattle. The largest herd of cattle numbered 465, and the smallest 36. The largest herd of milch cows was 60, but 2 had 20 and 14 respectively, although most of the others had from 1 to 5. Nine of the 12 ranches had milch cows, and 5 kept hogs.

The census figures on the number of cattle on each ranch are limited presumably to the home herds. In addition, some cattle from Texas and New Mexico were driven or shipped in for fattening. It is not known how many ranches followed this practice. Somewhat later information summarizes the procedure of the Inter-State Galloway Cattle Company on the enlarged Norton ranch in 1886. The home herd consisted of 600 head of thoroughbred Galloways and Shorthorns.[2] About 700 to 800 transient 3- and 4-year olds were driven in for feeding, and then shipped to market in the fall or winter. The field crops planted to support this livestock program included 150 acres of corn, 200 acres of sorghum, 100 acres of oats, and 60 acres of millet. The ranch also raised a large number of hogs and chickens, and had the only bearing orchard in the township, consisting of 6 peach, 4 plum, and 8 cherry trees.

The field-crop program of the other and more typical ranches may be presented on the basis of averages as 60 acres of corn, 34 acres of millet, and 37 acres of sorghum, together with either 36 acres of oats, 34 acres of winter wheat, or 26 acres of rye. Only two ranches grew potatoes. The average cut of prairie hay was 42 tons. The average hay rations for the winter would thus be 1 ton of prairie hay for 5 animals. Some of the variations should also be indicated. One rancher planted 200 acres of corn, 60 acres of oats, and 40 acres of sorghum. Another planted from 30 to 35 acres each of wheat, corn, barley, oats, and rye, 20 acres each of sorghum and millet, and cut 150 tons of prairie hay. A less favorable instance was a ranch that planted only 30 acres of millet and cut 200 tons of hay, although it went into the winter of 1884–85 with 300 head of stock. The death loss on this ranch was 65 head.

The ranch of Lewis, Price and Company emphasized dairying. It carried 60 head of milch cows in 1885 and had produced 8,000 pounds of butter during the preceding year. In addition to milch cows and field crops it had 250 other cattle. Of the 12 ranches only 3 had fruit trees, and 3 had 5 to 15 acres each in artificial timber, mostly cottonwoods. All of the ranches had some farm machinery, but the value of that on one ranch was only $40. The largest machinery valuation, that of the Lewis ranch, was $1,000. The average valuation was $336.

The ranches, not only in Wayne Township but in this section of the state, were of mushroom growth. Relatively few ranches provided shelter or adequate feed. The losses during the winter of 1884–85 were heavy. The township census enumerator wrote the following comment at the end of his report in the spring of 1885: "Most of the cattle died for want of food and not being acclimated & for want of shelter. Sheep ditto." After another hard winter, the *Kinsley Graphic* for January 25, 1886, reported that some stock raisers said the heavy losses meant a revision of the industry in western Kansas. The raising of vast herds of common stock would be discontinued, more attention given to better grades, and shelter provided during storms. On February 26, however, the same paper remarked, "Slowly the cattle baron has rounded up for the last time his thousands to give room to the vast corn fields and seas of grain."

In some ways the large farms possessed features little different from the smaller ranches and in others little different from the small farms. The 19 farms classified as large had between 320 and 640 acres, excepting one with 283 acres. Twelve were half-section farms, and 3 were full sections. For the most part the farm economy was of the mixed type, livestock and field crops. Five of the farms were partly fenced, the total enclosed acreage being 1,090, or an average of 200 acres for each. The remaining 14 had no fences.

The average large farm had 2 or 3 horses and sometimes a team of mules, although 2 farms had neither. Again, the average farm had 10 milch cows, 14 other cattle, and 5 hogs. The variations from the average were great, however, as one of the farms had 50 milch cows and 45 other cattle, while a second had 34 and 35 of each. The large farm usually had 3 milch cows, 3 other cattle, and 4 or 5 hogs, rather than the average. There were 2 farms with no milch cows, 4 with no other cattle, and 4 with no hogs, and several with only 1 each.

The large farmers planted a total of only 1,621 acres in field crops, or an average of 85 acres per farm. The percentage distribution of this acreage among the different crops was as follows: corn, 44.4; millet, 18.5; oats, 13; winter wheat, 11; sorghum, 6; barley, 5; and rye, 1. The average farm had 38 acres of corn, 17 acres of millet, 14 acres of oats, 14 acres of sorghum, either 26 acres of wheat or 11 acres of barley, and a few potatoes. The variations from the average were not so great in field crops as in livestock, probably not exceeding 50 percent in either direction from the average.

All of the large farms had machinery, although in several cases there was very little. The average valuation of farm implements was $85. Two large farms had $200 worth of machinery, while one had only $20 worth. Seven of the large farms had growing orchards, one with 538 fruit trees and another with 155, but most of them ranged from 5 to 60 trees. Six of these farms were growing artificial timber covering 1 to 8 acres.

The small farms were most numerous, as there were 29 farms consisting of 160 acres—the traditional homestead, tree claim, or preemption claim offered by the government as a subsidy to those who presumptively were too poor to otherwise acquire a farm home. The small farm represented the mixed type of agriculture—few livestock and some field crops, but very little of either. None of the farms in this group had a fence.

The average farm had one team of horses or mules, although 6 farms in the group had neither. It is not known whether these used oxen, depended upon exchanging work with neighbors, hired the necessary team work, or bought teams after the census was taken in March. Thirteen of the 29 farms had an average of 5 milch cows each, but the other 16 had none. Seventeen of the farms had an average of 8 other cattle, but 12 had none, 3 had sheep, and 16 had an average of 6 hogs each, but 13 had none.

The small farms had a total of 1,192 acres in field crops, or an average of 41 acres per farm. The percentage distribution of this acreage among the different crops was as follows: corn, 48; millet, 14; winter wheat, 13; sorghum, 9; oats, 8; barley, 4; rye, 2; and potatoes, 1.1. The average farm had 22 acres of corn, either 10 acres of millet or 8 acres of sorghum, but not both, and of the grains, 9 acres of oats, 19 acres of winter wheat, or 9 acres of barley. It may be said for emphasis that only 8 farms raised wheat at all, while 11 raised oats, and 5 raised barley. Thirteen farms of the 29 had 1 acre of potatoes. Only 5 of this group put up prairie hay.

The small farmers as well as the ranchmen and large farmers lost much livestock during the winter of 1884–85. One farmer lost 2 of his 3 horses, which left him with a horse and a mule for work stock. He had no milch cows, other cattle, or hogs. Of his flock of 650 sheep, he lost 200. Another farmer lost 2 of his 4 horses, 1 of 4 cattle, and his 2 hogs. A third farmer had no livestock except 6 cattle, and he lost 4 of them. It may be significant that not a single milch cow died. The historian can only speculate, but probably the milch cows received better care because the family living depended directly upon them. Another interesting fact is that no farmer lost a mule, but in spite of this record it was a long time before the farmers generally turned to mules for work stock. The total valuation of the farm machinery on the small farms in the township was $670, or an average of $35 each for the 19 farms that had any worth listing.

The settlers who came to the Kansas plains country from the timbered lands of the east missed trees possibly more than anything else. Just how many of the 29 small farmers tried to grow trees cannot be known, but 8 had planted 394 fruit trees by 1885, an average of nearly 50 trees per orchard. None of these trees had reached the bearing age. Five farmers had artificial timber, mostly cottonwood, making a total of 38 acres. Probably these plots were mostly tree-claim plantings.

A people engaged in subduing a new country were necessarily engrossed in the question of what crops to grow and how to grow them. The first move in the direction of an organized approach to their common problems appears to have originated with the sheep and cattle men who formed the Edwards County Wool Growers' Association, with J. M. Lewis, Sr. (Mass., Va.), as president, and I. B. Lawton (Ohio, Ohio), as secretary.[3] Both officers were ranchers, Lewis being interested in dairy and beef cattle, and Lawton in sheep. At the meeting in February 1884 this body decided to adjourn until March 1 to consider the organization of an association to include all farm and livestock interests.[4] This move seems to reflect in part the periodic shift from field crops to livestock which coincided with the recurrence of wet and dry years. With a returning period of wet years and a rush of small farmers into the predominantly range country, the field-crops cycle was being recognized.

The meeting on March 1 resulted in a new organization, the Edwards County Industrial Association, which recommended the holding of a county fair. When completed, Lawton and Lewis were president and vice-president, respectively, and J. Ferguson, secretary. Each township was authorized to have one representative to act with the officers as a board of directors.[5] For some reason the new organization did not function, and on December 6, the *Kinsley Mercury* suggested its revival and added the admonition, "Get together and wear off some of the rough edges and you will find yourself better, happier and richer men."

The next step was apparently taken on August 22, 1885 at a citizens' meeting in Kinsley, with J. M. Lewis, Sr., acting as chairman and the town business men taking a prominent part.[6] The Edwards County Fair Association was organized and the first fair was held on October 21–22. In order to secure the active participation of the entire county it was recommended that farmers' clubs be organized in every township to cooperate with the central body. Most townships acted on this suggestion during July and August 1886 and functioned for a while, but only one, the Wayne Township Farmers' Club, maintained its activities through a substantial period of time.[7]

In Wayne Township the preliminary meeting at which the organization of a club was discussed was held at the Ostrander School on July 2, 1886. C. S. Ostrander, for whom the school was named, was a New Yorker and took an active interest in the club. H. C. Leslie (Ill., Ill.) and B. B. Baum (Mich., Mich.) presided. After a two-hour session the meeting adjourned until July 13 at the same place. On this occasion a permanent organization was effected with officers as follows: H. L. Norton (N.Y., Ill.), president; J. L. Donnell (Ohio, Ohio), vice president; Ed Smith (N.Y., Texas), treasurer; and J. M. Lewis, Jr. (Wisc., D.C.), secretary. A committee was appointed to draft a constitution and bylaws and report to the third meeting to be held on July 20. It was agreed that the club should cooperate with the county fair association, discuss farm problems, and make the meetings social in character by holding them at the homes of the members. At that time there was no town of Lewis to speak of, where farmers could loaf on Saturdays after doing their weekly trading, and which could compete with the meetings of the club and the big picnic dinners which always lasted until well into the afternoon. In fact, the dinners were such an effective inducement to loyal attendance that comments appeared in the newspapers suggesting that many were more interested in the food than in the discussions of good farming which made possible the well-filled tables.

The Norton ranch, where the first regular meeting was held on August 7, had been acquired recently by the Inter-State Galloway Cattle Company with H. L. Norton retained as manager. The ranch buildings were surrounded by a "magnificent grove" of trees, set out seven years before, and under these trees four tables were spread, all well laden with food. The barn was arranged with seats and tables for the formal part of the meeting at 3 o'clock. The reporter for the meeting evidently felt that the occasion required special literary effort as he described the scene as follows:

It [the grove] gives one what we imagine to be the sensation experienced upon sudden transition from a desert waste into the aromatic bowers of the mythical gods. We found in this arcadian retreat at Mr. Norton's an assemblage of about one hundred and fifty persons, comprising the youth, beauty, and intelligence of Wayne township. Some were seated at the tables doing justice to the choice provisions made for the inner man, some were strolling beneath the wide spreading branches of the friendly shade trees, reveling among handsomely arranged flower gardens, listening to the heaven-born music of nature's plumaged songsters, as they flitted through the ambrosial bowers.

The entertainment included a reading of Bret Harte's poem, *Old John Burns of Gettysburg,* by Colonel Lewis, and piano and violin music by friends from Kinsley. At the business meeting the constitution and bylaws were adopted, the preamble being as follows:

Whereas it has been found convenient and advantageous through all time and by all people to associate themselves together for mutual improvement and protection, therefore we, the citizens of Wayne township, Edwards county, do hereby form this society for the following reasons: 1st. That we may promote a more thoroughly social feeling among the people of that township. 2nd. That by associating ourselves together, we may obtain a more thorough knowledge of farming, with its coordinate branches—cattle and dairying—that by an interchange of thought and sentiment each one may become possessed of a knowledge of them all. 3rd. To the end that all bickering and strife shall cease, and that the people of this township, mutually dependent, shall be a mutual help to each other.

To accomplish the third object the club set up a committee to arbitrate disputes among members. Its personnel consisted of M. C. Kennedy (Iowa, Mo.), Andrew Hardy (N.Y., N.Y.), and Mac Lewis (Wisc., D.C.). Unfortunately, no record of the proceedings of this committee has been found.

At this meeting the club decided to purchase two tents, as the residences and barns of the members were not large enough to accommodate the meetings, and members other than Norton did not possess a "magnificent grove" which would afford shelter. At this meeting and at each of those succeeding, a viewing committee made a report on the host's farm, and on occasion made recommendations for improvements. It was customary to consider a single topic and to have two or more farmers prepared to lead the discussion. During the winter months the club met at the newly established town of Lewis.

Of the twelve men having an official part in the organization of the club, all but three must be classed as easterners. All except three were also either ranchers or large farmers. They were well past the age when men's minds are usually thought of as being flexible and receptive to new ideas. They had come into the country during the most favorable weather conditions of thirty years. The weather cycle had already turned by 1886, and except for the years 1891–93 when rainfall was moderate, western Kansas was entering a decade of drouth and high temperatures. The adaptability of the easterners to the plains was being put to the supreme test.

So far as records are available, the topics of the discussions held by the club from 1886 to 1893 are listed.

| | | |
|---|---|---|
| 1886 | August | Wheat raising |
| | September | Swine |
| | October | Winter feeding, care, and management of livestock |
| | November | Corn stalk wheat (informal) |
| 1887 | March | Corn |
| | April | Best crop for early feeding of swine and cattle |
| | May | Horticulture |
| | July 4 | Livestock and field crops |
| | August | Curing fodder crops |
| | September | Cooperative creamery committee |
| | October | Cooperation of farmers in the manipulation of their products |
| | November | Continuation of the above |
| 1888 | May | Creamery committee report |
| | | Chinch bugs and the corn crop |
| | June | Poor corn stand (informal) |
| | July | How to make the farm profitable (farm planning; field crops and/or stock) |

|      | August    | Chinch bugs, corn, and wheat |
|      | September | Crop reports from the county |
|      |           | Cheese factory question |
|      | October   | Cheese factory question continued |
| 1889 | May       | Cultivation of broom corn |
|      | June      | Silos and ensilage |
|      | July      | Silos and ensilage |
|      | September | Butter and cheese |
| 1890 | June      | Future policy: questions of the day to be discussed as well as farm problems |
| 1891 | August    | Wheat culture |
|      | September | Wheat culture |
|      | October   | Butter and bread making (women) |
| 1893 | September | Wheat culture |

During the early years of the club, reports of its meetings usually appeared in the Kinsley newspapers, the *Graphic* and the *Mercury*. Although some sessions were not reported at all, others were covered sufficiently to convey the principal point involved, and a number were reported quite fully. There are no reports on the discussions of swine, horticulture, broom corn, butter and cheese, and bread and butter making (the reporter's attention being too fully occupied with the samples). Broadly speaking, the subject matter of these discussions can be grouped under five heads: adaptability of crops, field-crop culture, care of livestock, farm planning, and marketing.

On moving into the plains country it was natural for farmers to plant the crops that they had raised in their former home, such as corn, oats, soft wheat, barley, and rye. The emphasis in the grain division was on corn and oats, as is shown clearly by the Census of 1885, while in forage crops millet took precedence over sorghum. In view of the dominance of corn over wheat it may appear singular that wheat was selected for discussion at the first regular meeting in August 1886. This choice was not unnatural, however, because in the fall season wheat was the principal, if not the only crop to be sown.

The question of the choice of varieties of wheat for planting was presented by B. B. Baum (Mich.). He mentioned the Red or Early May, Kentucky Swamp, and Turkey wheat varieties, but recommended the Red May. This variety of soft winter wheat not only grew splendidly in Edwards

County, he said, but the millers liked it and paid good prices, and it was always considered "prime" in the Kansas City market. The Kentucky Swamp wheat had been grown in Hodgman County, northwest of Kinsley, and the Kinsley miller spoke favorably of it. Some farmers favored Turkey, a hard winter wheat, and Baum reported that "the Turkey is a passably good wheat to yield, but the millers do not like it very well, and shippers will not buy it unless they can get it in car load lots."

The next four years of drouth, hot summers, wind, and cold winters contributed a full quota of experience. By 1891 the local press indicated a shift from Red May to Turkey wheat and in the two meetings of the Wayne Township club in August and September 1891 the majority opinion favored Turkey. The reasons assigned were that it was hardier, stood winter and drouth better, yielded well, and in the current crop year excelled in both quality and price. So far as the question of variety was concerned, the Wayne Township farmers had reached a lasting decision, as the subsequent fame of Kansas wheat was based on the improved strains of this general variety.

Corn, the basic crop of the region, was discussed fully at the March meeting of 1887, but the question of varieties received little comment. The consensus of opinion favored medium yellow corn, although a variety called Golden Beauty was highly recommended. One member had raised white corn successfully. During the following years, no variety was found which was so outstandingly superior to the others as was Turkey wheat to its rivals. The corn tradition persisted in spite of the relative failure of its adaptation to the plains.

Unfortunately there was no discussion of the relative merits of millet and sorghum, but millet quickly dropped into the background. Sorghum served a triple purpose in the farm economy: syrup-sugar, fodder, and seed. There was at least one small sorghum mill operating in the township, in addition to the relatively large syrup factory at Kinsley. The variety grown was not recorded, but a few years of experience had taught the settlers that sorghum was one crop that never failed—that is, almost never. Thus they had found another certainty in crop selection. Closely associated with sorghum was the introduction of other members of the sorghum group. Jerusalem corn did not establish itself. Broom corn was raised in small quantities in the county, but comparatively little interest was taken in it by farmers on the sandy soil of Wayne Township. Kaffir corn was not discussed by the club, but the local press indicated that it was introduced permanently in the county about 1889, and within a few years it was widely grown. It was not included in the list of crops reported by the State Board of

Agriculture until 1893, when the county planted 465 acres, while in 1894 there were 1,761 acres. The discussion of early feed crops at the meeting in April 1887 added little information, except that rye, oats, sorghum, and corn were recommended by different members. The preeminence of sorghum was too definitely recognized, however, for extensive consideration of the others.

Next in importance to the choice of crops of suitable varieties was the problem of culture and tillage. Farmers from the east who had been accustomed to draining excess water from their fields had to learn how to conserve moisture which at best was deficient in quantity and how to prevent the dry soil from blowing away. The first settlers plowed for corn and wheat with a moldboard plow, turning the stubble under as far as possible in order to provide a garden-like seed bed. The wind blew the soil away or the sand cut the tender leaves to shreds, and the smooth fields did not hold the moisture effectively for the young corn. Furthermore the plow was a slow tool with which to prepare fields when moisture was at a premium. The lister, throwing up high ridges crosswise to the prevailing south winds, prevented the soil from blowing and protected the tender corn from excessive whipping, and planting in the bottom of the furrow gave the plants the most favorable access to moisture. Listing also made it possible to prepare ground about three times as rapidly as plowing and to plant the corn at the same time.

Eastern farmers, transplanted to the plains in the middle eighties, could not understand the value of listing, and at the meeting of March 5, 1887, the Wayne Township farmers after several years' experience were about equally divided between listermen and checkrowers. All agreed that listing was better in extremely dry seasons and on sandy soils, but all agreed also that eradication of weeds was more difficult. It was claimed that checkrowing was more universally and successfully practiced, that it caused less trouble during cultivation and in corn cutting, and that it left the ground in better condition for autumn planting. A number of farmers claimed that the quality of corn was superior when checkrowed. The reporter for the meeting commented: "The discussion was carried on with such spirit by both advocates of listing and check-rowing that one not posted would be inclined to try both."

The question of the best time to plant corn was canvassed at the same meeting, and on this matter opinion differed, ranging from April 20 to May 20. All agreed that corn should be cultivated three or four times. The screw harrow was recommended for small corn and especially for listed corn. The problem of weed eradication was only partially met by the knife sled during the nineties, and the disc sled for cultivating listed corn was not introduced until a decade later. A comparison of local experience showed that the average yield of corn was 22 bushels per acre in 1886.

Two years later, early spring rains directed attention to other aspects of the corn problem. One farmer reported at the May meeting that much of his listed corn had been drowned and would have to be replanted. He proposed to furrow one way and then plant in the furrow with a corn planter. The June meeting was largely devoted to an informal exchange of ideas on the reasons for the poor stand of corn. Several men placed the blame on the lister and some reported that they had replanted. One man said that he had listed too deep and the sand had washed over the corn and buried it. Others reported the best stand they had ever had and defended listing. The reporter of the meeting indicated that the listermen were in the majority. After a trip through the country, the editor of the *Kinsley Banner-Graphic* commented on July 6, that he was convinced that what Edwards County needed was scientific farming and a little more capital. To support his dictum he insisted that every piece of corn laid off both ways (check-rowed) and well cultivated was in excellent condition.

The chinch bugs, a frequent pest, were a serious problem in 1888 as they threatened the corn crop. They were discussed in the May meeting, but the opinion was expressed that the rains had disposed of them for the season. The reports of the August meeting indicated otherwise, however, as the bugs and the drouth had damaged the corn seriously. The highest estimate of yield reported was 40 bushels, the average was set at 20, but it was admitted that some corn was "very poor." G. H. Gilson (N.Y., Ky.) had burned off the prairie on his place in the spring, but this had not destroyed the bugs. Some farmers believed that burning did more damage than the bugs. The blame for chinch bug infestation was quite generally charged to wheat, and the secretary reported: "This led to a discussion as to whether it is best to sow wheat or not. The farmers were divided in opinion. A number of them will sow wheat, while a few will not, for fear of chinch bugs." Nothing can emphasize more emphatically the prevailing devotion to corn than that such a drastic proposal should have been made at all, and it must be understood that it was made in all seriousness in a county in the heart of what was to become the southwestern hard winter wheat area, whose proud boast is that "Kansas raises the best wheat in the World."

At the September meeting visitors from other townships were called upon for information. From Lincoln Township, in the southeast corner of the county, the corn crop was reported as the best ever raised. Corn was the principal crop, and was raised on light sandy soil. The visitor from Kinsley

Township, north of the river, reported that corn was a failure on the heavy land outside of the bottoms and that he did not attempt to raise it at all. These reports are indicative of the lesson experience was teaching Wayne Township farmers. Corn was more successful on the sandy soil, because the sand withstood drouth better than hard land. The presence of sandy soil was an important reason why corn persisted as a basic crop in Wayne Township long after it had been abandoned on the high, hard uplands north of the river.

At the wheat meeting in August 1886, G. D. Misner (Ohio, Ill.) led the discussion on the preparation of fields for wheat and seeding methods. He recommended June-July plowing to conserve moisture and early planting. On fallow ground he favored drilling, but with corn he broadcast the seed. G. H. Gilson agreed to early plowing and emphasized that late plowing in dry seasons meant total failure. In ordinary seasons he thought early plowing would yield a third better crop. He also stressed deep plowing. He sowed from 1⅛ to 1¼ bushels of seed per acre. He disagreed with Misner on the method of sowing in corn and recommended the one-horse drill. Volunteer wheat, he insisted, never amounted to anything. On most of the points enumerated, time has demonstrated that their opinions were well considered. The overwhelming difficulty in putting the early plowing theory into practice was that moisture seldom lasted long enough into midsummer to allow sufficient time to work the ground with the inadequate horse power and moldboard plows of the average small farmer.

The weather hazard frequently proved disastrous even after the wheat was sown under favorable conditions. The problem of winter killing is vividly illustrated by the note of the census enumerator of Wayne Township in March 1885, which reads: "Out of 471 acres of fall wheat there is not wheat enough to cover 15 acres. All winter killed." Part of the difficulty lay in the variety of soft wheat planted, and part in the handling of the soil. These it was possible to remedy, but disease, drouth, and unseasonable cold weather were beyond the reach of man to offset completely.

Wheat was also discussed at the two meetings in August and September 1891. Relatively good yields in 1889, 1890, and 1891 and fair prices gave it preference in depression farm planning. The acreage in wheat had increased phenomenally in 1890 and 1891, and the crop was discussed with interest. Emphasis was again placed on plowing immediately after harvest, and on pulverizing the ground a second time with either a disc or screw harrow before sowing. Clean corn ground without any preparation was also recommended. The best time to sow wheat was fixed at September 20 or later. No remedy was yet advanced, however, to overcome the inadequacy of equipment and horses. Although the disc plow which came into use near the end of the nineties did not increase the speed of plowing, it had two advantages over the moldboard plow. It left the stubble on top, which prevented blowing, and enabled the farmer to plow the ground long after it had become too dry and hard to plow with a moldboard plow. The practice of listing for wheat immediately after harvest and cutting down (busting) the ridges shortly before planting, thus working the ground twice and quickly between harvest time and planting—the first step toward speeding up operations—was not taken until 1905. The second important step was the introduction of the tractor as a substitute for horse power, mostly after the World War. The tractor might be used with either the lister or the one-way, a development of the disc plow.

The sessions on the care and feeding of livestock were not so adequately reported in the press as those on corn and wheat. It may have been accidental or the result of a lack of interest, but judging from the number of times these topics were selected it scarcely seems plausible that the latter could be the case. The second regular meeting was devoted to swine, and the papers merely reported that a dozen or more farmers participated in the discussion and that hogs were held in considerable numbers by the club members. The third meeting was devoted to the winter care and management of livestock and was led by E. F. Brown, who stressed shelter and feed as the prime requisites.[8] During the preceding winter he had carried sixty head of cattle on shocked fodder, corn, and sorghum during the early part of the season, and finished with stacked feed and grain. The sorghum had been sown thickly by broadcasting in order to insure small stalks. The next speaker, B. Craft (N.Y., Iowa), insisted that the best feed should be used first, and the season finished on what might be left. H. L. Norton, manager of the Inter-State ranch, reported that his mainstay was buffalo-grass pasture, with fodder, grain, and shelter in severe weather. He insisted that shelter was more important than feed.

The discussion of silos and ensilage which was continued through two monthly sessions, June and August 1889, was not reported, and the only comment recorded was that the formal paper received attention and that several men indicated their intention to build silos. So far as the writer has discovered, none were built in this period. The October meeting was devoted to a debate on butter and cheese. The former was defended by W. C. Johnson (N.Y., N.Y.) and Robert Corner (Ohio, Mo.), while cheese was championed by B. B. Baum (Mich., Mich.) and James Gray (Pa., Pa.), but the result was not reported.

Some aspects of the problems of farm planning and management have of necessity been included in the topics already treated. The first meeting in which farm planning received direct discussion was on July 4, 1887 when the speaker of the day, J. M. Lewis, Sr., referred to the fact that the cattlemen who first occupied the country had held that field crops would not grow and had used the argument as a means of discouraging farmers from settling there. He admitted that he had accepted this view during his first two or three years in the country, but he was not convinced that Edwards County was destined to become a great cattle-feeding center, because it produced feed and was half way between the regions of growth and consumption of beef.

A year later the question "How to make the farm profitable" brought out the most direct comments on the farm program. Three of the seven men mentioned by name—Gray (Pa., Pa.), Jared Malin (Ill., Ill.), and L. White (England)—defended corn as the principal farm crop. Gray who was one of the oldest settlers in the township, both in age (64) and residence (since 1877), maintained that, except for the last year, they had raised good crops for four or five years. Lewis and White insisted that the farmer should feed his corn crop to cattle, while Gray argued especially for hogs. This argument in reality placed Lewis with the corn men. Norton and Roberts, both livestock men, spoke for sorghum as a crop that never failed, the former emphasizing the seed crop as well as the fodder value. Only one of the group, G. H. Gilson, defended wheat, and Norton condemned it on account of chinch bugs. In defending wheat Gilson mentioned that he had raised 3,600 bushels one year and sold it for eighty cents to one dollar per bushel, but in spite of this success he insisted that farmers must not depend upon any one crop. Even though these farmers were discussing money crops almost exclusively, the fact is inescapable that they were living a relatively self-sufficient existence. Most of them kept cows, hogs enough for family meat and lard, chickens, gardens, and fruit trees. Watermelons were in a class by themselves. In a country where fruit growing was none too successful, and sweets and other delicacies expensive and unobtainable, the watermelon held a place with which no other product could compete.

Marketing problems appear in the record of the club, but they are less conspicuous than production problems. The meeting of August 1887 appointed a committee of five to investigate the sentiment of the farmers regarding the establishment of a cooperative creamery, and probably this move determined the choice of "Cooperation of farmers in the manipulation of their products" as the subject for the October meeting. There is no report of the discussion, except the comment that it was thorough and that it was continued to the November meeting. The creamery committee, reporting in May 1888, estimated the cost of a plant at $1,000 to $1,500, and recommended delay on the project until after harvest. The crop failure due to chinch bugs and drouth absorbed attention so completely during the following weeks that nothing further was said about a creamery.

It was not in keeping with the spirit of the frontier to quit after one or even several failures, so in September a cheese factory was suggested. Kinsley was undertaking one, but because of the distance it seemed impossible to participate in the enterprise. The Lewis brothers, Jim and Mac, pledged eighty cows, and others promised smaller numbers. The proposal of a man who offered to erect and operate a factory if five hundred cows were pledged was presented. The alternative was a cooperative association. The Kinsley plan was cooperative in form, the producers sharing the profits on the basis of the amount of milk furnished. A complete investigation of cheese factory management was voted, and the secretary was instructed to correspond with manufacturers and others and report at the next meeting. In October the committee reported 333 cows pledged, and the cooperative plan was apparently adopted.

During the following winter months the plant was completed in the town of Lewis, and on May 7, 1889 the first milk was delivered. At this time 480 cows were pledged. The subsequent history of the cheese factory is a bit hazy. It seems to have been operated during the summer of 1889, and probably was suspended during the winter. The *Banner-Graphic* of Kinsley on February 7, 1890 carried a notice of a meeting of the cooperative association for February 15 and announced that "the object of the meeting is to audit the books, elect officers . . . , and to come to some conclusion as to how the factory shall be run next summer." The following week the same paper announced that the meeting was postponed indefinitely. On April 12 it was held, and an offer from a private business firm was accepted to receive milk at fifty-five cents per hundred pounds. There seems to have been no further activity after the summer of 1890. During the next two or three years there was a wheat boom, and farmers were accused of having sold everything that would bring cash in order to expand the wheat acreage.[9] The Kinsley cheese factory was also closed, and when the drouth of 1893 proved disastrous to wheat, the farmers had no dairy stock to fall back on.

Marketing difficulties account partly for the perpetuation of the corn tradition. Prior to 1886 Wayne Township had no railroad outlet, except by hauling through the sand hills to Kinsley and Larned. Even after the railroad reached the south side of the river, the sandy roads discouraged long hauls. Often grain could be marketed to better advantage in the form of livestock, and the cattle ranches afforded a close market for surplus corn. This outlet placed a premium on corn rather than wheat until the cattle cycle had passed again and the farmer had learned more fully the wheat technique.

By January 1890 the Farmers' Alliance reached Edwards County, although as much as three years earlier Union Labor and People's Party tickets had disturbed the serenity of the selfish domination of the county-seat ring. As Wayne Township became stirred by political agitation, discussion of the improvement of agriculture ceased, and the farmers' club was not continued after 1893. During that summer, the farmers preferred baseball games to discussions of farm problems. The report of the September meeting on "Wheat Culture" bears the mark of a sense of futility in the succinct summary: "General opinion seemed to be that wheat should not be sown until after a rain."

Several important points not covered by the reports may be rounded out from the census data for 1895 and 1905. Of the 61 farm operators in Wayne Township in 1885, only 28 remained in 1895 and 14 in 1905.[10] There were 47 operators in 1885 in Wayne Township as reduced in size, 42 in 1895, and 72 in 1905. Stated in terms of new settlers: in 1895, 14 operators were new after 1885, and 58 in 1905. The newcomers found it necessary to learn the plains agriculture, but they had the advantage of the experience already gained. The operators of 1895 were born mostly in Ohio, New York, Illinois, Missouri, and Kentucky, and came to Kansas mostly from Ohio, Illinois, Missouri, and New York. In the next ten years Illinois and Missouri supplied many more immigrants than the states farther east.

The size of farms changed relatively little in the decade ending in 1895. The ranches were gone, although there were several nearby. There were 6 large farms (400 acres and up), 8 medium-sized farms (320 acres), and 25 quarter-section farms. The next ten years rectified somewhat the inadequate size of the farm unit, the distribution being 21 large, 28 medium-sized, and 23 small farms. It is clear from the history of agriculture in this region that inadequate capital resulting in small, badly equipped farms was almost as serious an obstacle to successful occupancy of the plains as the difficulties of adaptation. Although the farmers of Wayne Township must have talked of these matters among themselves, they did not list them among the subjects set for formal discussion. The Populist agitation placed the blame for hard times on money, the tariff, the trusts, and the railroads, but after the opening of the twentieth century when the country was prosperous, a half-section was considered as small a farm as could be expected to provide a living for a farm family.

The shift in the field-crop program is probably illustrated more accurately from the census data covering the county as a whole than from the smaller township unit. The average acreage per farm of corn, oats, and wheat in Edwards County was as follows:

| Year | Corn | Oats | Wheat |
|------|------|------|-------|
| 1885 | 16.5 | 7.2  | 4.0   |
| 1895 | 40.6 | 16.4 | 97.8  |
| 1905 | 45.2 | 5.5  | 145.0 |

The figures show that corn held its own in actual acreage between 1895 and 1905, but that wheat increased so rapidly after 1890 that corn played a relatively small part in farm planning.

The rivalry between field crops and livestock, farming versus ranching, is not clearly delineated in the discussions of the Wayne Township Club, but the subject can be clarified from other sources. In the earlier years as settlers moved into the plains, the predominance of one over the other ran in cycles with the weather, and during the last half of the nineties cattle were increasingly favored. A resident traveling across southeastern Edwards County, northeastern Kiowa County, and northwestern Pratt County in 1895 reported that this region was practically deserted, and that some other areas were sparsely occupied. Cattlemen proposed the repeal of the herd law to the county commissioners, but the farmers protested and with such vehemence that the matter was dropped. Later some of the large cattle companies secured control of extensive holdings, fenced their pastures, and deprived the small farmers with livestock of free pasturage on vacant land. The most significant conclusion to be drawn from this farmer-rancher rivalry is the fact that the farmers were able to hold their own. The "sod buster" had learned sufficiently how to adapt himself to the plains to enable him to stay and to maintain control.

## Notes

1. The original state census records are deposited with the Kansas State Historical Society at Topeka.

2. There may be some question whether all were pure blood. It is certain that many of them were good-grade stock. This ranch was only one of a chain owned by the company. A steer bred and raised on this ranch took the Grand Sweepstakes in

the dressed carcass class at the Chicago fat-stock show in the winter of 1887 and dressed 66 percent of live weight.

3. In naming the individuals who took a leading part in these activities, the state of birth and the state from which they came to Kansas are placed in parentheses after the name.

4. *Kinsley Graphic,* February 26, 1884.

5. *Ibid.,* March 4, 11, 25, 1884.

6. *Ibid.,* August 28, 1885.

7. *Kinsley Mercury,* July 10, 17, August 14, 21, 1886; *Kinsley Graphic,* July 9, August 13, 1886; *Wendell Champion,* July 30, 1886.

8. The identification of Brown is not positive, but probably there is a mistake in the initials and that E. H. Brown, a rancher, 55 years old, is meant. He was born in New York and came from that state.

9. *Kinsley Banner-Graphic,* February 8, 1895.

10. The township was divided about 1890, the west half retaining the original name and the east half taking the name of Belpre. The figures just given include the whole area. For the reduced Wayne Township the 1885 figure was 47 or near that, and for the later decades 19 and 14. No one in Belpre Township remained in 1905. Descendants are counted here as representing the 1885 operator.

# CHAPTER 10

# An Introduction to the History of the Bluestem- Pasture Region of Kansas

## *A Study in Adaptation to Geographical Environment*

[Because of its luxuriant native grasses, the bluestem region of Kansas became the center of the state's cattle business. This selection describes the ecological characteristics of the region and its white settlement history. In typical fashion, James Malin locates the region within its larger geographical context and describes the pattern of technological change that led to a grazing economy. Malin then shows how eastern forestmen struggled to overcome their erroneous "mental furniture" about the presumed superiority of tame eastern grasses over native bluestem grasses. When they finally accepted "nature's own careful selection based upon ages of experimentation in her own laboratories," the bluestem became one of the key cattle-producing regions of the nation for the next half century.]

The bluestem-pasture region of Kansas has come to be recognized as a natural region with rather clearly defined boundaries. On the map it appears as a somewhat elongated oval-shaped area about 200 miles from tip to tip, with Pottawatomie County, Kansas, at the northern end and Osage County, Oklahoma, at the southern end, the intervening country being some fifty miles, or somewhat more than two counties, in width. Roughly, this is the central third of the eastern half of the state, between 96° and 97° west longitude and 36° 30′ and 39° 30′ north latitude. The average annual rainfall varies from 30 to 35 inches except in the southern portion, but there the higher precipitation is offset, in part at least, by the higher temperatures and longer period of frost-free days—186 or more annually in the southern tier of Kansas counties, as against about 178 days in the central and northern sections. Topographically the region is rolling to hilly, with rather narrow valleys, but the most characteristic features of the typical pasture portions are hills, or bluffs, formed by outcroppings of rock of the Permian and Pennsylvania strata. For the most part this rock is lime-stone, but in places, especially in the southern end, there is sandstone. The soil is of the residual type derived from the limestones, shales, and sand-stones. In the typical limestone area outcroppings of stone appear near the top of the hills, the weathering process washing the decomposed materials down their sides to the lower ground.

Bluestem is the dominant native grass, represented by two major varieties: the Big Bluestem *(Andropogon furcatus)* which thrives in the lower lands, and the Little Bluestem *(Andropogon scoparius)* found on the high uplands. These are tall grasses, as contrasted with the short grasses, the buffalo and the gramas, which are present in greater or lesser numbers according to location and season, invading the region from the western side. Kentucky bluegrass has invaded the region from the eastern side, extending its occupation westward during wet periods and retreating eastward under the adversity of prolonged drought. Prior to the occupa-tion of the country by white settlement the bluestem grasses were widely distributed over the open prairie regions of the Middle West, occupying a dominant position over most, if not the whole of eastern Kansas. They were and still are present also in limited areas of the plains, especially in the sandhill districts, where the common name is bunch grass. For various reasons early descriptions of the grass associations of the West are often contradictory. Historical experience has indicated in part at least an explanation in the fluctuations of the weather. Descriptions written by observers during periods of prolonged drought would tend to emphasize the short grasses which thrived at the expense of the tall grasses and moved eastward under such influences, and similarly those descriptions written during favorably wet periods would reflect the reverse process. Several such cycles have occurred since white observers began writing descrip-tions, and consequently the first necessity in making interpretations of such materials is to fit them into the weather chronology.

The growing season of the bluestem grass is the spring and early summer months. During May, June, and July its nutritive value is strongest, declining until it reaches a minimum after frost. Bluestem makes the best hay when cut just after mid-summer and before it has seeded, while most tame grasses are at their best for hay during the blooming period. In hay making, early settlers followed Eastern tame hay practices and only after years of experience did they come to appreciate the importance of early cutting.[1]

The assumption is made frequently, indirectly if not directly, but without foundation in fact, that the bluestem region is unique and that even in the natural state it possessed the present limits as natural boundaries. The historical development of the area indicates, however, that the present limits are the result of a prolonged process of differentiation from the surrounding country. On the north and northeast, for example, the commercial cornbelt, utilizing glacial drift soils, encroached early upon the hill country; on the east a mixed farming area developed which invaded the hills from that direction; and on the west the wheat belt of central Kansas challenged the hills; while on the south the Indian reservation pastures of the old Indian territory and Oklahoma delayed the process of demarcation from the lower end. Within the region, the land most obviously suited to cultivation was occupied and the native sod broken. This included not only bottom land, but also upland. The principal barrier to general cultivation of the whole was the hills, with their outcroppings of stone, sometimes a succession or series like terraces up their slopes. In many places land was cultivated at one time that was later returned to grass.

At some points the stock country has persisted beyond the conventional limits of the bluestem region. To the eastward a spur of such country runs into Linn County along the divide separating the water sheds of the Marais des Cygnes and the Neosho rivers. In 1857 a local observer described the hill country of Linn County as follows—in terms almost identical with those so frequently applied to the bluestem-pasture region of the present:

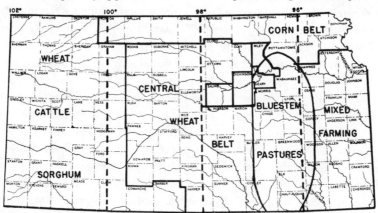

**Figure 10.1:** Map of Kansas, Showing Type-of-Farming Areas

Source: James C. Malin, *Winter Wheat in the Golden Belt of Kansas.*

Owing to the very singular position of the limestone—rock strata near the top of the "divide"—their constant washings and decomposition continue to enrich the land below, causing the grass to grow in great luxuriance, making the best feed for stock during the summer and winter.[2]

To the northwest across Clay County the hill country connects the bluestem-limestone area to the Dakota sandstone area of Ellsworth, Lincoln, and Cloud counties, which is also a bluestem country. To the southwest across Cowley, Harper, and Sedgwick counties the Arkansas Valley only briefly interrupts the bluestem-pasture region in its transition into the bluestem and short-grass pastures of the Medicine River red lands, and into the bluestem-bunch grass of the sandhills along the southern banks of the Arkansas and Cimarron rivers.

The bluestem-pasture region serves three significant functions, but the one that gives it distinction, if it does not render it unique, is that it occupies an intermediate position as a maturing ground or a grass-fattening area between the cattle-growing ranges of the southwestern plains and the central markets for grass-fattened cattle, or the feedlots of the cornbelt. Cattlemen have praised this unusual arrangement on the ground that the finishing weights are put on the animal near the market, saving freight and shipping shrinkage, and permitting flexibility in quick adjustment of shipping schedules to take advantage of favorable prices.[3] It is the largest such commercial grazing area for transient cattle in the United States. The time limits of the grazing season are about six months, April 15 to October 15, but the grass is ready earlier in the southern than in the northern end of the region. The movement of southwestern range cattle by rail into the bluestem grass begins in the latter part of April and is usually completed by mid-May. These cattle from a distance are supplemented to some extent by stock from local or nearby sources. The out-shipments to market usually begin in July, but vary with the season, the condition of cattle when delivered to the pastures, and the condition of the grass and are completed by October 15, leaving the pastures empty during the winter. The second function of the region is feed-lot finishing. This process is carried out on corn and alfalfa or other feeds, without grass or with grass. This is not done so extensively as in the cornbelt, but on a scale large enough to account for a substantial contribution to the market for full-fed beef. The third function is the maturing of young cattle by roughing through the winter, sometimes with grain added, pasturing through the following summer, and if not marketed as grass-fattened beef, full feeding into the second winter. The fourth and an important function is that the bluestem region serves as a breeding area for thoroughbred livestock. Although these functions have persisted together in varying proportions throughout the history of the area and often are hardly distinguishable from one another, the purpose of this address is to emphasize the evolution of the pasture function. The other aspects are included only as seems necessary to the principal objective.

The bluestem grass and the region have been the subject of many eulogies, some of which have gone beyond the limit of facts that can be or have been demonstrated scientifically. Furthermore, there is some disagreement concerning what factors give distinctive value to it as a grazing region. One school of thought, and the one most widely held, takes the ground that the limestone imparts to the bluestem grass its remarkable strength for fattening cattle. If this test were applied rigidly, it would restrict the limits of the region by excluding the sandstone country. The occupants of the sandstone pastures object, however, to the discrimination, holding that it is the grass itself that is distinctive, and that the bluestem grass has the same qualities whether grown on the limestone or the sandstone soils of eastern Kansas. Comparative scientific tests seem not to be available at present to determine conclusively the merits of the divergent views.

In the early days no particular name was applied to this pasture region, the term *Flint Hills* being a geographical name for the hills themselves in which flint or chert outcroppings occur. As a region it was not then thought of as conspicuously different from others. When the grazing for southwestern cattle was being referred to by livestock men of the 1880s, the terms used were usually "northern pastures" which meant primarily the northern Plains States and territories. At that time Kansas excluded "green" Texas cattle on account of the Texas fever except for shipment, either from designated western stations or through rail consignments. When Kansas came to be referred to in particular, which occurred rarely prior to the 1890s, the terms used were "Kansas pastures," or "Southern Kansas pastures," or some equivalent, and they were used so as including western short-grass as well as eastern long-grass grazing grounds.

The term *Flint Hills* as applied to pastures occurred only occasionally in the early accounts and then designated only the grazing in the hills themselves rather than the region. Thus the people of Chase County differentiated the Flint Hills as grazing grounds from the farming lands of the bottoms and the upland prairies.[4] As time passed, a broader usage of the term *Flint Hills* developed, especially on the part of those outside the area. During the second and third decades of the twentieth century the term was rather generally used, but was not altogether appropriate because the pasture district was more extensive than the Flint Hills.

The name *Bluestem* was used in the later years of the nineteenth century to describe the grasses from a botanical standpoint, but popularly the more frequently used names were *prairie grasses, long grasses,* or *tall grasses.* In the early years of the twentieth century *bluestem* was sometimes used to designate the grass of certain pastures, but not until after the World War did the term *bluestem pastures* gain general currency as applying to the region.[5] The J. E. Edwards eulogy of the bluestem grass, printed in 1918, contributed to grass consciousness among cattlemen, the more effective portions being frequently quoted.[6] A suggestion was made in 1923, but not acted upon, that the new hotel at Emporia be named "Blue Stem" and advertised nationally.[7] The term *Kansas Bluestem Region* or some variation was used with increasing frequency during the 1920s, gaining in popularity over the term *Flint Hills.*[8] Other possible names, the *Limestone Pastures* or the *Bluestem-Limestone Pastures,* did not find popular favor. In a sense, therefore, when in 1929 the Kansas State Board of Agriculture adopted the name "The Bluestem Pasture Region of Kansas," it was registering what was already well on the way to becoming an accomplished fact.

The first steps in white occupation of the bluestem region occurred in the northern part prior to the organization of the territory—at Council Grove on the Santa Fe trail and at St. Mary's mission, the latter in the late 1840s where stock raising and general farming, except wheat production, were carried on vigorously in order to provide support for the mission and to teach agriculture to the Pottawatomie Indians. With the organization of the territory, settlements were made immediately in the Kansas River valley as far west as Fort Riley. Only shortly afterwards settlements were made on the Neosho and Cottonwood rivers in the central area. Following the Civil War the settled area expanded rapidly, first occupying the bottom land and then pushing into the upland prairie. Part of the area was railroad land, but a substantial part could be acquired under the preemption law and after the Civil War under the homestead act, the taking of homesteads being reported in Chase County as late as 1880.[9] As had happened on earlier frontiers, livestock was for a time the predominant interest, but it was generally viewed as a temporary or transitional stage which would give way to general farming on all but the roughest of the uplands. On these matters opinion fluctuated somewhat with the weather, however, and during dry periods especially the advocates of livestock as a permanent interest had the opportunity to urge their views.[10]

During the decade of the 1870s the agricultural interests of eastern Kansas were relatively diversified. There were at least four types of activities represented: general farming on a small scale which was largely of the subsistence type, but which emphasized grain crops; farming which emphasized the raising of corn to be fed to livestock on a commercial basis; the breeding of fine stock; and the maturing and grazing of transient cattle.

In Chase County in the heart of the bluestem the small-farmer point of view was hostile to the transient herds driven in for grazing and demanded the herd law:

We want this law to protect us from the large herds that are driven in here by men who do not settle and help to improve the country, but merely to turn non-residents' and railroad lands into stockyards, and allow their cattle to run at large, destroying all crops that are not strongly fortified.[11]

A spokesman for the resident stockmen declared that nine of every ten men in Chase County depended upon stockraising as the basis of prosperity:

This is truly a stock raising county, we have thousands of acres of land that cannot be cultivated, but cannot be surpassed for grazing.[12]

Later an Elmdale correspondent reported that farmers were enlarging their cultivated fields "being convinced that farming will pay in this country."[13] Three weeks later the *Chase County Leader* announced through its boom column to prospective immigrants that the valleys of the watershed of the Cottonwood River were destined to be occupied by small farmers and that "the divides between them are excellent grazing grounds for cattle and sheep, and will always be open to the stock-raiser without cost."[14] On this assumption small farmers made no effort to secure title to the hills.

After the lapse of two years the herd law provided again the text for the argument that without it the county could never be settled and to be a first-class county the uplands, "the best wheat land in the state" must be occupied. "Give us the herd law and we can settle every quarter section of prairie land in the county."[15] Another correspondent endorsed this assertion but with some qualification, saying that "nearly every quarter section of arable land would be a fine farm."[16]

Calling attention to differences in geographical environment, another letter writer asserted:

Every new county and country is always opened up by men of moderate circumstances. In a heavily timbered country it takes a life-time; in a country like this, but a few years, if all work for the public good.[17]

The year 1874 with its drought and grasshoppers was one to make Kansas conscious of climatic differences and in protest against an Ohio man's clover theories, an old resident wrote:

The writer seems altogether ignorant of an important fact, which is about the first lesson taught to every practical farmer, viz.: that farming in Ohio, or any other state, is one thing, and farming in Kansas is something altogether different; and crops that pay in one section of the country are comparatively worthless in another.[18]

During 1875 farmers were searching for substitute crops that would make a profit in adverse years,[19] but with a more favorable year in 1876 a local correspondent reported that "the settlers are in hopes that in a few years all the land on this creek that will bear cultivation will be under fence [cultivated]."[20] At the opening of the next year grain prospects were bright, and again the *Leader* asserted that while the bottoms were better for corn, the uplands were better for small grain.[21]

However promising the early spring might be, unfavorable years for grain crops almost became a habit for Kansas during the late 1870s. By mid-summer of 1877 the *Leader* was proclaiming that Chase County was the best stock county in the state and was explaining why the wheat crop failed.[22] In another three years the admission was made that wheat had been practically abandoned as a crop.[23] In Greenwood County wheat was similarly abandoned.[24]

In the upper Kansas River valley, where the bluestem region now makes its transition into the wheat belt (Riley, Geary, and Dickinson counties) one observer in 1869 gave livestock not more than ten years of dominance, by which time the rising price of land would operate to eliminate livestock and favor grain as a more intensive land-use.[25] Four years later another insisted that Geary County was peculiarly a livestock country, only to be contradicted in turn by those who held that the livestock industry was perpetuated only by an artificial influence, the failure to adopt the herd law.[26] The winter wheat boom in Dickinson County was pointed to as proof of what would happen on Geary County hills if only the opportunity were given. Although Geary and Riley counties tried to evade the issue by laying the blame for retardation in wheat production upon the herd law, and other artificial factors, the passing years made clearer that more fundamental forces were at work.[27] In 1878 the *Manhattan Nationalist,* in commentary on the wheat propaganda of T. C. Henry of Abilene, insisted that "we are satisfied, however, that a large majority of the farmers of this section have lost money on wheat, taking year in and year out."[28] If these were merely isolated comments or expressions of discouragement over a crop failure, they might be subject to misinterpretation, but they are, in fact, representative of a trend indicating a more definite drawing of the line of demarcation between the pasture and the wheat country, a process that was in progress but not yet complete by the end of the decade of the 1870s.

During the decade of the 1880s far-reaching changes came to the bluestem area. There was more intensive encroachment by the small farmer upon the outer fringes, thus tending to differentiate more sharply than formerly the strictly grazing region from the surrounding grain farming. Within the bluestem region the influence of the small farmer declined. A livestock boom dominated the early part of the decade. It included horses, sheep, and hogs, but the major emphasis was upon fine cattle and the improvement of herds. This was based upon the expansion of some of the herds started during the previous decade and upon the coming of new men and money; some from the Southwest and Colorado, some from the East, and some from Canada, England, and Scotland. The volume of production increased until by 1883 heavy shipments of thoroughbred bulls to the range country was a reality. The Shorthorn breed had been the early favorite, then the Galloway and Angus gained a following. In a short time, however, the Hereford came to dominate the breeding for the range market. Combined with this breeding of fine cattle was an increased business in maturing pasturing cattle from outside the area, especially wintered Texas and Colorado cattle.

In order to provide the land for these extensive operations, free range quickly disappeared. The process of assembling acreages can be traced in part through the newspapers which record the purchase by stockmen of one small adjoining farm after another and the purchase of railroad land. The assembling of large acreages was facilitated also by syndicates which bought up railroad land from different roads, throwing it together for resale to those forming large ranches. Board and stone fences had been built around the earlier fields and pastures, but the thing that largely made possible this great enclosure movement and which characterized it was the introduction of barbed wire. Thus the herd problem of the 1870s was eliminated. The use of wire began slowly about 1879 and 1880 and reached boom proportions by 1883, and before the end of another two years the free range was gone. The passing of the free range marked also the end of many small farmers who had neglected their opportunities or had been financially unable to buy hill pasture land. Shut off from grass, they had to sell out.

This breeding-cattle boom was short-lived. It was dependent for its market upon the range-cattle boom which had reached its height by 1884 and run its course by 1886, and by that year a drought decade opened along with a world-wide economic depression. Few of the thoroughbred herds survived, and new adjustments had to be made in utilization of the grass resources of the region. The new era was introduced by railroads and Texas cattle with the accompaniment of Texas fever.

The main lines of the Union Pacific and the Santa Fe railroad systems ran east and west. The former had no southern connections, and the Santa Fe system could serve directly only the Colorado and the northern New Mexico ranges prior to 1880. The southern Kansas branches and subsidiaries of the Santa Fe reached the Indian territory border and the shipping points for Texas cattle at several places. The Texas cattle driven north could be loaded at these border points for through shipment to the terminal markets, but could not be unloaded within the state unless inspected and pronounced free of Texas fever. Pasture operations in transient cattle during the early 1880s were limited accordingly to those wintered north of the quarantine line and to Colorado range cattle. These were the same classes of cattle that were shipped in for winter feeding to be roughed through or half or full-fed on corn. In these days there was little distinction between the several classes of cattle, and the finishing processes were not clearly standardized as to either season or method. Cattle were being received and shipped out during every month of the year, but with an accent on the spring and fall movements.

Only slowly did the campaign against Texas fever enlarge the source of supplies for grass cattle, the success depending in turn upon the shutting off of the cattle-drives to northern Texas and the Indian territory and the substituting of rail shipment as a means of clearing these intermediate ranges of Texas fever. The cattle associations of the northern Indian territory took steps in the winter of 1883–1884 to restrict to two designated trails the drives from further south. The Texas Panhandle and western Indian territory cattle associations followed closely in 1885. During the same period New Mexico, Colorado, and northern range territories established quarantines, Montana following in the rear in 1886. Texas complained, but to no avail, that these quarantines were solely to monopolize free grass and not to protect cattle from disease. The western Kansas settlement boom of the middle 1880s served only to supplement the activities of the cattlemen who had effectively closed all but the most westerly cattle trails, and they were usable only under close restrictions.

During the 1870s Texas had secured rail outlets for its cattle to the St. Louis and Chicago markets by way of the Missouri Pacific (St. Louis, Iron Mountain, and Southern) railroad or by way of the Missouri, Kansas and Texas railroad across Indian territory and southeastern Kansas connecting with the Missouri Pacific road. Jay Gould had gained control of these roads and aroused the hostility of the cattle interests. The northern drive served as a more advantageous competitive marketing route for cattle intended for beef, fattening on northern grass along the trail and being shipped from western Kansas or Nebraska points to the Kansas City, Omaha, or Chicago markets. The closing of the ring of quarantines around Texas by 1885 was closing this competitive route and terminating bargaining power with the Gould interests.[29] Texas explored other alternatives. As trade in refrigerated dressed beef was becoming more important, one line of action suggested was to fatten beef on grain and cottonseed products, slaughter at home, and ship by water from a gulf port, thus circumventing both the dressed beef combine and the railroad extortion. Attempts in this direction were initiated, but failed.[30]

Another possibility was a change of procedure in the northern outlet. In 1883, and prior to the closing of the trails, competing Texas railroads experimented in a large way with rail shipments from south Texas by way of Fort Worth to rail heads on the Red River, particularly Wichita Falls from which the drive would commence. This would put the cattle on northern grass earlier and if rates were favorable, more cheaply than to drive the whole distance.[31] As the trails were closed such cattle were driven from the northern rail heads into the Indian territory as the only place left where Texas cattle might go legally.[32] Fattened on grass, they were shipped from Kansas border points or railroads in the eastern Indian territory where the Frisco offered competitive service to St. Louis as early as 1883.[33]

As the range cattle business shifted into the High Plains of western Texas and New Mexico in the later 1880s, more direct rail service from that area became insistent, and supplemented a growing demand from southern and central Texas for through competitive lines. The Kansas City livestock market interests had been aggressively challenging the St. Louis market and had been agitating during the same period to secure direct rail service from the Southwest to Kansas City in order to compete successfully with St. Louis and Chicago. As the rail situation stood prior to 1887, Kansas City had no direct connections and could only divert on unfavorable terms from the Gould–St. Louis combination a small part of the increasing rail shipments of cattle from southern Texas. The Santa Fe railroad was the best located strategically to take the lead, and with the support of the combined interests of southwestern cattlemen and Kansas City market men undertook a through line south from Arkansas City to Galveston, and one southwest across the Panhandle of Texas into New Mexico. The first connections were completed during 1887, and the year 1888 was the first full-length cattle season to be served by the new accommodations.[34] Much of the immediate significance of the new situation was lost, however, because of the economic depression of the period which was particularly severe on the range industry. The Rock Island railroad lines were extended into the Southwest as far as the Red River in 1892, making a second competing system and opening the Omaha market to Texas cattle by introducing competitive rates.[35] It is important, however, to distinguish between beef cattle and the stocker and feeder classes. Only beef cattle could be shipped to northern markets for slaughter. The stocker and feeder trade was subject to the restrictions of the quarantine systems, only a relatively small number moving into the northern ranges.

The first descriptions of Texas fever occur in the late eighteenth century when cattle from the Carolinas were taken north. Steps were taken to prevent further movement of such cattle, but the volume of the trade was not insistent enough to force a serious interstate issue. The southern borders of Virginia, Tennessee, and Missouri had the problem with them more or less constantly, but almost a century passed after the disease was first described on the Atlantic seaboard before the issue was joined at the southern Kansas-Missouri border on a scope which made of it a national problem in northern-southern intersectional relations.

Effective control of the disease was all but impossible prior to 1893 because little was known for certain of its nature or of the agency by which it was transmitted. The geographical distribution of the disease was determined by the federal bureau of animal industry and the boundary line of infested territory drawn upon maps, the first issued in 1884 for the section east and in 1885 for the section west of the Mississippi River. The fever was identified in 1889 as a blood disease caused by an intra-corpuscular parasite of the protozoan order, which caused a breakdown of corpuscles on so large a scale as to clog the organs of elimination. The cattle tick was suspected of serving as the transmitting agent, and experimental work proved the point, the announcement of the results being published in 1893. The federal quarantine line established in 1890 became the basis of cooperative federal-state action in segregating tick-free cattle and controlling the disease when it appeared in northern pastures.[36] Texans finally admitted the existence of such a disease and cooperated in controlling it by a quarantine line from north of which Texas cattle would move into the normal channels of the national cattle trade.[37] One phase of control work begun in 1892 was to inoculate susceptible cattle, later Southern cattle were dipped to free them of ticks, and lastly efforts were centered after the turn of the century in freeing the Southern land of tick infestation.

This background knowledge of the disease is important to the understanding of the history of attempts in Kansas to deal with the fever menace. As the settlers in territorial Kansas accumulated livestock, the Proslavery and Free-State men were able to agree on protective measures and set up vigilance committees to turn back herds of Southern cattle. Severe outbreaks of fever in 1858, 1859, and 1860 brought drastic legislation by the territorial legislature of 1859, and by the first state legislature of 1861, the latter prohibiting Southern cattle from entering the state at all. After the Civil War there were successive outbreaks of the disease, and the Kansas legislature amended the law repeatedly: 1867, 1872, 1873, 1876, 1877, 1879, 1881, 1883, 1884, 1885, setting a dead line, first at the sixth principal meridian, just west of Wichita, and in later enactments further west and prohibiting the movement of Texas cattle into Kansas at any point east of the line. The bluestem region was east of the line, but the driving of infected cattle into or across these counties occurred again and again, and the infiltration of cattle from the Indian territory across the border proved more or less continuous.

The fact that in the early 1880s so many Kansas stockmen were engaged in improving their native herds and in building up herds of thoroughbreds made imperative the exclusion of Texas fever. The pasturing of transient cattle was limited under such circumstances to animals from safe territory. The first steps on the part of the state to provide special machinery to safeguard the livestock interests against disease came in 1884 as the result of a foot-and-mouth disease scare. The Livestock Sanitary Commission thus created became an active agent in dealing with all livestock diseases and in combating Texas fever exercised the power of inspecting herds entering the state and of quarantining herds in which disease appeared. The federal law was enacted the same year creating the bureau of animal industry and vesting in it the power to exercise control over interstate transmission of disease. These two agencies, together with the discovery of the role of the cattle tick, gradually placed the cattlemen in a position to handle Texans without excessive risk, and the bluestem pastures were among the beneficiaries during the depression years of the late 1880s and the 1890s. Deprived of sharing in the heavy movement of Texans into the eastern Indian territory during the decade of the 1880s, the supply had come from the East and more largely from Colorado and the farther Southwest. Now the stock formerly diverted around Kansas could enter eastern Kansas directly. This did not occur all at once, but gradually through continuous readjustment in quarantine administration, and the bluestem grass lands resumed more completely the role geographical location and peculiar natural resources fitted them to serve in the national livestock economy.

From the standpoint of the bluestem region the railroad systems which served the grass sections were much the same ones that had become most important as outlets to the market for southwestern cattle, the pasture country lying on the way to the packing house. Because of this geographical relationship it was possible to ship stock from the ranges to the market destinations with privileges of pasturing in transit. The Missouri Pacific and the Frisco railroads had east and west lines in the southern part of the bluestem region of Kansas and the former across the central area. The Missouri, Kansas, and Texas lines had a diagonal road from Parsons running northwest by way of Emporia to Junction City. The Rock Island railroad served the west and northwestern section. The Santa Fe railroad system enjoyed the most complete coverage as far north as the Kansas River and the most strategic location of through lines connecting with the stock regions of the greater Southwest. The Santa Fe lines carried the largest volume of incoming cattle of any one system, but shared the trade widely with the others. Of the out-movement to market, however, the Santa Fe lines carried more than the others together.

In the twentieth century the pasturing of southwestern cattle was continued as the major interest, and the breeding of thoroughbred livestock was revived with new vigor. The pasture business was not static, however, and vigilance was necessary to make adjustments which would insure its continuance. Among these problems were the procedures employed in filling the pastures; the terms of the pasture contract; the methods of financing the business; the cumulative market preference for younger light-weight cattle instead of mature heavy-weight animals, and the difficulties of utilizing grass in producing this type of beef; the restoration of the grasslands after years of depletion and drouth; the effects of the changes in the South and Southwest in cattle production, markets, and packing facilities; the results of shifting population centers; and the outcome of the changing transportation facilities accompanied by the southern demand for remodeling of the rail rate-structure. Separate consideration should be given also to other livestock activities of the region, breeding of dairy cattle, hogs, sheep, and horses, and the production of feed crops that must be an integral part of any major livestock production program. In such an introductory survey as this, however, only a few problems can be selected from the list for treatment.

The methods of bringing the cattle to the grass vary with respect to the ownership of both, and may be described under four general types of combinations. The owner of southwestern cattle might lease the Kansas pastures, delivering the cattle to the pasture operator, who would take responsibility for them while on grass or, less frequently, the owner might retain management. The pastureman might buy the cattle and graze them himself. A man might own both the cattle and the grass, operating a ranch in the Southwest for cattle production and grasslands in the bluestem region for finishing, all under his own management. A fourth type involves a third party, the speculator, or middleman, who would buy cattle and lease pasture, leaving management of the cattle to the pastureman upon delivery. In years when cattle markets seemed to offer opportunities for profits a larger portion of cattle was bought from the producers, but when conditions were discouraging a large portion was left in first hands to be shipped to pasture by the southwestern owners. In the latter case if the economic outlook became too unfavorable after shipment to grass, the stock was wintered in Kansas or shipped to the home ranges as in 1930 or 1934.

The purchase of cattle for the pastures might be accomplished by different methods. The pasture operator might visit the southwestern ranges during the winter and contract his purchases for spring delivery. The same procedure might be followed by the speculator. The cattle trades might be made at the annual spring conventions of the cattlemen's associations in the Southwest or since 1916 at the Kansas Live Stock Association's spring meeting, usually at Wichita in March. The speculator might make purchases by either of the foregoing methods, reselling the cattle in smaller lots to third parties before delivery or at delivery time. On occasion, especially during a period of cattle shortage on the ranges, cattle might be purchased on the Kansas City stocker and feeder market to fill the pastures.

The leasing of grass was accomplished through several channels. A few cattlemen and pasturemen advertised in livestock journals. More leases were arranged at the stockmen's annual meetings, and others were handled through an information service of the livestock associations. Some were arranged through livestock commission houses at the markets. Once having established desirable connections, a large part of the contracts were renewed from year to year with adjustment to changing conditions. The historical development of the terms of the pasture contract is difficult to trace because few examples are available for study and the terms did not become fully standardized. Early herd and pasture advertisements sometimes announced terms. In 1872 herding was offered for 500 to 1,000 head of cattle, price not indicated, but the herder assumed responsibility for all losses except by disease. In 1879 another announced an intention to make up a herd of part-fed steers for the June and July market, assuring a supply of salt, the herding rate being one-half cent per head per day. Another offered to handle cattle for the season at seventy-five cents per head. Still another offered the service of a Shorthorn bull with the herd at one dollar per head per season. A similar offer was made in 1886 but did not announce the price.[38] The nature of the advertisements indicate the variety of the types of cattle being handled, part-fed steers, breeding cows, and miscellaneous stock. A number of advertisements of pastures for rent implied that the lessee would assume the management of the pasture and cattle while on grass. In other words he was renting land only, without services.[39] These transactions were limited to spring and summer grass, but if the number of newspaper items for the same period is any criterion, a larger number of farmers took cattle to winter on pasture and feed.

Another phase in the development of contract requirements appeared in 1890, when one advertisement specified three acres per head.[40] This was a period when Colorado and other western men, not Texans, were in the majority. Based upon payments through Strong City, Emporia, and Cottonwood Falls banks it was estimated that Chase County had 20,000 head from Colorado, New Mexico, and Arizona on grass with the result that a number of western cattlemen were spending much of their time there.[41] This indicated that many owners were supervising their own cattle on grass rather than transferring the full responsibility to the pasture owner. Another example of owner supervision resulted in taking the herd from the pasture because of dissatisfaction with the care they received.[42] An instance where the pastureman was taking full responsibility is illustrated by the theft of the hide from a dead steer. The importance of the episode did not lie so much in the value of the hide as in the fact that the pastureman must have the brand from it to present at settlement time when he must account to the owner for delivery of all steers received.[43]

In 1930 the pasture owners of the Northern bluestem region launched the "Kansas Bluestem Pasturemen's Association," one point in their four-point program being the formulation of a uniform contract. The decade of the 1930s introduced important variations in contracts, however, rather than uniformity, but in general the terms required the pastureman to receive the stock at the railroad station, transfer them to pasture, take care of them during the summer, and deliver a full count at the railroad at the end of the season. He was required to assume losses, except from disease. Minimum acreage allowances were required depending upon the age of the cattle, and rental prices were paid by head per season for each age class or by the acre. A newer procedure was some form of rental payment on the basis of pounds gained for the season, either at an agreed price per pound gained or for a part of the gain at the market price when sold. Contracts were usually made at a flat rate per season for the identical animal without respect to the actual number of days the cattle were on grass and without right of replacement of animals shipped early.[44] The rentals were usually deferred until marketing, and on occasion the pastureman advanced the freight.[45]

The price of pasture rentals fluctuated and was controlled primarily by the market price of beef rather than by the price of land.[46] About 1900 a rental of $1.00 per head per season was a good price on land worth $3.50 to $5.50 per acre. By 1911 the rates had advanced to $5.00 to $6.00 on land worth $18.00 to $30.00 and with cattle selling at $3.00 to $5.50 per hundred weight.[47] The World War lifted rentals to $14.00 to $20.00 per head with prevailing prices from $16.00 to $18.00,[48] and in some pastures the cattle were allowed five acres each, in consequence of the experience of the 1918 season which was dry.[49] By 1920 cattle prices were too high and leading pasture owners declined to buy, leaving cattle owners to rent the pastures. In Wabaunsee County rates ruled $12.00 and up.[50] The extension of the depression drove rentals down in 1921 to $6.00 to $12.00.[51] Further declines continued through 1922 when the ruling price was about $8.75.[52] By the middle 1920s more emphasis was being placed on young cattle, and a wider range in prices was emphasized accordingly. In 1925 there was some recovery from depression lows, young cattle being pastured at $5.00 to $8.00 with an average of about $6.25 and aged steers and cows from $7.00 to $10.00 with an average of about $8.50. Acreage allowances for young stuff averaged 3.25 acres and for steers 4.3 acres per head.[53] In 1927 the rate for aged steers was quoted at $6.00 to $10.00 with an average of $8.10 and an allowance of three to five acres, and young cattle at $4.00 to $8.50 with an average of $6.00 and an allowance of two to four acres. In the Osage limestone pastures the rates for aged steers were $4.00 to $8.00 with an average of $6.25 and an allowance of 5.1 acres and $3.00 to $6.00 with an average of $4.50 and an allowance of 4.5 acres. The sandstone pastures were quoted at lower rates.[54] By 1929 the rates reached $8.00 to $11.00 for aged steers. There had been only three prosperous years for cattlemen in the decade, 1925, 1927, and 1928; 1929 was favorable for those who marketed early.

As the depression of the 1930s deepened, pasture rates declined and by 1933 reached $2.50 to $5.00 for aged steers with an average of $3.50 to $4.00, and young cattle at $2.50 to $3.00. On account of dry weather the allowances were increased to six acres.[55] Prices recovered somewhat in 1935 and 1936, but allowances were further increased because of the prolonged and severe drought and some pastures were idle. The rates for 1937 were $7.00 to $9.00.[56] In 1941 prices began about $8.50, declining near the end of the leasing season to $7.00.

A long-time trend toward smaller, younger beef animals culminated after the World War and presented the bluestem region with a new crop of problems. On grass a mature steer took on fat, but a young animal added growth first and fat only if the feed provided nutrition definitely in excess of that necessary for growth. Grass needed a supplement for satisfactory finish. Systematic experimentation conducted by the state experiment station worked out new feeding procedures and rations. One important trend derived from these experiments was to prepare young cattle on dry feed before the grass season and later to finish them in the feed lot after grass. These adjustments assured the continuance of utilization of the bluestem grass in the maturing and fattening of the increasing proportion of young animals handled as well as grazing the continued run of mature cattle.

Financing the cattle business in any of its several phases requires facilities not necessary to other fields of agriculture. The turnover of capital is necessarily slow, as much as three years in breeding and maturing cattle and from six months to a year in handling grass and fed cattle. Large amounts of capital are employed and heavy risks involved because of the fluctuation of markets and price levels between the time of incurring first production costs and realizing final market returns.

These problems of financing have important social implications. While there was always a fair complement of small farms, the features that gave the character to the bluestem region were large stock farms and large pastures, both of which involved capital investment much beyond the means of the traditional family-size, family-owned-and-operated farm. Both land and cattle were figured not only in hundreds but often in thousands of units. A substantial number of old families survived through two or three generations. A much larger number had come and gone, many through the ordinary course of American farm population turnover, and many as the result of voluntary or forced liquidation—victims of depressions. Capital requirements and the nature of operations on large stock farms induced many fathers to associate their sons with them in the enterprise, or brothers to pool their interests. Urban capital was largely represented: grain and livestock commission men, doctors, lawyers and bankers—especially bankers—either as sole owners or as majority partners. Many of the commercial pastures, as distinguished from stock farms, were in similar hands. The words "banker and stockman" were used together so frequently as almost to constitute one word descriptive of the leading men of the region. From the standpoint of rurality, the families residing in country homes were in conspicuous degrees minority partners or agents managing the enterprises and employees, sometimes specialists in herd management and administration, but more numerous were relatively unskilled farm laborers. Conspicuous in the boom days of the 1880s were establishments of manorial proportions occupied by the owners, and in some degree these families survived.

The devastating effects of the prolonged drouth of the 1930s brought alarm to the bluestem region, an alarm not justified in the perspective of history. The grass problem had been ever present and ever a source of anxiety to stockmen. Much of the attitude of the early settlers toward grass was conditioned by the humid climate-timbered land point of view. There the grasses were not strictly native, but grass covering came only after the forests were cleared. Dependence upon tame grasses for pasture and meadow was the rule. Upon coming into the subhumid prairie-plains this type of mental furniture was carried west along with other farm properties. Allowing for a reasonable number of exceptions, there was a rather general assumption that the native grasses could not survive occupation of the country for purposes of agriculture. Writing from Osage County in June, 1880, prior to his long tenure as secretary of the State Board of Agriculture, F. D. Coburn expressed the view that the days were numbered when reliance could be placed upon wild prairie grass for pasture and hay.[58] A writer in Dickinson County in 1881 looked upon the wheat boom as temporary, insisting that "the time is not far distant when every farmer will have to depend on his own land for hay . . . and we predict that in ten years from now, there will be thousands of acres of clover and timothy growing, and cattle and sheep grazing thereon, where now are luxuriant and magnificent fields of wheat."[59] Three years later another writer repeated the Coburn view but went further in exposition: "The prairie grass must go. It is but a matter of a few years time when eastern Kansas will have to depend on tame grasses for hay. . . . Prairie grass does not make permanent pasturage. As soon as a tract of land is fenced and pastured, the wild grass soon dies and gives place to weeds and the pasture becomes almost worthless."[60]

The tame grasses of which so much was expected were bluegrass, clover, timothy and orchard grass, but it took extended and severe ministrations of time and nature to prove to these easterners the extent of their mistaken preconceptions. First introduced experimentally into the area in 1875, alfalfa, a rank outsider among tame grasses, had still to prove its worth and become second only to the native bluestem as a foundation grass for the cattle industry. A clear recognition of the permanence and significance of the bluestem grass was slow in materializing, a fact that is vividly illustrated by a report on western grasses made by an investigator for the federal Department of Agriculture in 1886 which depreciatingly declared that "although somewhat coarse it is considered valuable and everywhere cut for hay."[61] In view of such misconceptions concerning the behavior of nature there is little wonder at the confusion manifested concerning the future of grass. Nearer right than most, but still not sufficiently appreciative of nature's own careful selection based upon ages of experimentation in her own laboratories, was a writer who dismissed all the grasses from east of the Mississippi, insisting that "in view of the peculiarities of our climate, if not of our soil also, would we not suppose, *a priori,* that some of the many *native* grasses could be found that would be superior both for pasture and for hay?"[62]

At the opposite pole from these erroneous, early ideas concerning the native grasses are the equally mistaken views of the soil and grass conservation experts of the 1930s and 1940s who pointed back to the supposed golden age when the grass was plentiful and no question was raised respecting its permanence—only inexcusable abuse, they said, caused its depletion. In neither period was there sufficient appreciation of the alternation of favorable and unfavorable climatic conditions and their effect upon grass, nor of the remarkable recuperative powers of native grass. A grass covering is as natural to the prairie and plains as a forest covering to the humid East or jungle to the tropics. But in times of drought hysteria over depletion of grass there was only an occasional clear-memoried old-timer who insisted that these conditions were a recurring phenomena and that ninety percent of the problem depended upon nature and the return of favorable rains.[63] In other words, man's control measures could account for only ten percent. The exact figures might be challenged, but not the principle.

Various weeds thrived at the expense of grass during the drought of the 1930s, broom weed arousing particular comment from Council Grove to the south line of Greenwood County. The one favorable season of 1938 brought the following comment:

Broom weed, which last year caused alarm and no little damage is very scarce this season. Some report it entirely disappeared and other weeds which threatened many acres of good grass land, are not so prevalent this season. It all shows that when there is plenty of moisture in the ground the rugged native grass will take care of itself.[64]

The renewed vigor of the bluestem grass was so conspicuous that a number of people reported to the press on the extreme height to which it had grown: from Chase County, prior to the drought decade, eight feet, five inches; after the drought, six to eight feet; from Marshall County, nine feet tall; and in several pastures in Wabaunsee County, five to six feet tall even though it had been pastured all summer.[65] These measurements recall the statements of old-timers that the bluestem along the Cottonwood River would hide a man riding horseback.

The original carrying capacity of the grasslands varied widely because of the differences in soil quality and depth and in topography, the extremes being found in the rocky hilltops and in the river bottoms. Another type of extreme was to be found in periods of favorable rainfall in contrast with periods of severe drought. In the course of years much of the best grass-producing land was brought into cultivation, leaving the less fertile to carry the grazing load. Waste land developed in pastures around watering places and feeding grounds.[66] These factors are an important reminder that comparisons of carrying capacity for different periods seldom apply to identical acres. During boom periods carrying capacity was greatly over-rated, and under adverse conditions the depletion was represented in correspondingly pessimistic terms. Experimental work in pasture restoration lacked the essential elements of perspective afforded only by the lapse of a long period of time. The oldest controlled pasture experiment in the bluestem area was begun so recently as 1915.[67] To be fully convincing it would be necessary to have records of a reasonable number of samples representing different sections of the region, records that would in each case apply to identical acres, and records which would embrace at least a century of climatic experience. Making a moderate allowance for error, the tentative conclusion from this historical study of the bluestem region is that no substantial long-time change has taken place in the carrying capacity of pastures which have had reasonable treatment. Furthermore, experience indicates that not only may depleted pastures be restored, but that bare places and even plowed fields may be reseeded and restored successfully in a comparatively short time when the essential weather conditions are favorable.

By way of conclusion to this introductory survey of the history of the bluestem-pasture region, attention is directed to the volume of the pasture movement of southwestern cattle at different periods and some evaluation of it in comparative terms. Probably there is no phase of Western history with which the public has a more general interest and at least a superficial familiarity than the Texas cattle drives from the time of the opening of the Abilene market in 1867 to the closing of the cattle trails to Dodge City in the

1880s. Around this phase of American history there has grown up an amazing accumulation of history, legend, and folklore. The exact volume of those drives can never be known, but estimates are available which indicate some approximation of numbers.[68] Except for three isolated big years, the estimates of the annual drives of Texas cattle northward range from 150,000 to 350,000 for the years 1869 to 1884. From other estimates the conclusion is derived that not over 25 percent of such cattle were shipped to market for beef, or 50,000 to 75,000 head each year.[69]

Systematic estimates are lacking of the volume of southwestern cattle shipped by rail to the Kansas pastures for grass fattening as they proceeded on their way to market, but significant fragments can be pieced together for the earlier periods, and for the recent period the federal agricultural marketing service has provided rather full data. In the 1890s the Kansas inspection service reported on the number of permits granted for entrance into the state, but the figures were on a calendar year basis and did not segregate cattle for pasture from those for feeding, and the pasture regions within the state were not designated separately. The admissions into the state for 1891 and 1892 averaged 325,000 for each year. The movement for the year 1895 was evidently one of the smallest as only 58,481 were admitted for pasture and feeding. Big volume was attained again in 1897 with 424,249 admitted, the sources of this movement being distributed as follows: Texas, 233,444; Arizona, 82,048; Oklahoma, 30,497; New Mexico, 29,819; Missouri, 7,351; and Old Mexico, 31,090. The numbers for 1898 were larger, but the annual volume for the four years 1900–1903 ranged from 213,000 to 319,000.

Skipping over two decades to the five-year period 1925–1929 the federal marketing service figures are more explicit and are available for the bluestem region and for the Oklahoma Osage pastures separately. The combined figures for these pastures ranged from 423,000 to 486,000 annually. The bluestem's share of these ranged from 263,000 to 278,000 annually. During the depression years of the 1930s the numbers of cattle sent to the Kansas-Oklahoma pastures fluctuated widely and the general trend was downward until 1939. The ten-year average, 1930 to 1939 inclusive, was 287,000 head for the combined pastures and 209,000 for the bluestem, but the low year was 1938 with 196,000 and 131,000 head respectively. The cattle movement for the current year 1941 credits the two pasture regions with 240,000 transient cattle, the bluestem with 177,000 head, and the Osage with 63,000. This reflects a partial recovery in volume, but there is still a question, because of the economic changes that have occurred in the South during the depression decade, whether the volume will again reach the levels of the earlier years.

In comparing periods it is evident that the numbers of southwestern beef cattle handled annually by rail through Kansas in 1897 was six to eight times as great as during the Texas-drive period, when as pointed out above not over 50,000 to 75,000 of those driven annually were suitable for beef. The numbers for the bluestem region alone in the late 1920s were four to five times those for the wild years at Abilene, Ellsworth, and Dodge City. A comparison of the size of the animals and the percentage of commercial beef dressed out of each gives an even greater advantage to the more recent periods. In quality of beef the Texas steer could not be compared with the modern steer. On all points the more recent procedures for fattening cattle account for more and better beef, and the Kansas bluestem grasslands serve as the maturing and fattening ground in a more efficient style than was ever possible under the drive regime.

Unfortunately for good history, the general public has overvalued the ephemeral, the sensational, and the pathological features of the short-lived cowboy boom days. At most the Texas drives of song and story lasted not more than twenty years, while the practice of rail shipments through the bluestem pastures has already functioned more than half a century. The bluestem-pasture business is more efficient, it is relatively standardized and avoids the sensational and the spectacular as the herds are moved by train to pasture to insure the least possible shrinkage. The shipments are delivered at numerous small railway stations which serve the pastures. When the cattle leave the pastures for market the shipment is usually accomplished by an overnight haul. None of these operations come to the attention of the public, and like most of the stabilized institutions of a complex social system they are taken for granted so long as they continue to deliver beef to the consumer's table. Outside the ranks of the cattlemen themselves, few understand the significance of this beef-producing process. It is not a local industry only, but a vital intersectional link in the national economic system. The history of the bluestem-pasture region is important in its own right as Kansas history, but is more than that. To the extent that the Kansas bluestem contributes to the essential meat supplies of the nation, it is also national history. Nevertheless, there are few regions in the United States that are more important and less known than this bluestem-pasture region of Kansas.

## Notes

1. The grama and buffalo grasses retain more feed value than bluestem when cured on the ground (in the pasture), and therefore make better winter pasture. The Kentucky bluegrass makes an earlier spring growth and a later fall growth, being nearly dormant during the summer, and during mild seasons remains green well into the winter.

For winter pasture the bluestem region is more valuable in proportion to the amount of grama and buffalo grass that may be intermixed with it, and for early spring and fall pasture in proportion to the mixture of Kentucky bluegrass with the bluestem, but for summer pasture the bluestem with the minimum of mixture is best.

2. John O. Wattles, Moneka, Kan., in the *New York Tribune,* March 31, 1857.

3. *Kansas Stockman,* Topeka, May 1, 1933.

4. *Chase County Leader,* Cottonwood Falls, March 1, 29, 1872.

5. *Junction City Union,* November 16, 1872; *Ottawa Daily Republic,* April 2, 1884; *Texas Live Stock Journal* (Fort Worth), November, 1886; George E. Tucker, "Blue[stem] Grass and the Beef Steer," *Greenwood Magazine* (Eureka), April, 1905, pp. 7–10.

6. *Kansas Stockman* (Topeka), April 5, 1918, December 15, 1922. *Cf.* eulogies of the bluestem by T. H. Lampe, *ibid.,* February 15, June 15, 1927, April 15, 1931, November 15, 1935, February 15, 1941.

7. *Ibid.,* January 15, 1923.

8. *Ibid.,* August 1, 1919, June 15, 1921, August 15, 1922, April 15, 1925, February 1, June 15, 1927, February 1, 1928.

9. *Chase County Leader* (Cottonwood Falls), April 29, 1880.

10. *The Nationalist* (Manhattan), January 25, 1878, June 23, 1881; *Dickinson County Chronicle,* Abilene, February 10, 1882.

11. *Chase County Leader,* (Cottonwood Falls), March 1, 1872.

12. *Ibid.,* March 29, 1872.

13. *Ibid.,* May 17, 1872.

14. *Ibid.,* June 7, 1872. A later statement to the same effect was made as a reminiscence and was reported by Vandergrift in the *Atchison Globe,* reprinted in the *Chase County Republican* (Strong City), May 15, 1890.

15. Unsigned letter to the *Chase County Leader,* (Cottonwood Falls), May 8, 1874.

16. *Ibid.,* May 22, 1874.

17. *Ibid.,* May 15, 1874.

18. *Ibid.,* February 4, 1875.

19. *Ibid.,* February–March, 1875.

20. *Ibid.,* June 15, 1876.

21. *Ibid.,* February 22, 1877.

22. *Ibid.,* June 21, July 26, 1877.

23. *Ibid.,* April 22, 1880. In the issue of September 15, 1881, it was stated that "many have quit sowing wheat and but little ground is being plowed for it."

24. *Livestock-Indicator* (Kansas City, Mo.), December 6, 1883.

25. *Junction City Union,* September 11, 1869.

26. *Ibid.,* March 15, 22, 29, June 28, 1873, May 9, 1874.

27. *Ibid.,* November 27, 1875 — "Mize on Junction City Grain Market," a reply to John Davis in the *Junction City Tribune.*

28. *Nationalist* (Manhattan), January 25, 1878.

29. Quarantines: *Texas Live Stock Journal* (Fort Worth), August 9, 1884, May 2, 9, 23, 30, June 13, July 4, 1885, June 5, 1886, April 5, 1890, June 20, July 4, 1891. Gould railroad difficulties: *Ibid.,* May 19, 26, November 24, 1883, March 1, July 12, 1884.

30. *Ibid.,* August 9, 1884, December 26, 1891.

31. *Ibid.,* January 27, February 24, April 21 (railroad map), May 5, 1883, May 10, 17, 24, 31, June 14, 28, 1884, January 10, April 25, 1885.

32. *Ibid.,* April 2, 1892.

33. *Ibid.,* June 2, 9, 1883.

34. *Live-Stock Indicator* (Kansas City, Mo.), July 3, 1884, September 24, October 1, 8, 1885, April 1, 1886; *Texas Live Stock Journal* (Fort Worth), January 26, 1884, July 3, 1886, April 23, 30, September 3, 1887; map of the railroad situation is in *ibid.,* October (special Panhandle edition), 1887; *Annual Reports of the Board of Directors of the Atchison, Topeka and Santa Fe Railroad Company, 1885–1887* (Boston, 1886–1888).

35. *Texas Live Stock and Farm Journal* (Fort Worth), June 17, 1892.

36. *Second Biennial Report of the Live-Stock Sanitary Commission of the State of Kansas, 1889–90* (Topeka, 1891).

37. *Texas Live Stock Journal* (Fort Worth), December 5, 12, 1891, April 16, 1892.

38. *Abilene Chronicle,* May 16, 1872, February 2, 1879; *Junction City Union,* March 1, 1879; *Chase County Leader* (Cottonwood Falls), February 11, 1886.

39. *Dickinson County Chronicle* (Abilene), March 24, 1882, Alioth ranch; *Chase County Leader* (Cottonwood Falls), May 27, 1886, S. A. Stephenson.

40. *Ibid.,* April 24, 1890.

41. *Chase County Republican* (Strong City), June 26, 1890.

42. *Chase County Leader* (Cottonwood Falls), August 8, 1901.

43. *Ibid.,* August 30, 1900.

44. *Cf.* A. D. Weber, "Problems in Leasing Blue Stem Grass," *Kansas Stockman* (Topeka), March 1, 1936; T. H. Lampe, *ibid.,* January 15, 1933, from *Livestock Leader.*

45. T. H. Lampe, "Blue Stem Grass," *Kansas Stockman* (Topeka), April 15, 1931, from *Livestock Leader.*

46. A. D. Weber, *loc. cit.*

47. *Daily Drover's Telegram* (Kansas City, Mo.), January 10, 12, April 18, 1911. Rental prices represent reports from Wabaunsee and Greenwood counties.

48. *Kansas Stockman* (Topeka), February 15, May 1, 1919.

49. *Ibid.,* January 15, August 1, 1919.

50. *Ibid.,* April 15, July 15, August 16, September 1, 15, 1920.

51. *Ibid.,* April 15, 1921.

52. *Ibid.,* April 1, 1922.

53. *Ibid.,* April 15, 1925.

54. *Ibid.,* April 15, 1927; *Kansas City* (Mo.) *Star,* February 13, 1929; *Kansas Stockman* (Topeka), March 15, 1929.

55. *Ibid.,* April 1, May 1, 1933.

56. *Kansas City* (Mo.) *Star,* April 15, 1937.

57. *Kansas City* (Mo.) *Times.* May 6, 1941.

58. *Stock, Farm and Home Weekly* (Kansas City, Mo), June 19, 1880.

59. *Dickinson County Chronicle* (Abilene), February 25, 1881.

60. *Kansas City* (Mo.) *Live-Stock Indicator,* July 24, 1884.

61. *Texas Live Stock Journal* (Fort Worth), November, 1886. An article based upon the report of Prof. George Veasey.

62. *Kansas City* (Mo.) *Live-Stock Indicator,* October 4, 1888.

63. *Kansas Stockman* (Topeka), October 15, 1937; *Cf.* Francis H. Arnold, "Conditions in Southwest," in *ibid.,* April 1, 1938.

64. *Ibid.,* July 1, 1938. *Cf.,* also, September 15, 1938. A similar thing happened in the short grass of the High Plains. The cactus menace was the subject of vigorous eradication measures. During the wet season of 1941 an apparent miracle happened, the cactus died out, in some regions almost completely, and in and around where each clump of cactus had been the buffalo grass and grama grass appeared in most vigorous condition, the cactus having served as protection and nurse crop to the new grass. The author made a tour of observation of these grasslands during the mid-summer of 1941. *Cf.,* also, *Topeka Daily Capital,* August 17, 1941.

The Russian thistle served much the same nurse crop function on both the grass lands and the fallow fields in the Great Plains region, the outcome being conspicuous in the summer of 1941. Old settlers told the author that the same thing occurred in connection with the restoration after the drought of the 1890s.

65. *Kansas Stockman* (Topeka), December 15, 1929, October 15, 1937, September 15, 1938.

66. *Cf.* Henry Rogler, "Pasture Situation in Kansas," in *ibid.,* April 1, 1938, covers some of these points.

67. Kling L. Anderson, "Deferred Grazing of Bluestem Pastures," *Bulletin* 291, Kansas Agricultural Experiment Station (Topeka: State Printing Plant, 1940). The introductory statements in this study are lacking in historical background and make assertions regarding carrying capacity which would be difficult to prove and which ignore weather cycles.

68. E. E. Dale, *The Range Cattle Industry* (Norman: University of Oklahoma Press, 1930), pp. 59, 60, and footnotes. Dale used Nimmo's figures as the most accurate.

69. *Wichita Eagle,* June 14, 1872. Not over twenty-five percent were beef cattle according to Dale, *The Range Cattle Industry,* p. 82. The analysis of herds and the disposition of driven cattle in part based upon the tenth U.S. Census, v. III, p. 21 cited by Dale.

# CHAPTER 11

# Rural Life & Subhumid Environment during the Decade of the Seventies

*"The Clean Shirt and Good Living"*

[The factor requirements for successful farm-making in the humid, timbered East in the 1870s differed from those in the subhumid, treeless plains. In the East the necessary raw materials were a "free gift of nature," available by human labor which had a very low opportunity cost. On the plains, by contrast, nature provided the land; everything else required for farming—building materials, fencing and fuel, water and sometimes even food—had to be imported from outside the region or produced by technology such as windmills that were manufactured elsewhere. To finance these capital requirements was the challenge of the plains farmer.

None faced a greater struggle than farmers in the transition region between humid and subhumid areas where yearly fluctuations in climate created a particularly sanguine and hardy folk. In this chapter Malin emphasizes the folk process of the evolution of winter wheat farming in the four-county locale between the bluestem-pasture lands in eastern Kansas and the central wheat belt to the west. Malin viewed this local case study, and others like it elsewhere in Kansas, as preliminary steps in the broader goal of writing a satisfactory history of agriculture for the state as a whole.]

In the presentation of the problem of adaptation of agriculture to a subhumid environment, the thought has been kept constantly in mind that a good case may be spoiled by claiming too much, by over-statement, and failure to make careful discrimination. Certain things are characteristic of all frontiers or of agriculture anywhere in temperate climates; others are peculiar to subhumid environments alone; still others affect both types of environments, but differently, being usable or convenient for living in the humid environment, but essentials to the subhumid environment to survive at all.

In the humid, timbered eastern portion of the continent the most substantial part of the necessities for the making of the farm home of the first pioneers was a free gift of nature, already on the ground, and available only at the cost of man's labor in utilization. The labor cost was heavy, and in consequence life was not idyllic, but time and labor did not cost money. There was little surplus produced for outside markets, but nature, with some encouragement, provided the means of transportation—livestock might be driven or commodities moved over waterways. In the subhumid region, however, nature supplied only the land, and allowing for the transition belt between humid and arid, man was required to provide all the materials and facilities by artificial (man devised) means, or mostly by importation from other regions, commodities and services which required out-of-pocket capital, and even though only in small amounts in each individual operation, the sum total was substantial. For dwelling purposes timber was imported from outside. For fences, after using for a time Osage orange hedge fences in the transition country, barbed wire was invented and imported from outside, and even posts had to be imported. Natural fuels were either negligible or were quickly exhausted, and dependence upon coal from outside was imperative. This accounts for the enthusiasm with which every indication of coal, however slight, was always exploited in the press. It meant the possibility of essential fuel and the elusive hope of industrial development to process commodities at home and to free the region from paying tribute to the outside world for all essentials. It is this that gives significance to the decision of Salina in 1889, so vehemently expressed after the failure of the industrial boom, that it was useless, with existing resources, to talk of manufacturers until the fuel question was solved. The Henry Oltman "coal bank" was ridiculed when urged as a new source of fuel—the editor spoke from experience in pointing out that about every five years for at least the last twenty this same "coal bank" had been promoted in a similar fashion—the development of fuel requirements called for capital not wind, he reminded his readers, and Salina should bore for gas or coal in hopes of locating an adequate fuel supply.[1]

As late as 1877 a Manhattan editor was discussing the question "What Shall We Burn?" in terms of wood and coal:

The indications are, that at no distant period, the denizens of Manhattan will discard the use of wood for fuel, almost altogether, and burn coal. To the great neglect of their fortunes, the farmers prefer to sit around the fire on stormy days, when any number of cold-looking men may be seen prancing around town, ready to sacrifice their last nickel for a load of wood. On a bright day, there is plenty of wood in town, but the average Manhattanite thinks he does not need wood just then, which leaves the disgusted countryman to stand around nearly all day, knocking his heels together, and swearing that he will be "gol dummed" if he ever brings another load of wood to town. The next stormy day finds the citizen trading off his wood stove for a coal burner and making a business call on Mr. Howard. This will be a good thing for promoting the growth of timber in this country, and the development of the mining interests. Many dislike the use of coal for cooking purposes, as it makes such a dirt; but ultimately the bulk of our coal will come from Colorado, which is free from dirt, hard and shiny, easy to kindle, and gives out a bright, clear, heat. Our hardware dealers report an increased sale of coal burners, and it will not be long before king coal will drive our present friend, wood, almost entirely from the market.[2]

The views expressed in Wichita on the relation of fuel and transportation were equally applicable throughout central Kansas:

Fuel is the great desideratum in this prairie country. Cheap fuel is an absolute necessity. What we want and what we must have is competition in coal. Canon City coal must come in competition with Cherokee and Missouri coal at every railway station in Kansas. Osage City dirt must not control the prices of coal in this state.[3]

Attention was called likewise to lumber rates which were fully as significant to the development of the Plains.

The subhumid environment meant fewer and fewer natural springs and streams such as had provided water in the humid climate. The conquest of the subhumid upland in particular was even more dependent, if it were possible, upon specialized machinery to make available an adequate supply of water than upon materials for housing and fuel. The drive well and pumps came first, and then the windmills, with the opening of the decade of the eighties. This substantial achievement of adjustment to a working basis was assured by the outlawing of the drive-well patent and the emergence of mass production of windmills at a price level low enough to be within the reach of the farmer.[4]

Large machines, drawn by horses at this state of development, were an essential, not merely a convenience, in subhumid agriculture. Soil must be worked quickly while moisture was sufficient and with a view to conserving what was available. Lower yields per acre and more frequent crop failures, particularly before experience had shown the way to greater certainty, enforced a cheaper per acre expenditure on crops and a larger acreage. The economic solution of that problem in production was to increase the machinery and horse power investment and reduce the labor charge, spreading the machinery cost over the larger number of acres which machines made practicable.

Capacity to produce its own food had been the test of the desirability of any country where measured in terms of traditional humid environment. Most of the staple vegetables, fruits, berries, and nuts upon which Americans had lived were native to humid climates. Only a few of them were adaptable to a subhumid region, and at successive points in the transition from the humid to the arid one plant after another passed the point critical to its survival. The occupation of the subhumid country was dependent, therefore, to varying degrees upon the outside for certain foods, that dependence being controlled by the degree of moisture deficiency and accompanying climatic factors. A traditional subsistence agriculture was not possible as a regular system, and in years of cash-crop failures, when subsistence was critical, these crops had usually already failed. They were conspicuously less drouth resistant than the field crops. A subsistence agriculture was not even available under these circumstances as a crop insurance. This emphasizes one of the most important deficiencies in environmental adjustment, inasmuch as most attention and the greater success has been associated with the cash crops and as yet relatively little intensive experiment has been devoted to such reserve subsistence food crops. Possibly the botanical world does not have plants with a sufficient range of adaptability to meet this challenge.

All these forms of equipment, supplies, and services could be furnished at a price cheap enough to permit development of the Plains only when the industrial East had reached a true mass-production basis with its resultant low cost per unit.[5] By the decade of the seventies this stage had not been fully attained, and the resultant costs were beyond the capacity of the West to finance successfully. It was that problem of meeting these cash capital costs that became another test of survival in the Plains environment.

During the early formative period of settlement successive new farmers brought cash which was spent in the community for improvements, current supplies, and subsistence until crops matured. The cash of these newcomers invested in land purchased from first hands, the government and railroads or non-resident investors, did not augment the community fund of capital. Land sales served this function only in commissions to local dealers and when land was held and transferred within the community by residents, especially to non-residents. The settler who sold out and moved on took his capital with him, his receipts being reflected locally only to the extent that he paid local debts as a result of receipt of new money. Capital advanced from the East to new purchasers on mortgages likewise was reflected only slightly in terms of the community pool of capital. Another important source of new cash was construction of railroads, private buildings, and public works and wages paid by business enterprises using outside resources. After a community reached a stage of relative stabilization many of these cash sources were cut off. Clearly the key to the capital problem was the production of a sure cash crop, and the volume of balance due to the East meant that the cash crop must be produced on large acreages per farmer and at the minimum of cash outlay per acre. Crop failures meant that the limited supplies of cash were soon absorbed in fixed charges payable in the East: interest, insurance, transportation, food. New capital imports ceased, new immigration fell off, land sales ceased or were made at forced sale at reduced prices, wiping out capital gains, the fruits of labor expended, and the increase in value attributable to community development. Cash transfers even within the community diminished or ceased— tax payments, wages, and salaries. The vicious cycle quickly brought destitution to all who were without substantial cash reserves, and most new settlers came with scarcely enough capital to meet expenses until the first crop should have matured. The settler with cash reserves sufficient to weather one or a series of adverse years might survive and prosper over a period of years. Emphatically, one key to survival was some means of subsistence together with a setting up of reserves that might serve as a sort of crop insurance to the rank and file.

Kansas climate was such that the inhabitants were kept constantly aware of it, only at some times more vividly than at others. The recognition of peculiarity which was so clearly in evidence among the first comers of the fifties and sixties persisted, but was tempered increasingly by the growing conviction that the climate was changing for the better. Thus there were two schools of thought, those who insisted there was no long time change and those who held the opposite, but with the climate-change sentiment in the majority in the seventies and particularly during the mid-eighties. T. C. Henry was in the former group. Others who have been less recognized were Professors E. M. Shelton and E. Gale of the agricultural college. Shelton's importance to the problem of agricultural adaptation has not been adequately appreciated in Kansas. He should be known for his work with livestock; grasses, especially alfalfa, and wheat. His realistic point of view is best expressed in his own words as showing his understanding of Kansas climate:

They argue that this is the way the thing is done in the East. Now, no eastern farmer can live in Kansas a couple of years without learning a good deal; but what he learns is as nothing compared with what he unlearns. I have got so far in this myself that I feel like commending from the first, any agricultural project of which it can be said "They don't do so in the East."[6]

T. Dunlap, a farmer in the Willowdale community, Dickinson County, summed up his conclusions on crop experience in 1881:

We have got to adapt ourselves to the country we are living in. There are several kinds of crops that we know will grow here in Kansas, one of them is sorghum or sugar cane, which grows right along through drouth, hot winds or grasshoppers, and will no doubt soon be a profitable crop for a farmer to raise. Another is the sweet potato which we had better raise pretty largely next year and let the potato bugs rest one year. Another crop that grows well here is peanuts, and still another is broom corn. While wheat, corn and hogs may be the leading crops, these other ones may be mixed in so as to help fill out the programme.

As dry as this season is it will not interfere with the cattle and sheep business.[7]

Gale's interpretation of climate as unchanging was presented in a convincing manner as the result of his study of tree rings from the timber of the Republican River valley and the vicinity of Manhattan. He formulated a tree ring calendar from 1760 showing growing years and unfavorable years concluding:

That for a period of one hundred and fifty years, at least, the wood growth of our native forests, in the variableness of its successive seasons, is almost a perfect repetition of what we have witnessed for the last twenty years... It remains for man, so far as he has the power, instead of indulging in quixotic dreams of cosmic revolutions, to counteract on the one hand unfavorable influences, and, on the other, make all possible provision for the contingencies of the climate. We may also come to the conclusion that it is not wise to infer, because we have enjoyed three or four bountiful years, that the order of nature has been changed, for the testimony of the forest is that there were years, long ago, just as fruitful, before the white man had come with his plow, and smoke, and electricity.[8]

Among those who believed climate was changing, the principal arguments were that the plow opened the soil to absorption and retention of moisture, that trees induced rainfall, and that rainfall followed civilization.[9] Wishful thinking fell in with this theory of the favorably changing climate just as political considerations during the nineteen thirties sponsored an opposite view of the effect of cultivation of the soil and presented it to the public in the government sponsored film "The Plow That Broke the Plains," and Tugwell's prediction that within 300 years the eastward march of the desert would bury St. Louis in oblivion under a blanket of sand—unless, of course his program was adopted.[10]

The periods of particularly unfavorable weather resulted in giving concentrated attention to adaptation problems. Periods of favorable weather meant a return to the customary procedures of the humid agriculture. With the next recurrence of a dry year the farmer was the victim of weather, unprepared to meet the emergency. This uncertainty makes the transition region between the definitely humid and the permanently subhumid areas the critical region which usually was harder hit in years of drouth than the less humid country which was committed exclusively to dry farming methods. In this respect it is clear that the transition country did not necessarily provide the means of a gradual process of achieving adaptation, and the most optimistic interpretation must recognize these limitations.

Neither the plainsman nor his climate can probably ever be understood by an easterner. In 1881 a review of the season recounted a succession of disasters, but concluded with the perennial note of hope:

The gloomy forecasts in respect to the wheat crop is more than justified by the daily returns of the threshing machines. Taking a fair view of the whole county, the yield of wheat will not reach half a crop. There is a wide diversity of success in different localities, but the above estimate is a safe average. The late spring, cold, frosty winds, excessive rains; burning, blighting winds; violent storm, and the vast army of chinch bugs, have all combined to destroy or diminish the wheat harvest; while the present excessive dry weather is playing sad havoc with the growing crops. This has been an extraordinary, and in many particulars a disastrous year. Cyclones, tornadoes, rain and hail storms combined with freshets, have been particularly destructive; the electric fluid has been the occasion of an unusual loss of human life; the intense cold of last winter has had a match in the excessive heat of this summer, and the hardship to man and beast has been uncommon and discouraging. But, on the whole, those of us who escape under these adverse circumstances with our lives, health, and a good share of our property, should feel grateful, and be prepared to forego the large crops we expected this year, and hope for better success in the years which are to follow.[11]

Another instance from 1880 formulated the "true philosophy" applicable to Kansas zephyrs which was characteristic:

The Kansas Zephyrs blew with unusual force on Monday and Tuesday, the wind being from the south. Real estate was lively, and a few persons were somewhat inclined to grumble. We have always felt friendly toward the zephyrs. We have enjoyed an immense amount of happiness by trying to look on the bright side of life—and especially upon the bright side of the sighing, singing, musical zephyrs. We prefer a bouyant, active and breezy atmosphere in Kansas, to the dark, rainy, dismal, muddy, chilling weather of other less favored States. This is the true philosophy, and every live Kansan ought to adopt it—and be happy.[12]

Such reactions were still characteristic of the Kansas Plains in the drouth decade of the nineteen thirties:

When God made Western Kansas, He held it in reserve for a great people. The conditions imposed try out men's souls as with fire. We are poor as the Lord Himself, was. We are buffeted with winds, burned out with drouth, pounded out with hail, froze out with wintry blasts, baked with summer heat, starved out by the grain gamblers and yet through it all, with faith in the future and a hope that next year conditions will be better, we spit on our hands, stiffen our backbones, give our overalls a hitch, smile at the hardships of life and tell the world that we are ready for whatever comes next.[13]

Some easterners are so unkind as to call this stupidity—plainsmen call it courage.

## Machinery and the Plains

The problems of machinery have appeared in numerous forms in the history of the Plains, but have not been interpreted adequately. The machinery costs were a frequent subject of complaint and controversy as has been seen in connection with the exchanges arising out of the "Golden Belt" episode of 1877, and T. C. Henry's recognition of the issue in his Farmers' Institute address of 1878. Walking plows were advertised at from $12 to $24; a sulky at about $60; and a binder at about $250. A country locals writer, in 1879, commented upon the number of binders being taken out by farmers to harvest a half-crop, which he argued could not more than pay for the interest on the machine.[14] Another reference was made to the problem in complimenting certain men who had bought a binder and had cut enough wheat for others, the first harvest, to pay for it:

There is a good deal of talk indulged in about buying machinery being the ruination of farmers, but we reckon it is bad management and not the machinery. Of course, if a fellow buys a costly machine merely to harvest a little dab of wheat for himself, and then leaves it out doors to the merciless weather, it will "get away with him," as it ought to.[15]

At this stage of developments there would seem to be no basis for charges of monopoly. Advertisements show that there were several lines of all types of implements available to the community and the larger dealers handled frequently two or more competing lines. The prices were high, but in the case of harvesting machines in particular, a rapid evolution was in progress from the self-rake reaper through the harvester, the wire binder to the twine binder, all in the course of approximately a decade. Most of these machines were experimental, inefficient, short-lived, and changes outmoded them even then they were not worn out from use. Many of the companies manufacturing such machines were inefficient, inadequately financed, mismanaged, or unscrupulous in sales methods, and farmers buying from them often lost most of their investment. Whether it is necessary or not, every new, important industry has gone through such an experimental mushroom stage of instability. The decade of the seventies was notoriously a period of inventive fertility and mechanical experimentation, and the user of the output was both the beneficiary as well as the victim of phenomenal, technological change.

In all parts of the country mechanization was in progress, but in the sub-humid West the environment tended to emphasize machinery as a means of producing money crops—something to ship out—to pay the balances chargeable against the region. The climate further emphasized machines, and for that era large machines, as a means of completing large scale operations rapidly while the necessary moisture was available; or harvesting rapidly to save large acreages of grain ripening at one time.

All of these new machines of the seventies were horse drawn, and the period marked substantially the passing of strictly hand operations and ox-power. This change extended largely to the practice of the operator riding the machine instead of walking. Of course, many could not afford to buy the more expensive riding equipment and many conservative farmers refused for years to accept the machines, but the younger generation came more and more to insist upon them. One comment in 1883 insisted that "the average Kansas granger don't propose to hoof it around his fields for any purpose if he can find a machine that will permit him to ride."[16] In corn growing one farmer compared 1877 with fifty years earlier. Then a farmer with two or three boys worked from sun-up to tend ten or twelve acres, but in 1877 with horse machinery one man alone could tend sixty to seventy acres and not go to the field until seven o'clock. And in special comment on a new cultivator he remarked that now all that was needed was a sun-shade of canvas over the driver. In some machinery advertisements even that deficiency was remedied.[17] An interesting instance of conservatism was supplied by a farmer who possibly did not plow his own corn: "We use the common walking cultivator, as we consider this the best, at least when boys and hired men are used as drivers."[18] Wheat growing was particularly adaptable to riding machinery. Corn growing still required hand harvesting, both husking and cutting, and no doubt that fact contributed to the attractions of wheat over corn farming.

During the early seventies oxen supplied much of the farm power used, but they were too slow-moving for successful operation of the new power machinery, and besides, saving of labor was only one of the reasons for these machines. One of the most compelling reasons for using such machinery in a subhumid environment was the necessity for speed in completing the job while conditions were favorable. Horses and mules were more satisfactory. Many horses were brought west by the wagon immigrants. Horses were driven in from Texas or other range states. Most of these were small, and a realistic survey of the size and quality of the horses casts grave doubt upon many of the claims made with respect to the depth of plowing practiced. Two and three-horse teams seem to have been the standard, and the patent three-horse evener salesmen, as well as lightening rod salesmen, appear to have been among the major rural pests of the late seventies. A sulky plow used three horses, a gang plow three or four, in the latter case probably tandem, the eight-hoe drill two horses, the eight-foot header two horses. As speed in completing operations was one of the most pressing factors in successful farming in the region, the fact must be recognized that even horse machinery in such sizes and pulled by such power fell far short of requirements for most efficient results.

The necessity for better horses was recognized. In 1876 they were being shipped in from Missouri. Later in the decade and in the early eighties emphasis was placed more and more conspicuously upon the breeding of Normans (Percheron), Shires, and Clydesdales; larger, fast stepping draft horses.[19]

In humid climates, title to and control of land was considered the essential of an agricultural system. In the desert, land is worthless without water and therefore control of water came to be accepted as the key to occupation of arid regions. If there is any one factor which occupies a similar place in the semi-arid country, it is dry-farming machinery—mechanization, through power machinery eventually, but at this stage, horse power. The only function of a generalization is to focus attention upon a controlling factor in a situation, and it is valid only to the degree to which it serves that purpose. It is not intended to mean that this factor of mechanization as applied to a semi-arid country is universal and without exception—only that it is both important and significant to an understanding of the basis of regional development of the Great Plains area.

## Marketing

In the subhumid interior region, without natural waterways, the railroad was essential to transportation. It was not, as in the humid country, merely a more efficient system. On the basis of wagon-train transport, commercial agriculture had been all but impossible. In its early stages, after the first rail lines were completed, the cost of service was only a little less expensive, so the great benefits anticipated by the first enthusiasm for railroads turned into disappointments. One of the early reactions to this outcome was the narrow-gauge boom for "the people's road," which crystallized in Kansas during 1871, continued through the mid-seventies and resulted in the building of the Leavenworth and Western on a route north of the Kansas river. There was only confusion as a result of this "craze" because another school of thought insisted that the combined influence of the narrow gauge agitation and the depression of 1873 discouraged the building of standard-gauge lines. This group insisted that cheap rail rates would come only through more railroads and competing lines. A third approach was the advocacy of governmental regulation.

The Union Pacific railroad had reached Junction City in 1866, and the first competing road by way of Emporia in 1870. This had brought the first reduction in rail rates, but the one town Junction City, the point of intersection, was the principal beneficiary. In 1875 the two roads came under the same control and rates were raised, to be reduced again only in 1879. In 1883 the inauguration of state regulation brought further reductions. Other factors were even more fundamental to the situation, however, in the increased efficiency resulting from the gradual change from iron to steel in railroad construction and equipment, making possible larger locomotives and cars, longer trains, and greater speed. A car of wheat in 1875 was said to be 340 bushels; in 1882, 400 bushels; and in 1883, 500 bushels.[20] In 1879 a train a half-mile long broke a record on the Kansas Pacific and consisted of 15 loaded and 58 empty cars, requiring two engines, one at either end, to move 102 miles in nine hours.[21]

**Table 11.1:** Freight Movements, 1869

|  |  | April (Pounds) | May (Pounds) | June (Pounds) |
|---|---|---|---|---|
| Salina | Forwarded | 44,417 | 48,211 | 312,302 |
|  | Received | 750,467 | 485,728 | 265,833 |
| Junction City | Forwarded | 881,282 | 933,947 | 919,088 |
|  | Received | 2,215,416 | 3,924,477 | 3,332,557 |
| Manhattan | Forwarded | 297,314 | 373,950 | 780,583 |
|  | Received | 554,260 | 486,293 | 490,982 |

Source: *Junction City Union,* 17 July 1869.

In a new country one of the first concerns of both the farmer and the railroad was something to ship out. Table 11.1 of incoming and outgoing freight at Salina, Junction City, and Manhattan during the spring months of 1869 emphasizes concretely the one-way nature of freight traffic and the fact that rates on incoming freight must pay largely the operating costs of trains both ways.

Of course a large commercial crop to be marketed in the East might balance or even reverse the account, but in any event such a condition must await the development of agriculture to surplus status unless some non-agricultural commodity might be produced to supply something to ship out. During the seventies prolonged general economic depression presented little demand in the East for western commodities of any kind. Contrary to the Texas cattle trade traditions, that business did not provide either a very large or consistent volume of business, and it was seasonal. Frequent crop failures did not insure uniform volume of outgoing freight even after the wheat boom had provided such traffic. The Kansas Pacific railroad was fully aware of the importance of the problem, and during the crop failure year of 1874, R. S. Elliott, its industrial agent, was investigating the possibilities for processing gypsum near Solomon City, but a profitable business was dependent upon eastern railroads giving Kansas the same rates as from Iowa to St. Louis. It was in this connection that the remark was made, "There is nothing so important to this country as finding something to ship out."[22] This comment had an application broader than the welfare of the railroad and one which was long recognized. The *Lawrence Republican* had discussed "the true basis" of prosperity in Kansas in 1859 in the following terms:

Frontier towns always enjoy a season of commercial sunshine not at all of their own creation. It is during the time when, from myriad avenues, there flows into the common centre streams of foreign wealth. It is the point in their existence when speculation is rife, when the fever of buying lots today for one hundred dollars and selling them for a profit of one hundred per cent to-morrow, runs highest—that time when much is fictitious and uncertain. But all this is temporary. The show of prosperity is there, but the sources of it are extraneous.

It is perfectly well settled that no place can rise to permanent importance without producing the elements of that importance within itself. The proposition may not hold invariably true with respect to large commercial emporiums, . . . though even in those instances there is in a limited sense a production of wealth growing out of their natural position and ability to meet the demand for that transfer of productions.[23]

The conclusion of the argument was an assertion of the necessity of manufacturing and especially the processing of local raw materials at home.

From the standpoint of transportation another aspect of marketing must be emphasized. The *Junction City Union* declared in 1869 that "our market is west; when it isn't right at the farmer's door." As respects the home market it was asserted:

For five years to come, every man who cultivates a farm can safely calculate on the fact that the new and neighboring settlers will gladly purchase his crop, and not even trouble him to hitch up his team.

As respects the markets west it was admitted that they were prospective because at the time the Junction City area was shipping in, not out. When the mills were improved so as to produce a superior flour, the prediction was made that the market would be in the West.[24] In 1874 the Fogarty mill was shipping flour to Texas, the next year to Mexico by way of Colorado, and for a number of years thereafter large shipments followed.[25] In this way processed products were contributing something to be shipped out, but only in years of good crops and even then such shipments as went west and south, by dividing the outgoing traffic, did not improve the east-bound freight situation.

As soon as the farmers of the valley began producing a substantial commercial surplus of grain, they were confronted with the newly developing agencies for marketing. Elevators were first established in connection with mills: at Junction City in the fall of 1874.[26] Two years later a public meeting was called to consider the building of an elevator, and the claim was made that a saving of five cents per bushel would result.[27] During 1876 five elevators were built in Dickinson County, one of them by the Grange.[28] During the following winter a storm of protest was raised against the requirement imposed by the railroad that all grain be shipped through elevators and this resulted in the building of a farmer's elevator at Salina.[29] Direct shipping by farmers was in operation again the next crop year and comparative risks of the different methods discussed in the background of sharply fluctuating grain markets.[30] Again in 1882 there were protests against the requirement that grain be shipped through elevators.[31] The farmer complained against the weight given by dealers at local shipping points for both grain and live-stock, and demanded installation of public scales.[32] Dealers had their grievances also against weights and shortages on cars shipped to terminal markets,[33] and against conditions existing at the Kansas City stock yards.[34] The fluctuation in local prices as repercussions from speculation on the futures markets was noted from time to time and the losses resulting to local dealers and farmers stimulated an interest in reports of agitation in the New York legislature to abolish futures trading.[35]

\* \* \*

## Size of Farms

Data are not readily available for a comparative statistical study of the number and size of farms in these four counties at different dates.[36] The federal census material for 1880 is summarized in table 11.2 for the four counties and for the state as a whole. Although the average in each of the counties is somewhat above the state average, it is not conspicuously so in any one, and is largest in the pasture county of Geary. It is regrettable that the size group 100–499 acres is not broken down into quarter, half-sections, and three-quarter farm-size groups, because the point that would be of particular interest is the number who would fall into the traditional quarter-section group. Attention should be called, however, to the number of 40-acre and 80-acre farms.

Table 11.2: Number and Size of Farms

| | Total No. | Under 3 | 3–9 | 10–19 | 20–49 | 50–99 | 100–499 | 500–999 | 1,000 plus | Ave. size |
|---|---|---|---|---|---|---|---|---|---|---|
| Geary (Davis) | 767 | — | 12 | 8 | 41 | 238 | 452 | 12 | 4 | 170 |
| Riley | 1,333 | — | 10 | 14 | 63 | 348 | 875 | 20 | 3 | 164 |
| Dickinson | 2,308 | — | 6 | 11 | 81 | 731 | 1,427 | 43 | 9 | 168 |
| Saline | 1,986 | — | 12 | 4 | 44 | 596 | 1,295 | 32 | 3 | 160 |
| State | 138,561 | 62 | 997 | 1,658 | 9,539 | 31,078 | 93,823 | 1,169 | 235 | 155 |

Source: *United States Census 1880*, 3:86–89.

Table 11.3: Buckeye Township: Number and Percentage of Farms by Size Group

| Farms (in Acres) | 1875 No. | 1875 % | 1880 No. | 1880 % | 1885 No. | 1885 % |
|---|---|---|---|---|---|---|
| 40 | 1 | 1.4 | 0 | 0 | 0 | 0 |
| 80 | 32 | 43.3 | 30 | 38.3 | 37 | 33.1 |
| 160 | 31 | 41.8 | 31 | 39.9 | 43 | 38.4 |
| 320 | 10 | 13.5 | 17 | 21.8 | 21 | 18.7 |
| 640+ | — | — | — | — | 10 | 8.9 |
| No data | — | — | — | — | 1 | .9 |
| Total | 74 | 100 | 78 | 100 | 112 | 100.0 |

Source: *United States Census 1880*, 3:86–89.

The results of a study of Buckeye Township, Dickinson County, are presented in table 11.3. These are based upon the manuscript federal and state
census returns, farm by farm for the years 1875, 1880, and 1885. The prevailing size of the farm units, based upon operation, not ownership, was
the eighties and quarter-sections. The increase in the total number of farms
of each group on account of more intensive settlement conceals the size
trend which becomes clear when reduced to percentages. The eighty and
the quarter-section sizes were on the decline throughout the decade, but
only at a slow rate, and at the end of the decade the larger sizes were only a
little more than one out of four. For practical purposes it can be said that
this county had been settled after the Civil War, the railroad serving it for
the first season in 1867, so this evolution of the land system to 1885 represents the situation approximately twenty years from first settlement.

A historical sketch of the Fairview School district, Dickinson County, in
1880 reported 35 owners in the three-mile square district (36 quarters),
seven farms called large were eunumerated; one of a section, one of 400
acres, and with slight variations five averaged half-sections, the remainder
being eighties and quarters.[37]

The fact of these prevailing sizes raises the question whether they were
sufficient for a family living, and whether the operators were satisfied that
these sizes were suitable. The reading of farm notes for the period leaves
the impression that few thought of the problem in terms of an ideal size. In
taking government land each took the largest size unit available under the
law, and in buying land the largest he could buy with the money available.
Few thought of the farm in terms of a permanent home, even for a lifetime
and probably none to be handed down from generation to generation in

the family, but rather as a speculation which would be improved and developed with a hope of a sale sooner or later at a profit. Not infrequently the successful farmer added land, and the purchase of 480 acres making a total of over 2,000 acres in one case drew the admiring comment, "He will have a farm yet."[38]

On two different occasions one rural correspondent did discuss explicitly the question of ideal farm sizes and adequacy of rural living. The first occasion was in 1879 in consequence of general discontent over a bad year. Farmer T. Dunlap wrote:

I have become satisfied that we as farmers of Dickinson county are trying to farm too much land. We must sell off part of our land, go on a smaller scale, and farm a good deal better. Farming has not paid very well this season as far as the wheat crop is concerned, but we must not depend wholly on wheat, nor on corn, hogs and wheat, but we ought to have . . . something to fall back on.

A farmer should not have any more land than he can make use of either for culture or for pasture, for the taxes will be a burden to him.

Admitting that farming does not pay every year, still I think the farmer is much better off than our loose men that are roaming around the country seeking for jobs and helping to create strikes.[39]

Two years later meant the accumulation of two severe years, and yet the same writer stood his ground:

What a country Kansas is for stock. And what a chance there is for the young man or the middle-aged man with a family, that has any desire to settle down on a farm, and is willing to work for a living, to secure himself a good home. For several weeks past I have been led to wonder at the "gold fever excitement," that has taken so many of our young men, and even married men, who leave their families behind them, off west to try and make a fortune in the mining country. A man with a family, with 160 acres of land in Dickinson county, (with a contented mind, and a will to work,) is far better off than the Astors or Vanderbilts, or even President Garfield, as far as the real substantial enjoyments of life is concerned. Why is it that men who have a competency, enough to make themselves and family comfortable, are not willing to "let well enough alone," but will sell out and risk all they have got in some new venture, and will in probably forty-nine cases out of fifty, come home strapped, broken down in constitution and in morals, to spend the remnant of their days in poverty and want.[40]

When T. C. Henry attacked the federal land system, advocating the repeal of the homestead and preemption and other acts, and insisted that 160 acres was not sufficient to support a family west of Fort Riley, J. W.

Robson came forward in defense of the land system and the quarter-section farm, half grass and half crop-land, as one on which a farmer could live in comfort and luxury.[41] In response to the *Topeka Commonwealth* commentary on his address, Henry withdrew his quarter-section farm statement as applied to Dickinson and similar counties. The *Atchison Champion* had insisted upon the adequacy of the quarter-section farm and the *Saline County Journal* had been more specific in defending the 80 and 160 acre farm in Saline County.[42]

In 1881 a descriptive picture was drawn of the statistically average Dickinson County farm based upon the assessor's rolls for the year. This imaginary farm consisted of 160 acres, grew 50 acres of wheat, 36 acres of corn, 1 acre of potatoes, 3 or 4 acres of other crops, kept 4 horses or mules, 7 or 8 head of cattle, 12 hogs, 6 sheep and had an orchard of 30 apple trees, 60 peach trees, 12 cherry trees, some plum and pear trees and raspberry, gooseberry and blackberry bushes, besides some grape vines.[43] This is the kind of farm that should have made Dunlap and Robson happy. There was an unreality in these discussions, however, which was already becoming evident in 1881, but a few years more were to teach many of these farmers in the school of stark reality. Robson called attention to the fact that "the range for stock is rapidly diminishing. Most of us who have been depending hitherto on the 'commons' adjoining our homes for pasturage, will soon have no commons."[44] This was an admission that undeveloped railroad and absentee-owned lands were serving an important function which was not candidly recognized by the land reformers who made outcry against land monopoly. Robson thought mistakenly that tame-grass culture would supply the pasture deficiency, but the sale of these raw lands and development by resident owners was gradually forcing an increase in farm size in self-defense and the squeezing out of the smaller farmers.[45]

A second factor injecting error into the statistical picture of farm sizes was the "sidewalk" and absentee farmers of whom there were an undetermined but substantial number in the region. As they did not maintain a farm establishment, but had all their farm work done on the contract system, their operations only serve to confuse the object of this discussion, which is the size of a self-maintaining farm unit best adapted to the environment and the requirements of the prevailing system of agriculture.[46] The picture was obscured further by the widespread conviction that climate was undergoing a change favorable for agriculture as practiced in humid climates. It was this factor more than any other that caused confusion between the two interpretations of the nature of the problem of the region—was it merely a new frontier like any other encountered in the westward march across the continent and therefore only experiencing much the same growing pains, or was it, not temporarily but permanently, a new environment to which adjustments must be made fundamentally different from anything heretofore experienced by the race? On many things the environmental view was accepted, but even where accepted for some things it was not consistently and logically applied to all aspects of the situation. The adjustment had to be arrived at the hard way by experience in each and every department, one place at a time.

By way of conclusion the fact should be stressed that there was clearly no popular demand for congress to change the laws relative to size of the farm unit under which government land was being distributed. Furthermore, it is evident that there was no general agreement in the region itself that a change in size was necessary to adapt more accurately to the requirements of subhumid environment. The conviction that the land laws were wrong in this respect did not become general until a later period, and any such conclusion changed with technological innovations, particularly mechanical power farming. It is equally evident also, that the rank and file of the farmers did not have the capital to invest in larger farms, and if they had acquired them, even under liberality of the land laws, they did not have the capital to meet the operating charges, especially machinery and horsepower on larger farms. The most intangible, but certainly not the least important factor in success anywhere commercial agriculture is practiced is that of managerial ability and business judgment. Some have it—a sort of sixth sense—some do not. Some can manage a large farm, some a small one, and others can farm excellently under capable and sympathetic direction. One is tempted to assume that the management factor is more critical to farming success in a subhumid environment than elsewhere, but possibly that cannot be proved. The question of the size of farm was much more, therefore, than that of size theoretically adequate to maintain a farm family in the subhumid environment. There could be no such absolute ideal size. There could be only successive practical adjustments by which men of limited resources, agricultural skill, and managerial ability could somehow make some kind of a living, sometimes out of crops produced, sometimes out of earned increment in land values realized through sales, and there were always many who failed.

## Turnover of Farm Operators

The populations of frontier communities were largely on the move.[47] Of the farm operators in Dickinson and Saline counties in 1865 only 43

Table 11.4: Buckeye Township, Dickinson County Turnover of Farm Operators, 1875–1940
(Upper Line, Italic: Number of Farm Operators; Lower Line, Arabic: Percentage)

| Base | 5 yrs. later | 10 yrs. later | 15 yrs. later | 20 yrs. later | 25 yrs. later | 30 yrs. later | 35 yrs. later | 40 yrs. later | 45 yrs. later | 50 yrs. later | 55 yrs. later | 60 yrs. later | 65 yrs. later |
|---|---|---|---|---|---|---|---|---|---|---|---|---|---|
| **1860** { *12** / 100* | *7** / 58.3* | *5** / 41.6* | | | | | | | | | | | |
| **1865** { *79** / 100* | *34** / 43* | | | | | | | | | | | | |
| **1870** | | | | | | | | | | | | | |
| **1875** { *73* / 100 | *42* / 57.5 | *32* / 43.8 | | *22* / 30.1 | | *13* / 17.8 | | *10* / 13.7 | *6* / 8.2 | *5* / 6.8 | *4* / 5.5 | *5* / 6.8 | *5* / 6.8 |
| **1880** { *79* / 100 | *46* / 58.2 | | *33* / 41.8 | | *18* / 22.8 | | *16* / 20.2 | *12* / 15.2 | *11* / 14.0 | *10* / 12.7 | *10* / 12.7 | *7* / 8.9 | |
| **1885** { *108* / 100 | | *47* / 43.5 | | *29* / 26.9 | | *21* / 19.4 | *19* / 17.6 | *19* / 17.6 | *15* / 13.9 | *15* / 13.9 | *13* / 12.0 | | |
| **1890** | | | | | | | | | | | | | |
| **1895** { *100* / 100 | | *38* / 38.0 | | *29* / 29.0 | *29* / 29.0 | *25* / 25.0 | *21* / 21.0 | *20* / 20.0 | *17* / 17.0 | | | | |
| **1900** | | | | | | | | | | | | | |
| **1905** { *100* / 100 | | *46* / 46.0 | | *37* / 37.0 | *35* / 35.0 | *29* / 29.0 | *26* / 26.0 | *21* / 21.0 | | | | | |
| **1910** | | | | | | | | | | | | | |
| **1915** { *130* / 100 | *83* / 63.8 | *62* / 47.7 | *51* / 39.2 | *46* / 35.4 | *36* / 27.7 | | | | | | | | |
| **1920** { *125* / 100 | *88* / 70.4 | *67* / 53.6 | *62* / 49.6 | *47* / 37.6 | | | | | | | | | |
| **1925** { *117* / 100 | *77* / 65.8 | *70* / 59.8 | *52* / 44.4 | | | | | | | | | | |
| **1930** { *104* / 100 | *75* / 72.1 | *57* / 54.8 | | | | | | | | | | | |
| **1935** { *111* / 100 | *68* / 61.3 | | | | | | | | | | | | |
| **1940** { *98* / 100 | | | | | | | | | | | | | |

*Whole county

**Table 11.5:** Walnut Township, Saline County Turnover of Farm Operators, 1875–1940
(Upper Line, Italic: Number of Farm Operators; Lower Line, Arabic: Percentage)

| | Base | 5 yrs. later | 10 yrs. later | 15 yrs. later | 20 yrs. later | 25 yrs. later | 30 yrs. later | 35 yrs. later | 40 yrs. later | 45 yrs. later | 50 yrs. later | 55 yrs. later | 60 yrs. later | 65 yrs. later |
|---|---|---|---|---|---|---|---|---|---|---|---|---|---|---|
| 1860 | | | | | | | | | | | | | | |
| 1865 | *70\** / 100\* | *30\** / 42.9\* | | | | | | | | | | | | |
| 1870 | | | | | | | | | | | | | | |
| 1875 | *70* / 100 | *39* / 55.7 | *32* / 45.7 | | | | *14* / 20.0 | | *13* / 18.6 | *7* / 10.0 | *8* / 11.4 | *7* / 10.0 | *6* / 8.6 | *5* / 7.1 |
| 1880 | *88* / 100 | *50* / 56.8 | | | | *20* / 22.7 | | *16* / 18.2 | *12* / 13.6 | *10* / 11.4 | *11* / 12.5 | *10* / 11.4 | *8* / 9.1 | |
| 1885 | *140* / 100 | | | | *35* / 25.0 | | *23* / 16.4 | *18* / 12.9 | *15* / 10.7 | *13* / 9.3 | *11* / 7.9 | *10* / 7.1 | | |
| 1890 | | | | | | | | | | | | | | |
| 1895 | | | | | | | | | | | | | | |
| 1900 | | | | | | | | | | | | | | |
| 1905 | *91* / 100 | | *42* / 46.2 | *37* / 40.7 | *29* / 31.9 | *25* / 27.5 | *23* / 25.3 | *20* / 22.0 | | | | | | |
| 1910 | | | | | | | | | | | | | | |
| 1915 | *104* / 100 | *59* / 56.7 | *44* / 42.3 | *41* / 39.4 | *35* / 33.7 | *31* / 29.8 | | | | | | | | |
| 1920 | *97* / 100 | *54* / 55.7 | *44* / 45.4 | *39* / 40.2 | *34* / 35.1 | | | | | | | | | |
| 1925 | *82* / 100 | *59* / 71.9 | *49* / 59.8 | *39* / 47.6 | | | | | | | | | | |
| 1930 | *82* / 100 | *59* / 71.9 | *41* / 50.0 | | | | | | | | | | | |
| 1935 | *94* / 100 | *60* / 63.8 | | | | | | | | | | | | |
| 1940 | *88* / 100 | | | | | | | | | | | | | |

\*Whole county

percent remained in those counties five years later. For the base years 1875 and later, the population turnover data have been compiled for a single township in each of these counties: Buckeye Township north of Abilene and Walnut Township south of Salina. Tables 11.4 and 11.5 give the numbers and percentages of those continuing in the township or represented by a male descendant. For the years from 1875 through the first quarter of the twentieth century there was not much change in the rate of turnover, but beginning in 1925 a high level of stability was attained. Note should be made of how little rather than how much the depression of 1930–40 and power farming undermined community stability in comparison with the depressions of pioneer periods. It was a very different thing to have 60 percent leave within five years as in the pioneer period and have 60 percent remain as in the last decade. The pioneer period was a time when there was a truly great body of migratory farmers, both in total numbers and in percentages of the whole number of farm operators. The press admitted that "a few people are going East, and some of their friends claim they are deserting the country. But like the raw recruit, 'they are only going to the rear to rally.' "[48] Such rapid turnover of farm operators in the pioneer period necessarily meant that the larger part of them were always new men inexperienced in farming in the new environment. As Shelton pointed out, they spent their first years unlearning what they thought they knew about farming. This could only retard adjustment and stabilization of agricultural practices and of community life. In the background of such rapid change in the composition of society, the remarkable thing is the degree of survival and continuity in the various activities of the community which depended upon the cooperation of the social group, schools, churches, granges, or other organizations.

As there were no census data on land tenure until 1880, there is little that can be drawn from that source. In 1880, of 79 farmers in Buckeye Township 71 were listed as owners and only 8 as tenants. After five years only 46 of these land owners remained and none of the tenants. Conclusions drawn from this single sample would be misleading, however, because in several other samples from other parts of the state the persistence of tenants in a community was approximately equal to owners, and samples have been found where the tenants were the more persistent portion of the farm population.[49]

The total number of farm operators in each of the townships under consideration fluctuated in cycles, reaching the high point in 1885, 1915, and 1935, and it will be noted from the tables that a great percentage of turnover always followed such extremes. Naturally there are several factors interrelated in these situations, but two considerations are of special significance. Instability was always higher among newcomers than among seasoned residents. The fact of the number increasing to a peak at these dates meant that replacements of new settlers had exceeded departures during the years preceding these dates. In other words, at such peaks the community was composed of a larger proportion of new and unadjusted settlers than at any other time. The second important factor is the reduction in the size of farms which necessarily resulted from increasing the number of farms in a given area. These two factors, new unadjusted settlers and small farms, added up to community instability. By contrast, in periods of depression when community replacements had been few, farm sizes increased, and land was in strong hands of seasoned residents, the turnover was relatively low.

The high rate of turnover of farm population together with the inefficiency of agricultural management suggest that there would not have been necessarily any virtue in stability. In view of the quality of so large a portion of the migrant farmers it was not a misfortune to a particular community that they quickly moved on. If their places were filled successfully by better quality, the exchanges were clear again. The community as a whole did develop, but there was probably little improvement in status of the individual farmer who moved on from place to place. Some who remained did not learn effectively the environmental adjustments necessary to success, and continuity in development rested substantially, therefore, upon the few who could lead in re-education of a succession of newcomers.

Whenever the unstable native American came into competition with the immigrant stock of Germans, Swedes, and Bohemians, the American lost out, and many of these newcomers to America were settling in the Kansas and Smoky Hill valleys during the decade. The American did not possess the tenacious love of the soil for its own sake that was so conspicuous among these European stocks. The histories of the land policies of the United States are replete with references to plans for providing land and a home to the poor actual settler as distinguished from the speculator. Such studies as this reveal, however, that actual settlers who were desirous of land upon which to establish a home for their lifetime and for their descendants to the first, second, and third generation were virtually nonexistent. With few exceptions, an American was always ready to sell at a profit in time of prosperity. In times of depression he frequently sold out on any terms from necessity or discouragement. Many moved to the towns. A vivid example of competition with the foreign stocks occurred in western Marion County when the Mennonites moved in and the railroad was built from Marion to McPherson providing for the founding of the new town of Hillsboro. The Risley Township locals reported, "About two thirds of the American population of Risley are talking of moving to the new town to go into business."[50] Much has been written about migrant American farmers, but historians have ignored the villages and small towns and the rate of mortality of business enterprises launched by these Americans who abandoned the soil, for whatever reason, for the even greater, but unknown hazards of the supposed rise in social and economic status attendant upon getting into some business in town.

## Pioneer Farming

The average quality and efficiency of farming operations necessarily fell far below the best that was theoretically possible under existing conditions, and the poorest must have been bad indeed. The *Manhattan Nationalist* quoted an unidentified Kansas exchange describing a type of farmer asking "How many Riley county farmers recognize themselves?"

He "houses" his farm implements in the corners of the fence; his fowls roost in trees during the storms of winter; his manure pile leaches into the roadside ditch, and, wiping his nose on his coat sleeve, he makes plaintive complaint that "farming don't pay."[51]

The fact that some farmers, possibly most of them, were always behind in their work, plowing for wheat and sowing wheat, is evident from the frequent comment in the press during the summer urging early plowing and sowing, and later recording late operations and then early in the spring the admission that some would not get their corn out in time to plant a new crop. One editor said, "These are the farmers who are fond of coming to town, sitting around in grocery stores, and complaining of the hard times."[52] Whatever may have been the reason, there was no exaggeration about husking corn in March, because country locals recorded such practice nearly every year there was a corn crop.

Admiration for Pennsylvania barns was the occasion for a plea for better farm management. Such barns were built on two levels, the lower floor for livestock and the upper for storage and some large enough to drive a team into and turn around:

Whenever Pennsylvania barns are seen all over our prairies, we shall not fear insect pests, or any other disaster, for our farmers will always have enough in store to tide a bad year.[53]

It was one thing to argue theoretically on how farming should be done, but it was quite another to do it at a profit with the facilities at hand. The adjustment to crop and tillage had not been fully accomplished; the type of managerial ability necessary to efficient farming was scarce in the type of migrant pioneer settler who constituted the rank and file of operators; and capital available to most was not adequate to finance land and machinery. There was no reasonable course open even to the best farmers, but to spend as little cash as possible under the uncertainties of pioneer agriculture and of climatic hazards. At a farmers' institute session at the agricultural college in 1881, the question was put explicitly whether it would not pay to adopt more expensive and scientific methods. Of course, the primary purpose of holding the institute at all was to encourage better farming, but Professor Fairchild met the query with a practical answer: "This [is] a question of time and place," and in making this reply he was not evading the issue.[54]

The more substantial type of citizen was impatiently desirous of a higher standard of living available to him only through more consistent profits which the agricultural techniques of the time were not yet capable of producing. Partial adjustments to environment had been accomplished, but in the opening years of the eighties more time must elapse for confirmation of the validity of those already under trial, and several major changes were yet to be introduced. Only then would there be justification for extensive capital investment in scientific farming and a reasonable expectation of success.

## Notes

1. *Saline County Journal* (Salina), February 7, 1889. Abilene claimed small quantities of gas and oil in the "city hole" at 300 feet. *Ibid.,* March 15, 1888. Halstead was prospecting for coal, gas, or salt on the theory that "it is certainly entirely within the bounds of reason to suppose that there is something under ground worth working for," *Halstead Independent,* October 12, 1888.

2. *Manhattan Enterprise,* January 24, 1877.

3. *Wichita Eagle,* February 21, 1884.

4. E. W. Hayter, "The Western Farmers and the Drivewell Patent," *Agricultural History* 16 (January, 1942): 16–28; *Manhattan Nationalist,* May 12, 1876; *Topeka Daily Commonwealth,* January 4, March 2, 1880; *Wichita Eagle,* April 1, 1880; *Wichita Beacon,* April 28, 1880.

5. Walter Prescott Webb, *The Great Plains* (Boston and New York: Houghton Mifflin Company), p. 271.

6. *Industrialist* (Manhattan), January 11, 1877, Lecture on "Grasses."

7. *Abilene Chronicle,* September 9, 1881. In other places Dunlap committed himself to the climate-change theory, but his statement here is significant as emphasizing the necessity of adaptation.

8. *Nationalist* (Manhattan), February 22, 1878. See Gale also in the *Nationalist,* February 24, 1881. A biographical sketch of Gale is found in the *Manhattan Enterprise,* September 27, 1878. Born in Vermont in 1824, educated to the ministry, he had been interested in horticulture and had lived in Kansas since 1864. Gale's construction and use of a tree-ring calendar in 1878 is interesting because such calendars are usually associated in the public mind with Dr. A. E. Douglas, for work published in the second quarter of the twentieth century.

9. "Civilization and Rain," *Lawrence Republican,* August 16, 1860. More seasonable climate, *Salina Herald,* October 20, 1877; Desert vanishing, *Atchison Champion,* quoted in the *Industrialist* (Manhattan), January 19, 1878, and in *Salina Herald,* April 12, 1879; Climate changes, 1874–1887, *Salina Journal,* July 14, 1887.

10. Speech delivered at Albany, May 15, 1935, A.P. report in *Kansas City* (Mo.) *Times,* May 16, 1935.

11. *Abilene Chronicle,* August 26, 1881.

12. *Abilene Gazette,* April 16, 1880.

13. *Greeley County News, Tribune,* quoted by the *Kansas Stockman* (Topeka), February 1, 1932.

14. *Marion County Record* (Marion), June 27, 1879.

15. *Ibid.,* July 20, 1883.

16. *Salina Herald,* March 29, 1883.

17. *Abilene Chronicle,* June 22, 1877. T. Dunlap, "Willowdale Items." The *Marion Record,* August 18, 1876, gives advertisements of sulky plows with umbrellas.

18. J. S. Foster, Jewell County in *Report of the Kansas State Board of Agriculture for the Quarter Ending March 31, 1887* (Topeka, 1887), p. 24.

19. *Saline County Journal* (Salina), July 13, 1876; *Junction City Union,* March 30, December 7, 1878; June 7, 1879; *Manhattan Nationalist,* May 7, 1880; February 24, 1881; *Abilene Gazette,* December 2, 1881; *Marion Record,* February 15, 29, 1884.

20. *Chase County Leader* (Cottonwood Falls), September 30, 1875; *Junction City Union,* July 22, 1882; *Marion Graphic,* February 2, 1883. It was not until 1889 that seventy-pound steel rails replaced the first light-weight steel rails on the Union Pacific (Kansas Pacific) main line up the Kansas Valley. *Junction City Union,* February 16, 1889.

21. *Saline County Journal* (Salina), February 20, 1879.

22. *Junction City Union,* July 18, 1874.

23. *Lawrence Republican,* April 14, 1859.

24. *Junction City Union,* September 11, 1869.

25. *Ibid.,* July 25, 1874; August 7, 1875; April 1, 1876; November 17, 1877; July 27, 1878; February 15, 1879.

26. *Ibid.,* September 5, 1874.

27. *Ibid.,* July 15, 1876.

28. *Abilene Chronicle,* January 12, 1877.

29. *Salina Herald,* December 23, 30, 1876; January 13, June 9, 1877.

30. *Ibid.,* November 3, 1877; January 25, 1879.

31. *Marion Record,* July 21, 1882.

32. *Abilene Chronicle,* March 24, 1882.

33. *Junction City Union,* October 22, 1881, based upon *Topeka Commonwealth* articles.

34. *Topeka* (Daily) *Commonwealth,* January 26, 31, 1882, in commentary on charges of the *Lawrence Journal.*

35. *Saline County Journal* (Salina), January 17, March 28, 1878. *Topeka Daily Commonwealth,* April 30, 1882.

36. The federal census for 1870 is seriously deficient. The author has not had available the trained clerical help nor the means of financing the necessary studies of whole counties based upon the state census data of 1875 and 1885. Only one township in Dickinson County has been given such treatment.

37. *Abilene Chronicle,* March 2, 1880. Possibly a part of the land belonging in farms of the district lay outside of the three-mile square.

38. *Abilene Chronicle,* March 7, 1879.

39. *Abilene Chronicle,* July 18, 1879.

40. *Abilene Chronicle,* June 3, 1881.

41. *Abilene Chronicle,* February 10, March 3, 1882.

42. *Topeka Daily Commonwealth,* February 4, 1882. *Saline County Journal,* February 16, 1882.

43. *Abilene Chronicle,* June 24, 1881.

44. *Abilene Chronicle,* May 13, 1881.

45. James C. Malin, "An Introduction to the History of the Bluestem-Pasture Region of Kansas," *Kansas Historical Quarterly* 11 (February 1942): 9, 12.

46. An unsigned article of 1879, *Atlantic Monthly* 44 (December 1879): 717–25, at p. 722, referring to south central Kansas, particularly along the Santa Fe railroad system, said some estimated that half the wheat was raised by the contract farmers. Probably this was an over-estimate, but conditions varied. There is no reason to believe that such a situation prevailed in Buckeye Township of the Fairview district of Dickinson County.

47. James C. Malin, "The Turnover of Farm Population in Kansas," *Kansas Historical Quarterly* 4 (November 1935): 339–72.

48. *Salina Herald,* May 10, 1883.

49. See "Land Tenure, Operator Turnover, and Farm Organization" (Chapter 19 below).

50. *Marion Record,* March 7, 1879.

51. *Manhattan Nationalist,* April 12, 1878.

52. *Salina Herald,* March 10, 1877.

53. *Saline County Journal,* March 7, 1878. Exchange.

54. *Manhattan Nationalist,* February 24, 1881.

# CHAPTER 12

# The Lower Missouri Valley

[Local history was James Malin's forte. In this essay, written for a popular audience, he has provided a concise statement of his ecological interpretation of history, in the context of the development of the Mississippi River Elbow region centered in Kansas City. In keeping with his methodology, Malin first carefully defines the region and its terrain, climate, soil, and plants. The historical development and particularly the technological innovations are then described within the ecological context from the beginning of white settlement into the modern era.]

The portion of the Lower Missouri Valley presented here as the Missouri River Elbow (having as its focus the metropolitan center of Greater Kansas City) is assigned the following boundaries (fig. 12.1): on the northeast the boundary lies along the channel of the ancient Missouri River from the vicinity of St. Joseph, Missouri, eastward to the present Grand River and thence southeastward to the present Missouri River, and thence down that river to Cooper County, whose county seat is Booneville. The southeastern boundary follows roughly a southwesterly course from Cooper County, skirting the Ozark region and passing through Jasper County and the corner of Kansas. In Oklahoma, "the Bluestem Bowl" sits upon the city of Tulsa as its base, the Frisco railroad through Vinita approximating its eastern side, and the Arkansas River its western side. The western

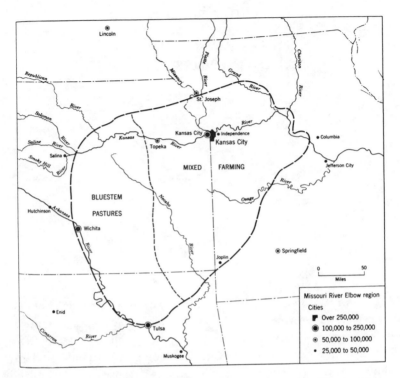

**Figure 12.1**: Missouri Elbow region. The Elbow region of the Lower Missouri Valley centers on Kansas City.

boundary of the Missouri River Elbow in Kansas lies approximately along the 97th meridian, the western edge of the Kansas Bluestem Pastures. The northern limit is the southern side of the northern tier of Kansas counties, the northern tier being primary commercial corn counties which belong to the western Corn Belt.

## Regional Delimitations

The basis for such a regional delimitation is multiple, and, of course, no two criteria determine boundaries that coincide exactly: bedrock, terrain, climate, vegetation, soils, agriculture, and the metropolitan influence of markets, trade, newspaper circulation, and the like of Greater Kansas City. In spite of the fact that such limits are necessarily zones rather than specific lines that can be surveyed, distinctiveness of character is conspicuous. The boundary that is least definite, in other words, the most arbitrary, is the northern.

## The Terrain

The surface geology of the area is relatively simple and uniform, the rocks being Pennsylvanian and Permian. The eastern limits of the outcrop of lower Pennsylvanian rocks lie along a line from Hannibal, Missouri, past the southeast corner of Kansas, which coincides closely with the southeastern boundary of the region. The western limits of the Permian rocks lie near the 97th meridian and west of the Flint Hills outcrop. To the north and south there are no distinct geological boundaries since the Pennsylvanian formations extend without interruption into Iowa and Oklahoma except that glacial drift completely covers the north. The Permian rocks disappear near the Nebraska line but extend into Oklahoma. The glacial drift covering the Pennsylvanian and Permian rocks at the north, however, has been removed largely by erosion as far northward as the boundary of the region.[1]

Physiographically the area is part of the Central Lowlands of the Mississippi valley, bounded on the southeast by the Ozark Plateaus of the Interior Highlands and on the west by the Great Plains Border province, whose eastern boundary is not yet well established on the maps although it lies near the Permian-Cretaceous geological boundary.[2] The Central Lowlands lie in a northeast-southwest direction without a physical northern or southern boundary so far as the Elbow region is concerned.

In detail, according to Branson's classification for Missouri, the Missouri portion of the Elbow area south of the Missouri River is Old Plains and, north of the same stream, Old Plains modified by glaciation. The old Missouri Grand River, northern boundary for the Elbow region, is relatively arbitrary except for the degree of erosion of the glacial drift cover. In Kansas, according to Schoewe, the Osage Plains occupy the major part of the area, corresponding to Branson's Old Plains, and the dissected glacial till plains occupy the whole of the portion north of the Kansas River, penetrating slightly south of that stream, and correspond to Branson's Old Plains modified by glaciation. The western boundary of the Osage Plains lies near the Permian-Cretaceous boundary.[3]

The elevation of the country along the western border of the Elbow is between 1,200 and 1,300 feet above sea level; but at Kansas City, Kansas, it is 771 feet; at Jefferson City, Missouri, 730 feet; at Coffeyville, Kansas, 730 feet; and at Tulsa, Oklahoma, 698 feet.[4] The surface slopes east and southeast, although the dip of the underlying rock strata is west and northwest. The topography is rolling, and in some parts the hills are substantial, but there is little of the area that is level in the sense in which easterners traditionally think of Kansas, and to them the geographers' term *plains* as applying to the area is often misleading.

## Climatic Conditions

The annual average rainfall for northern Missouri, north of the Ozark plateaus, diminishes northwestward from 42 to 32 inches at the northwest corner of Missouri, and, in Kansas, from the same position, northwestward and westward from 42 to 30 inches near the 97th meridian. As in other parts of the area between the Mississippi River and the Rocky Mountains, the rainy season is the spring and early summer months.[5]

The average number of hours of sunshine daily during the summer months, June–August, is 10.5–11, and for the winter months, December–February, 5.5–6, whereas the average annual number of clear days is between 140 and 160 and the average annual number of cloudy days is 80–100.[6] In all instances, the eastern and western regional boundary corresponds closely with the specified limits of the daily sunshine, clear days, and cloudy days. The average growing season in western Missouri is 180 days, and in southeastern Kansas 186 days, diminishing to the northwestward to 178 days.[7]

## Native Vegetation

From the standpoint of vegetation, the Missouri River Elbow is prairie. At the eastern and southeastern edges, the forest was relatively dense, but, westward toward the Missouri state line, the grassland became conspicuous. The story is told that the county seat of Jackson County, Missouri, where Kansas City developed, was to have been located in the center of the county, which at that time also included what is now Cass, Bates, and part of Vernon counties. Independence was chosen, not because it was at the geographical center, but because it was at the center of the westernmost body of dense timber in western Missouri. Typical forest men made the decision! In eastern Kansas, grass predominated, and timber occurred only along the streams, diminishing in quantity and quality and changing in composition of species to the westward. The Missouri–Eastern Kansas trees were deciduous hardwoods, oak, hickory, and walnut predominating. Near Fort Riley and Council Grove, Kansas, occurred the last of these species, either of quality or quantity, which indicated rather sharply a vegetational boundary at or near the 97th meridian. The native grasses were the bluestems (*Andropogon* spp.), Big and Little, side-oat-grama, and associated grasses and herbs of the typical tall-grass prairie.[8] These extended to the Fort Riley–Council Grove line, west of which the short grasses of the plains mingled conspicuously with the tall grasses in the mixed-grass prairie.[9]

## Soils

The entire Elbow lies east of Marbut's solum line dividing pedalfer (acid) from pedocal (alkaline) soils, the line running irregularly from a point just west of the 97th meridian at the northern boundary of Kansas to a point near 98° 20′ on the southern boundary. All the soils within the region are northern prairie soils, according to Marbut, except near the southern limits where the transition to southern prairie soils occurs. Southern prairie soils penetrate from Oklahoma well up the Verdigris valley into Kansas. In Missouri the Ozark Highland boundary marks the southern limit of the prairie soils.[10] According to Marbut, the only areas of the Elbow with normal soil profiles are those north of the Kansas River in Kansas and north of the Missouri River in Missouri. Approximately the western half of the Bluestem Pastures has soils with imperfectly developed profiles. The rest of eastern Kansas, south of the Kansas River, and the Missouri portion south of the Missouri River are classed as soils with claypan.

According to the local Missouri soil classification, the Marshall silt loam, Wabash and Knox silt loams group, and the Cherokee, Oswego, and Bates group comprise almost exactly the glaciated portion of the Elbow region. The soils along the northwestern border of the Ozark Highlands are Cherokee, Oswego, and Bates. They are of relatively lower fertility, the Bates soils having a more friable subsoil. The soil region along both sides of the Missouri River is dominantly Marshall silt loam, with Wabash soils in the bottoms except for Knox silt loams, a wind-laid soil most prominent in Platte and Buchanan counties, close to the Missouri River. "All things considered, this (soil) region contains the most productive soils of the state.[11]

## Regional Patterns

Without too great a stretch of the imagination, orientation of the Missouri River Elbow may be thought of as an ellipse whose axis runs northeast–southwest, Kansas City occupying the eastern focus. Within the region similar elliptical patterns of behavior prevail, whether of trade territory or college-student distribution. People do not move far to the west, north, or south for any purpose but face relatively long distances northeastward or eastward. In a real sense in everything but topography, the area faces northeast or east, utilizing communication lines by way of Chicago and St. Louis. This generalization applies primarily, however, to the era of railroads, because the earlier river communications faced east and southeast, focusing on New Orleans. Roughly the historical dividing date between water and rail communications is the decade of the 1860s. But probably that is getting ahead of the story.

*Political Antecedents*

While the western valley of the Mississippi River was under the dominion of France, St. Louis was founded in 1764 by men interested in the fur trade. With the purchase of Louisiana by the United States, the French leadership continued for a time but was partly displaced by Anglo-Americans. French trading posts were established on the Charitan, the Grand, the Missouri (in the vicinity of Kansas City and at St. Joseph) and on the Kansas rivers, and the French settlement in the Kansas City area became a permanent component of that town's early population. The admission of Missouri as a state in the Union occurred in 1821, at which time white population had not yet reached the western line of the new state. Indian title in western Missouri, north of the Missouri River, was extinguished in 1815, and south of the river in 1808 except for a 25-mile strip along the western boundary which continued in Indian hands until 1825. White settlements were made in the counties west of Jefferson City as the Indian frontier retreated: Saline County in 1810, Cooper County in 1812, Lafayette County in 1815, Carroll and Ray counties, north of the river, in 1816, Clay County in 1819, and, south of the river, Jackson County after 1825. Lexington, Liberty, Independence, Westport, and Kansas arose as county seat or commercial towns. In 1837, the Platte Purchase added the northwest counties to Missouri and steered settlement in that direction. In the late 1850s, the southwestern counties along the border were settled, paralleling the development of the Territory of Kansas.

The Indian country, west of Missouri, was organized by the Act of May 30, 1854, under the name of Nebraska and Kansas, and within the first two years settlement moved in from the northeast by way of the Missouri River boundary at that point, up the Kansas River as far as Manhattan and Junction City, and into the upper Neosho River valley to Council Grove. The presidential campaign of 1856 and the Kansas Civil War marked the close of the first phase, and then settlement pushed into southeastern Kansas facing the Missouri border, and the border conflict of 1857–1860 followed. The population was predominantly antislavery and anti-Negro from the Ohio Valley and from border states farther east. Rivalries among the towns of Leavenworth, Atchison, Lawrence, and Wyandot were gradually resolved by the rise of Kansas City, Missouri, and eventually of Greater Kansas City, which included Kansas City, Missouri, Kansas City, Kansas, and several satellite towns. According to the United States Census for 1950, Metropolitan Kansas City covered 1,662 square miles in 4 counties and contained 814,357 people.

The early population of Missouri was predominantly from Kentucky and Tennessee, and local institutions reflected that fact. The population of early Kansas was predominantly of closely related origins, the antislavery and anti-Negro elements of the Ohio Valley and the border states farther east. Many eastern Kansas county seats, built around a public square, rather than along a main street, reflect the same cultural heritage, as well as the fact that the criminal code of Kansas was based upon that of Missouri, which was based upon that of Kentucky, which in turn was derived largely from Virginia. The Kansas constitution of 1859 was modeled, however, largely upon the Ohio institution, and Kansas was admitted to the Union January 29, 1861.[12]

## Agriculture

Agriculturally, the Missouri River Elbow lies at transitional crossroads, both east–west and north–south. In the mid-latitudes its southern boundary lies near the line where traditionally cotton and corn meet, but it would be more accurate to say where wheat and cotton meet, because corn is the common crop primary to both areas. In the east-west orientation the tall-grass prairie was transitional between the Corn Belt proper and the Winter Wheat region. Corn is predominant among field crops for the area as a whole, but to a diminishing extent westward. Missouri has 24 of the 77 commercial corn counties as designated by the United States Department of Agriculture for corn production controls in the Elbow, and Kansas has 21 of 33. In Missouri the cash-grain areas, especially wheat, occupy the river bottoms where the soil is more easily worked in the fall than in the spring. The uplands farms are meat-production type based upon mixed agriculture. In eastern Kansas, the three eastern tiers of counties are mixed farming areas with a strong emphasis on dairying in the counties tributary to urbanized areas. The wheat varieties grown were soft winter wheats until after World War II, when a new variety of hard winter wheat, Pawnee, became available. Since then a rapid shift has been in progress.

Specialty farming consists of the growing of vegetables, fruits, potatoes, and tobacco. Tobacco growing, mostly in Missouri, has the longest history and dates from the time of slave labor. Modern tobacco culture in Missouri is concentrated primarily in the one county of Platte and centers upon the auction market at Weston, the only market west of the Mississippi River. Platte County had 3,013 acres of Missouri's 5,700 acres of tobacco in 1949. The dominant type is white Burley. Mechanization has been extended to the setting of the plants and to cultivation. Part of the Missouri crop is sold at the Weston auction, and part is trucked to Kentucky markets, especially to Lexington.

In Missouri, the commercial potato crop is limited largely to a small area in Ray County. In Kansas, the Kaw Valley potato area lies mostly north of the Kansas (Kaw) River between Topeka and Kansas City. The Missouri potato acreage allotment for 1950 was 3,200 acres and for Kansas 2,600 acres. This is small compared with 120,400 acres in Maine and 130,300 acres in Idaho but it provides early maturity.

Before the turn of the century, commercial fruit production had occupied a substantial place in the agriculture of the area. Competition among other local crops and with fruits of other specialized commercial regions, made accessible through cheap transportation and changing public taste in fruits, had reduced all or even extinguished some branches of the business. Apple orchards had been extensive at points along the Kansas River and on both sides of the Missouri River until the second decade of the twentieth century. Only a few had survived in Kansas by mid-century at most favored points, and relatively more in Missouri. The extreme drought of the 1930s and severe winters took further toll in both states. After World War II, new insecticides which produced clean apples with 12 to 18 applications per season and new marketing organization brought some revival in Missouri; however, it would be premature to generalize on this promising revival.

Soil conservation became an issue. Soil analysis, terracing, contour farming, rotation, planting of legumes, treatments with minerals, and the like were emphasized in both states, and the stories of rehabilitation of individual farms were given special emphasis in farm publications as case histories which would encourage others to undertake similar operations. In certain parts of southeastern Kansas where soils were derived from shales, there are deficiencies in trace elements. In 1949, the state opened an experiment station in that area to test the effects of feeds grown on these soils upon livestock and to experiment with the special problems involved in their utilization.

## Livestock Raising

The Elbow is historic as a livestock-breeding area, especially for beef cattle, serving both the specialized requirements of the Corn Belt and of the short-grass plains to the west. Colonel William A. Harris had built a Shorthorn herd of national significance at Linwood, Kansas, in the 1880s. He was one of the national leaders among Shorthorn men in importing the Scotch, or Cruikshank, strain, which displaced the fashionable Bates and Booth strains. Charles Gudgell and Thomas Alexander Simpson, of Independence, Missouri, during the same decade, had led in importation of Aberdeen-Angus cattle, but their greatest fame rests upon the importation in 1882 of Anxiety IV, the greatest Hereford bull of them all. With this and other distinguished Hereford strains, that breed came to dominate the western range cattle industry to the extent of more than three-fourths of all range cattle from the Rio Grande River northward into Canada. The Robert H. Hazlett herd at El Dorado, Kansas, founded in 1898 and dispersed in 1937 after the owner's death, was another of the most influential Hereford herds of America. Near Kansas City, Missouri, the Sni-a-Bar farms of William Rockhill Nelson of the *Kansas City Star* specialized in Shorthorn cattle and agricultural experimentation. The Sni-a-Bar farm was sold by the Nelson estate in 1945 after the expiration of the 30-year provision of the founder's will that the program of the farm be carried on.

Dairying in the Elbow was of lesser importance, relatively, until after World War I, when a major shift came in dietary habits of the nation as well as rapid urbanization of the region. In 1949, 30 Missouri and Kansas counties constituted the milkshed of the Kansas City metropolitan area with a sales volume of $50,000,000 each year and 500,000 quarts of milk daily, 99 percent of which is pasteurized. The relatively small city of Lawrence, Kansas, with a population over 15,000, draws more than 14,000 quarts of grade A milk daily from a 6-county milkshed. Other cities are somewhat comparable.

Kansas City is the home of the American Royal Livestock Show, held annually in the fall. The Royal had its beginnings in 1898. The American Royal Building constructed in 1922 was burned and rebuilt in 1923. The show specializes in meat animals, and entries are made by individual exhibitors. In 1949, the American Royal Dairy Show was launched as an annual event. The exhibits are by districts into which the 4-state area, Missouri, Kansas, Oklahoma, Arkansas, was divided, and the selections in each breed are made competitively within each district. The Hereford Breeders Association maintains its offices at Kansas City.

The unique feature of the livestock industry of the Elbow is the Bluestem Pastures area (fig. 12.1) near the western edge of the tall-grass country. It is an area of hill topography, consisting mostly of limestone outcrops with much sandstone exposed toward the south end. This country has been left mostly in native grass, dominantly bluestems, but with other grasses sharing the vegetational cover.[13] One result of the cattle drives from Texas in the 1870s was the discovery that cattle fattened on northern grass. After the rail era intervened, cattle were shipped north or northeast from Texas and the Southwest to be grass-fattened before they were put on the markets. The procedure became well standardized after cattle-tick controls had been established, and since World War I the standard contracts call for pasture leases to run for 6 months from April 1 to October 1. The cattle may be pastured by the ranch owner or by buyers who assume the risk, or they may be purchased outright by pasture owners. The annual in-movement begins about April 1 and is completed by the end of May. The out-movement begins in July, reaches its peak late in August or early September, and the pastures are empty by October 1. The destinations vary. Some go directly to the slaughter market as grass-fat beef, others are sold to Corn Belt feeders for full-finishing, whereas younger cattle may be held over for maturity to be grass-fattened or corn-fed the following summer.

Lease prices vary with the season and the quality of the pasture. The prices for 1949 were the highest in 25 years of record. In the Kansas Bluestem Pastures, leases for cows and steers varied from $12.00 to $17.00 per head for the season with an average of $14.50, whereas for young cattle they were from $8.00 to $12.00, averaging around $10.20 per head. In the Oklahoma Bluestem Bowl, or Osage Pastures, prices were from $10.00 to $15.00, averaging $12.50, and from $8.00 to $10.00, averaging $9.00 per head, for the respective classes. The acreage guarantees per head vary also with the quality of the pastures. In Kansas, for 1949, they were from 3.5 to 6.5 acres per head for cows and steers and from 2.5 to 4.5 acres for young cattle. In Oklahoma, the figures were from 5 to 7 and from 4 to 6, respectively. The in-movement of cattle in 1949 for the whole Bluestem Pasture area of the two states was 351,000 head, compared with 379,000 in 1948, 377,000 in 1947, and a 10-year average (1938–1947) of 321,000 head. The in-movement for the Kansas Bluestem Pastures separately in 1949 was 308,000 cattle and calves, compared with 332,000 in 1948, and 332,000 in 1947. The 10-year average (1938–1947) was 260,000 head. The Osage Pastures received 43,000 head in 1949, compared with 47,000 in 1948 and 45,000 in 1947. The 10-year average (1938–1947) was 61,000 head. Neither the national nor the historical significance of the Bluestem Pastures in the role of beef production is adequately appreciated. Both the number of animals and especially the volume of prime beef handled annually through these pastures as a permanent system are far greater than the volume involved in the sensationally pictured but ephemeral long drives of the 1870s to Abilene and to Dodge City.[14]

## Kansas City, the Nucleus

In its beginnings Kansas City was founded upon merchant functions in relation to communications. Kansas City as a primary assembling point gathered commodities to be forwarded that were the natural products of its trade territory. Consumption goods from the East were forwarded in exchange. As the Indian and wildlife were displaced by white civilization, similar basic functions were still performed; only the nature of the articles was different. In order to perform the functions more effectively upon a larger scale, organized markets, including warehousing and commission houses, the stockyards and livestock exchange, and the elevators and Board of Trade were set up. To these were added as a new function the processing of the major products of the trade territory, the milling of grain, and the packing of meat products.

With the rise of the Texas cattle trade, the railroads as livestock carriers built stockyards at Kansas City in 1868. In 1871, the Kansas City Stockyards Company was organized, and the specialized functions of the business were separated from the railroad business. The original 18-acre tract had a reputed capacity of 15,000 cattle and 4,000 hogs. In 1848, the yards covered 242 acres in the two states with a daily capacity of 175,000 animals. The livestock interests built a Livestock Exchange Building in 1876 to accommodate commission houses and banking facilities, and in 1886 the Livestock Exchange was organized. Although pork packing had begun in 1858, beef packing did not begin until 1868. By the mid-twentieth century, Kansas City ranked second in the United States as a livestock and meat-packing center. Even under the influence of tractor and truck, Kansas City remains the principal market for horses and Missouri mules, which became famous during Santa Fe Trail days.

The first grain elevator in Kansas City dates from 1871, but any substantial grain surpluses were not available for shipment out of the county until the big soft-winter-wheat crop of 1875 in central Kansas. The next year the Board of Trade was reorganized, a call board authorized, and an exchange building begun. By the 1940s, elevator capacity was 61,632,000 bushels, mostly located on the Kansas side of the line, and Kansas City was the primary hard-winter-wheat market and milling center and held first rank as a cash-grain market.

Dehydration of alfalfa began in Kansas in 1933 with one plant in the southeastern district and reached its peak in 1948. In 1949, the eastern third of the state operated 37 plants using 47 units. Soybean processing began in Kansas at Emporia in 1941, and with one exception at Wichita, the 6 plants in operation in 1950 are in the eastern third of the state at Hiawatha, Emporia, Fredonia, Coffeyville, and Girard. Big production of soybeans in Kansas began with World War II: 1941, 540,000 bushels; 1942, 2,438,000 bushels; and 1949, 3,436,000 bushels.

As a wholesale center Kansas City early became the leading city between St. Louis and the Rocky Mountains. By the second decade of the twentieth century, it became necessary to share this trade with Salina, Hutchinson, Wichita, Enid, Tulsa, and Oklahoma City.

## Fuels and Energy

The energy requirements of the area are supplied by coal, oil, gas, and water since hydroelectric power produced within the area is negligible. The Pennsylvanian rocks underlie most of the area with their eastern limits close to the eastern boundary of the Missouri River Elbow. Although coal occurs in several horizons, the best quality comes from the Cherokee shales near the bottom of the series in Missouri, Kansas, and Oklahoma. In Missouri, 86 per cent comes from two beds, which are mined at several points in the three states. The westernmost Kansas field is the Osage coal, which occurs near the top of the Pennsylvanian series. The Santa Fe railroad built its first section of road from Topeka southward to Carbondale in 1869 to exploit this coal for railroad fuel. Thus, from the beginning, the Santa Fe was a coal-burning road. Coal mining in Missouri and Kansas is mostly by the strip method, although some is mined by drifting and deep shaft. Domestic coal needs are supplied mostly from Arkansas semi-anthracite. Large quantities of Eastern coal are used for various purposes. Railroads are the largest users of coal from this area, but other large users include steam electric power plants and manufacturing industries. None use good coking coal. The high point of 7,561,947 tons of coal produced in Kansas in 1918 was reduced to about 3,000,000 tons annually in the late 1940s, although large quantities of coal are still available as reserves. Since World War I, coal has become much less important relatively than oil and gas. Cooperative research under the auspices of Federal and State governments and the coal producers is developing methods of producing synthetic fuel at Louisiana, Missouri, and gas by burning coal in the mine at Hume, Missouri. The resulting gas is to be used for fuel and other purposes aboveground. Among other things, these substitutes for mined coal would by-pass the labor union exactions from the coal industry.

Drilling for oil in Kansas began in 1860, within the year after the Drake well in Pennsylvania was brought in. Although both oil and gas were soon found, the supply was not in major quantities. The first major gas discovery was at Iola in December, 1893, but big production did not come until later. The first long-distance pipe line from the south-central Kansas fields reached the Kansas River and the Missouri River cities in the winter of 1905–1906. Big production of oil was still later, in 1914 and 1917 in the El Dorado field. Between World Wars I and II, the pipe-line distribution system from the southwestern fields to the great population centers north and east of Kansas City made that city an important center. After World War II, additional pipe lines for both oil and gas were completed. With reliable supplies of oil and gas for domestic and industrial fuel, coal consumption was sharply curtailed. The first major change-over occurred after World War I as a result of the prolonged coal strikes, and more rapid conversion took place after World War II for similar reasons.

## Manufacturing

Manufacturing in the Elbow region, which began with the processing of forest and agricultural commodities produced in the area, consisted of meat packing, flour milling, and furniture manufacturing. The furniture industry still draws largely from the walnut lumber of the area for veneer. Of the mineral production, the only metals are lead and zinc of the tri-state fields of Missouri, Kansas, and Oklahoma. In the competition of postwar economic conditions, the mining and smelting of these metals is distinctly marginal, and in early 1950 the industry was closed down for a time. The clay-products industry boomed in the last years of the nineteenth century and the first quarter of the twentieth century, when vitrified brick became a favorite paving material for city streets and for highways for a short time after World War I. Hollow tile for building purposes provided another expanding branch of the business. The Portland cement boom of 1905–1910 launched another big business, which came into its own with Federal highway construction and the expanding use of concrete in building of all kinds.

Repeatedly, but without marked success, the towns of the Elbow region attempted to launch manufacturing enterprises other than processing of agricultural and forest commodities and clay products and cement for local consumption. Although the automobile industry established assembly plants, the major approach to heavy industry was the Sheffield Steel Corporation in 1925, which grew out of the Kansas City Bolt and Nut Company established in 1888 during the boom of the 1880s. The sole source of raw material for this steel enterprise in the early stages was scrap collected from the Kansas City trade territory. In 1930, Sheffield Steel became a subsidiary of the American Rolling Mills Company, and a program of expansion carried it to St. Louis, Tulsa, and Houston. With World War II, the Defense Plant Corporation built a blast furnace and coke oven on the Houston ship channel, which Sheffield leased for war production and in January, 1949, bought together with the iron ore fields at Jacksonville and Linden, Texas, and coal properties in the McAllister, Oklahoma, area. Thus the present steel plant at Kansas City occupies an important position in the Southwest and in the Armco steel family.

World War II and the shifting of war industry into the interior of the continent seemed to be the great opportunity for the Missouri River Elbow region. It did bring a number of new war plants into the area and provided the means for expansion of small industries already in production. The Darby interests in Kansas City, Kansas, built LCT and LCM boats. New defense plants in the area were the Lake City Ordnance plant in Missouri, the Sunflower and the Jayhawk Ordnance plants in Kansas, the North American Bomber plant, and the Pratt and Whitney Engine plant near Kansas City. Some of these facilities were continued in operation under conversion to peacetime industries. The Jayhawk Ordnance plant near Pittsburg was operated by the Spencer Chemical Company, an offshoot of the Pittsburg and Midway Coal Mining Company, who bought it after the war and expanded it into a major member of the chemical industry of the United States. Among other things, it is the second largest producer of synthetic ammonia from natural gas.

Efforts to share in war industries brought home the significance of research in science and technology to small businesses not able to finance their own research facilities. An estimate of the figure that businessmen of the 6-state area of Missouri, Kansas, Nebraska, Iowa, Oklahoma, and

Arkansas were spending for eastern aid was set at $200,000 annually. In 1943, the solution of this fundamental aspect of business competition was sought by the incorporation of the Midwest Research Institute at Kansas City. As a supplement to the research institute, the Linda Hall Library, which was already devoted to science and technology, achieved an added significance.

## Communication

Missouri River navigation afforded the historic basis for the communication system of the Elbow region. Although the steamboats employed in the early days were self-contained common carriers, they gave way quickly to railroads as soon as reasonably efficient service was available after the Civil War. The tradition of cheap water transport did not pass, however, with the steamboat. In Kansas City, a movement developed between 1872 and 1875 that culminated in the creation of a corporation to operate barges propelled by towboats. The unit no longer was the self-contained steamboat, but a combination of a power boat and one or more cargo barges. Although the experiment failed, a contemporary observer urged further experiment with new designs in equipment. In 1949, the experiment in new designs was still going on with its following of hopeful believers in cheap water transport.

The Missouri early gained an unenviable reputation as an unpredictable, unmanageable stream.[15] The story of attempts to secure channel improvements is long and tedious. Under the stimulus of the breakdown of the national transportation system during the crisis of World War I, Congress made a declaration of policy relative to rails and water, which was incorporated into section 500 of the Transportation Act of 1920: "to foster and preserve in full vigor both rail and water transportation." A comprehensive plan for the whole Mississippi River system was formulated, and preliminary work was begun on the Missouri as far as Kansas City during the later 1920s. The goal of a 9-foot channel from St. Louis to Kansas City and Sioux City was set. Work was curtailed during the war decade of the 1940s, and by 1950 the goal had not been reached. The Federal Barge Lines began operating on the Missouri River in 1936, but the service was restricted. In February, 1948, the newest river equipment, an integrated tow, the *Harry S. Truman,* christened at New Orleans by Miss Margaret Truman, was given a trial. It is built in two units separated by barges. The bow or lead unit is spoon-shaped, and the driving unit at the rear pushes the combination. It is powered by two 1,600-hp Diesel engines which operate two 9-foot propellers.[16] A speed of 7 mph was claimed against a 6-mph current. The full capacity was 9 barges, about a 1,200-foot tow, with a capacity of almost 12,000 tons. Because of the sharp bends of the Missouri River, only 4 barges were used on the trial run, creating a 620-foot tow drawing 7½ feet of water. On the return trip with 153,832 bushels of wheat, one or more barges dragged bottom, three broke loose, and one hit an abutment of the Liberty Bridge 15 miles downstream from Kansas City and sank. One of the largest upstream cargos was a 4-barge tow of 2,000 tons of steel from the Pittsburgh area by the *Franklin D. Roosevelt* in 1949. Steel was brought up to Kansas City from the Chicago area also by way of the Illinois and the Missouri rivers.

By the second quarter of the twentieth century, Greater Kansas City as a communications center had arrived—a rail, highway, and air center. Twelve major railroads serve the area. The so-called transcontinental railroads from the Atlantic and Pacific coasts to the interior meet along two north–south axes, roughly the Mississippi and the Missouri rivers. Thus some eastern lines end at St. Louis, and others extend through Kansas City. Similarly some western lines end at Kansas City and others at St. Louis or Chicago. The double-hinge or overlapping of these systems is particularly significant to the rail service afforded to the Missouri Elbow region at the geographical center of the United States. Kansas has 5 rail lines west to Denver and the Rocky Mountains, 4 lines east to St. Louis, 7 lines northeast to Chicago, 3 lines north to the Twin Cities, 2 lines to Memphis and the southeast, and 4 lines south to the Gulf of Mexico, which is the shortest haul to salt water. To handle this traffic, Kansas City completed its new Union Station (Jarvis Hunt, architect) and Terminal in 1914 on a scale large enough to absorb expansion. After World War II, the Santa Fe and Rock Island railroads built new "hump yards" to speed up sorting and switching of cars. The Santa Fe applied for the right of entry into St. Louis, which was denied by the Interstate Commerce Commission. However, in 1949, the Burlington was granted a more direct freight line between these cities as well as the right to shorten its line from Kansas City to Chicago.

The land transportation system would be incomplete without mention of highway service by 14 bus lines and by more than 100 truck lines.

The position of the Elbow region as almost the geographic center of the United States gave it significance in the air age. In 1927, the Kansas City, Missouri, Municipal Airport was dedicated, and across the river in the opposite bend was the Fairfax Airport of Kansas City, Kansas. Finally, in 1943, the Grandview Airport south of the city was completed. The Municipal Airport is the commercial operating center of air travel for 5 lines, and the Fairfax Airport is the overhaul base of Trans World Airlines, the United States Air Force having been transferred from Fairfax to the Naval Airbase at Olathe in 1950. The postwar reorganization of the national air defense system in 1948 brought the Strategic Air Command headquarters to Omaha. Two units of the command are based at Topeka, and the operating commands are based at Fort Worth, Texas, and Colorado Springs. It is the function of the SAC to be able to strike from this central axis of the United States with heavy bombers at objectives in any direction throughout the globe.

The Missouri River Elbow is well supplied with educational institutions. The University of Missouri at Columbia is at the eastern edge, Kansas State College of Agriculture at Manhattan is at the western edge, and the University of Kansas occupies a central position at Lawrence. Other state schools are the teachers colleges in Kansas at Emporia and Pittsburg and in Missouri at Warrensburg, and Washburn Municipal University at Topeka. Besides these, there are the University óf Kansas City, the junior colleges of both the Kansas Cities and of several smaller cities, as well as a number of colleges under the auspices of the several churches. The major art center of

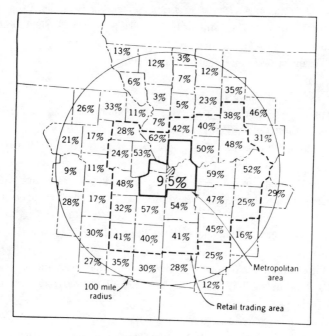

**Figure 12.2:** Circulation of the *Kansas City Star.* Percentage of households by counties that subscribed to the evening edition of the *Kansas City Star,* 1952.

the area is the William Rockhill Nelson Gallery of Art and Atkins Museum, which was formally opened in 1933.

The Elbow region is essentially a one-newspaper area. That paper is the *Kansas City Times–Star (Morning Times, Evening Star)*, which was made dominant by William Rockhill Nelson (1841–1915). Although other cities have their papers, no other has the intensive coverage of the *Star* for the area in question (fig. 12.2).

In 1950, Kansas City celebrated its Centennial as a chartered town, and the State of Kansas celebrated its one-hundredth anniversary of territorial organization in 1954 and will celebrate 100 years of statehood in 1961. The span of a century tends to emphasize the fact that the entire culture of the region has been developed within the lifetime of three generations, grandparents to grandchildren. Although other people have sometimes called it by different names, the region has called itself "the heart of America."

## Notes

1. Walter H. Schoewe, "The Geography of Kansas, Part II, Physical Geography," *Transactions of the Kansas Academy of Science* 52 (September 1949), fig. 12, p. 262.

2. John C. Frye and Ada Swineford, "The Plains Border Physiographic Section," *Transactions of the Kansas Academy of Science* 52 (1949): 71–81.

3. E. B. Branson, *Geology of Missouri* (1944), p. 350, map on p. 352. Schoewe, *op. cit.*, fig. 22, p. 276.

4. Schoewe, *op. cit.*, table 11, pp. 277–79.

5. J. A. Hodges and others, "Types of Farming in Kansas," *Kansas Agricultural Experiment Station Bulletin*, no. 251, August 1930, fig. 19, p. 24.

6. S. D. Flora, "Climate of Kansas," *Report of the Kansas State Board of Agriculture*, vol. 67, no. 285 (June 1948).

7. C. H. Hammar and others, "Types of Farming in Missouri," *Missouri Agricultural Experiment Station Research Bulletin*, no. 284 (October 1947) 3d ed., fig. 24, p. 45; Hodges, fig. 21, p. 27.

8. J. E. Weaver and T. J. Fitzpatrick, "The Prairie," *Ecological Monographs*, vol. 4, no. 2 (April 1934).

9. James C. Malin, *The Grassland of North America*, chapters 7 and 9.

10. C. F. Marbut, "Soils of the United States, Part III," *Atlas of American Agriculture* (1935), plate 2.

11. Hammar, *op. cit.*, pp. 31–39.

12. J. C. Malin, *John Brown and the Legend of Fifty-six*, chapters 25 and 30; *Grassland Historical Studies*, vol 1, Geology and Geography.

13. Weaver and Fitzpatrick, *op. cit.* This is the best ecological study that is applicable to most of the area.

14. James C. Malin, "Introduction to the History of the Bluestem Pastures Region of Kansas," *Kansas Historical Quarterly* 11 (1942): 3–28.

15. Flood control problems were enmeshed in the total plans for the whole Missouri River valley which include diking and straightening of the Missouri itself, control of floods, soil conservation, and hydroelectric power production on the Grande, the Osage, and the Kansas tributaries. Opponents of large dams, especially those large enough for power production, charged that the costs were excessive for the benefits to be derived not only in money but in agricultural acreage flooded, forests destroyed, and coal deposits inundated. These opponents argued that soil conservation and flood control could be accomplished more effectively in other ways. Meanwhile Federal power agencies were extending the coverage of government-financed cooperatives in the distribution of electricity throughout northwestern Missouri and in February, 1950, made the largest loan ever granted by the Rural Electric Administration for a 257-mile transmission system and a steam-generating plant near Missouri City, the whole to be linked with the Southwestern Power Administration to permit exchange of excess power. The private utilities protested that they had been supplying adequately and economically the power requirements of the cooperatives in question.

16. Others on the river are 6 or 6½ feet in diameter. In contrast some of the early steamboats on the river were designed to draw less than 20 inches of water.

CHAPTER 13

# Kansas: Some Reflections
# on Culture Inheritance
# & Originality

[Was Kansas a child of New England? In this sprightly essay, James Malin answers this perennial question in his characteristically oblique manner by describing the factors of ecology, demography, and technology that shaped Kansas culture in the nineteenth century. Population characteristics and the coming of railroads are singled out as key ingredients in the construction of Kansas society, but the powerful influences of legends and myths, many of them false, are not overlooked. Malin's approach is true to his dictum that historical research must encompass "the complete relatedness of all the facts" in a situation as they "*act* simultaneously."]

## Introduction

The purpose of this chapter is too complex to express adequately in any simple title. The first assumption essential to an orientation upon the subject matter is that of culture as defined by the cultural anthropologist—the way of life as a whole of any people. In this case the geographical setting or area in which that culture developed is Kansas, whose boundaries are completely artificial, except for the short river section at the northeastern corner, which may or may not be considered a natural boundary. The concept of culture deals with men and what they did in their geographical area with properties of the earth which they were able to make available to their use. A sharp distinction must be observed between determinism and factors that merely influence history. In no sense is determinism admissible to the history of this culture and area during its one century plus as space partitioned according to existing arbitrary lines. A natural resource has its origin in an idea held by men, and in the cultural technology men use to bring the properties of the geographical area into the horizon of utilization. Thus natural resources depend upon the inventive genius of men and are inexhaustible, unless men's minds become exhausted.

## Kansas as a Geographical Area

Kansas as a geographical area is an accident of politics, or possibly, a consequence of a series of accidents. Its boundaries have not made sense according to any frame of reference based upon tangible facts and logical conclusions drawn from facts. For many reasons the eastern boundary would lie more appropriately about fifty miles east of its historical position, but repeated attempts to effect even modest adjustments were futile. In terms of types of farming, the northern tier of counties has belonged to the Nebraska corn belt. On the other hand, however, serious consideration was given at least twice to proposals for the annexation to Kansas of that part of Nebraska that lies south of the Platte River. Several plausible, if not sound, reasons were advanced for such a change. But many Kansans objected that the area in question contained too many Democrats. The southern boundary line was bungled on account of the slavery prohibition, the Indian barrier, and misunderstanding about Indian reservation limits. The territory of Kansas extended to the Rocky Mountains, but for peculiar reasons, when Kansas became a state, Kansans voluntarily restricted themselves to the country east of 102° west longitude. The foregoing citations applied to Kansas limits in relation to other states and territories, but still other boundary schemes referred primarily or only to internal matters. Numerous proposals were made to divide Kansas either into an East and West Kansas, or into a North and South Kansas. But tangible facts and logic made little headway against emotional attachments to the combinations of historical traditions associated with a geographical area and its people.

Subsequent to Lincoln's dictum of 4 July 1861, denying the sacredness of a state, so-called state government in the nation was restricted by successive assumptions of power on the part of the central government until all true self-government disappeared. The vestiges of state structure survived, to be sure, but as little more than administrative agencies of the central authority. Yet, the symbols and legends of state sovereignty survived, so far as they had any meaning, and were filled in by each generation and social group according to the subjective need of the hour. In states other than Kansas, each in its own peculiar character, the people behaved in a similar fashion. Persistent always, however, was an overriding loyalty to the symbols and legends embodied in its traditions. Few, and Kansas was not among them, were willing to discard even their antiquated constitutions.

## Kansas in an Ecological Perspective

Plant and animal life of Kansas necessarily is that of mid-latitudes regardless of whether or not "native," in the popular pre-Columbian discovery sense, or introduced by recent European man. Thus the species and varieties of life found in the area represent those peculiarly adapted to such a geographical habitat, as well as outliers of those most specifically adapted to the high and low latitudes. In this latter sense, Kansas lies in a transition zone, or a belt of overlapping margins of dispersion patterns occupied by marginal species of life forms. In this belt, the more distinctly northern and southern life forms meet and intermingle.

The Kansas area is transitional also in its east-west variations of both diminishing moisture and rising elevation to the westward. Thus such species as lie in the fringes of optimal environment, both in a north-south and an east-west orientation, represent elements of unusual risk as pertains to survival in relation to the short-term fluctuations of weather and other hazards.

Kansas is situated in the central portion of the North American grassland. In its mid-latitude position, between the Platte River on the north and the Canadian-Arkansas rivers on the south, both the east-west zoning and the north-south zoning of life forms are more sharply differentiated than in any other part of the grassland. This is particularly conspicuous as relates to the east-west orientation. The true forest country lies to the east, and the true moist-desert to the west.

## Kansas according to Primitive Peoples

In this area called Kansas the occupancy by primitive peoples who had attained a Folsom-type culture dates from about ten thousand years ago. Within some two thousand years of the present, later primitive cultures had invaded the area from the desert southwest, from the forested southeast, and from the woodlands of the continent east of the Mississippi River.

Probably these invasions occurred more than once. If so, this central grass-land was long a meeting ground where an intermingling of cultures occurred. Individual village sites reveal to the archeologist successive periods of occupance, in some cases, interrupted by periods of apparent abandonment in which the site was covered by several inches of wind-blown material. Thus the dust storms of the grass country, and of major proportions, are demonstrated to have occurred long before Europeans appeared on the scene. For several centuries prior to the modern European discovery of the western world, the Great Plains as well as the prairie was occupied by people living in villages and dependent largely upon agricul-ture for food supply, but supplemented by wild game. These were the peoples who were displaced by European culture within the four centuries usually labeled modern history and documented by written records. In this perspective it would not be unexpected if resemblances occurred in some of the patterns of behavior of European man in America.

## European-American Forest Culture in the Grassland

In the process of displacing an occupying Indian population and of resettling the area with men of European-American culture, each of the invading people was a unique individual and new to the area. He brought with him his peculiar personality and his cultural heritage. By the experience of living together, diverse elements were blended into a new culture. Even people coming from the same eastern state brought variants of their unique localities. Differences, not likeness, were the rule. Railroads within land-mass interiors had not exercised extensively their leveling effects until late in the nineteenth century. These points are more than commonplaces and have usually been lost from view. More attractive have been the over-simplified generalizations about Puritan, slaveholder, aboli-tionist, northerner, southerner, Republican, Democrat, etc.

The high degree of mobility of population poses problems for the consideration of the historian. To what extent did first comers determine or impose a pattern of culture that would survive in spite of a rapid turnover of population? To be more specific, do the political institutions once estab-lished mold the culture regardless of the changing population that imple-ments them? Stated in opposite extremes, did the changing population modify and direct the functional operation of the institutions regardless of their origin and their first institutional form as established in Kansas? If the answer rejects both extremes, may the pragmatic adjustments be deter-mined quantitatively, or only subjectively?

**Table 13.1:** Sources of Kansas Population in 1860

| | | |
|---|---|---|
| New England | 3.9% | |
| Northern tier of states west of New England | 8.4 | |
| Iowa | 3.7 | |
| *Total, northern states* | | *16.0%* |
| Lower South | | 13.5 |
| Border states east of Appalachian Mountains, north | 6.5 | |
| Border states north of Ohio River | 28.8 | |
| *Total northern border* | | *35.3* |
| Border states east of Appalachian Mountains, south | 5.0 | |
| Border states south of Ohio River | 8.5 | |
| *Total southern border* | | *13.5* |
| Missouri | | 10.6 |
| Total border states | | 59.5 |
| Foreign-born | | 11.8 |

The sources of Kansas population (107,209), according to the federal census of 1860, assigned to states of birth are shown in Table 13.1.

The first generalization to be made from these figures is both the absolute and relative statistical unimportance of the New England contribution, 3.9% of the whole. The contribution of the strictly northern states' 16% is only slightly larger than the lower south's 13.5%. Clearly, the border states peopled Kansas, and most conspicuous as a group were the three Ohio Valley states north of the river of that name: Ohio, Indiana, and Illinois, totaling 28.8%. A special explanation is in order about that group of states. They had been peopled largely from south of the river and south of the Mason-Dixon line. A conspicuous culture trait is critical to this discussion. Although they were antislavery in sentiment, they were even more pronounced anti-Negro. So far as generalization can be accurate in the matter, they tended to take a position that the only way in which Negroes would be tolerated among them was as slaves—but emphatically, they did not want Negroes, either free or slave. The seeming paradox involved in this situation is that people sometimes found themselves to be antislavery and proslavery at one and the same time. A similar generalization holds largely for the population of all border states, including Missouri, except that possibly after 1850 the balance turned in Ohio. It is only in this context that the position of Missouri can be reinterpreted in accordance with facts. Missouri was not so much interested in slavery as such as in being embarrassed by a large free Negro population. In this context also, Missouri's interest in making Kansas a slave state is intelligible.

The peopling of Kansas by the border states was decisive, therefore, in giving the free white-state point of view an overwhelming majority. In December 1855, in adopting the Topeka state constitution, the free-state party voted separately on the Negro question and by a vote of three to one decided to exclude free Negroes from the state if admitted under that instrument. The Wyandotte state constitution of 1859 incorporated a modified white-state proviso in restricting participation in political affairs to white men. This position was confirmed by popular vote twice after the Civil War, and Negro suffrage came to Kansas only with the fifteenth amendment to the federal constitution. Racial integration in the public schools of Topeka came only in 1954 in consequence of a ruling of the United States Supreme Court. The basic culture trait had a way of persisting in spite of the legends about John Brown, and the relation of Kansas to the American Civil War and the abolition of slavery.

As a whole, the Wyandotte constitution had been derived primarily from the Ohio constitution of 1850 as a model. The civil code of the territory adopted by the first free-state territorial legislature (1858) and continued thereafter under statehood was based also upon that of Ohio. The criminal code, however, followed a different pattern, being based upon the Missouri code, which in turn reached back to Kentucky and Virginia. In view of the course of Kansas territorial history and the prolonged war on the "Bogus" legislatures of 1855 and 1857 and their laws, this adoption of the Missouri criminal code in 1858 and its continuance was one of the most remarkable occurrences of the territorial controversy.

The foregoing population analyses and interpretations of culture traits and institutions are related to the census of 1860 and state beginnings. Analyses of successive census enumerations of 1870 and later, national and state, reveal a migration pattern that was little different. Thus the original culture traits were reinforced by people similarly oriented. In other words, the original culture pattern as registered in 1860 did not necessarily determine the attitude for the next century. The major additions to the population only continued in the basic pattern. But this whole situation, additions to population—and losses—requires further consideration in its own right, featuring population structure and the meaning of mobility.

The quantitative extent of population change and of turnover is little appreciated and must be given explicit formulation as a preliminary to further discussion. From the table of population (Table 13.2) the increase of numbers between 1860 and 1870 should be noted. If every person listed in 1860 were still present, 257,193 new residents were listed, or more than $2\frac{1}{3}$ times the number present in 1860. In other words, of every ten persons

Table 13.2: Kansas Population, 1860–1950

| | Total | Increase over Preceding Decade | |
|---|---|---|---|
| Year | Population | Number | % |
| 1860 | 107,206 | | |
| 1865 | 135,807 | | |
| 1870 | 364,399 | 257,193 | 239.9 |
| 1875 | 528,349 | | |
| 1880 | 996,096 | 631,697 | 173.4 |
| 1885 | 1,268,530 | | |
| 1888 | 1,518,552 | | |
| 1890 | 1,428,108 | 432,012 | 43.4 |
| 1895 | 1,334,734 | | |
| 1900 | 1,470,495 | 42,386 | 3.0 |
| 1905 | 1,455,968 | | |
| 1910 | 1,690,949 | 220,454 | 15.0 |
| 1915 | | | |
| 1920 | 1,769,257 | 78,308 | 4.6 |
| 1925 | | | |
| 1930 | 1,880,999 | 111,742 | 6.3 |
| 1940 | 1,801,028 | 79,971 | |
| 1950 | 1,905,299 | 104,271 | |

present in 1870, seven would be newcomers. In 1880, with almost one million present, 631,697 or 173% had been added after 1870. Or, of every eleven present in 1880, seven were newcomers. Comparing 1880 with 1860, in the same manner, of every nine persons present in 1880, eight were new. So far as numbers were concerned, the old settlers of 1860 would appear to be a relatively insignificant proportion. For example, if measured by votes in the ballot box, they would seem to be negligible. But these figures tell only a small fraction of the story.

The mobility of population was fundamental to the changing structure of the society, and this subject has received scarcely any consideration. Materials are available for such research, but the task is formidable, and no overall attempt has been made to undertake it.

I have made studies of the turnover of farm operators, using selected townships and county samples. This procedure was most revealing, but necessarily had its limitations. By comparing the farm operators of 1860 as a base year, name by name, with the subsequent census enumerations it was possible to determine who and how many persisted in their residence in the particular township or county at the subsequent enumeration dates. Where both state and federal manuscript census records were available, this means the comparisons were at five-year intervals. Otherwise at ten-year intervals. The heavy losses occurred during the first five or ten years, the rate of loss being reduced later until a lapse of about twenty years when the list of persistent individuals or a family representative became relatively stable. In eastern Kansas a loss of 60% during the first ten years was

Table 13.3: Kansas Population, 1885

| Population: | State total | 1,268,530 |
|---|---|---|
| | Native-born | 1,135,855 |
| | Foreign-born | 132,675 |

| *Born in* | | *Where from to Kansas* | |
|---|---|---|---|
| Kansas | 336,344 | Kansas | 330,057 |
| Illinois | 134,703 | Illinois | 194,089 |
| Ohio | 112,323 | Missouri | 136,729 |
| Indiana | 100,271 | Iowa | 109,067 |
| Missouri | 76,777 | Indiana | 94,186 |
| Pennsylvania | 62,425 | Ohio | 74,633 |
| Iowa | 61,932 | Pennsylvania | 42,483 |
| New York | 42,367 | Kentucky | 25,020 |
| Kentucky | 40,116 | New York | 24,086 |
| Tennessee | 19,537 | Nebraska | 20,938 |
| Foreign | 132,675 | Foreign | 60,218 |
| Germany | 39,159 | Germany | 16,142 |
| England and Wales | 18,963 | Scandinavia | 10,630 |
| Scandinavia | 18,690 | Russia | 8,623 |
| Ireland | 15,092 | British-American | 6,925 |
| British-American | 12,387 | England and Wales | 6,623 |
| Russia | 9,623 | Austria-Hungary | 3,933 |
| | | Ireland | 3,083 |

Source: Fifth Biennial Report of the Kansas State Board of Agriculture, Population, pp. 9–60.

**Table 13.4:** Kansas Population, 1895

| Population: | State total | 1,334,734 |
| --- | --- | --- |
| | Native-born | 1,206,332 |
| | Foreign-born | 128,402 |

| *Born in* | | *Where from to Kansas* | |
| --- | --- | --- | --- |
| Kansas | 529,865 | Kansas | 525,662 |
| Illinois | 111,945 | Illinois | 145,449 |
| Ohio | 90,354 | Missouri | 123,356 |
| Missouri | 78,748 | Iowa | 81,744 |
| Indiana | 76,825 | Indiana | 69,951 |
| Iowa | 54,199 | Ohio | 63,801 |
| Pennsylvania | 48,357 | Nebraska | 35,588 |
| Kentucky | 30,423 | Pennsylvania | 34,410 |
| New York | 29,600 | Kentucky | 20,508 |
| Nebraska | 14,641 | New York | 18,029 |
| Foreign | 128,402 | Foreign | ca. 64,000 |
| Germany | 39,527 | Germany | 20,235 |
| Scandinavia | 18,285 | Scandinavia | 11,480 |
| England and Wales | 15,348 | Russia | 9,743 |
| Ireland | 11,800 | England and Wales | 6,438 |
| Russia | 10,740 | British-American | 5,326 |
| British-American | 9,283 | South European | 4,625 |

Source: Decennial Census, 1895. Tenth Biennial Report of the Kansas State Board of Agriculture, pt. 8, p. 541.

not unusual. This was true, not only for the 1860 census used as a base, but for subsequent enumerations, and only in the twentieth century was this pattern modified, the losses being somewhat reduced. Arranged by rainfall belts from east to west, substantially the same story was told for each. In other words, geographical factors exercised a remarkably slight apparent influence.

This analysis should be carried a step further. In each census subsequent to 1860, used as a base year, the newcomers during the decade should be separated from the old settlers. The latter, then, when compared with later enumerations, were relatively the more stable. The newcomers of each enumeration always were highly unstable, the rate of losses being substantially the same as the first census after settlement, the pioneer decade for each area. In other words, the newcomers of any decade, and the original settlers of the area behaved in the same fashion in terms of population losses for the particular area.

Furthermore, in relating losses to periods of drouth and economic depression, the rate of loss was not necessarily greater than for periods of favorable weather and prosperity. In fact, many samples revealed a lesser rate of loss for drouth and depression than for favorable weather and prosperity.

The aspect of population change that is most in need of clarification is that of population replacement in relation to losses. The rate of loss was relatively stable; but the rate of replacement was highly variable, and that accounted for the net gain or loss of population for a particular area, and for the state as a whole.

Table 13.5: Kansas Population, 1905

| Population: | State total | 1,554,968 |
| | Native-born | 1,400,441 |
| | Foreign-born | 118,378 |

| *Born in* | | *Where from to Kansas* | |
|---|---|---|---|
| Kansas | 739,795 | Kansas | 733,608 |
| Missouri | 113,176 | Missouri | 162,629 |
| Illinois | 108,709 | Illinois | 129,837 |
| Ohio | 76,666 | Iowa | 79,083 |
| Indiana | 69,201 | Indiana | 61,378 |
| Iowa | 59,151 | Ohio | 53,262 |
| Pennsylvania | 41,677 | Nebraska | 39,786 |
| Kentucky | 27,923 | Pennsylvania | 29,592 |
| New York | 24,098 | Kentucky | 19,033 |
| Nebraska | 21,243 | New York | 15,541 |
| Foreign | 118,378 | Foreign | 68,709 |
| Germany | 43,124 | Germany | 24,411 |
| Scandinavia | 17,929 | Scandinavia | 11,144 |
| England and Wales | 13,203 | Russia | 10,242 |
| Russia | 11,535 | England and Wales | 5,920 |
| Ireland | 8,958 | British-American | 4,369 |
| British-American | 7,444 | Ireland | 2,756 |

Source: "Decennial Census, 1905." Fifteenth Biennial Report of the Kansas State Board of Agriculture (bound in, but paged separately), p. 44.

Returning, then, to the general population growth figures, the proportions of old settlers and newcomers take on a different significance in this turnover perspective. Could the whole of the Kansas census for 1860 be compared name for name with that of 1870, the operation would reveal quite exactly how few of the 100,000 were still in Kansas in 1870. As that has not been done, however, resort must be had to the farm operator turnover statistics, supplemented by less reliable but significant tentative generalizations about urban business establishments. Exploratory studies of the latter have been made, but are not in a form that lend themselves to statistical presentation. Nevertheless, this much may be said, that businesses using fairly substantial capital investments were on the whole much more stable than those requiring small capital outlays. The most unstable of all were the service occupations where labor was the prime investment: barbers, restaurant operators, real estate agents, etc. From all these sources, the conclusion seems reasonable as a tentative working hypothesis that the farm operator loss rate of 60% or more for the first ten years from any base census year is not excessive for newcomers. On this basis, of the 100,000 population of 1860, approximately 40,000 might still be in the state in 1870. But such a small number would be virtually lost in a population of 364,399 in 1870, a ratio of something like one in nine, or one in ten.

A comparison of the populations of 1870 and 1880 would be more hazardous because of the larger number of seasoned settlers involved. The figure already calculated for 1880, of eight newcomers for every nine present in that enumeration, would be drastically modified; just how much would be a guess, possibly fourteen out of every fifteen. Conceding even the roughest approximation of accuracy, the possibility of early settlers, pre–Civil War population, acting as the determinant of Kansas culture as of 1880 or later, seems preposterous. Yet, a concession must be made to the influence of aggressive individuals and to the power of legends and symbols that had become an important emotional factor in the Kansas tradition, such as Memorial Day orators eulogized as Kansas ideals. Supporting this point of view also, was the sound statistical fact that until 1910 at least, the replacement population of newcomers came from substantially the same border states, with an emphasis on the northern border states that had comprised the original 100,000. The newcomers were new to Kansas to be sure, but allowing for variants, personal and locality-wise, the overall cultural trends embraced strong similarities.[1]

If the same techniques could be applied to the territorial population, comparing the settlers of the first three years with those of the census of

1860, an even more telling and drastic situation would be revealed. The newcomers of those first three years were induced to come to Kansas under undue excitement, and their disappointments and disillusionments were notorious. There is good reason to believe that the number who returned to the East or who went elsewhere was greater than from most other new settlements. Furthermore, numerically, the numbers who arrived in Kansas during those first three years was not large, whether from north, south, or border areas. Volume migration to Kansas came first in 1857 and the newcomers of 1857–1859 inclusive did not come under the abnormal conditions which had climaxed in the presidential campaign and its induced Kansas Civil War of 1856. It was this new population of 1857 that became critical in turning the scales, deciding that the free-state party should participate in the elections of the winter of 1857–1858 by which it seized control of both the territorial legislature of 1858 and the Lecompton state government under the nominally proslavery Lecompton constitution.[2] The number of fifty-sixers and earlier settlers who were present in the Kansas population of 1870 or 1880 was so small as to appear negligible statistically, either in absolute numbers or percentagewise.

Having looked at the population problem statistically and arrived at these conclusions, the fact must be recognized that statistics do not tell the whole story. Qualifications have already been noted. At the time of the second inauguration of John A. Martin as governor of Kansas, January 1887, the nine men who had preceded him in that office were invited to attend the ceremonies. Of the first ten state governors, including Martin, except for Anthony and St. John, all had come to Kansas prior to the census of 1860. Of these first ten governors, three were born in Ohio, and two each in Pennsylvania and Indiana. One each was born in Massachusetts, Virginia and New York. Of the two post-war arrivals, St. John, of Indiana background, became notorious as the prohibition governor. The only New England–born governor among the first ten, Charles Robinson, was opposed to prohibition, and near the end of his career ran for governor on the Democratic ticket. Also, he was a religious liberal. Where, if anywhere, in the record of Kansas governors is to be found the New England Puritan stereotype so often ascribed to Kansas? Statistically, this small group was insignificant, yet, placed in society as they were, the influence of these persistent men was out of proportion to numbers.

Newspaper editors afford another group that is worthy of attention. A list of eleven may be compiled, of men arriving prior to 1860 and still present in 1889, whose careers were sufficiently important to give them some state-wide attention. Pennsylvania and New York contributed three each, Massa-

Table 13.6: Kansas Press: Territorial Comers Still Active in 1889

| | | |
|---|---|---|
| D. R. Anthony | Massachusetts | 1824–1904 |
| John S. Gilmore | New York | 1848–1913 |
| Vincent J. Lane | Pennsylvania | 1828–1914 |
| G. W. Martin | Pennsylvania | 1841–1914 |
| John A. Martin | Pennsylvania | 1839–1889 |
| Sol Miller | Indiana | 1831–1897 |
| S. S. Prouty | New York | 1835–1889 |
| John Speer | Ohio | 1817–1906 |
| Jacob Stotler | Maryland | 1833–1901 |
| T. D. Thacher | New York | 1831–1894 |
| D. W. Wilder | Massachusetts | 1832–1911 |

chusetts two, and Ohio, Indiana, and Maryland one each. Although their papers were primarily local in circulation, several of them received much wider recognition. Unquestionably of greatest importance throughout the whole period were D. R. Anthony of Leavenworth, John A. Martin of Atchison, Sol Miller of Troy, and G. W. Martin of Junction City and Kansas City. Others moved about or otherwise interrupted their editorial activities. Over-emphasis on these men should be avoided, however, because, by the eighteen eighties the papers having an approximation of statewide coverage were edited by men who arrived after the Civil War—the *Topeka Capital* and the *State Journal*. The three Kansas City, Missouri, papers, the *Journal,* the *Star,* and the *Times,* drew a part of their staffs from Kansas journalism.

## Town Planning

Another approach to the study of Kansas culture is an analysis of town planning. Three types appear: those oriented to river navigation, to the public square, and to main streets. By coincidence, Kansas was being settled during the eighteen fifties when the steam locomotive on rails was challenging the steam boat on rivers and before the outcome of that new technology was fully evident. The lag in culture evaluation of rail innovation was conspicuous, accentuated by the fact that the "old" system itself had been an innovation to the preceding generation. So substantial had been the advantages of steam navigation that it appeared secure. And besides, it was in the age-old tradition of water communication as fundamental to the organization of all society. The novelty of rail communication was thus doubly difficult to appraise. Familiar to all, however, was the orientation of river towns on the levee, just as on the seacoast all towns were oriented on the harbor water front. The street system must serve the river front and the levees. Wholesale and retail business establishments must occupy locations most convenient for unloading and breaking bulk for retail trade. Conversely, collecting and reshipment businesses must find places convenient for their peculiar requirements. Choice residence sites often occupied bluffs overlooking the river upstream from the commercial levee. The Kansas cities, both in Missouri and Kansas at the junction of the Kansas and the Missouri rivers, Leavenworth and Atchison, and lesser rivals on the right bank were all planned as typical river towns. Their immense advantage over inland towns was conspicuous during the first two decades of Kansas history. The coming of the railroad changed all that. Probably most town promoters thought that rails would be important primarily to supplement or complement river navigation. Only a few bold souls, who thought of rails as displacing altogether the river communication system, pointed out that in a railroad-oriented culture, a river location might be a handicap—expansion being possible only in one direction. For the towns serving Kansas, on the west bank of the Missouri River, a railroad bridge was imperative, and the town that was first with such a facility might gain the decisive lead over rivals. The City of Kansas, Missouri (the old Westport Landing) dedicated its bridge in July 1869. Leavenworth and Atchison lagged, acquiring railroad bridges in 1872 and 1875 respectively.

Once the river town acquired its railroad, the next question was the effect of the new technology on the town's orientation. What, if anything, was the railroad equivalent of the levee as a unifying focus of the whole city's activities? In the beginning, each railroad insisted upon serving itself first, and the town might be divided in support of the claims of the several roads. The idea of a jointly owned terminal railroad, switching, and transfer facility was slow in coming. Slow also was the conception of a union passenger station. Leavenworth's internal quarrels and rivalries certainly damaged its competitive strength, and to put the matter in that language may be an understatement.

The town built around a square was in the southern tradition where the county was the minimal unit of local government. This type of town planning had been carried north of the Ohio River along with other traits typical of southern culture. Thus, regardless of whether the immigrants to Kansas were from the southern states directly, or from the border states, they were accustomed to the public square orientation. Inland eastern

Kansas towns of the territorial period were mostly built around squares, the so-called proslavery towns, and the towns founded by free-state immigrants from the Ohio River border areas.

The third type of town planning was to build the business houses along a main street: Lawrence, Topeka, and Manhattan being the most notable examples of New England design. Again, note should be taken that the New England type of planning was not conspicuous during the period of territorial beginnings. Circumstances altered cases, however, and the proslavery town of Franklin, about five miles east of Lawrence, was built along the California Road as its main street. The local situation, not imitation of New England, determined the plan.

After the Civil War, when central and western Kansas were settled, both of the latter town plans were used. County seat rivalries fostered the public square type, but often, even success in that enterprise did not always result in the dominance of the square, as in Hill City, Ness City, Kinsley and Meade. Possibly the public square design was too pretentious. The village or small town could be accommodated in one or two blocks of business houses along a single street.

The railroad had its influence upon all inland towns. From them, unlike river towns, theoretically, railroads might radiate in all directions. In practice, where there was only one railroad, the main street often intersected it at approximately right angles, with the railway station near the point of intersection. Where there were two or more railroads, each tended to maintain its own service facilities regardless of town planning, and often destroying any unity of town orientation that might have been planned. But in these respects, after the Civil War, Kansas was no different from other western states. After World War I, motor highways have introduced a series of further reorientations of town organization, and the end is not yet. Highways might be routed through the town, around the town, or might by-pass it altogether.

## Theatre as an Example of the Role of the Railroad in Reorienting Kansas

Returning the description to the first decades of Kansas history, the rivalry between railroads as innovators in competition with river navigation worked a reorientation of the whole area in relation to the southern and the eastern United States. This may be illustrated meaningfully by reviewing, as one example, what happened to the theatre, a theme that involves more than commerce in commodities of the field and of the factory. During the eighteen fifties, the resident theatrical company reigned at Leavenworth, and later was combined with the traveling star system. By the eighteen seventies the complete traveling dramatic company was coming into its own.[3]

During the decades of the eighteen fifties and the eighteen sixties the fact is conspicuous that the Missouri River and water communications influenced, if they did not actually dominate, not only the orientation of theatre and other entertainment, but most aspects of the outlook and activities of the inhabitants of the Missouri Valley. Until well along in the eighteen sixties most travel necessary to entertainment was dependent upon the river almost as literally as showboats. The resident theatre associated with the traveling star system required the least possible dependence upon mobility, especially during the winter months when the river was closed to navigation. Theatre that required travel was peculiarly a summer institution. The orientation was upon New Orleans by way of Cincinnati or by way of St. Louis, and was based upon long practice and upon established personal relations.

Recruitment of actors for the resident company at Leavenworth was from St. Louis, Louisville, Cincinnati, or New Orleans. A study of the New Orleans theatre of the eighteen fifties, and the eighteen sixties, both before and after the American Civil War, reveals the major role of that city in relation to the interior river cities, extending to the Missouri River Elbow region, and including Leavenworth. Many, if not most, of the stars who played in the Leavenworth Theatre played at the St. Charles and DeBar Theatres and others in New Orleans and in St. Louis. Except for physical equipment and size of the house, the theatergoer might not be able to distinguish which of the three cities he was in: New Orleans, St. Louis, or Leavenworth.

By 1870 a revolution had occurred. The complete traveling dramatic troupe was taking over, was oriented upon Chicago, and was traveling by rail. These companies provided entertainment during the winter months and frequently recruited actors from the towns in which they played. By the early eighteen eighties the specialized one-play company, originating in New York City, became a competitor of the traveling dramatic company that played a different bill each night for a week or ten days. But the specialized one-play company could not afford one-night stands in small towns, and thus tended to be limited to cities large enough to present the play more than once. In Kansas, the organization of theatre circuits provided a maximum of assured box office receipts with the minimum of travel expense for the specialized company. The multiple-play traveling companies found difficulty in securing accommodation in the theatre of the larger towns, but still were without competition in the small towns.

Studies of the relations between Chicago and New York City need to be done. New York City dominance over Chicago in theatre paralleled closely in time the centralization in New York City of so many other functions of society in the United States during the last third of the nineteenth century. The railroad was certainly a major factor in this whole process of reconstruction of society.

## Conclusion

The question that emerges from such an analysis as is presented here is not whether Kansas is a child of New England, but takes on a different form: how did New England wield as much influence as it did, and how was the legend about New England parentage and Puritanism imposed upon the Kansas tradition contrary to so conspicuous a weight of available facts?

The Civil War, the so-called reconstruction issues that came in its wake, the settlement of Kansas by an unusually large proportion of Union soldiers, the dominance of the Republican party, making Kansas virtually a one-party state, all worked to crystallize thinking along a fairly uniform pattern in which no doubt was entertained about the moral imperative— the North won the war, saved the Union, freed the slave, therefore the North was morally right, and the Republican party claimed the credit, virtually equating the Republican party with the North. In terms of the mental conditioning of a whole people, this process was most effectively carried out. The mind of the Kansans, if not committed already to this point of view before coming to Kansas, was thoroughly indoctrinated, not in the facts of this history, but in the legend about history.

In referring to the Union veterans of the Civil War in this connection, it is necessary to differentiate between Union veterans as a whole and the G.A.R. The latter as an organization had only a small membership or scarcely any representation in Kansas until late in the eighteen eighties and nineties. Its influence even at that date lay, not in numbers, but in organization which often arbitrarily assumed the role of speaking and acting for all Union veterans, and the public and historians have tended to accept this generalization without investigation of the facts. Also, action of veterans as such was sometimes, and more often than realized by historians, erroneously attributed to the G.A.R. So far as the Civil War legend was involved, with its moral concerns, the influence that had shaped thought was not New England Puritanism in the direct conventional sense, but rather, patriotism cast in the mold of the moral imperative and associated directly with living issues, the Union and the abolition of slavery. And, parenthetically, emphasis is in order that this moral commitment even about abolition of slavery was largely in consequence of the course taken by the war and postwar retrospect, and should not be confused with the debated issue of the "cause" of the American Civil War. So much that crystallized in people's minds after the event—results—has been read back chronologically into prewar years and attributed to causes.

The complex of attitudes associated with the Civil War tradition— patriotism—attained, almost if not quite, the status of a secular religion. So far as theology in the conventional sense was concerned, to be sure, Kansans were overwhelmingly Protestant, not Puritan, in any legitimate sense of that much-abused word. And the new scientific and philosophical ideas that were so potent in the nineteenth century in challenging theology came from Europe—Great Britain, Germany, and France. The conclusion seems justified that the challenge to theological orthodoxy by science and the higher criticism met with less intolerance than the challenge to patriotism as a secular orthodoxy.[4]

The subject of education—formal education—would require an essay at least as long as the present paper to present even its minimal outlines—the net conclusion of such a discussion being that education was not adminis- tered conspicuously in the proper sense as learning, but illustrated rather the power of indoctrination, confused by a conflict between imitation of Eastern models and pragmatic functionalism, all of which discouraged originality.

At this point the chapter is brought to an arbitrary close—time has run out with only a sampling of features of Kansas culture. In dealing with the facts of history as differentiated from the legends about them, the observa- tion has often been made that the legends, even though false, may them- selves become causes. In the present connection the argument would run, that although Kansas is not a child of New England, the legend about it being such operated as though the legend was true. From this line of reasoning a paradoxical conclusion might be drawn, that facts of history are false and that the legends, the false, are true, both in the causal sense.

The mode of thought injected by this point of view involves the concept of action and reaction, or reciprocal action in the naïve space-time frame of reference. A space and a time interval is implied between cause and effect. Reactions and reciprocal actions require further extensions of time. All this is futile and interposes a bar to effective thought. It is syllogistic manipula- tion in a near vacuum and is unrelated to the essential facts. Either party may assert and his opposite number deny, without arriving at a resolution of differences, each choosing his premise and scrupulously observing the rules of formal logic. The outcome must necessarily be intellectual defeatism.

A different approach is essential and one that preserves throughout the complete relatedness of all the facts present in the field. At the instant of decision, all the factors present in a situation *act* simultaneously. Sometimes this approach to the conceptualizing of causation is called field theory. Regardless of the name, however, the principle utilized, simultaneity of action in the field, transcends the limitations of naïve space and time and their relativisms. No priority in time, nor time intervals between any two or more factors are involved. Literally, all factors present in the field *act together*—simultaneity is an absolute. Once this mode of thought is pursued to its conclusions, the frustrations of the conventional theories of causation are dissolved.[5]

Such a reorientation of thought about causation cannot be pursued further at this time, but the reader is challenged to apply the principles to the subject matter of this paper and to other facts that are omitted but are equally pertinent. The opening of the second century of the history of Kansas would seem to be an appropriate time for some innovation.

## Notes

1. These population analyses are drawn primarily from the present author's studies: *John Brown and the Legend of Fifty-Six* (Philadelphia, 1942); "The Turnover of Farm Population in Kansas," *Kansas Historical Quarterly* 4 (November, 1935): 355–72; *The Grassland of North America: Prolegomena to Its History* (Lawrence, 1947), chapters 16–19. Compare with A. D. Edwards, "Influence of Drought and Depression on a Rural Community: A Case Study in Haskell County, Kansas," USDA Farm Security Administration, *Social Science Research Report,* No. 7 (Washington, 1939). Edwards used the same methodology.

2. See the present writer's *John Brown and the Legend of Fifty-six,* chapter 30, and "Notes on the Writing of General Histories of Kansas," part 1, "The Setting of the Stage," and part 2, "J. N. Holloway, *History of Kansas* (Lafayette, Ind., 1868)," *Kansas Historical Quarterly* 21 (Summer, Winter, 1954): 184–223, 264–87.

3. James C. Malin, "James A. and Louie Lord: Theatrical Team—Their Personal Story, 1869–1889"; "Theatre in Kansas, 1858–1868 . . . ."; "Traveling Theatre in Kansas"; *Kansas Historical Quarterly* 22 (Autumn 1956), 242–75; 23 (Spring, Summer, Autumn, Winter 1957): 10–53, 191–203, 298–323, 401–38.

4. The present author has dealt with aspects of philosophy and theology in

several articles which afford some background for these conclusions: "Kansas Philosophers, 1871–... , *Kansas Historical Quarterly* 24 (Summer 1958): 168–97; " 'Creative Evolution': The Philosophy of Elisha Wesley McComas, Fort Scott," *Kansas Historical Quarterly* 24 (Autumn 1958), 314–50; "William Sutton White, Swedenborgian Publicist ... ," *Kansas Historical Quarterly* 24 (Winter 1958): 426–57, 25 (Spring, Summer 1959): 68–103, 197–228; "Ironquill's 'The Washerwoman's Song,' "*Kansas Historical Quarterly* 25 (Autumn 1959): 257–82; "Eugene Ware and Dr. Sanger: The Code of Political Ethics, 1872–1892," *Kansas Historical Quarterly* 26 (Autumn 1960): 255–66.

5. Other discussions related to this one are to be found in the present author's *The Contriving Brain and the Skillful Hand* (Lawrence, 1955), chapter 11, and in "Adventure into the Unknown by Relativist 'Man-afraid-of-his-mind!' " in an Emory University Symposium volume, *Relativism and the Study of Man* (Princeton, N.J., 1961).

# PART III

# Quantitative Methods in Grassland Population Studies

History "from the bottom up" has been the motto of social science historians during the past several decades. For the first time the lives and actions of the inarticulate common people have moved to the center of the historical stage to take their place beside articulate elites. This restoration has required a shift in sources and methodology as well. People at the bottom rungs of society seldom leave written records of their lives, and scholars must therefore reconstruct their life courses and behavior from government records collected for administrative purposes, such as civil and census registers, land and tax records, and the like.

Frederick Jackson Turner and his students first undertook a few case studies, based on the census manuscripts and land records, but their work was limited. James Malin in the mid-1930s realized the potential of these nominal sources for social scientific studies of farmer behavior. He devised research techniques of areal sampling, individual-level analysis, and multi-file nominal record linkage. Malin traced individual farm operators from one census to the next (including both federal and Kansas state censuses) and linked farm operators in the population and agricultural censuses of the same year. These innovative methods enabled him to chart rural persistence and turnover patterns, to determine the initial migration fields of pioneer Kansans, to measure changes in land tenure and farm size, and to describe the demographic characteristics of farm operators.

Malin also began studies of urbanization in 1935; his work on the Kinsley boom is an example. But he expressed frustration later in life for not being "able to work out any new [statistical] methodology that was particularly effective for studying urban populations," as he had done for rural populations. Despite his modest disclaimer, Malin's powerful techniques of census analysis became the mainstay of the new social history. Malin's work served as a guide for the succeeding generation—Frank L. Owsley, Merle Curti, Allan G. Bogue, Stephan Thernstrom, and Peter Knights, among others.

Malin placed his social scientific technique in the service of regional history at a time when local history was out of favor. He also synthesized his historical findings with the natural sciences of biology, climatology, geology, geography, and pedology (soil science). His guiding principle, as he once stated, was to use any and all appropriate tools, provided that they helped the historian to "eliminate the subjective element of personal opinion or philosophical interpretation, . . . and to arrive at objective and positive conclusions" (*Grassland of North America*, p. 324). Although Malin seemed to overlook the subjectivity inherent in his serial sources and quantitative tools, he did prove that behavioral methods that can be replicated by other scholars serve to advance knowledge. In this direct way, Malin demonstrated that historians, like other scientists, could build upon each other's research and develop more precise generalizations about past human behavior that would command greater acceptance by colleagues. While not achieving the unattainable goal of objectivity, he reached a degree of precision unrivaled at the time and thus offered a powerful alternative to the rank historical subjectivism of his era.

In addition to the scientific and quantitative analysis of pioneer farmer behavior, Malin also integrated scientific knowledge with the folk knowledge that he found embedded in local newspapers and reports of farm organizations. The folk process of cultural and technological adaptation was as significant as scientific knowledge in shaping behavioral adjustment in the central grassland. Malin, in brief, sought an interdisciplinary synthesis of science, technology, and regional history. He urged historians to acquire a competence in the natural sciences and natural scientists to take training in history and the social sciences.

As an advocate of quantitative methods, interdisciplinary studies, and comparative behavioral analysis, James Malin was truly a father of the new social science history that has flourished in the decades after World War II.

# CHAPTER 14

# Local Historical Studies

## &

# Population Problems

[The strength of James Malin's regional case study method of charting agricultural and cultural adaptation in the central grassland was his pioneering use of disaggregate behavioral records at the community level. Historical demographers customarily had relied upon published aggregate, or "mass," statistics, in order to measure changes in population structure and mobility patterns over time. Malin chose to study population behavior "from the bottom up" by reconstructing the lives of thousands of individual Kansas farm operators in sample communities. In this chapter, Malin details the promising possibilities of this new methodology and briefly summarizes his major conclusions, many of which modified Turner's frontier hypothesis at a number of key points, notably the theory of settlers as "rolling stones" across successive frontiers and the picture of increasing Americanization of the soil. Kansas pioneers came mainly in a single long-distance move from noncontiguous eastern states, and within a generation foreign-born newcomers gradually displaced the original native-born farmers.]

As a historian participating in the discussion of population studies, the first aspect I wish to emphasize is one of materials and procedure. For the most part, demographers have drawn upon the mass figures of the printed Census when dealing with the United States. Necessarily these are net figures, which do not reveal the contradictions or differences existing among the component elements of the population or among the local units other than the arbitrary political subdivisions into states and counties. The behavior of one element in the population or local unit may be canceled by that of another, or the net result of the mass data may be determined by the decisive behavior of a relatively small element of the whole. As in outline surveys or general histories, it is writing from the top down and partakes too much of the fitting of generalizations to particular cases rather than arriving at the generalization from the study of the underlying detail. Not only does American history as a whole need to be written from the bottom up, but population studies, as an aspect of history, need such treatment. The mass statistics tell only part of the story, and it is necessary to balance one type of procedure against the other, recognizing that both are essential to a complete and balanced treatment of population problems.

The local-community approach makes possible the analysis of units small enough so that they can be dealt with in the entirety of their behavior. As people do not live their lives in separate compartments—economic, social, cultural, or religious—the study of history and of population behavior must be envisioned as a whole. As single communities are small enough to make comprehensive studies practicable, but too small to afford the basis for generalization, a number of sample communities may be selected, each of which may be studied separately, and then the samples grouped together in sufficient numbers to afford a reasonable basis for statistical validity. The materials for such local studies are varied, including records of local government, of probate of wills and settlement of estates, of churches, of schools and other organizations, of private diaries, news-papers, and so forth; but for population problems, in particular, land records and, most important of all, the original Census schedules, the manuscript record as it was taken down name by name, family by family, in the periodical enumerations by house-to-house canvass under either state or Federal authority, are appropriate. Kansas has taken a decennial state census from 1865 to 1925 inclusive. These are deposited in the Archives Department of the Kansas State Historical Society, Topeka, and the society has also the Federal Censuses of 1860 and 1870. All are open without restriction for the use of students of population problems. By statute, the Federal Government has closed the later Federal Census records to use by any but government employees. As decennial enumerations such as those of Kansas have not been made by the states generally, and as Kansas has abandoned its census,[1] it is highly desirable that the Federal Census records be opened for the use of accredited private investigators.

The present writer is engaged upon local studies, employing the materials and procedure described above, and some of the possibilities may be illustrated from results already published or in progress.[2] The studies of migration of population based upon mass statistics emphasize increasing interstate migration and mobility, while the local Kansas farm population studied demonstrate a high degree of stability of farm operators. The Kansas communities studied seem to pass through three stages: the frontier period of extremely rapid turnover, a second period of relative stabilization at low levels, and a third state, entered upon by the older eastern communities about 1915, of a high degree of stability, which increased after the World War. The younger western communities of the semiarid west followed essentially the same pattern as the eastern communities sampled, but had not reached the same community age or quite the degree of stability of the older samples. The important point is that, for any given community age, the rate of turnover was essentially the same for any rainfall belt, whether in the humid east or the semiarid west. Seemingly the mass statistics and the local studies lead to opposite conclusions, but in fact they are both valid. This is a striking instance of the importance of rounding out population studies by utilizing both approaches, and placing the whole in its historical perspective.

The Federal Census data on interstate migration is particularly defective because it records only the state of birth and the state of residence at the time of the particular enumeration. Attempts to measure, from mass statistics drawn from such sources, the volume and direction of migration cannot trace removals from state to state between these dates. These difficulties have been recognized, but not to their full extent, because there have been no means of filling the gaps, even in part. The Kansas state census enumerations, 1875–1925 inclusive, however, give both the state of birth and the state from which migration was made to Kansas. It is thus possible to scan the lists, name by name, and determine the numbers respectively who migrated direct or migrated by way of another state or states. In the case of large families, it is possible to go a step further in analyzing the indirect migration and, by examining the birth states of successive children, to trace with surprising completeness the record of the migration of such families through several states. For present purposes, however, the discussion is limited to the simplest classification into direct and indirect migration from state of birth.

As Kansas is 400 miles long, reaching from the humid Missouri River to the semiarid high plains, sample townships were selected in seven successive stages of the westward push of population. In this way, if there are any substantial differences in the relation of these successive frontiers to the sources of migration, they should be revealed. The percentage curves follow the same general pattern, however, the proportion of direct migration rising after 1875 to a peak and then declining, the decline being quite sharp after 1915. The principal difference in the curves is found in the exact date at which the high point of direct migration was reached. In the three successive groups of sample townships in the eastern third of the state, the high point is registered in the census of 1895, which means that this migration had reached its climax during the eighties and early nineties. In the central third the census of 1905 is the high point, and in the high-plains third, west of the one hundredth meridian, the crest was recorded in 1915.

Two types of conclusions may be drawn from these facts: first, regarding the nature of the migration; second, regarding the birth-residence index. On the first point, between the Civil War period and the high point in the direct migration curve, the migration to Kansas was increasingly of a type of people who had not been on the move before—obviously they were relatively stable people, in the sense that they had not wandered permanently from the state of birth. On the other hand, since those high-point dates, in increasing proportions the migrants to Kansas were of a type who had been on the move, to the extent of at least one removal prior to the census in which they were found in Kansas.[3]

Further analysis of direct native migration, on the basis of whether it came from substantially contiguous states (Nebraska, Iowa, Missouri, and Arkansas) or from noncontiguous states, reveals that the movement from contiguous states was a relatively small proportion of either the total native migration or of the direct migration until the census of 1905 and after, varying somewhat with the groups of samples. The movement from noncontiguous states was much the greater and for the most part increased in proportion to the whole native migration, following much the same curve as the total direct migration except that the peak and reversal of trend were reached in some groups about ten years earlier. By 1915 in some samples and by 1925 in others, the contiguous migration had increased to such an extent as to exceed the noncontiguous movement in the extreme eastern and extreme western samples. From its nature, the birth-residence index, based on the Federal Census, cannot give any indication of this fluctuation and composition character of interstate migration. It is evident that since the decline set in for direct migration to Kansas from the state of birth, the birth-residence index has become more and more defective for Kansas and for any other state that may possess similar characteristics. For satisfactory migration analysis, it is essential to determine whether comparable changes took place or whether behavior was substantially different in other sections of the United States.

This analysis possesses significance for evaluation of the Turner frontier interpretation of American history, by which individuals are represented as following successive frontiers, each new frontier being peopled by the last adjacent frontier. None of the results for Kansas studies conform to this simple formula. At the peak, direct migration constituted 46 percent to 60 percent of the native migration in the several samples, and over 50 percent in four of the seven groups; and direct migration from noncontiguous states accounted for approximately half of the native migration at the highest point of its flow. If the increased direct migration is explained, as some of the Turner school have suggested, by the consolidation of rail-roads which promoted long-distance movement, then the still greater efficiency of transportation in later periods does not explain the reversal of the trend.

Still another aspect of population movement may be studied by tracing the succession of people who occupy any given community. Either the manuscript census records or local land records afford the material for such studies.[4] From the standpoint of sectional sources, emigrants from New England or from the lower South found difficulty in establishing themselves in Kansas and were rather easily displaced by midwestern native or foreign farmers. Farm occupants of urban origin likewise found difficulty in competition. Probably the most significant consideration from the standpoint of American agriculture is the outcome of racial competition. Negroes and Jews usually failed to maintain themselves as farm operators, while Germans, Scandinavians, and Czechs, those European rural immigrants among whom love of the soil was conspicuous, usually drove out Anglo-Americans, who to an increasing degree have lost their soil-hunger under the influence of urbanization of the United States and inefficiency in economic competition.

There is no general appreciation of the extent to which these foreign racial strains influence or even dominate the agriculture of the trans-Mississippi West,[5] and only in part have the first and second generations of the native-born been sufficiently Americanized to lose the soil tradition. To what extent have the migrant American farmers, emphasized by mass statistics, been these native Americans who have failed in competition? To what extent have drought and depression been excuses, rather than reasons, for this migrancy, along with monopoly, trusts, railroads, money, and other traditional agrarian issues? There is peculiar irony in the fact that the operation of governmental policies over the last half century or more, in subsidizing the American tradition of the family-size farm, have aided these immigrant strains in the process of displacing the native Anglo-American farmers.

The manuscript census materials open new possibilities for the analysis of the internal structure of society, as well as of its population movements. In interpreting American history in terms of the frontier hypothesis, generalizations have been formulated which are in themselves contradictory, but so superficial have been the critical examinations of the composition of frontier populations that the inconsistencies have passed almost unchallenged. If the movement to new lands had been that of individuals migrating through several successive frontiers, then necessarily the newest frontier must have been composed of mature people. Yet it has been asserted more insistently that the frontier was young, composed in large measure of young married couples just starting out in life to grow up with the country, their children in turn to begin life on a newer frontier. Studies of farm operators in Kansas demonstrate a relatively normal age distribution. The median ages for men in 1860 (within six years of first settlement) was about thirty-five, and later Kansas frontiers to the westward (the fourth and fifth rainfall belts) were thirty-six and forty respectively. As the communities matured, the median ages advanced, in some cases as much as ten years, then declined for a time, and between 1915 and 1925 most of the samples turned slightly upward again, but not above the earlier highs. In general terms, it might be said that the median age of farm operators stabilized between forty-three and forty-five and that fluctuations were within a comparatively narrow range. In age distribution, the number of men under twenty-five was very small, and even the bracket twenty-five to twenty-nine was altogether too small to conform to the youth formula of the frontier hypothesis. On the other hand, the fact should be emphasized that, in samples of similar community age, the farm operator of 1925 was not older than the farmer of 1885 or 1895.

In the United States general interest in population problems is not only of recent origin, but it has spread under the influence of the abnormal conditions of the depression of the 1930s and has been too closely associated with social and economic planning. Some of the work has been scientifically and objectively done, but much of it, being inspired by a cause, has been controlled largely by zeal in promotion and defense of a particular type of social policy. Historians have neglected this type of investigation, and much of the work is in the hands of those belonging to the presentist school, who scorn history and tradition. Yet, without historical perspective, even the most careful investigators may misinterpret their results. The question of migration, discussed above, is a case in point. Many sensational things have been written about migrating farmers during the present depression, and grandiose schemes of resettlement have been proposed and some inaugurated. In the light of historical studies of farm communities, however, the Kansas farmers have achieved for the first time in history a high degree of stability. The sensational exploitations of migrant farmers deal with an extremely small minority, most of whom are of the type which in earlier times always have been on the move in larger relative numbers. The remarkable thing about this present depression, from the standpoint of population movement, is the relative minuteness of the volume in comparison with previous historical periods, either before or after the passing of the frontier. The fact that the Turner hypothesis has been used extensively as a justification for social planning, as a substitute for the frontier, gives particular pertinence to the fact that much that has been claimed for the significance of the frontier in American history does not bear investigation.

The rapid turnover of frontier population and the increasing stability in mature communities present many problems. During the early periods of extreme instability, little permanence or continuity in community organization and culture could be expected. With the coming of population stability, however, other disruptive forces appeared upon the scene. Automotive transportation was a leading factor in all but closing the country school and church and destroying the village as a rural community center. With school, church, trading, and entertainment focused upon large towns, the farmer's social and cultural life became urbanized. At the opening of the century, the Country-Life Movement, under the pioneer leadership of Liberty Hyde Bailey and Kenyon Leech Butterfield, emphasized this characteristic and the resulting discontent with farm life among rural people. The factors dominating the fourth decade of the century only accentuate the tendencies then so conspicuous, and under the new circumstances the possibilities of preserving or readjusting a distinctly rural culture in the United States are even more remote.

## Notes

1. Partly because of the overshadowing of the state by the extension of Federal activity and partly as an economy measure, Kansas abandoned its census in 1935, thereby breaking the continuous record of population data.

2. James C. Malin, "The Turnover of Farm Population in Kansas," *Kansas Historical Quarterly* 4 (November 1935): 339–72; "The Adaptation of the Agricultural

System to Sub-humid Environment," *Agricultural History* 10 (July 1936): 118–41; "The Kinsley Boom of the Late Eighties," *Kansas Historical Quarterly* 4 (February, May 1935): 23–49, 164–87. *Cf.* A. D. Edwards, *Influence of Drought and Depression on a Rural Community: A Case Study of Haskell County, Kansas,* Farm Security Administration, Social Research Report no. 7, (Washington, D.C., 1939). This study by Edwards applied the procedure of the present author, together with some improvements which were suggested by experience with the pioneer project.

3. Neither of the above statements deals with intrastate movement, either in the state of birth prior to removal to Kansas or within Kansas after arrival.

4. A. B. Hollingshead, "Changes in Land Ownership as an Index of Succession in Rural Communities," *American Journal of Sociology* 43 (March 1938): 764–77. Hollingshead used land records for this purpose, in a study of Nebraska communities.

5. The role of Asiatics on the Pacific Coast and of Southern Europeans in New England agriculture has received more attention.

# CHAPTER 15

# The Turnover
# of Farm Population
# in Kansas

[James Malin considered this essay on farmer turnover as one of his "most important innovations." It has become a classic in its own right and serves as the methodological cornerstone of the new social history that has flourished in recent decades. The direct measurement of geographical and social mobility rates over time among various populations rests directly on the research techniques devised by Malin in the early 1930s. He reported the first results of his individual-level census research at a national meeting of American historians in 1935, and for the next fifteen years he continued to raise new behavioral questions and to expand his data base spatially and chronologically.

This seminal essay details the differential patterns of intra- and inter-generational farmer persistence rates in forty-eight selected townships in the five rainfall belts of Kansas between 1860 and 1935. In his conclusions, Malin stresses that historical factors, more than ecological conditions, affected the number of pioneer settlers who chose to leave or stay in the community. The pioneer period witnessed high turnover; the filling-in stage brought relative stability; but when the community reached full maturity, out-mobility virtually ceased. The effects of such high mobility rates in the early years of frontier communities were significant, Malin suggested, and deserving of detailed study.]

Although there is much discussion of the improvement of farm conditions and of the stabilization of agriculture, there is remarkably little specific information of historical character about the behavior of farm population and of the factors which influence that behavior. This study of the turnover of farm population in Kansas presents only one of many phases of an investigation undertaken in that field.

The state of Kansas was divided into five belts, or zones, from east to west, and townships were selected in each in sufficient number to make a fairly representative sampling of each area. Except for the third or central belt, the selection resulted in the inclusion in each division of upwards of one thousand farms after the belt was fully settled, the number varying, of course, from time to time. The method for determining the division of the state presented many probelms. Which should be used: arbitrary rectangles, time of first settlement, type-of-farming areas of contemporary times, soil, topography, temperature, altitude, or rainfall? Arbitrary division into rectangles, while frequently used for statistical purposes, did not appear to have any meaning for this study. From the standpoint of the frontier alone, the division on the basis of time of settlement would seem to be most desirable, but such an arrangement would have a limited relation to subsequent development. As settlement moved from northeast to southwest, the process did not conform with the natural geographical conditions. Type-of-farming areas are more suitable for investigations where time and change do not enter. Soil areas are not sufficiently definite and uniform. Temperature belts in Kansas run northeast and southwest, with the longest growing season in the southeast corner and the shortest in the northwest corner. Altitude belts are similar, although they run more nearly north and south, but in this respect also Kansas faces the southeast rather than the east or northeast. Rainfall belts in the eastern part of the state run northeast and southwest also, but near the middle of the state, they change directions to north and south.[1]

For the present purpose, rainfall has been chosen as the basis of division because of the close relation of rainfall to agriculture and because this division more nearly conforms to some of the other possible divisions; time of settlement, temperature, and altitude, without their exaggerated extremes. The first rainfall belt of 35 inches per year and upward runs from the northeast corner of the state southwestward. This region includes the section most heavily populated during the territorial period. The second rainfall belt of 30 to 35 inches includes Brown and Nemaha counties in the northeast and extends southwest into the east central section, including such cities as Emporia, Newton, and Wichita. The third rainfall belt of 25 to

30 inches extends westward to a line nearly north and south through Ellsworth, Great Bend, and Pratt. The fourth belt of 20 to 25 inches extends to a point slightly west of the one-hundredth meridian. The fifth belt of less than 20 inches rainfall includes the remainder of the state west to the Colorado line.[2]

The selection of the township samples presented its difficulties. The boundaries of the townships must remain unchanged through the years for which census data are available, or if divided, the subdivisions must include the original area. The sample townships must be strictly rural in character without being isolated. The presence of a small town is permissible, but a city of any size would introduce the suburban factor which is a problem in itself. The township should be large enough to be fairly representative, and foreign populations or other unusual influences must not be present in sufficient degree to dominate or distort the results. In practice it has been found all but impossible to find townships that have not been influenced by foreign population to some degree at some time in their history.

The materials used are the original federal and state census records giving names and other data for all farm operators, at five-year intervals from 1860 to 1885 and for ten-year intervals thereafter until 1915, after which five-year intervals are resumed. Lists of names of farm operators were compiled from each census for all townships analyzed and these lists compared with succeeding name lists to determine operators who were represented in the township in their own right or through male descendants.[3] From resulting statistics the following types of data could be established: firstly, the total number of farm operators at successive census dates; secondly, the persistence of farm operators; and thirdly, the proportion of the farm operators of any period who are descendants from those of any prior period.

The whole number of farm operators, both for the townships taken separately as well as for them taken as groups, increased through the settlement period, frequently, if not usually, to a number in excess of what the land would support under the existing stage of economic development. The second phase was usually a recession in numbers accompanied by an increase in the size of the farm unit. Beyond that point few generalizations seem possible. When the numbers were plotted in graphic form, the curves showed no uniformity of pattern. After the frontier or settlement period the townships took on characteristics of established communities, but not necessarily of stabilized communities. Only in the eastern part could the term *stabilization* be applied with any degree of accuracy, because only there has sufficient time elapsed for fairly adequate adjustments to environment to be completed. The peculiarities of agricultural problems on the plains require a longer period of adaptation than has elapsed since the original settlement. And furthermore, throughout the state, both east and west, the advent of power machinery disrupted much of the adaptation already supposedly achieved.

The period of depression between 1870 and 1875 recorded moderate losses of farm operators in the first and second belts. The next five years brought increases in population along with partial economic recovery for most of the state. The five years 1880–1885, generally prosperous, present a different picture. The first and fourth belts lost farm operators. In the fourth it was the result of reaction from the boom in the northwest counties. The decade 1885–1895, mostly one of national and world-wide depression, shows increases in the first, second, and third belts, the older region, but decreases again in the fourth or younger part of the state. The decade 1895–1905 recorded decreases in four belts, but substantial increases in the fourth. This was the period in which the fourth belt was achieving relative stabilization on a basis of hard winter wheat farming, and succeeded in running counter to the trends of the country both to the east and to the west of it. The decade 1905–1915 was the first one in which all belts registered the same trend, a substantial increase, especially in the fifth. Decreases occurred during the next five years, the World War period, except in the fifth, and increases during the first half of the twenties, except in the second and third. The period 1925–1930, another period of national prosperity, brought declines in numbers in all belts. It is a period of rapid mechanization of agriculture and correspondingly enlarged farm units. In the depression years 1930–1935 the decline in numbers was reversed except in the second belt. The 1930–1935 change in direction was substantial, otherwise it might not be significant as census rolls were probably more complete in 1935 than in former years on account of the federal agricultural allotment policy. For emphasis it may be well to stress the fact that the number of farm operators increased between 1930 and 1935 even in the semiarid fifth rainfall belt, the so-called "dust-bowl."

Although only limited generalizations may be permissible from these variegated data, a few things stand out. Economic depression was usually associated with declining numbers of farm operators during the frontier or settlement stage of development of the country, but increasing numbers usually occurred in older parts of the state. On the other hand, national prosperity was associated with increasing numbers in all parts of the state between 1905 and 1915, and with declining numbers in most of the state between 1925 and 1930.[4]

These conclusions have an important bearing on the so-called safety valve theory of the frontier hypothesis. It has been rather generally assumed by the followers of F. J. Turner that unfavorable conditions in the east or older regions resulted in a flow of population westward to free or cheap land, thus affording relief to the east and providing opportunity to the migrants. The data collected in this study do not seem to bear out such a theory. On the frontier the number of farm operators declined more often than it increased during periods of general economic stress. On the other hand the increases occurred in most substantial numbers in the older counties and especially those containing a town of some size. The significance of the shift resulting from depressed economic conditions appears to lie therefore in urban to rural rather than old-country to frontier readjustment. This urban-to-rural movement was conspicuous while there still was an open frontier, and it was conspicuous in the 1930–1935 period after the frontier was gone.

The study of the agricultural census rolls, name by name and farm by farm, reveals many changes which cannot be presented statistically. For the decade 1925–1935, some of these furnish significant background for interpretation of the data. During the twenties rapid mechanization and increased size of farms necessarily reduced the number of farm operators. Many of the less efficient were squeezed out and found it difficult to make a living at any other occupation. The towns received most of them and thereby added to marginal urban population. Much of the tradition of agricultural depression of the twenties was associated with these who were eliminated or who were on the borderline. More accurately, these farmers were the victims of a revolutionary advance in agricultural technology. Also the period seems to have encouraged the early retirement of many older operators from active management of their land. The depression of the thirties seems to have reversed to some extent both of these tendencies. Near larger towns especially, there was subdivision of farms associated with the town-to-country movement. Another tendency seems to be an attempt on the part of the head of a family to provide for all members through subdivision of the farm. In other cases farmers who had retired appear to have returned to active operation of their land. In still others, instead of older farmers retiring outright, many seem to reserve a small plot of ground which they operate separately from the original farm. There was an increasing tendency also for the sons in a family to operate a farm jointly under such a title as Jones Brothers, or a father and sons to handle the farm jointly. Obviously there are conflicting factors present in these cases of joint management. In some it seems to have been a substitute for sub-division of the land, while in others the situation suggests that the joining of forces was a means for carrying on large-scale operations. Subdivision, consolidation, and preservation of the size of farm units went on at the same time. The effect of subdivision and consolidation is to cancel or offset each other in the statistics. The figures for the number of farms in any township or county, therefore, may be unchanged, but the farm situation may be changed radically.

The second phase of the problem of population turnover, the persistence of farm operators, affords more that is unusual. General conclusions are presented first. In all rainfall belts, the rate of turnover was high, but was declining during the first twenty-five years from the time of settlement. At about twenty to thirty years after settlement, the rate of turnover may be said to have become somewhat stabilized, although the word *stabilized* must again be used loosely. In some cases, instead of stabilization, there was an increase in the rate of turnover after that high point twenty-five years from settlement. After the World War persistence increased substantially.

For purposes of summarizing persistence of population by rainfall belts, the data on the several sample townships were added together for each belt, and the persistence was expressed in percentages of the total of persons included in each base census list who remained at successive later census periods. In the first, or eastern, belt in 1860 there were 478 operators in the five sample townships. Five years later only 35 percent remained; at the end of ten years 26 percent; at the end of twenty-five years 20 percent; in 1920, or after sixty years, 10.6 percent, and in 1935, or after seventy-five years, 8.3 percent. Taking in succession the years 1865, 1870, 1875, 1880, and 1885 as base years, the percentage of persistence increased to a high point in 1885. There were 953 farm operators in 1885, and of these ten years later 51.4 percent remained, after another ten years 40.8 percent, in 1920 after thirty-five years, 24.6 percent, and in 1935, or after fifty years, 19 percent. The next base year, 1895, showed increasing instability; only 47.7 percent remained after ten years. It was not until after 1915 that the 1885 level again was reached. The last three base years, 1920, 1925 and 1930, showed little variation from the high mark of about 66 percent after five years and 56 percent after ten years (fig. 15.1).

The five different townships in the first rainfall belt varied quite widely. Doniphan is the northeast county of the state along the Missouri River. Center Township includes the county seat, Troy. Its leading economic

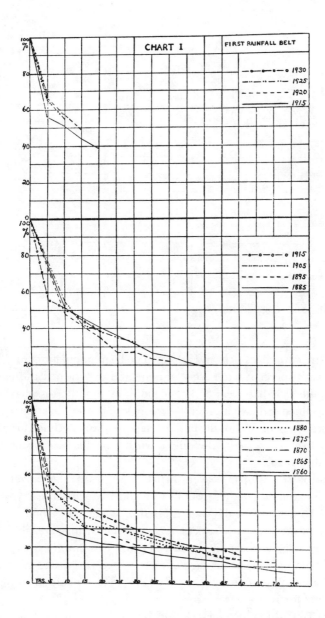

**Figure 15.1:** Persistence of habitation, first rainfall belt. Five townships are represented in this chart, all starting from 1860.

**Table 15.1:** Persistence of Farm Operators,
First Rainfall Belt (35″+: Eastern Kansas)

|      | 1860   | 1865  | 1870  | 1875  | 1880  | 1885  | 1890 | 1895  |
|------|--------|-------|-------|-------|-------|-------|------|-------|
| 1860 | 100.0% | 35.5% | 26.0% | 24.2% | 22.1% | 20.7% |      | 16.4% |
| 1865 |        | 100.0 | 42.5  | 36.2  | 30.8  | 27.8  |      | 21.2  |
| 1870 |        |       | 100.0 | 52.0  | 44.1  | 37.4  |      | 30.0  |
| 1875 |        |       |       | 100.0 | 56.0  | 48.3  |      | 37.5  |
| 1880 |        |       |       |       | 100.0 | 52.5  |      | 31.3  |
| 1885 |        |       |       |       |       | 100.0 |      | 51.4  |
| 1890 |        |       |       |       |       |       |      |       |
| 1895 |        |       |       |       |       |       |      | 100.0 |
| 1900 |        |       |       |       |       |       |      |       |
| 1905 |        |       |       |       |       |       |      |       |
| 1910 |        |       |       |       |       |       |      |       |
| 1915 |        |       |       |       |       |       |      |       |
| 1920 |        |       |       |       |       |       |      |       |
| 1925 |        |       |       |       |       |       |      |       |
| 1930 |        |       |       |       |       |       |      |       |
| 1935 |        |       |       |       |       |       |      |       |

interests are corn, livestock, and apples. The farm population was highly stabilized at 55 percent at the five-year point and 46 percent at the ten-year point for the 1865 base year and changed little until the 1915 base year, when it declined somewhat. After the World War the stabilization reached a high percentage of 70.8 for the period 1920–1925 and declined to 67.1 for the years 1930–1935, being the only township in this belt to decline in stability after 1920.

Alexandria Township in Leavenworth County lies in the Stranger Creek valley, just to the west of the city of Leavenworth. Much of the township is rough and in the early day was timbered. Water and wood made it especially attractive to early settlers. It is a general farming area. It did not reach a high degree of stability as early as Doniphan County, but the level rose steadily to a high percentage of 71.6 for the 1920 base year for the period 1920–1925. After irregularity for 1925–1930, it made a new high of 72.4 percent for 1930–1935.

Eudora Township in Douglas County is mostly bottom land, settled by Germans in the north part and Quakers, the Hesper community, in the south. It is a general farming township. In level of stability it was between

| | 1900 | 1905 | 1910 | 1915 | 1920 | 1925 | 1930 | 1935 |
|---|---|---|---|---|---|---|---|---|
| 1860 | | 14.4% | | 13.2% | 10.6% | 9.6% | 9.0% | 8.3% |
| 1865 | | 20.6 | | 17.2 | 14.4 | 14.0 | 13.1 | 12.5 |
| 1870 | | 24.5 | | 19.9 | 16.8 | 15.3 | 14.0 | 13.0 |
| 1875 | | 29.7 | | 23.7 | 21.5 | 20.1 | 19.3 | 16.4 |
| 1880 | | 30.9 | | 23.4 | 20.3 | 18.9 | 17.1 | 15.8 |
| 1885 | | 40.8 | | 31.5 | 26.5 | 24.7 | 21.5 | 19.0 |
| 1890 | | | | | | | | |
| 1895 | | 47.7 | | 35.0 | 27.0 | 27.2 | 23.4 | 21.9 |
| 1900 | | | | | | | | |
| 1905 | | 100.0 | | 54.8 | 42.0 | 38.6 | 35.2 | 32.6 |
| 1910 | | | | | | | | |
| 1915 | | | | 100.0 | 55.9 | 50.9 | 44.1 | 38.3 |
| 1920 | | | | | 100.0 | 66.3 | 56.9 | 48.8 |
| 1925 | | | | | | 100.0 | 65.6 | 54.7 |
| 1930 | | | | | | | 100.0 | 66.8 |
| 1935 | | | | | | | | 100.0 |

Doniphan and Leavenworth, with a percentage of approximately 66 for each five-year period after 1920.

The most irregular population movements of the five were found in Valley Township of Linn County. This community occupied the north watershed of the Marais des Cygnes River on the Missouri border and contains the village of Trading Post, made notorious in territorial days by John Brown's "Parallels." The first high point of stability was reached at the 1875 base year with 51 percent at five years and 49 percent at ten years. The second high point was 1905 at about the same level as 1875. The third high was the 1925 base year with 58 percent for the five years 1925–1930, but with a low figure of 37 percent for 1930–1935. The 1930 base year showed a decline also for the 1930–1935 quinquennium.

The most stable township of the group was Kanwaka in Douglas, a general farming community, lying on the ridge dividing the Wakarusa and the Kansas river valleys and between the historic towns of Lawrence and Lecompton. A very high stability was found for the base years 1865, 1870, and 1875 of 58 percent to 65 percent at the five-year point and 46 percent to 53 percent at the ten-year point. The second and third high levels were the 1885 and 1905 base years with 71.2 percent and 63 percent at the ten-year mark. Beginning with the 1915 base year the five-year level of 70 percent was practically unchanged for the succeeding base years.

The second rainfall belt, represented by six townships, started with 1860 also, as its first base year, and the curve of persistence was similar to the first rainfall belt, differing only in details. A high degree of stabilization occurred by 1885, and the curves for the base years 1895 to 1915 were almost identical with 1885. At the end of fifteen years the four stood close to 45 percent. At that point the 1915 curve diverged, but the others continued close together. The level of the 1920, 1925, and 1930 lines rose to a high point in 1930 of 71 percent at the end of five years (fig. 15.2).

Brown County, in this belt, is in the heart of the Kansas corn belt and lies just west of Doniphan County. The 1875 base year showed the highest percentage of stability until the postwar period, with 73 at five years, 61 at ten years, and 47 at fifteen years. Thereafter there was some irregularity at lower levels until the 1905 base year, which opened a period of increasing stability to almost the 1875 level. The 1925 base year was definitely lower, but the 1930 base year was again high at 72 percent for 1930–1935.

Lyon County, lying in the blue-stem pasture region, contributed three townships to this group. Agnes City Township is mostly pasture, Pike Township is largely bottom land with more general farming and alfalfa. Reading Township partakes somewhat of the characteristics of both. These townships were outstanding in showing an unusually high level of stability in the earliest year. Pike Township maintained a higher level of stability for 1860, 1865, and 1870 than for any base years since. This may be accounted for in part by the fact that it contained a closely knit Quaker community. The 1860 base year retained 60 percent at five years and 51 percent at ten years. The 1865 base year retained 68.8 percent at five years and 66.2 percent at ten years. The 1870 base year retained 67.1 percent at five years and 59.6 percent at ten years. The middle years 1875–1905 were highly stable, but at a lower level. By 1915 the stability had risen to 60 percent retained after five years and 50 percent after ten years, and succeeding base years remained almost unchanged until 1930, which advanced to 64 percent at the five-year point. The record of Agnes City Township was very similar except the level of stability was not so high in the early years. Reading Township, which was given present boundaries by 1875, reached higher levels but was more irregular.

Harvey County is in the eastern part of the wheat belt. Macon Township lies between two towns, Newton and Halstead. After a somewhat irregular beginning it achieved a very high stability by 1915. That base year retained 67 percent of its farm operators after five years and 58 percent after ten

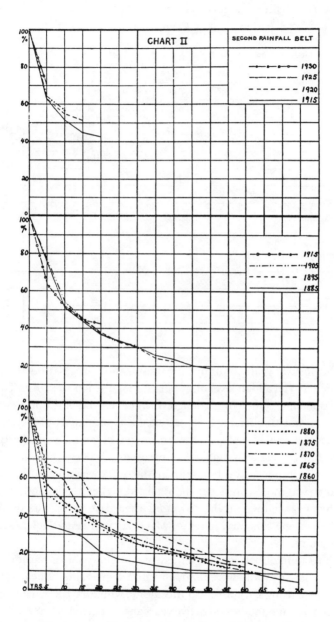

**Figure 15.2:** Persistence of habitation, second rainfall belt. The 1860, 1865, and 1870 curves represent only two townships in Lyon County, Agnes City and Pike. The 1875 and later curves represent six townships in three counties, Brown, Harvey, and Lyon.

**Table 15.2:** Persistence of Farm Operators,
Second Rainfall Belt (30" to 35": East Central Kansas)

|      | 1860   | 1865  | 1870  | 1875  | 1880  | 1885  | 1890 | 1895  |
|------|--------|-------|-------|-------|-------|-------|------|-------|
| 1860 | 100.0% | 34.5% | 31.0% | 28.7% | 20.7% | 17.2% |      | 13.7% |
| 1865 |        | 100.0 | 67.4  | 64.0  | 60.0  | 43.0  |      | 34.9  |
| 1870 |        |       | 100.0 | 66.0  | 58.6  | 41.3  |      | 31.3  |
| 1875 |        |       |       | 100.0 | 57.0  | 46.8  |      | 35.3  |
| 1880 |        |       |       |       | 100.0 | 51.4  |      | 38.4  |
| 1885 |        |       |       |       |       | 100.0 |      | 51.2  |
| 1890 |        |       |       |       |       |       |      |       |
| 1895 |        |       |       |       |       |       |      | 100.0 |
| 1900 |        |       |       |       |       |       |      |       |
| 1905 |        |       |       |       |       |       |      |       |
| 1910 |        |       |       |       |       |       |      |       |
| 1915 |        |       |       |       |       |       |      |       |
| 1920 |        |       |       |       |       |       |      |       |
| 1925 |        |       |       |       |       |       |      |       |
| 1930 |        |       |       |       |       |       |      |       |
| 1935 |        |       |       |       |       |       |      |       |

years. The postwar years continued the stabilization process until the 1930 base year achieved a high level of 75 percent retained in 1935. Alta Township is about the center of a triangle formed by the cities of Newton, Hutchinson, and McPherson. In its early years it was settled by Mennonites from Russia and Germany. The percentages of persistence are quite irregular, but are relatively high. In the early years, 1880 to 1905, inclusive, the Alta Township level was higher than Macon Township, but since that time Macon was more consistent and retained higher percentages, except for the five-year figures on the 1920 and 1930 base years. The number retained after ten years was higher for Macon than for Alta even for these two exceptions.

The third rainfall belt is represented by four townships, but for early years two whole counties were used, Dickinson and Saline. The first base year was 1860, using Dickinson County alone, which gave a percentage of 58.3 percent retained at the end of five years and 42 percent at the end of ten years. The 1865 base, using both counties, retained 43 percent at the end of five years. By 1875 the township lines were sufficiently established to change to the township units, and one township in Phillips County was introduced for 1875 and one from Kingman in 1880. The high point of persistence was the 1875 base year, for which 57 percent remained after five

| | 1900 | 1905 | 1910 | 1915 | 1920 | 1925 | 1930 | 1935 |
|---|---|---|---|---|---|---|---|---|
| 1860 | | 11.5% | | 11.5% | 11.5% | 9.2% | 6.9% | 5.7% |
| 1865 | | 26.7 | | 20.0 | 16.2 | 16.2 | 12.8 | 10.4 |
| 1870 | | 24.6 | | 20.0 | 14.6 | 13.3 | 11.3 | 10.0 |
| 1875 | | 25.3 | | 20.9 | 18.4 | 17.0 | 14.9 | 13.6 |
| 1880 | | 28.4 | | 22.9 | 19.7 | 17.8 | 15.1 | 14.3 |
| 1885 | | 37.0 | | 30.2 | 25.7 | 23.7 | 20.2 | 19.0 |
| 1890 | | | | | | | | |
| 1895 | | 51.0 | | 37.9 | 32.8 | 30.4 | 24.3 | 22.9 |
| 1900 | | | | | | | | |
| 1905 | | 100.0 | | 53.8 | 45.1 | 36.7 | 32.8 | 30.8 |
| 1910 | | | | | | | | |
| 1915 | | | | 100.0 | 62.9 | 51.7 | 44.7 | 42.5 |
| 1920 | | | | | 100.0 | 63.0 | 55.0 | 51.7 |
| 1925 | | | | | | 100.0 | 64.0 | 56.4 |
| 1930 | | | | | | | 100.0 | 71.0 |
| 1935 | | | | | | | | 100.0 |

years, 47 percent after ten years, 37 percent after twenty years, 21 percent after thirty years, and 11 percent after forty-five years. All base years from 1875 to 1895, inclusive, showed a lower rate of persistence. Beginning with 1905 the level of stability rose steadily to the last base year, 1930, with 73.5 percent after five years.

The third zone is in the east central wheat belt. Dickinson and Saline counties lie in the lower Smoky River valley, which in the seventies received the name the Golden Belt as descriptive of its leading crop. Jewell County, on the Nebraska line, raised less wheat and more corn and livestock. Kingman County is predominantly a wheat country. The record of these counties was so nearly uniform that they need not be treated separately. From the time of settlement to the World War each base year retained 55 percent to 58 percent of its farm operators after five years, and 41 percent to 46 percent after ten years. Kingman County, the one farthest southwest, was highest in stability, closing in 1935 with 80.8 percent of the farm operators of 1930 (fig. 15.3).

The fourth rainfall belt started from an 1875 base, losing in five years all but 38 percent, in ten years all but 24 percent, in twenty years all but 14 percent, and after sixty years there remained 4 percent. The 1880 base year

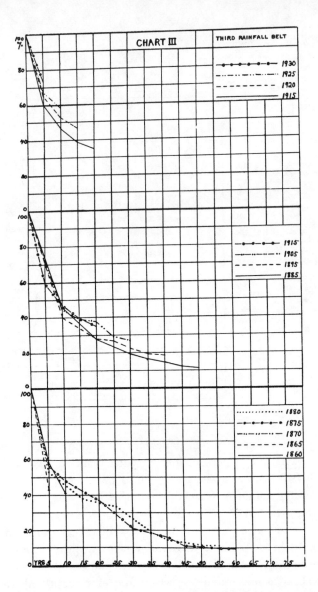

**Figure 15.3:** Persistence of habitation, third rainfall belt. The 1860 and 1865 curves represent the whole of two counties, Dickinson and Saline. After 1870 the population became so large that it did not seem practicable to carry them further in that form. The 1875 curve represents one township each from Dickinson, Jewell, and Saline counties. The 1880 curve represents one township each from Dickinson, Kingman, and Saline counties. The census roll for Sinclair Township in Jewell County is missing for that year. The 1880 and later curves are based on one township each in the four above-named counties, except 1895 for which the census roll for Walnut Township in Saline County is missing.

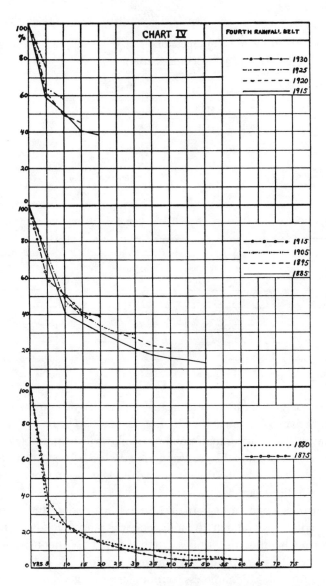

**Figure 15.4:** Persistence of habitation, fourth rainfall belt. The 1875 curve represents four townships, one each in Ellsworth and Barber counties, and two in Edwards County. The 1880 curve represents eight townships, one each from the counties of Barber, Ellis, Ness, Phillips, and Russell, and three from Edwards. Ellsworth is not included because of changes in township lines. The 1885 curve represents ten townships, the same ones named for 1880 with the addition of one from Ellsworth and one from Decatur County. The remaining curves on this chart are based on the same ten townships.

**Table 15.3:** Persistence of Farm Operators,
Third Rainfall Belt (25″ to 30″: Central Kansas)

|        | 1860   | 1865  | 1870  | 1875    | 1880   | 1885  | 1890 | 1895  |
|--------|--------|-------|-------|---------|--------|-------|------|-------|
| 1860   | 100.0% | 58.3% | 41.6% |         |        |       |      |       |
| 1865   |        | 100.0 | 43.0  |         |        |       |      |       |
| 1870   |        |       |       |         |        |       |      |       |
| 1875   |        |       |       | 100.0 % | 56.6%  | 47.7% |      | 36.8% |
| 1880   |        |       |       |         | 100.0  | 53.0  |      | 38.0  |
| 1885   |        |       |       |         |        | 100.0 |      | 45.6  |
| 1890   |        |       |       |         |        |       |      |       |
| 1895   |        |       |       |         |        |       |      | 100.0 |
| 1900   |        |       |       |         |        |       |      |       |
| 1905   |        |       |       |         |        |       |      |       |
| 1910   |        |       |       |         |        |       |      |       |
| 1915   |        |       |       |         |        |       |      |       |
| 1920   |        |       |       |         |        |       |      |       |
| 1925   |        |       |       |         |        |       |      |       |
| 1930   |        |       |       |         |        |       |      |       |
| 1935   |        |       |       |         |        |       |      |       |

followed closely the same curve at the ten- and twenty-year points, but held up to more than 6 percent at the fifty-five-year mark. The base years 1895, 1905, and 1915 reached a high point of stability for the prewar period at more than 47 percent. In the postwar period the level of persistence rose in each successive census until the 1930 curve reached 76.1 percent in 1935 or at the end of five years (fig. 15.4).

The fourth belt is in the heart of the Kansas wheat region, and in area it is the largest of the five rainfall divisions. The selection of ten townships was made from eight different counties. On the northern border two counties, Phillips and Decatur, produce corn and livestock as well as wheat. Ellsworth, Russell, Ellis and Ness counties include a good representation of cattle country. Edwards County is devoted almost altogether to wheat. Barber County produces cattle and wheat. Five of the individual townships, in Barber, Decatur, Edwards (Trenton), Ellsworth, and Russell counties, were moderately irregular in turnover until 1905 or 1915, and thereafter increased consistently in stability to a high level of 70 percent to 80 percent for the five years 1930–1935. In the others the irregularity from base to base continued through their whole history, but all arrived at a level of 70 percent or more for the final five years. In 1905 the level of stability declined in the townships from Barber, Decatur, Edwards (Kinsley and

|  | 1900 | 1905 | 1910 | 1915 | 1920 | 1925 | 1930 | 1935 |
|---|---|---|---|---|---|---|---|---|
| 1860 |  |  |  |  |  |  |  |  |
| 1865 |  |  |  |  |  |  |  |  |
| 1870 |  |  |  |  |  |  |  |  |
| 1875 |  | 20.7% |  | 16.2% | 11.7% | 10.8% | 10.0% | 9.9% |
| 1880 |  | 23.4 |  | 18.6 | 15.0 | 13.3 | 11.7 | 11.7 |
| 1885 |  | 27.7 |  | 18.8 | 16.4 | 14.6 | 12.3 | 11.4 |
| 1890 |  |  |  |  |  |  |  |  |
| 1895 |  | 40.0 |  | 27.7 | 26.4 | 22.3 | 19.2 | 18.4 |
| 1900 |  |  |  |  |  |  |  |  |
| 1905 |  | 100.0 |  | 44.2 | 39.0 | 37.6 | 29.2 | 26.8 |
| 1910 |  |  |  |  |  |  |  |  |
| 1915 |  |  |  | 100.0 | 59.5 | 46.3 | 39.2 | 35.0 |
| 1920 |  |  |  |  | 100.0 | 65.2 | 53.3 | 46.8 |
| 1925 |  |  |  |  |  | 100.0 | 66.7 | 57.7 |
| 1930 |  |  |  |  |  |  | 100.0 | 73.5 |
| 1935 |  |  |  |  |  |  |  | 100.0 |

Wayne), Ness, and Phillips counties, but increased in the other four. In 1915 the decline occurred only in the townships from Barber and Decatur counties, and in 1920 only in Ness, Phillips, and Russell counties.

The fifth rainfall belt, represented by two whole counties, and five townships from two others, was settled in the late eighties. As the federal census for 1890 is closed to investigators, the first base year available is the state census of 1895. At the ten-year mark this belt retained 33 percent of its members, at twenty-five, 16 percent, and at forty years (1935) 8.8 percent. The succeeding base-year curves were consistently higher, and that of 1925 substantially higher—with 59.1 percent retained after five years and 50.5 percent after ten years. The record for 1930–1935 was only eight-tenths of a point lower. For the region as a whole the record of stability for post–World War years is lower than for the belts farther east, but an analysis by separate counties presents a different view (fig. 15.5).

Three of the counties represented lie on the west line of the state, Cheyenne in the Republican River valley, Wallace in the Smoky River valley, and Hamilton in the Arkansas River valley. Gove County is the third county east from Wallace, in the Smoky River valley. The cattle industry was dominant in this region until the wheat boom under the influence of

**Table 15.4:** Persistence of Farm Operators,
Fourth Rainfall Belt (20″ to 25″: West Central Kansas)

|      | 1875 | 1880 | 1885 | 1890 | 1895 | 1900 | 1905 | 1910 | 1915 | 1920 | 1925 | 1930 | 1935 |
|------|------|------|------|------|------|------|------|------|------|------|------|------|------|
| 1875 | 100.0% | 38.0% | 24.0% |  | 14.1% |  | 8.7% |  | 5.5% | 4.3% | 5.5% | 5.5% | 4.3% |
| 1880 |  | 100.0 | 29.6 |  | 17.2 |  | 13.1 |  | 10.0 | 8.6 | 7.6 | 6.7 | 6.1 |
| 1885 |  |  | 100.0 |  | 39.3 |  | 30.0 |  | 21.0 | 17.5 | 15.9 | 14.8 | 13.7 |
| 1890 |  |  |  |  |  |  |  |  |  |  |  |  |  |
| 1895 |  |  |  |  | 100.0 |  | 47.4 |  | 33.6 | 30.0 | 26.7 | 23.0 | 21.6 |
| 1900 |  |  |  |  |  |  |  |  |  |  |  |  |  |
| 1905 |  |  |  |  |  |  | 100.0 |  | 47.0 | 39.4 | 33.7 | 30.0 | 29.9 |
| 1910 |  |  |  |  |  |  |  |  |  |  |  |  |  |
| 1915 |  |  |  |  |  |  |  |  | 100.0 | 59.6 | 50.7 | 41.1 | 38.8 |
| 1920 |  |  |  |  |  |  |  |  |  | 100.0 | 62.3 | 49.3 | 45.3 |
| 1925 |  |  |  |  |  |  |  |  |  |  | 100.0 | 64.4 | 58.3 |
| 1930 |  |  |  |  |  |  |  |  |  |  |  | 100.0 | 76.1 |
| 1935 |  |  |  |  |  |  |  |  |  |  |  |  | 100.0 |

power farm equipment in the twenties. Throughout the whole history of these counties, however, there was a wide divergence between them in stability of population, but the record was quite consistent within each one. Cheyenne County was always most stable, Wallace next, and Gove, farther east, was third. Hamilton County was substantially lower than the others, and as it turned out its numbers in the post–World War period had too much influence as against the four townships of Cheyenne County in the combined figures for the fifth rainfall belt. Cheyenne County, represented by four townships, not only had the highest level of stability in this belt, but it ranked near the top for any rainfall belt. Only four townships were higher in the fourth belt, those in Ellis, Ellsworth, Ness, and Russell. Two were higher in the third belt, those in Dickinson and Kingman. Three were higher in the second belt, those in Brown and Harvey. Only Kanwaka Township in Douglas County was higher in the first belt. The record for Wallace County would average well with townships in any part of the state.

    A study of individual townships presents additional interesting data. Jaqua Township, in the southwest corner of Cheyenne County, while somewhat irregular from year to year, achieved the highest level of persistence of any township in the state represented in this study, regardless of location (fig. 15.5, inset). It had no near rival in the fourth rainfall belt. Vinita Township in Kingman County was nearest to it in the third belt, Macon Township in Harvey County in the second, and Kanwaka

Township in Douglas County in the first. In spite of its low average, Hamilton County had one township, Bear Creek, with an exceptionally high stability which would place it favorably in any rainfall belt.

Several factors enter into the situation in the fifth belt that are either absent or less pronounced farther east. In age of settlement it had scarcely passed the frontier period when the World War came, if the same time is allowed for that process as in the eastern belts. On the contrary it might be argued that modern industrialism had shortened the period necessary for

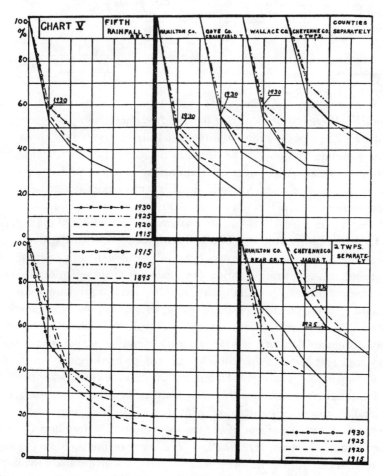

Figure 15.5: Persistence of habitation, fifth rainfall belt. This chart contains only two divisions because of the short period since its first settlement. The inserts at the right of the figures for the belt as a whole present the curves for individual counties, and for certain individual townships.

**Table 15.5:** Persistence of Farm Operators,
Fifth Rainfall Belt (20″ —: Western Kansas)

|  | 1895 | 1900 | 1905 | 1910 | 1915 | 1920 | 1925 | 1930 | 1935 |  |  |  |  |
|---|---|---|---|---|---|---|---|---|---|---|---|---|---|
| 1895 | 100.0% |  | 33.3% |  | 20.0% | 16.6% | 14.2% | 11.7% | 10.7% |  |  |  |  |
| 1900 |  |  |  |  |  |  |  |  |  |  |  |  |  |
| 1905 |  |  | 100.0 |  | 39.4 | 29.8 | 27.0 | 21.7 | 19.8 |  |  |  |  |
| 1910 |  |  |  |  |  |  |  |  |  |  |  |  |  |
| 1915 |  |  |  |  | 100.0 | 53.1 | 40.9 | 34.6 | 30.5 |  |  |  |  |
| 1920 |  |  |  |  |  | 100.0 | 55.5 | 43.0 | 38.7 |  |  |  |  |
| 1925 |  |  |  |  |  |  | 100.0 | 59.1 | 50.5 |  |  |  |  |
| 1930 |  |  |  |  |  |  |  | 100.0 | 58.3 |  |  |  |  |
| 1935 |  |  |  |  |  |  |  |  | 100.0 |  |  |  |  |

frontier adjustment. At least, there were some very different influences at work, but there is little or no clue to what their effect should have been on stability of farm population. In connection with the later period, the World War stimulated somewhat the emphasis on wheat, but the wheat boom proper, associated with power farm equipment, did not come until the last half of the twenties and the early thirties. It was more extensive in the southwest counties, such as Hamilton, than in the northwest. The depression did not begin to make itself felt in a serious way until the winter of 1931–1932.

In connection with the wheat boom two unusual factors were introduced, the absentee farm operator (often called the suit-case farmer) and the farm corporation. Adequate treatment of these is not possible because complete information of a nature required for this kind of a study was not collected by the census enumerators, and some of the names of these classes may not have been placed on the rolls. In Wallace County only a few absentee operators, who can be clearly identified as such, were listed, and none was listed in the Cheyenne townships used, nor in Grainfield Township in Gove County. In Hamilton County quite a number appeared.

The rolls for 1935 are probably most complete because of their use by the federal allotment administration. In Wallace County eighteen absentees were listed, or 4.3 percent of the farm operators. In Hamilton County twenty-five absentees were listed, or 6 percent of the operators of the county. In Lamont Township in the latter county ten of the ninety-five farm operators, or 10.5 percent, were of this class in 1931 and in 1935 fourteen of ninety-one farm operators, or 15.4 percent.

The wheat-farming corporations were present in Wallace and Hamilton counties, but held the larger acreage in the former. In 1930 one corporation was listed in Hamilton County with 3,360 acres, or the equivalent of five 640-acre farms. By 1935 its holdings had been disposed of, but a second corporation which acquired acreage after 1930 still held 2,800 acres in 1935. In Wallace County in 1930 one corporation held 25,610 acres distributed through three townships, or an equivalent of forty 640-acre farms. By 1935 it still held 3,200 acres. The census rolls do not show how many farm operators were displaced when these corporations accumulated their acreage, nor how many new operators returned when the corporations were carrying out forced liquidation of their holdings under the requirements of the legislative act of 1931. There can be no question, however, that the net effect of both absenteeism and the corporation farming episode was to increase instability of farm operators, even though the extent of that influence cannot be determined.

The history of the turnover of farm operators seems to fall into three periods, except in the fifth belt: the settlement period of exceptionally rapid change, a middle period of relative stabilization at rather low levels, and the recent period of higher stability. During the settlement period exceptionally heavy losses of population are registered for the first and second base years in the first, second,[5] and fourth rainfall belts, and relatively moderate losses in the third and fifth. The Civil War period occupied the four years following the 1860 census and might seem to account for the great losses in the first and second belts, but the same fact could not account for the opposite effect in the third belt.

In most of the curves the losses of population during the settlement period are especially heavy for the first ten years, and then the curve flattens out during the second decade. For the curves representing the period of relative stabilization, the losses are not so great during the first decade, and are relatively greater for the second decade than for the first base-year curves. In other words, these losses after stabilization are distributed more evenly over the first twenty years, rather than being concentrated in the first ten years as in the curves for the settlement years.

The second period has been characterized as one of relative stabilization. The rate of turnover was still high. Few townships retained more than 55 percent to 60 percent of their farm operators for five years or 45 percent to 50 percent of them for ten years. The period 1915 to 1920, the World War era, seems to mark a division point for most townships between the second and third periods. With relative suddenness the percentage of persistence for five years increased by ten to fifteen points, many townships retaining between 65 percent and 82 percent. For the first time it could be said that the emphasis was on stability rather than change. In the older eastern part of the state this new development appeared in a few cases as early as 1905, but a number of instances are found in 1915 and by 1920 it was general.[6] The general trend was for stability to increase with the age of the community.

The outstanding fact to be derived from this analysis of the persistence of farm operators, however, is that the general pattern presented by the curves of persistence is very nearly the same for the five rainfall belts. The two extreme western belts show results only slightly lower on the whole than the eastern belts, although some of them are actually higher. In other words, the persistence of farm operators was a relatively constant factor, except for the immediate settlement period. While the total number of farm operators fluctuated, the rate of turnover was constant. When the total was declining, it meant only that the losses from the normal turnover were not being replaced by new arrivals, and when the total number rose, it meant that they were more than being replaced. In either case the losses from any particular base period were going on at a fairly constant rate.

Further analysis of the curves does not indicate any uniform reflection of the influence of economic cycles or of rainfall cycles. If anything, after the communities became established, periods of drouth and depression such as 1895 and 1930 when taken as a base tended to show a higher stability than some other periods. The same is true of the post-war depression in many townships using 1920 as a base. The periods of reputed prosperity, such as those beginning with 1905 or 1925, displayed an unusually high rate of turnover in many communities. The relation of soil and land tenure to turnover requires further study. The foreign population was usually more stable than the native-born, but not so much so as is usually supposed. The second and later generations seemed to take on rather quickly many of the characteristics of the native-born. When the combined data for each of the rainfall belts is broken down into the individual township samples, the separate curves of persistence show wide fluctuation, but the fluctuations within a rainfall belt, with a few exceptions, are as wide on the whole as between rainfall belts.

From the facts available, it would appear that the problem is primarily one of group behavior, apart from specifically assignable accidents of farm life in the separate communities or regions involved. In other words, under any given set of general conditions, the farm operators in all parts of the state reacted in much the same manner, the variations of local physical environment exercising only a secondary or minor influence. For any conclusions that may be drawn, that assumption may well be employed as the point of departure. An interesting suggestion in this connection may be derived from a study of persistence of students in college. The data on a freshman group entering the college of liberal arts of the University of Kansas in 1928 provides a curve of persistence over a period of four to six years identical in shape with the curves for Kansas farm operators over a period of twenty to thirty years. Whether the matter has any significance or not, the fact remains that the students as a group in their brief career in college behave in much the same manner as their parents in their career as farm operators. Unfortunately, comparable data are not available for other social groups.

The third phase of the problem of turnover of farm operators is to determine the proportion of farm operators of particular periods who are descendants of those of an earlier period. This procedure makes the approach from the opposite direction from the second. Three base years were chosen, 1885, 1915, and 1935, for the eastern belts whose settlement dated from 1860. The absence of data from the federal census of 1910 made it necessary to choose a prior or later date. The year 1915 was taken because it represented more nearly the base used for comparative purposes in most of the post–World War discussions of agriculture. The later-settled parts of the state presented other problems, and for part of the third rainfall belt and for the fourth belt two periods were taken, dividing the life of the communities as near the half-way point as possible. The fifth belt was handled similarly, only the mid-point fell at 1915 instead of 1905 as in the fourth. Tables 1–6 report the results in detail and therefore only brief interpretations will be presented here. In all parts of the state the original or early settlers and their descendants constitute an extremely small proportion of the later or contemporary community. Except for Kanwaka Township, 8 percent is the highest representation the settlers of 1860 held seventy-five years later.[7] These facts run contrary to much of the tradition about the character of a community being determined by the people who settled it and established its original institutions. Obviously, the pioneers constituted too small a proportion of the later community to exercise a controlling influence. The proportion of a community that can be traced back to later base points rose rapidly as those dates approached the present. It is notable, nevertheless, that in few townships does the proportion of the community which traced its origin to 1915 or 1905 appear as high as might be expected from the percentages of persistence of farm operators indicated in the previous section. In many cases the older families were represented in the community by only one operator, while newer families might have two or more. The opposite is true, however, in a few cases where one or more prolific families came to constitute a large proportion of the community. In one particular case, Wheatland Township, Ellis County, the male lines of two families constitute 35.4 percent of the operators of 1935.

A comparison of figures for the five rainfall belts shows quite similar percentages for the different belts, except for the fifth (fig. 15.6). If age of the community is recognized, however, the percentages there are much higher than for any of the eastern belts at a similar community age.

The fact of the high rate of turnover of rural population during the early period and the middle periods of Kansas history suggests numerous questions about the effects such instability has had on institutions: political, economic, and social. As Edwards County has been studied most intimately, some illustrations are chosen from there. During the frontier stage of development, scarcely a mention was made in the press concerning reform of local political institutions. The sole question at issue in elections was the county-seat ring against the field, for the maintenance of power, and incidentally, the money income from offices and county contracts. This was particularly important in the early years during hard times when

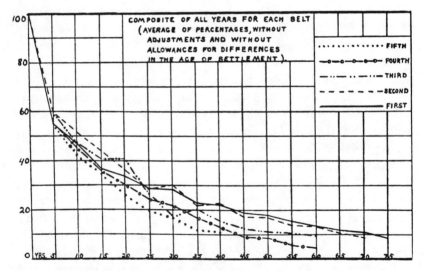

Figure 15.6: Persistence of habitation, composite of rainfall belts. This chart presents a summary of the charts for the five individual belts in the form of a composite of all years for each belt arrived at by averaging the percentages of persistence for each base year. This procedure is open to criticism, but it is sufficiently accurate to assist in presenting general trends. As the data for the first three belts begins with 1860, the fourth with 1875 and the fifth with 1895, the instability associated with the frontier period has too much influence in the averages for the western belts.

public money, derived mostly from taxing the railroads, was about the only cash in circulation in the community. In 1880 an unusual situation was presented when the old county ring, which called itself Republican, was crumbling, and the drouth entered its second year. Emigration of politicians was so extensive that when the time came to call the Republican county convention in the midst of a national campaign, no member of the county committee was a resident of the county. The people got a new deal in politics when a group of citizens assumed the responsibility for calling a mass meeting to reorganize the party. The net result, however, was just to establish a new ring on a basis similar to the old. Whenever the newer settlers in the county tried to get control, the county ring raised the cry of "carpetbaggers" trying to exploit the "old settlers." One editor denounced in language more vigorous than elegant such attempts "to show that unless a man ran wild with the buffalo years ago, he is not eligible to office."[8] A correspondent closed the incident with the remark that if the candidate in question was a "tenderfoot" then three-fourths of the voters were also. A few years later, after the Populist reformers had been in office for some time, a disgusted member of the party protested the failure to reduce taxes and to reform the fee system. One of the officials made a formal reply in which he invoked that age-old political wisdom so dear to reformers as well as to old party men that discussion "may create dissension in our party," and that the writer of the protest "implies that it would greatly please him . . . for the present incumbents . . . to preach their own funeral sermons and proclaim themselves fools at one and the same time by taking less than the Republican statute makes it lawful for them to take."[9]

Certainly the instability of the frontier population, together with the bare bread-and-butter existence of the community as a whole, retarded the progressive adaptation of local political institutions to meet the obligations expected of them as a result of rapidly changing economic and social conditions. This influence was not limited to the frontier, because the older eastern communities were demoralized by competition with western agriculture. And furthermore, even after the frontier had achieved the status of established rural communities, the high rate of turnover of population kept at a minimum the interest which this moving farm population generated for its changing, yet unchanged, local institutions.

The economic development of the farm communities was not promoted by the high rate of turnover of farmers. Possibly agricultural methods did not suffer so seriously in the humid areas of the East as they did in the more arid country west of the Missouri River. Each new crop of Eastern farmers found that they must unlearn most of what they thought they knew about

Table 15.6: Percentage of Farm Operators in Each Rainfall Belt Representing Operators of Earlier Periods

| First Rainfall Belt, 35"+ | 1860, numbers | 25 years later, percentage of 1885 | 55 years later, percentage of 1915 | 75 years later, percentage of 1935 | 1885, numbers | 30 years later, percentage of 1915 | 50 years later, percentage of 1935 | 1915, numbers | 20 years later, percentage of 1935 |
|---|---|---|---|---|---|---|---|---|---|
| Doniphan County, Center Township | 137 | 20.4 | 12.7 | 6.5 | 250 | 43.3 | 28.4 | 325 | 45.5 |
| Douglas County, Eudora Township | 88 | 10.6 | 4.9 | 4.2 | 264 | 51.1 | 38.3 | 223 | 60.3 |
| Douglas County, Kanwaka Township | 88 | 27.2 | 22.4 | 17.0 | 125 | 43.7 | 37.3 | 169 | 57.7 |
| Leavenworth County, Alexandria Township | 90 | 13.2 | 10.4 | 6.6 | 189 | 44.4 | 30.0 | 173 | 60.0 |
| Linn County, Valley Township | 75 | 8.8 | 6.7 | 4.7 | 125 | 27.2 | 27.4 | 147 | 50.0 |
| Total | 478 | 15.6 | 11.3 | 7.9 | 953 | 43.0 | 32.1 | 1,037 | 53.5 |
| **Second Rainfall Belt, 30" to 35"** | | | | | | | | | |
| Brown County, Walnut Township | * | 10.1 | 5.4 | 5.7 | 237 | 45.0 | 33.2 | 227 | 64.1 |
| Lyon County, Agnes City Township | 40 | 0.0 | 0.0 | 0.0 | 198 | 32.0 | 25.7 | 238 | 66.8 |
| Lyon County, Pike Township | 47 | 19.4 | 12.6 | 8.1 | 134 | 37.7 | 24.5 | 159 | 46.0 |
| Total | | | | | 569 | 38.1 | 28.1 | 624 | 59.7 |
| | | | | | 1875, number | 30 years later, percentage of 1905 | 60 years later, percentage of 1935 | 1905, numbers | 30 years later, percentage of 1935 |
| Harvey County, Alta Township | | | | | 62 | 27.4 | 23.0 | 91 | 61.0 |
| Harvey County, Macon Township | | | | | 87 | 21.5 | 14.0 | 116 | 44.8 |
| Total | | | | | 149 | 24.1 | 18.6 | 207 | 53.1 |
| **Third Rainfall Belt, 25" to 30"** | | | | | 1875, number | 30 years later, percentage of 1905 | 60 years later, percentage of 1935 | 1905, numbers | 30 years later, percentage of 1935 |
| Dickinson County, Buckeye Township | | | | | 73 | 14.0 | 7.2 | 100 | 30.0 |
| Jewell County, Sinclair Township | | | | | 79 | 23.3 | 20.9 | 103 | 36.0 |
| Kingman County, Vinita Township | | | | | (1880) 80 | 29.4 | 17.3 | 85 | 45.2 |
| Saline County, Walnut Township | | | | | 70 | 24.1 | 13.7 | 91 | 34.7 |
| Total† | | | | | 222 | 20.5 | 13.3 | 379 | 35.7 |

## Fourth Rainfall Belt, 25″ to 30″

| | 1875, numbers | 30 years later, percentage of 1905 | 60 years later, percentage of 1935 | 1905, numbers | 30 years later, percentage of 1935 |
|---|---|---|---|---|---|
| Barber County, Sun City and subdivisions | 19 | 5.5 | 3.0 | 72 | 40.0 |
| Edwards County, Kinsley Township | 39 | 4.4 | 2.2 | 68 | 21.8 |
| Edwards County, Trenton Township | 40 | 0.0 | 0.0 | 40 | 36.0 |
| Total | 98 | 3.8 | 1.8 | 180 | 35.4 |

| | 1880, numbers | 25 years later, percentage of 1905 | 55 years later, percentage of 1935 | 1905, numbers | 30 years later, percentage of 1935 |
|---|---|---|---|---|---|
| Edwards County, Wayne Township | 95 | 16.6 | 14.0 | 72 | 52.8 |
| Ellis County, Wheatland Township | 189 | 52.8 | 68.0 | 65 | 82.8 |
| Ness County, Highpoint Township | 90 | 23.0 | 12.0 | 96 | 32.8 |
| Phillips County, Long Island Township | 110 | 35.2 | 19.0 | 142 | 40.4 |
| Russell County, Big Creek Township | 218 | 30.5 | 16.1 | 108 | 56.5 |
| Total | 702 | 31.2 | 24.0 | 483 | 51.0 |

| | 1885, numbers | 20 years later, percentage of 1905 | 50 years later, percentage of 1935 | 1905, numbers | 30 years later, percentage of 1935 |
|---|---|---|---|---|---|
| Decatur County, Center Township | 51 | 6.4 | 6.0 | 47 | 44.0 |
| Ellsworth County, Lincoln Township | 59 | 38.3 | 19.3 | 47 | 44.0 |
| Total | 110 | 22.3 | 13.1 | 94 | 44.0 |

## Fifth Rainfall Belt, 20″—

| | 1895, numbers | 20 years later, percentage of 1915 | 40 years later, percentage of 1935 | 1915, numbers | 20 years later, percentage of 1935 |
|---|---|---|---|---|---|
| Cheyenne County, four townships | 236 | 38.9 | 24.8 | 190 | 41.9 |
| Gove County, Grainfield Township | 28 | 11.8 | 6.1 | 67 | 31.7 |
| Hamilton County | 197 | 11.8 | 3.6 | 321 | 21.6 |
| Wallace County | 355 | 22.0 | 10.5 | 317 | 34.3 |
| Total | 816 | 21.2 | 10.7 | 895 | 31.1 |
| Cheyenne County, Jaqua Township | 40 | 36.0 | 23.4 | 39 | 48.9 |
| Hamilton County, Bear Creek Township | 22 | 16.0 | 14.6 | 50 | 30.5 |

*County undivided.    †Omitting Vinita Township for figures derived from 1875 base.

agriculture and adapt themselves to new methods and to new crops. A large proportion starved out or moved out for other reasons without ever learning. It is well to remember that the tillage methods and the varieties of wheat that have given outstanding distinction to the Kansas hard winter wheat belt have become standard only since 1905. Forty years is a long time to discover what crops to raise and how to grow them.

Social institutions suffered more seriously if anything than others. Again and again lyceums, debating societies, literary clubs, and dancing clubs were organized, only to break up within a few months. Each new organization usually carried a large proportion of new names indicative of the rapidly changing population. Churches suffered along with other institutions. In Wayne Township, Edwards County, the first religious organization was Methodist church, South. Why this should have been is difficult to explain, because there were scarcely any southern people in the community. Possibly a preacher on a nearby circuit was willing to add this community to his other charges as an additional source of income. During the cattle boom of the middle eighties the ranch element and large farmers organized a Protestant Episcopal church, and hauling stone from a distance built a little Gothic church amid the sand hills. It had its six gables and a cross, a vestry room, an organ room, paneled ceilings, stained glass memorial windows, and rented pews. With the crash in the cattle business, the ranches came into the possession of the 160-acre farmers and the loan companies, and aristocracy in religion disappeared with the cattlemen. The 160-acre farmers organized a Methodist Episcopal church and put up a little frame building. After 1900, Missouri immigrants came and with them the Christian church and the Baptist church. With the shifting of population both of the latter failed in a few years, leaving only the Methodists. Probably the Methodists survived only because of a strong centralized organization and an emotional religion which provided the psychological compensation necessary in the arid life of the plains. Across the river in the German communities, the Catholic church, also a strong centralized organization with a genius for reaching the masses, maintained its position. Churches organized on a relatively independent congregational basis had little chance of survival amid an unstable and changing population, except in the larger towns. This discussion of churches suggests further that changing community characteristics are closely related to changing sources of interstate migration, but that is a problem of sufficient importance to require a separate treatment.

The foregoing discussion applied to the period prior to the World War, when instability was the outstanding fact. The recent period of relatively high stability may produce different results. In any event, if the higher level of stability persists, it provides a substantially different population environment within which economic, social and political institutions must function and develop. What the results may be, only time can tell.

Under prevailing conditions in agriculture it would be remarkable indeed not to recognize the question whether the conclusions reached concerning the turnover of farm population have any significance for current agricultural policies. On April 11, 1935, a Midwest economic conference held at Kansas City devoted a session to the subject of land utilization policies. The plan of the national resources board was outlined, explaining how the government planned to purchase seventy-five million acres of submarginal land, to extend grass areas as protection against erosion, to relocate farmers on more economically planned farms, and for other purposes. In the course of the discussion S. L. Miller, of the University of Iowa, was quoted in the press as saying: "I was brought up in western Kansas and I know you have a lot more failures where you fail to get rain. The problem is whether or not we intend to conserve our resources." The opposite side of the question was taken by E. S. Sparks, of the University of South Dakota, who was quoted as saying: "It has always been my experience that good farmers succeed almost anywhere you put them and poor farmers will fail on the best land in Iowa. Why shift them around? You still have the problem of farm management." He developed his theme further by declaring that until the government knew more about what it was doing the program looked like folderol.[10]

It is clear that Sparks was looking at the problem from the standpoint of the farmer as an individual and as a member of a group whose behavior is determined by forces among which national land utilization and other economic policies and conditions are largely incidentals. The results of this investigation of the turnover of farm population do not constitute proof, of course, but so far as they may contribute to enlargement of knowledge about the conditions within which agricultural policies must function, they tend to give support to the Sparks contention. Possibly one further observation might be added, that the whole discussion might well lead to a reconsideration of the time-tried National Grange dictum that the farmer is more important than the farm.

In certain respects the relation of farm population movements to agricultural policy is reasonably clear. The mere fact of a high degree of persistence or of mobility of farm operators does not necessarily mean either prosperity or failure. A highly mobile population may be prosperous, and a highly stabilized community may be stagnant and backward. On the other hand, the reverse may be true in both cases. At least there is nothing in this study to the contrary except during the early frontier stage. Much that has been proposed in the way of agricultural policy implies either directly or indirectly that a causal relationship does exist. If policies designed to increase rural prosperity are expected to stabilize rural population, there is little hope of success. If resettlement or land utilization projects require operators to remain over a period of years, they will not hold out much hope thereby of insuring prosperity. Attempts to stabilize population in such resettlement plans run counter to the group habits of Kansas farmers, and there is no reason to believe that they differ widely from other farmers of the major agricultural areas. It is vital to such policies to know first why farmers move as they have done and why a rapid stabilization occurred during the post–World War period, and whether there is reason to assume that the high level of stability will continue. Without a fairly exact analysis of the factors determining such movements, any agricultural policy which directly or indirectly involves movement or resettlement of farm population is obviously a step in the dark.

## Notes

1. Maps showing types-of-farming areas, rainfall and growing seasons may be found conveniently in J. A. Hodges, et al., "Types of Farming in Kansas," *Kansas Agricultural Experiment Station Bulletin* 251 (August 1930). A soil map is to be found in the *Twenty-eighth Biennial Reoort of the Kansas State Board of Agriculture,* opposite p. 100, in conjunction with an article on soils of Kansas by R. I. Throckmorton, pp. 91–102.

2. Group I, *First Rainfall Belt:* Doniphan County, Center Township; Leavenworth County, Alexandria Township; Linn County, Valley Township; Douglas County, Eudora Township, Kanwaka Township.

Group II, *Second Rainfall Belt:* Brown County, Walnut Township; Lyon County, Pike Township, Agnes City Township, Reading Township; Harvey County, Macon Township, Alta Township.

Group III, *Third Rainfall Belt:* Jewell County, Sinclair Township; Dickinson County, Buckeye Township; Saline County, Walnut Township; Kingman County, Vinita Township.

Group IV, *Fourth Rainfall Belt:* Phillips County, Long Island Township; Ellsworth County, Lincoln Township; Russell County, Big Creek Township; Ellis County, Wheatland Township; Edwards County, Kinsley Township, Trenton Township, Wayne Township; Barber County, Sun City Township, Deerhead Township, Turkey Creek Township; Decatur County, Center Township; Ness County, High Point Township.

Group V, *Fifth Rainfall Belt:* Gove County, Grainfield Township; Cheyenne County, Jaqua Township, Benkelman Township, Calhoun Township, Cleveland Run Township; Wallace County, Harrison Township, Morton Township, North Township, Sharon Springs Township, Stockholm Township, Vega Township, Wallace Township, Weskan Township; Hamilton County, Bear Creek Township, Coolidge Township, Kendall Township, Lamont Township, Liberty Township, Medway Township, Richland Township, Syracuse Township.

3. The shift of farm operation from father to children is usually very small during the first ten years from any particular census date and only somewhat larger during the second ten years. By the end of twenty years relatively few of the families in question are represented in the township, as will be seen from the analysis of data later in the paper, so the element of error inevitable through inability to follow the female line is relatively small. If a family includes male children, the possibility of the male succeeding to the farm instead of the females tends to minimize this constant error.

4. In this discussion the words "result" or "cause" have been excluded and the phrase "associated with," or an equivalent, is used in order to avoid any implications of "cause-effect" relationships.

5. The 1865 base year is an exception in the second rainfall belt.

6. The federal census of 1910, if open to research, would be of particular interest at this point.

7. These figures are too low, but they are the nearest possible, because the female lines of descent cannot be traced from the census rolls. Investigation of this problem in one township, through the aid of old settlers, points to a conclusion, however, that the error is relatively small for the average community, because the extent of population movement was so nearly complete. Furthermore, if the farm continued in the hands of the family the probability was in favor of a son continuing rather than a daughter. For later base points this kind of error is probably greater than for the old-settler period. The amount of error of this kind is probably greater here, however, than it is in the previous section of this study.

8. *Kinsley Weekly Mercury,* November 3, 1887.

9. *Kinsley Graphic,* March 29, 1895.

10. *Kansas City* (Mo.) *Times,* April 12, 1935.

# CHAPTER 16

# Introduction to
# J. A. Walker's Early History
# of Edwards County

[Malin prepared this introduction when he arranged for the reprinting in 1940 of J. A. Walker's "Sketch of the History of Edwards County, Kansas," which had first been published in the March 14 and 28, 1878 issues of the *Edwards County Leader* (Kinsley), approximately five years after the founding of the community. Malin's stated objective in his editorial remarks was to provide the "modern reader" with "some additional information by way of giving a setting for this pioneering account." This introduction merits attention because in it Malin reports on his census research findings regarding Edwards County on the topics of occupational and age distributions, place of birth data, and cropping patterns, all of which challenged the "accepted wisdom" of frontier scholars in the Turnerian tradition.]

There are occasional instances where an early historical sketch of the beginnings of a community are of sufficient importance to justify reprinting. The one offered here fits the test—J. A. Walker's "Sketch of the History of Edwards County, Kansas."[1] In many respects the history was excellent and served as a source of supply for local historians for some time thereafter.[2] Necessarily, however, as the settlement had been in existence only five years, anything written so close to the events was lacking in perspective, but on the other hand, it preserved facts that almost certainly would otherwise have been lost completely. In fact, few Kansas communities have had the good fortune to have such a history written within five years of the beginnings. The years 1877 and 1878 offered a first false promise of prosperity to the pioneers who had come just prior to the panic of 1873, and whose cup of adversity had been filled to overflowing by drought and grasshoppers. Obviously Walker was writing for booming purposes, and certain reticences were desirable concerning the starving period and local political frauds. For the modern reader it seems helpful therefore to provide some additional information by way of giving a setting for this pioneer account.

J. A. Walker, the author of the first history of Edwards County, was forty-three years of age when he came to Kansas in the spring of 1873. Born in New Hampshire, he had married a Vermont-born woman, but had lived in Massachusetts, which was the birthplace of his five children. He entered a soldier's homestead on Section 14, Township 24, Range 19, but supplemented his income by holding local office: Assessor of Kinsley Township in 1875 and county clerk under the original county organization. On his farm he sowed seven and one-half acres of winter wheat in the fall of 1874 and twelve acres of corn in the spring of 1875. Two mules provided his farm power, and two cows contributed to the support of the family.[3] The Kansas climate has ever been a subject of discussion, but Walker kept careful records of rainfall at Kinsley from May, 1876, to November, 1877 (Table 16.1).

The rainfall of 1879 and 1880 was not as favorable, however, and much of the population migrated, among them Walker, who became an emigration agent of the Northern Pacific railroad, assigned to his native New England.[4]

In describing the beginnings of Kinsley a conspicuous place was given by Walker to the Chicago workingmen's colony and particularly to the Massachusetts colony, of which he was a member, sent out by the Homestead and Colonization Bureau of Boston. A more idealistic experiment was that of the Fraternal Home and Land Association of Philadelphia under the leadership of a Prof. J. R. Wentz, who arrived with his first contingent March 5, 1877, and established the seat of the colony, Freemansberg, southeast of Kinsley across the river and the main ridge of sand hills. Two other groups came in April and May, after which there were no further records of arrivals.[5] The colony was designed upon some kind of mutual or cooperative plan by which Wentz thought workingmen with small capital might succeed in agriculture, but the details were not explained sufficiently in the local press to be enlightening. A large colony house, 24 by 40 feet,

**Table 16.1:** Rainfall at Kinsley

|                | Days of Rainfall | Total, in Inches |
|----------------|:----------------:|:----------------:|
| May, 1876      | 5                | 5.55             |
| June           | 4                | 2.75             |
| July           | 4                | 0.75             |
| August         | 8                | 2.50             |
| September      | 4                | 2.62             |
| October        | 6                | 2.25             |
| November       | 5                | 0.42             |
| December       | 0                | 0.00             |
| January, 1877  | 2                | 0.38             |
| February       | 2                | 0.56             |
| March          | 0                | 0.00             |
| April          | 8                | 3.55             |
| May            | 8                | 8.73             |
| June           | 8                | 4.19             |
| July           | 3                | 1.25             |
| August         | 5                | 2.75             |
| September      | 5                | 1.00             |
| October        | 6                | 4.06             |
| November       | 3                | 0.73             |

Source: *Valley Republican* (Kinsley), December 8, 1877.

with an ell wing 14 by 24 feet, was built by the first party. Plans were announced later for the building of sod houses, plastered inside and outside with lime, a means of overcoming the absence of timber on the plains for building materials and of giving more permanence than the ordinary unprotected sod house of the short-grass country. The outcome is not known, as the press did not report further on this proposal. Wentz hoped to secure a steam plow for the use of his colony, but apparently failed. In fact, within a very short time the whole project collapsed, but here again the local press failed to report, and posterity is left without information on what became of the people who had been brought out from the far East. It is even unknown whether there were any substantial number of city workingmen. The most interesting aspect of the experiment was the recognition at the outset, even though unsuccessful in their solution, of three of the most important problems involved in the adaptation of agriculture to the plains: A device to make available the advantages of adequate capital to the small farmer, native building materials which would free the plains from economic vassalage to the humid, timbered country, and mechanical farm power.

Other projects mentioned in the local papers were a Baltimore working-men's association and a French Catholic colony, but there is no evidence that any settlers were ever brought out under their auspices.[6] More tangible were German colony associations credited to St. Louis, Cincinnati, and western New York, and to the advertising activities of the German Emigration Society of Edwards County.[7] The German settlements were mostly in the western and southern parts of the county, the first Germans being the Plags, father and sons, who settled south of Kinsley. The *Kinsley Graphic,* May 4, 1878, discussed the colony question in an editorial, saying that "as a rule they are successful failures. That is, as failures they are a success." This generalization was qualified only by admission of a limited success of colonization among Germans.

The organized-colony idea was a type of social idealism which was attractive to many people of that decade who were interested in social reform and the betterment of the condition of the poorer classes. Many of these schemes were designed to facilitate the migration of industrial working-men of the East to western agricultural lands. The Chicago and Massachusetts enterprises were launched in 1872, prior to the panic and depression which began in 1873, but neither transplanted industrial workers. The Chicago association appears not to have sent any settlers except the location committee, and the Massachusetts colonists were mostly farmers. After the depression set in there is no record of additional colonists sent out by the Massachusetts organization, and later census records show that very few came from that area. None of the projects originating in the depression period resulted in migration. Exceedingly few individual settlers came during the depression period proper. This is only another historical illustration of the fact that the frontier did not serve as a safety valve through which the problems of recurrent American depressions were solved. On the contrary, the evidence of population movement is conclusively in the opposite direction, and the locals in the Kinsley newspapers made frequent mention of the return to the East of those who turned their faces toward their old homes.

The establishment of the neighboring town of Offerle near the western edge of the county was mentioned by Walker. Lawrence Offerle and his sons were among the most influential, if not the dominant members in the early life of the community, operating a general store as well as agricultural enterprises. The post office called Belpre near the eastern edge of the

county was established as early as 1879, but the town was not laid out until
the railroad was built south of the river in 1886. The origin of Nettleton is
not indicated, but during the winter of 1876–1877 John Fitch, of Hyde Park,
Ill., settled there and undertook to promote the place in a big way. His
house, intended for a hotel, was reported to have been 28 by 42 feet and
three stories above a full basement, and illuminated by gas manufactured
on the premises. A three-story mill was built, with equipment for grinding
flour, feed and for shelling corn. The plan was to use wind power, but the
windmill was supplemented by a steam engine. In 1877 Fitch raised corn,
barley, millet, sweet potatoes, cabbage, tomatoes, and other products, and
became postmaster and railroad station agent. There seemed to be no limit
to his ambitions and energy. Disaster pursued him, however, his wife dying
in March and he being killed in an accident in July, 1878. His estate was
liquidated the following year, and Nettleton (Fitchburg) soon fell into
obscurity.[8]

As most of the county lay south and east of the Arkansas River, the
bridging of that stream was an essential public improvement. The bonds
were voted by the county July 29, 1876, and the structure was reported
completed in March, 1877. The contractors had used timbers shorter than
specified in the contract, and defective material, even after it had been
condemned, had been built into the bridge. The county declined to accept
the bridge until alterations had been made to increase its strength and
efficiency, and until concessions had been made in the cost.[9] In a later
report the county commissioners stated that of the $12,000 worth of bonds
voted, $9,000 had been sold at 87½ net, yielding $7,875, of which $484.13
was still on hand.[10] The weakness of the bridge was not remedied in full,
evidently, because in March, 1881, eleven of the twenty spans were washed
out, requiring another $2,000 to make repairs and reopen it to traffic.[11]

The brick school building at Kinsley was constructed of local materials
and was a source of pride when it was built at the cost of $4,400. At first only
two rooms were finished; the undivided second floor, 35 by 50 feet, was
used as a public hall. On April 30, 1877, the women of the community celebrated the completion by holding a community supper, social, and
dance.[12] During the first term only the east room on the main floor was
used, but before the winter passed, complaints were made because of
crowding 75 children into one room, and the school was closed February 1
for a two months' vacation, during which the school board proposed to seat
and furnish the west room. On April 1 a three months' spring term was
scheduled to open.[13] School teaching must have been a relatively strenuous
profession in those days as some of the children carried firearms and

practiced using them during recesses and on the way to and from school. The editor of the *Republican* protested in June, and again in September, 1878, appealing to the parents for cooperation in terminating the practice and warned that in case of failure arrests would follow.[14]

City pride in the school building was soon dissipated when the walls cracked and crumbled. In 1887 it was torn down, the local paper commenting that the work was proceeding rapidly because the bricks were loose from the mortar:

The tearing down of the old central school building discloses a rascally piece of work on the part of the contractor who built it. Thousands of brick in the walls never were burned at all. They are simply mud bricks. . . . Anyone who will put such brick in the walls of a public school building deserves a term in the legislature.[15]

Of the eighty-five families in Edwards County in 1875, seventy-five had taken land and, according to occupation, the landed families were distributed as follows: fifty-two farmers; five carpenters; three painters; nine other trades represented by one each (hotelkeeper, lawyer, mason, millwright, shoemaker, surveyor, clerk, chairmaker, railroad agent); and six with no occupation designated.[16] Of the ten families in the county without land, two were listed as farmers, five other trades represented by one each (railroad agent, printer, bricklayer, carpenter, painter), and three with no occupation designated.

According to land tenure, of the seventy-two for whom records are available, twenty-six (about 36%) had made preemption entries, five (about 7%) homestead entries, thirty-seven (about 51%) soldiers' homestead entries, two timber claim entries, and three men apparently had bought land outright. In one case a man had filed on both a soldier's homestead and a timber claim. Conspicuously, these first settlers took government, not railroad land, and therefore it was the liberal land laws and particularly the soldiers' homestead law that served as the original attraction in this particular instance. The further indication of the drift of land occupation was announced from time to time by summaries of locations made by the local real-estate agents. Thus, for the month of March, 1877, the record stood: preemption, eleven; homestead declaratory, seventeen; homestead entries, eight; timber culture, thirteen.[17] On May 3, 1878, the *Edwards County Leader* remarked that five-eighths of the available acreage was government and the remainder Santa Fe railroad land. Near the end of April, 1877, the report was that more than one hundred persons had settled over the river and all government land was taken along the Comanche County road southward to within a few miles of the Rattlesnake.[18] By the end of the year a similar report was published regarding government land between Kinsley and the Sawlog or South Fork of the Pawnee.[19]

The state census data of 1875 show an average age for eighty farm operators of 36.5 years, and for their wives of 34.0 years. The age distributions are given in table 16.2 and show comparatively few in the twenties, the largest group being in the thirties, although twenty percent of the men were forty-five or above, or almost exactly the same proportion as were below thirty. The eldest was sixty-five and the youngest man or woman was twenty-two. The separation of single from married men emphasizes that sixteen of the nineteen in the twenty-year-old group were single and that twenty-seven of the thirty-five of the thirty-year-old group were married. In other words, the permanent backbone of this frontier was not young married couples starting life and expecting to grow up with the country, but rather middle-aged people with families. Twenty-nine families had sixty-two children of their own, or about two per family, besides a total of five other children being raised in these families.

The sources of Edwards County population as of 1875 were somewhat unusual. Of seventy men whose place of birth was recorded, thirty-four were born in New England, mostly in upper New England, and nineteen of the forty women. The next largest groups were from the North Atlantic states, and foreign-born from Germany, England, and Ireland. Forty-eight of the seventy men came to Kansas from New England, particularly from Massachusetts as their place of last residence, and the next largest group, seventeen in number, came from the North Central states east of the Mississippi River. Only three of the sixteen foreign-born came direct from the country of birth, and nineteen of fifty-four native-born men and eleven of thirty women came direct from their birth states.

The agricultural schedules of the county for the census of 1875 recorded the crop program of seventy-two farms. Of these, sixty-four farmers planted corn that spring, averaging thirteen acres each; twenty-six farmers averaged eight acres each of winter wheat planted in the fall of 1874, and one farmer planted spring wheat in 1875; sixteen farmers planted barley and twelve planted oats, in each case an average of three acres. Of other crops, three farmers planted rye, and one farmer each planted sorghum, millet, potatoes, and sweet potatoes. On ten farms orchards had been started. Unquestionably, corn was the predominant crop, and twenty-five farmers planted nothing else, the corn acreages on these farms ranging from three to ten acres. Even if the season had been favorable, which it was not, the county would not have produced enough grain to feed itself.

The livestock equipment of these farms consisted of seventy-eight horses

**Table 16.2:** Age Distribution of Farm Operators and Wives

| Age Groups | Farm Operators | Women | Single Men | Married Men |
|---|---|---|---|---|
| 21–24 | 10 | 7 | 9 | 0 |
| 25–29 | 9 | 6 | 7 | 3 |
| 30–34 | 20 | 15 | 7 | 13 |
| 35–39 | 15 | 11 | 1 | 14 |
| 40–44 | 10 | 4 | 3 | 7 |
| 45–49 | 3 | 1 | 0 | 3 |
| 50–54 | 5 | 2 | 2 | 3 |
| 55–59 | 5 | 1 | 3 | 2 |
| 60+ | 3 | 1 | 0 | 3 |
| Total | 80 | 48 | 32 | 48 |

distributed among thirty-eight operators, supplemented by eight mules on five farms; sixty cows scattered among twenty-nine owners; seventy-two other cattle among twenty-six owners; and twenty-nine hogs among eleven owners. Four farmers owned sheep, but most of the 419 sheep and 1,270 pounds of wool were credited to two men. No livestock of any kind was listed on twenty-five farms. Three farmers reported poultry or eggs sold, and eight a total of 830 pounds of butter made during the preceeding year. Clearly, the meat supply was as deficient as the grain supply.

Although the dollar figures for the value of machinery equipment of farms may not be reliable, yet their general significance is inescapable. Thirty-five farmers reported no machinery, while thirty-seven reported an average value of about $26. The total value of personal property listed was $10,952 distributed among forty-nine farmers, the smallest being $5 and the largest $834, with an average of $226. Twenty-one listed no personal property. In view of the deficiencies in other respects this item was more favorable than might be expected, as twenty-five of the whole number reported $200 worth or over.

During the first winter after the main bodies of colonists arrived (1873–1874) many were destitute. Appeals were made to the President of the United States for aid to be distributed from army stores at Fort Larned, but requests were denied, as Congress had not provided supplies for that purpose. Gov. Thomas A. Osborn wrote to one group of settlers under the date of December 20, 1873, saying that he understood that a local relief board was functioning at Petersburg under the direction of Capt. P. H. Niles, who would give aid in case of necessity. No further information has been forthcoming regarding this situation, but the reference to Niles suggests that possibly the source of funds was the Boston organization which had sponsored the Massachusetts colony.

In the season of 1874 the drought, followed by the grasshopper scourge, added to the distress which would in all probability have been serious enough in this primitive plains settlement because the nation as a whole was in the depths of economic depression. A state relief committee as well as the federal government through the various army posts distributed food, clothing, and coal. On December 13, 1874, C. L. Hubbs, who had been appointed by Governor Osborn to act in Edwards County, reported to the governor that fifty-nine persons were in need. In view of the fact that there were only 234 persons in the county, this would indicate that one-fourth of the population was on the list. The Santa Fe railroad advanced seed wheat in the fall of 1874 to settlers along its line, allowing a maximum of fifteen bushels per farm. Not until 1876 did the county begin to show signs of recovery, but by 1877 immigrants were coming into the region in large numbers.[20]

It is evident that the organization of Edwards County was accomplished by means of a fraudulent census, and for some reason it was allowed to stand, although the legislature declined to seat the representative until 1877. Without rivers to afford natural facilities for transportation, the railroad had been the necessary preliminary to settlement as applying to the whole subhumid West. That fact has been rather generally recognized by historians, but an equally important one not clearly understood is that so small a population and so little property could not have maintained either the settlement itself or a local government had it not been for the railroad. In 1877 J. A. Walker called attention to the distribution of property holdings in the county. The railroad valuation constituted over eighty-six percent of the whole.

Nonresident property was negligible, and resident property was mostly personal rather than real estate and was mostly lost to taxation because of legal exemptions. It was pointed out that homesteaders would avail themselves of the maximum time of seven years to prove up and take patents and only then would their land become taxable. Preemptors would take advantage of the grasshopper law which extended the time for making payments so that such land would not generally become taxable until 1879.[21] There is probably no exaggeration therefore in the contemporaneous statement that the railroad took "the burden of the taxes off the farmers and producers. The company pays about 95 percent of the taxes."[22]

The particular occasion for bringing this situation out into the open was

**Table 16.3**: Taxable Property of Edwards County, 1877

|  |  |
|---|---|
| Santa Fe railroad and its subsidiary the Arkansas Valley Town Co. | $380,000 |
| Business men | 10,000 |
| Nonresidents | 10,000 |
| Residents | 40,000 |
| Total | $440,000 |

the controversy over the voting of bonds for a courthouse and jail. An "Old Settler" argued that there were not enough people, that the most of the county lay across the river and the settlers had not been there long enough to qualify for voting and that later it might be desirable to remove the county seat to some point across the river nearer the center of the county.[23] The answer of Kinsley to any suggestion of taking the county seat across the river requires no comment. The editor of the *Leader* advocated forcefully the cause of the courthouse, insisting that rentals and expense of transporting prisoners to Great Bend would meet the interest on the necessary bonds. Referring to the voting of bonds for the bridge, he stated:

Then, as well as now, the greater part of the taxes in Edwards county was paid by the railroad land company, and it was expected that said company would object to the building of a bridge until the prospects looked more favorable but not so, when counseled, they said build your bridges, make your improvements throughout the county, and although we pay the bulk of the taxes, all we want is clean hands, economy and no stealing on the part of county officials.

On the courthouse question he declared:

We have no fears of the railroad land company objecting and if they do not, why should we. It will be a long time before those who have taken Government land or before those that may take, will have to prove up and in the meantime the railroad company will be taxed from year to year for the payment of the bonds issued, and many of the old settlers as well as the new ones will find when the proper time comes for proving up their claims, that by the judicious management of our county officials, in the year 1877, that the public buildings have all been erected and that they are in possession of good farms with no taxes to pay for such improvement.[24]

No statement has been found from an official of the Santa Fe railroad or of its subsidiary land company, and there is no means of knowing whether the editor of the *Leader* may have been under obligations to the company and may have been speaking under inspiration, but however that may have been, all of the independent facts available point to the conclusion that the general picture of the situation was essentially true, although in specific detail it may have been overstated.[25] J. A. Walker's statement was that rentals and other expenses were costing $1.13 per thousand, while the direct levy would be about $1.82 per thousand, or a net increase in taxes of 69 cents per thousand.[26] The county treasurer's printed statement of the tax rate for 1877 was:[27]

| | |
|---|---|
| For State of Kansas | 0.55 |
| Edwards County | 1.00 |
| Kinsley Township | 0.15 |
| Trenton Township | 0.10 |
| County poor | 0.10 |
| Bridge bonds | 0.20 |
| School District No. 1 | 1.10 |
| School District No. 1 bonds | 0.40 |
| School District No. 2 | 1.00 |
| School District No. 2 bonds | 0.60 |
| School District No. 3 | 1.60 |
| School District No. 4 | 0.50 |
| School District No. 5 | 1.30 |

On petition of July 7, the county commissioners ordered an election to be held August 4, 1877, on the question of the issuance of $8,000 in courthouse and jail bonds. The proposition was defeated, and apparently very badly, because the *Leader* recorded the momentous event with a three-line local and a cut of a sick rooster, but no figures or comment.[28]

On the basis of experience, the agricultural system was undergoing some modification and especially with the temporary turn of more favorable climatic conditions. As table 16.4 shows, winter wheat increased rapidly, but as time was to demonstrate, not in fulfillment of hopes for this crop. The Early Red May, a soft wheat, did not prove altogether successful, although it was the best variety then given any widespread trial in the area. Spring wheat and barley had a substantial following, but oats made comparatively little headway. Clearly, corn was still the principal crop in the county. Among the new crops that showed promise were millet, broomcorn, and sorghum. This early experiment with sorghum was sig-

**Table 16.4:** Acreage in Field Crops, Edwards County, 1875–1878

|                     | 1875  | 1876  | 1877  | 1878  |
|---------------------|-------|-------|-------|-------|
| Winter Wheat        | 202   | 524   | 704   | 2,205 |
| Spring wheat        | 4     | 39    | 283   | 1,460 |
| Oats                | 39    | 65    | 148   | 504   |
| Barley              | 46    | 158   | 529   | 1,273 |
| Corn                | 855   | 1,229 | 1,770 | 2,908 |
| Sorghum             | 0.5   | 18    | 41    | 73    |
| Broomcorn           | 0     | 2     | 32    | 47    |
| Millet and Hungarian| 0     | 21    | 123   | 724   |

Source: *First Biennial Report of the State Board of Agriculture* (Topeka, 1878), p. 198.

nificant, because it was not a native of the Western hemisphere, had been introduced only recently, and was soon to prove one of the most reliable of the Plains crops. It is evident that by 1878 only the beginnings had been made in the baffling problem, still only partially solved, of adaptation of the agricultural system to the subhumid environment.

## Notes

1. Published first in the *Edwards County Leader* (Kinsley), March 14, 28, 1878, under the title, "Views of Kinsley and Vicinity, and a Sketch of the History of Edwards County, Kansas." The views (pictures) are not reproduced here.

2. The *Kinsley Republican,* January 4, 1879, a rival paper, reprinted the most of the history, with some variations and without giving credit to Walker.

3. "Kansas State Census," Edwards County, 1875, in Archives division of the Kansas State Historical Society.

4. *Kinsley Graphic,* January 1, 1881.

5. *Edwards County Leader,* April 12, May 17, 1877.

6. For announcements, see *ibid.,* September 13, 1877, and *Valley Republican* (Kinsley), January 26, 1878.

7. *Valley Republican* (Kinsley), November 10, December 15, 1877; January 5, 1878. *Edwards County Leader* (Kinsley), October 4, 1877; February 14, September 5, 1878. *Kinsley Graphic,* September 7, 1878.

8. *Valley Republican,* (Kinsley), November 3, 1877; January 12, March 30, 1878. *Edwards County Leader* (Kinsley), September 20, December 20, 1877; March 7, August 15, 1878. *Kinsley Republican,* February 15, 1879.

9. *Edwards County Leader* (Kinsley), March 29, 1877.

10. *Ibid.,* August 2, 1877.

11. *Kinsley Graphic,* March 5, July 23, 1881.

12. *Edwards County Leader* (Kinsley), April 19, May 3, 1877. Walker's history gave the size of the building as 35 by 40 feet, and stated that there were four rooms. Possibly the upper rooms were finished the second year.

13. *Valley Republican,* (Kinsley), January 19, February 2, 1878.

14. *Kinsley Republican,* September 21, 1878.

15. *Kinsley Weekly Mercury,* August 18, 1887.

16. "Kansas State Census," 1875. Single adults were counted as families for census purposes.

17. *Edwards County Leader* (Kinsley), April 5, 1877.

18. *Ibid.,* April 26, 1877.

19. *Valley Republican* (Kinsley), December 15, 1878.

20. Official correspondence concerning relief is found in "Correspondence of Kansas Governors" (Archives division, Kansas State Historical Society). The records of the Kansas Central Relief Committee, 1874–1875, in the possession of the Historical Society, contain material on the relations of that organization to Edwards County.

21. *Edwards County Leader* (Kinsley), July 26, 1877.

22. *Ibid.,* May 3, 1877.

23. *Ibid.,* May 24, 1877.

24. *Ibid.,* May 31, 1877.

25. Most of the county records burned in a town fire in 1879 so that the author has not been able to verify specific figures given except as they appear in the public prints. Some of these seem contradictory in detail, but without changing the larger aspects of the matter.

26. *Edwards County Leader* (Kinsley), July 26, 1877.

27. *Ibid.,* November 8, 1877.

28. *Ibid.,* July 19, August 9, 1877.

CHAPTER 17

# Methodology for History
# of Social Change

*Population Studies*

[The following excerpt serves as a synopsis of James Malin's methodological and substantive contributions to grassland history during the decade from 1935 to 1944. His revisions of Turner's theories are cited, and he included previously unpublished research findings on interstate migration and age of farm operators in Kansas. Although the Kansas census records that formed the primary source for his work were not unique to the Jayhawk State, as Malin mistakenly assumed, nevertheless he was right on target when he recommended that future scholars should exploit such individual-level record series by using mechanical data processing equipment and statistical calculators. Not only would such labor-saving techniques permit large-scale research projects, but, as Malin rightly noted, they would also permit subsequent scholars to replicate the initial quantitative results and thus to test the validity of their findings.]

Some examples of methodology for the study of the history of social change are described in this chapter. The first aspect is the study of the population problems. The initial study in the series was published in 1935, some other phases being treated from time to time thereafter (Malin, 1936, 1940a, 1940b, 1940e, 1944b). The second aspect was agricultural studies focused upon the comparative analysis of internal differences from area to area and internal changes in time from the first recorded census enumeration after.

pioneer settlement to the last ones available when the study was closed (Malin, 1942a). The third aspect was the reconstruction in some kind of narrative form of the history of the process by which the population worked out possible adjustments to the exigencies of environment and circumstances (Malin, 1935, 1936, 1940, 1944). In this phase, attention was focused especially, and necessarily, upon these procedures as concrete and realistic samples of the folk process of history in action.

Out of these investigations grew the consideration of the problem of the community as a historical concept, and one which must differ necessarily from the concepts held by sociologists. The latter discipline is not bothered by the time factor, which intervenes to prevent the historian from formulating similar definitions. Closely related, and growing out of the community problem, is the city or urbanization, an equally difficult concept to reduce to a workable definition. Historical samples of these problems appear in incomplete form in two published studies, Kinsley and Abilene (Malin, 1933, 1944).

In the presentation of all these studies the present author is keenly aware of the handicap of verbalism and ideologies already firmly established. The language does not possess words that are satisfactory to designate the process of change in a frontier as it was transformed in the course of time into the society of the 1940s. The words *mature, develop, evolve,* or any similar ones are freighted with a traditional ideology associated with the idea of progress, or the Darwinian evolution, from an alleged lower to a higher form, which also involves progress, or the organismic concept of the life cycle of birth, youth, maturity, old age, and death. The word *stabilized* does not express adequately the process, because factors intervene which disrupt the general tendency toward stabilization with age and the achievement of an appropriate harmony of the folk culture with the environment. Furthermore, there is a limit beyond which stabilization cannot go. Equilibrium is always unstable. Irrespective of the words used, it is imperative to deal with the social process as one of indeterminate and continuous change—an open system.

An aspect of methodology in Jenny's *Factors in Soil Formation* is suggestive for history. After challenging organismic ideology and the concept of maturity in soils, he discussed the question of when parent materials became soil, and gave the answer, whenever soil-forming factors begin to operate. Also, soil already formed would be reduced to the status of parent material whenever a change occurred in the soil-forming factors, initiating a new sequence in soil formation. In time, soil was parent material in relation to the future, and product of the operation of soil-forming factors in relation to the past. Change in society may be viewed similarly in relation to society-forming factors. As social history, the American frontier represents a relatively short span of historic time. The period occupied by the settling-in process was highly unstable, especially the first years, after which a relative equilibrium might be achieved. Major modifications in any existing factor, or variable, or the introduction of a new variable, must necessarily upset the unstable equilibrium, initiating a new sequence of succession toward reestablishment of a new unstable equilibrium in its areal setting. New settlers who arrived from time to time in any community represented major changes in the factors operating in a community, and changes of variable proportions. Power farming, during the second quarter of the twentieth century, represented the introduction of a new independent variable, highly disturbing to equilibrium. In either case, a new sequence in re-forming society was initiated. At any given instant, in relation to the future, the state of society is parent material, and in relation to the past, it is the product of the operation of society-forming factors. And in any case, within the circle of known facts, the social process is one of indeterminate and continuous change—an open system.

## Population Studies

Population studies in the sense of historical demography have received little attention from American historians. Turner's frontier approach, as expounded in his essays, included the growth and development of a frontier community into a mature society. In practice, however, Turner did not develop a specific methodology for tracing the process of such development, or for reducing the process to a problem, or series of problems stated in an operational form, to which objective quantitative methods could be applied. He did not take particular communities or restricted geographical areas and follow their evolution through a period of time with a view to presenting systematically the growth of the principal features of the culture complex. Without such more or less standardized quantitative methodology it was impossible to measure in an objective manner what happened to the population on any particular frontier, and what changes occurred as it grew older. It was even more impossible to study the population of different frontiers comparatively, either as frontiers or as societies developing through periods of time, in order to determine specifically the continuities and the differences, either of time or of geographical environment, or of relations to the technological development of the background society. The most elaborate project that has been undertaken, but not completed, which was making some contribution in that direction, was Joseph Shafer's Wisconsin Domesday project. In the case of Webb's *The Great Plains,* he did not address himself to that problem at all as his attention was occupied with other aspects of the regional approach.

The present author has undertaken pioneer studies in historical demography, and the adaptation of the agricultural system to Kansas as a specific area of the central grassland. Some attention has been given to the town, to the facilities of entertainment, and to strictly social life. The most fruitful contributions thus far, both as respects methodology and historical conclusions, have been in the first two departments, population and agricultural studies. The basic procedure is described most fully in "The Turnover of Farm Population in Kansas," (Malin, 1935), and "Local Historical Studies and Population Problems" in *The Cultural Approach to History,* edited by Caroline Ware (1940).

The sampling method is the basis of operations, using a township or community area of fixed geographical boundaries as the unit small enough that it can be manageable in the entirety of its social behavior. Several such samples can be thrown together for statistical purposes, but handled separately for narrative purposes. They can be combined as seems desirable on different kinds of classifications to emphasize community age, type-of-farming area, rainfall belts, soil types, immigrant or native populations, or other aspects that may be of interest. The sources of the data are the state and federal census records. Other records that might be used are local records of land titles, or tax lists, and probate court cases.

The procedure for studying population behavior was to list the farm operators from the agricultural schedule of the census, and then gather the data from the population schedules for each operator, his wife, and his family, by name. As Kansas took a decennial census from 1865–1925 inclusive, the federal and state census enumerations provided lists at five-year intervals to 1885, after which period the federal census records were closed to investigation. For the later period the state census was depended upon exclusively. After 1925 statistical rolls of farm operators were available in Kansas for each year, but not general population data. The census list of farm operators for the first enumeration after settlement afforded the first base for comparison, and each list thereafter was compared with the base list to determine the individual operators remaining within the census area, but not necessarily upon the same farm. In turn, each census list was used as a base list for comparison with subsequent lists. Upon the death or retirement of an original operator, a son was counted as representing the family succession in the area. Tables were then prepared showing the total number of operators at each base enumeration interval, and the number remaining at each successive enumeration; another table was prepared in terms of percentages persisting; and then graphs were constructed, plotting comparative curves for each base year.

The conclusions from these population studies are illuminating, and a few of them are summarized here; but the more complete treatment of the published portions are to be found in the original monographs. In the population turnover studies, there were variations from sample to sample, but there was a general uniformity of the curves illustrating farm-operator persistence, irrespective of whether the community was settled just prior to the census of 1860 or of 1895. The rate of turnover of population (or persistence as one may choose to call it) was associated primarily with community age; very high turnover during the pioneering period, a period of relative stabilization at low levels of persistence, and lastly a period of a high degree of stabilization, especially after 1915 or later. Of course, there were limits beyond which stabilization with age could not go. New independent variables entered from time to time, such as mechanical powered farming, following which new adjustments must be made. The turnover pattern of communities of a comparable age persisted to a remarkable degree, irrespective of depressions or of drouths, and there was very little difference as respects rainfall belts of 35 inches or over and 20 inches or less. Among the most stable found were some communities in the high plains where rainfall was less than 20 inches. New settlers were always more unstable that the old residents. Thus, with every replacement by new settlers, the movers were weeded out, leaving the more permanent element. It is not safe, however, to jump at conclusions as to why some moved and others stayed, or to assume that the best stayed and the worst moved. In most samples and periods there was a tendency toward greater stability during depressions, and mobility during periods of prosperity.

A second group of conclusions has to do with the total numbers of operators in each sample. The behavior was not uniform. On the pioneering frontier, numbers usually declined during depression and drouth. As already pointed out, the rate of loss, or turnover, was not greater necessarily when a drouth, or depression, year was used as the base from which to measure, and, on the contrary, was generally less. The real issue was the flow of replacement population. With a consistently high rate of loss, complete depopulation would have resulted if new settlers had not arrived promptly. An increase in the total number of farm operators meant that the flow of replacement population exceeded the losses. This usually occurred in the pioneer period, during booms. The decline in the total numbers of farm operators meant that the flow of replacement had diminished or ceased. This occurred in the pioneer period during drouth and depression periods. The rate of turnover in either case, based on the whole number of any particular census list, fluctuated little. In other words, the frontier was not a safety valve in the sense in which that theory has been used by the Turner school of history.

No satisfactory method has been devised for tracing what became of those who moved. The local newspapers record that many returned to the East, moved to towns, went to the mines in the mountains, or worked for the railroad, during depressions, but sufficiently exact data are not available from such sources to afford reliable quantitative treatment. Significant increases in numbers occurred frequently in older samples during depressions, in part, at least, reflecting an urban-rural movement. In most respects the depression of the 1930s was no exception to the general behavior pattern. The newest settled areas suffered the highest rate of turnover and net losses, but the conspicuous characteristic was the stability regularly associated with older communities, the propaganda to the contrary notwithstanding. There were fewer farmers on the move, proportionally, than in any previous depression in Kansas. Again it should be emphasized that replacement population had cesased to flow into the region, and that, rather than instability, accounted for population losses.

A third group of conclusions relates to what proportion of the total population of a sample, at any given date, were descendants of the operators of any prior date. Allowing for wide variations in individual samples, it is clear that the high rate of turnover of operators during the pioneering phase left a very small proportion of the original settler descendants among the farmers fifty to seventy-five years later. The assumption so often made that the original settlers determined the character of a community is unsafe as a generalization. After a substantial stabilization of the community had been achieved, even though the turnover might still be relatively high, the proportionate influence of the subsequent population was much greater.

The principal foreign-born groups of farm operators in Kansas who were sufficiently concentrated to dominate the communities were Germans, Swedes, and Bohemians. On the whole, they were highly persistent, but the second and third American-born generations reflected much the American pattern of behavior (Malin, 1935, 1940a). With the cessation of a large replacement population from the mother countries, these communities rapidly lost much of their distinctive character. As a rule, Negroes and Jews did not appear conspicuously in farm population.

Negro colonies were established during the period of the Civil War and reconstruction migrations, but the population mostly drifted to the cities. Partly, the explanation lay in inability to carry on independent farming enterprise; partly, it was failure to adapt to environment; but, more largely, the answer probably lay in the cessation of the flow of replacement population to compensate for the high turnover characteristic of all newly established enterprises.

Studies of the internal migration of the United States are handicapped by the fact that federal census enumerations recorded only the state of birth and the place of residence at the time of the enumeration. Also, all the later federal enumerations were closed to investigation, except to federal employees, so only the printed mass statistics were available. Kansas census records, 1875–1925, recorded the additional data of the state from which the individual moved to Kansas. As the Kansas census and the early federal enumerations are open for examination of individual names, it was possible to make more satisfactory studies than have ever been made elsewhere. Even much of the migration intervening between birth and the removal to Kansas can be pieced together, for persons with families, by noting the birth states of the children. In connection with local studies, data on these matters were printed in 1936, 1940, and 1944 as pertained to Edwards, Dickinson, and Saline counties. The present author reported at the annual meeting of the American Historical Association, in December, 1939, on the broader aspects of interstate migration of native Americans direct from the state of birth to Kansas. This was published in abstract in *The Cultural Approach to History* edited by Caroline Ware, without the detailed statistical table (17.1) which is now printed (Malin, 1940e). The sample areas were grouped from east to west across the length of the state in seven successive frontiers. The most significant points of emphasis were that the native migration to Kansas, direct from the state of birth, increased in proportion after 1875, both 1895 and 1905 being high, and thereafter the proportion declined, and furthermore, the part of that migration that moved into Kansas from adjacent states was small in proportion to that coming from non-contiguous states. These general conclusions confirmed fully the more specific ones relative to Edwards (two samples), Dickinson, and Saline counties (Malin, 1936, 1940a, and 1944b).

In the second statistical table (17.2) is presented, for the first time, the data on interstate migration to Kansas from the state of last residence. The conclusions drawn from these data support those presented in 1939 at the American Historical Association meeting, and printed in 1940. The migration was not from one frontier to the next adjacent states but from

Table 17.1: Interstate Migration of Native Farm Operators (Men) to Kansas, Direct from State of Birth (Percentages Based on Total Native Farm Operators)

| | 1875 | | 1885 | | 1895 | | 1905 | | 1915 | | 1925 | |
|---|---|---|---|---|---|---|---|---|---|---|---|---|
| | No. | % | No. | % | No. | % | No. | % | No. | % | No. | % |
| *First tier counties, three townships* | | | | | | | | | | | | |
| Total farm operators | 442 | | 535 | | 489 | | 541 | | 605 | | 569 | |
| Total native | 345 | 100.00 | 429 | 100.00 | 413 | 100.00 | 468 | 100.0 | 539 | 100.00 | 539 | 100.00 |
| Native direct | 135 | 39.13 | 184 | 42.89 | 192 | 46.48 | 195 | 41.66 | 202 | 37.47 | 160 | 29.68 |
| Contiguous | 42 | 12.17 | 66 | 15.39 | 65 | 15.73 | 88 | 18.8 | 111 | 20.59 | 107 | 19.85 |
| Non-contiguous | 93 | 26.96 | 118 | 27.50 | 127 | 30.75 | 107 | 22.86 | 91 | 16.88 | 53 | 9.83 |
| *Second tier* | | | | | | | | | | | | |
| Total farm operators | 467 | | 611 | | 616 | | 629 | | 596 | | 566 | |
| Total native | 330 | 100.00 | 458 | 100.00 | 465 | 100.00 | 520 | 100.00 | 541 | 100.00 | 534 | 100.00 |
| Native direct | 132 | 40.00 | 253 | 55.24 | 253 | 54.40 | 258 | 49.61 | 212 | 39.18 | 162 | 30.33 |
| Contiguous | 14 | 4.24 | 37 | 8.08 | 33 | 7.09 | 45 | 8.65 | 48 | 8.87 | 52 | 9.73 |
| Non-contiguous | 118 | 35.76 | 216 | 47.16 | 220 | 47.31 | 213 | 40.96 | 164 | 30.31 | 110 | 20.60 |
| *Extreme territorial frontier 1860* | | | | | | | | | | | | |
| Total farm operators | 393 | | 695 | | 615 | | 645 | | 714 | | 688 | |
| Total native | 305 | | 539 | | 511 | | 534 | | 634 | | 629 | |
| Native direct | 160 | 52.45 | 277 | 51.39 | 307 | 60.07 | 312 | 58.42 | 275 | 43.37 | 184 | 29.25 |
| Contiguous | 4 | 1.31 | 17 | 3.15 | 41 | 8.02 | 45 | 8.42 | 65 | 10.25 | 56 | 8.90 |
| Non-contiguous | 256 | 51.14 | 250, | 48.24 | 266 | 52.05 | 267 | 50.00 | 190 | 33.13 | 128 | 20.35 |

*First post-war*
*frontier, 1865–70*

| | (1) n | (1) % | (2) n | (2) % | (3) n | (3) % | (4) n | (4) % | (5) n | (5) % | (6) n | (6) % |
|---|---|---|---|---|---|---|---|---|---|---|---|---|
| Total farm operators | 268 | | 251 | | 245 | | 252 | | 248 | | 234 | |
| Total native | 218 | | 139 | | 126 | | 130 | | 165 | | 189 | |
| Native direct | 65 | 30.00 | 53 | 38.13 | 37 | 29.36 | 63 | 48.46 | 52 | 31.51 | 40 | 21.16 |
| Contiguous | 2 | .91 | 6 | 4.31 | 20 | 15.85 | 24 | 18.46 | 22 | 13.33 | 22 | 11.64 |
| Non-contiguous | 63 | 29.09 | 47 | 33.32 | 17 | 13.51* | 39 | 30.00 | 30 | 18.18 | 18 | 9.52 |

*Second post-war*
*frontier, mid-70s*

| | (1) n | (1) % | (2) n | (2) % | (3) n | (3) % | (4) n | (4) % | (5) n | (5) % | (6) n | (6) % |
|---|---|---|---|---|---|---|---|---|---|---|---|---|
| Total farm operators | | | 632 | | 687 | | 744 | | 881 | | 700 | |
| Total native | | | 438 | | 421 | | 508 | | 700 | | 624 | |
| Native direct | | | 174 | 39.72 | 213 | 50.60 | 269 | 52.95 | 307 | 43.85 | 198 | 31.73 |
| Contiguous | | | 11 | 2.51 | 27 | 6.41 | 63 | 12.40 | 106 | 15.14 | 74 | 11.85 |
| Non-contiguous | | | 163 | 37.21 | 186 | 44.19 | 206 | 40.55 | 201 | 28.71 | 124 | 19.88 |

*First recovery*
*frontier, 1878–79*

| | (1) n | (1) % | (2) n | (2) % | (3) n | (3) % | (4) n | (4) % | (5) n | (5) % | (6) n | (6) % |
|---|---|---|---|---|---|---|---|---|---|---|---|---|
| Total farm operators | | | 194 | | 134 | | 207 | | 250 | | 281 | |
| Total native | | | 159 | | 106 | | 169 | | 203 | | 213 | |
| Native direct | | | 75 | 47.17 | 52 | 49.05 | 86 | 50.90 | 97 | 47.76 | 79 | 37.08 |
| Contiguous | | | 12 | 7.54 | 13 | 12.26 | 27 | 16.00 | 39 | 19.21 | 37 | 17.37 |
| Non-contiguous | | | 63 | 39.63 | 39 | 36.79 | 59 | 34.90 | 58 | 28.55 | 42 | 19.71 |

*West of 100°*

| | (1) n | (1) % | (2) n | (2) % | (3) n | (3) % | (4) n | (4) % | (5) n | (5) % | (6) n | (6) % |
|---|---|---|---|---|---|---|---|---|---|---|---|---|
| Total farm operators | | | | | 726 | | 581 | | 833 | | 916 | |
| Total native | | | | | 515 | | 439 | | 711 | | 817 | |
| Native direct | | | | | 186 | 36.11 | 185 | 42.14 | 345 | 48.55 | 316 | 38.66 |
| Contiguous | | | | | 65 | 12.62 | 72 | 16.40 | 175 | 24.61 | 199 | 24.35 |
| Non-contiguous | | | | | 121 | 23.49 | 113 | 25.74 | 170 | 23.94 | 117 | 14.31 |

Omitted: Kansas-born, foreign-born, and native indirect migration.

*This figure of 13.51% is out of line with probabilities, but no satisfactory explanation has been found.

Table 17.2: Interstate Migration of Farm Operators (Men) from State of Last Residence (Percentages Based on Internal Migrants, Native and Foreign-born)

| | 1875 No. | 1875 % | 1885 No. | 1885 % | 1895 No. | 1895 % | 1905 No. | 1905 % | 1915 No. | 1915 % | 1925 No. | 1925 % |
|---|---|---|---|---|---|---|---|---|---|---|---|---|
| Total farm operators | 442 | | 534 | | 489 | | 541 | | 604 | | 569 | |
| Kansas-born | 1 | | 32 | | 105 | | 159 | | 253 | | 318 | |
| Foreign-born direct to Kansas | 18 | | 40 | | 32 | | 34 | | 52 | | 18 | |
| Internal migration to Kansas | 423 | 100.0 | 462 | 100.0 | 352 | 100.0 | 333 | 100.0 | 296 | 100.0 | 288 | 100.0 |
| From adjacent state | 214 | 50.5 | 215 | 46.5 | 158 | 44.9 | 179 | 53.7 | 169 | 57.1 | 162 | 71.0 |
| From non-contiguous state | 209 | 49.5 | 245 | 53.5 | 194 | 55.1 | 154 | 46.3 | 127 | 42.9 | 66 | 29.0 |
| Total farm operators | 466 | | 611 | | 616 | | 628 | | 596 | | 566 | |
| Kansas-born | 1 | | 25 | | 88 | | 169 | | 271 | | 324 | |
| Foreign-born direct to Kansas | 27 | | 53 | | 57 | | 59 | | 40 | | 24 | |
| Internal migration to Kansas | 438 | 100.0 | 523 | 100.0 | 470 | 100.0 | 400 | 100.0 | 284 | 100.0 | 217 | 100.0 |
| From adjacent state | 104 | 23.7 | 123 | 23.5 | 115 | 26.6 | 106 | 26.5 | 92 | 32.4 | 87 | 40.0 |
| From non-contiguous state | 334 | 76.3 | 400 | 76.5 | 355 | 73.4 | 294 | 73.5 | 192 | 67.6 | 130 | 60.0 |
| Total farm operators | 393 | | 694 | | 614 | | 644 | | 715 | | 689 | |
| Kansas-born | 0 | | 7 | | 36 | | 94 | | 227 | | 341 | |
| Foreign-born direct to Kansas | 24 | | 46 | | 42 | | 60 | | 48 | | 38 | |
| Internal migration to Kansas | 369 | 100.0 | 637 | 100.0 | 536 | 100.0 | 478 | 100.0 | 446 | 100.0 | 257 | 100.0 |
| From adjacent state | 60 | 16.2 | 107 | 16.8 | 106 | 19.7 | 102 | 21.3 | 161 | 36.1 | 95 | 36.9 |
| From non-contiguous state | 309 | 83.8 | 530 | 83.2 | 430 | 80.3 | 376 | 78.7 | 285 | 63.9 | 162 | 63.1 |

| | | | | | | | | | | |
|---|---|---|---|---|---|---|---|---|---|---|
| Total farm operators | | | 250 | | 245 | | 257 | | 248 | | 234 | |
| Kansas-born | | | 2 | | 10 | | 28 | | 96 | | 138 | |
| Foreign-born direct to Kansas | | | 75 | | 96 | | 103 | | 68 | | 41 | |
| Internal migration to Kansas | | | 167 | 100.0 | 138 | 100.0 | 128 | 100.0 | 84 | 100.0 | 54 | 100.0 |
| From adjacent state | | | 65 | 38.9 | 58 | 42.0 | 46 | 36.0 | 29 | 34.5 | 32 | 59.2 |
| From non-contiguous state | | | 102 | 61.1 | 80 | 58.0 | 82 | 64.0 | 55 | 65.5 | 21 | 40.8 |
| Total farm operators | 270 | | 632 | | 687 | | 744 | | 885 | | 701 | |
| Kansas-born | 0 | | 8 | | 10 | | 64 | | 241 | | 345 | |
| Foreign-born direct to Kansas | 19 | | 85 | | 153 | | 142 | | 131 | | 45 | |
| Internal migration to Kansas | 251 | 100.0 | 535 | 100.0 | 524 | 100.0 | 538 | 100.0 | 509 | 100.0 | 296 | 100.0 |
| From adjacent state | 60 | 24.3 | 132 | 24.6 | 134 | 25.7 | 177 | 32.9 | 207 | 40.6 | 119 | 40.2 |
| From non-contiguous state | 191 | 75.7 | 403 | 75.4 | 390 | 74.3 | 361 | 67.1 | 302 | 59.4 | 177 | 59.8 |
| Total farm operators | | | 194 | | 134 | | 207 | | 250 | | 281 | |
| Kansas-born | | | 0 | | 1 | | 13 | | 57 | | 96 | |
| Foreign-born direct to Kansas | | | 2 | | 5 | | 15 | | 34 | | 55 | |
| Internal migration to Kansas | | | 192 | 100.0 | 127 | 100.0 | 177 | 100.0 | 159 | 100.0 | 126 | 100.0 |
| From adjacent state | | | 56 | 29.1 | 55 | 43.3 | 71 | 40.1 | 69 | 43.4 | 59 | 46.8 |
| From non-contiguous state | | | 136 | 70.9 | 72 | 56.7 | 106 | 59.9 | 90 | 56.6 | 67 | 53.2 |
| Total farm operators | | | | | 723 | | 538 | | 833 | | 913 | |
| Kansas-born | | | | | 9 | | 33 | | 157 | | 274 | |
| Foreign-born direct to Kansas | | | | | 71 | | 37 | | 57 | | 48 | |
| Internal migration to Kansas | | | | | 638 | 100.0 | 511 | 100.0 | 620 | 100.0 | 554 | 100.0 |
| From adjacent state | | | | | 347 | 54.3 | 276 | 54.0 | 351 | 56.6 | 359 | 64.8 |
| From non-contiguous state | | | | | 291 | 45.7 | 235 | 46.0 | 269 | 43.4 | 195 | 35.2 |

Note: Defects in the census data leave some unaccounted for.

non-contiguous states, except for the farthest west frontier, which meant mostly that the settlers made the long jump from some state east of the Mississippi River to Kansas. In the case of the west tier of counties of Kansas forming the seventh group, two factors are sufficient, probably, to explain that behavior: the building of the Burlington and Rock Island railroads into the area from Nebraska and Iowa; and secondly, after 1895 the change in all migration was setting in, especially by 1915. The decisive aspect of the table as a whole is that, for the census dates 1875–1905, the probabilities were that very nearly three of every four, or four of every five, of the migrant operators listed on those dates had migrated from a distance to Kansas, and that the adjustments necessary to so marked a change in environment were substantial. Conspicuous also was the number of Kansas-born operators in the enumerations of 1915 and 1925, a fact which contributes to an explanation of stabilization of population to its environment. Three points relative to migration need to be emphasized because of the tradition in Turner circles that one frontier supplied the population for the next. The Goodrich (1936) and Thornthwaite (1934) studies in migration employed an inadequate methodology, but made the best use possible of the mass statistics from the printed federal census enumerations. Thornthwaite's (1934, p. 10) conclusion that the trans-Mississippi states received settlers chiefly from eastern states, which had been settled forty or fifty years earlier, is so vague as to be virtually meaningless. He did not define the word *settled*. Shannon (1945) followed Thornthwaite in part, concluding that only the occasional family made the long jump from non-contiguous states. The Shannon conclusions are so far out of line with the facts derived from the Kansas census data that the error must be emphasized. Whether or not studies based upon an adequate methodology would reveal different conclusions for states north or south of Kansas cannot be forecast with certainty, but the probabilities are that they would differ little from the Kansas results.

The age of the population of the frontier has been the subject of much inconsistent or contradictory treatment. One contention is that the frontier was settled by men who had made several successive removals. If so, then the frontiersman must have been anything but young. Another extreme held that the frontier was composed conspicuously of young couples who were just starting out in life. Paxson (1930, pp. 29–31) defined the frontier in terms of a cycle, from the coming of the cabineer until his firstborn, in turn, married and set out on a new frontier. The present author, in 1936, 1940, and 1942, presented quantitative data on the subject for Kansas and for the first time removed this phase of the frontier problem from the realm of merely speculative generalization. In the samples analyzed, the young couples just beginning life were conspicuously in the minority. Table 17.3, of median ages, gives the most complete body of data on that aspect of the age question, both for comparative areas in Kansas and for successive stages in community age, 1860–1925. It should be noted that children and other members of the communities were eliminated, the data applying only to farm operators and their wives. This segregation gives the results statistical meaning. The men were conspicuously middle-aged, and in only two entries in the table did the median fall below 35. The age distribution clustered rather closely around the median.

After the publication of "The Turnover of Farm Population in Kansas" (Malin, 1935b), the USDA, through its division of farm population and rural life, undertook a study of farm population in Kansas. A. D. Edwards was in charge, and he applied largely the methodology just described. The present writer cooperated fully, explained the procedures and illustrated them by materials published and unpublished, pointed out errors and difficulties that had been encountered in the experimental work, and suggested improvements. Edwards's study covered Haskell County as a whole, with an intensive concentration on one township sample, and was published as Social Science Research *Report* No. 7, January, 1939. In evaluating the report, distinction should be made between the research results and the policy conclusions, the latter of course conformed in general with the departmental policy. The important conclusion is that the methodology in the hands of another investigator produced essentially the same research results as obtained by its originator. The present writer emphasized to Edwards the importance of studying the replacement population in the community, from census to census. The older population had made some adjustments, but the new population was composed of beginners. He made this differentiation and presented the data and graphs (pp. 17–23) showing the quantitative difference between these two segments of the operators under examination. The new, or replacement, population always followed approximately a new frontier type of curve, and the old population followed a stabilized society type of curve. He found also, what the present writer pointed out, that periods of prosperity seemed to show, for the most part, greater instability than periods of drouth and depression.

It is important that anyone organizing a research project of any size, according to this method, should master fully the possibilities of the punch card and statistical machine methods of compiling and computing data. The study is less liable to result in errors—but the all-important factor is

Table 17.3: Median Age of Farm Operators and Wives by Rainfall Belts: Kansas

| Date | 35+ in. | | 30–35 in. | | 25–30 in. | | 20–25 in. | | 20– in. | |
|------|---------|-------|-----------|-------|-----------|-------|-----------|-------|---------|-------|
|      | Men | Women | Men | Women | Men | Women | Men | Women | Men | Women |
| 1860 | 37.0 | 34.0 | 33.0 | 31.0 | 32.8 | 31.2 | — | — | — | — |
| 1865 | 39.0 | 35.0 | 37.0 | 34.0 | 35.0 | 29.0 | — | — | — | — |
| 1870 | 40.0 | 35.5 | 38.0 | 35.0 | 35.5 | 32.5 | — | — | — | — |
| 1875 | 44.5 | 38.0 | 39.0 | 35.6 | 35.0 | 33.0 | 36.0 | 34.0 | — | — |
| 1885 | 45.0 | 39.0 | 41.0 | 37.0 | 40.0 | 36.0 | 40.0 | 36.0 | — | — |
| 1895 | 43.0 | 38.0 | 43.0 | 38.0 | 43.0 | 38.0 | 42.0 | 39.0 | 40.0 | 37.0 |
| 1905 | 44.8 | 41.0 | 43.0 | 39.0 | 44.0 | 39.0 | 42.0 | 36.0 | 44.0 | 39.0 |
| 1915 | 45.0 | 41.0 | 42.0 | 39.0 | 42.0 | 37.0 | 39.0 | 37.0 | 44.0 | 38.0 |
| 1925 | 45.6 | 40.5 | 43.0 | 39.5 | 41.5 | 38.5 | 40.6 | 37.5 | 42.5 | 37.0 |

Note: The same sample townships and counties were used
in this as in the other phases of the population studies.

labor-saving that may mean the difference between failure and completion of the project.

The kind of population studies thus briefly described are in progress only for Kansas. The full value of these can be brought out only through comparative studies by substantially the same method for other areas, states to the north, to the south, and to the west of Kansas, and especially samples from eastern states, and for social groups other than farm operators. So far as can be determined by preliminary surveys, no other state has quite so complete a record of data essential to the purpose as appears in the Kansas census, but such federal census materials as are available, and county records, seem to indicate that similar studies are feasible for other areas. For Kentucky, with its long axis running east and west in the general direction of population movement, it would seem that a county basis of study would have to be devised. Louis Warren's effective use of county records in his book, *Lincoln's Parentage and Childhood* (1926), indicates that in those records lies an opportunity to make valuable population studies. The most effective thing that could be done to make possible the tracing of migration within states, as well as between states, would be the making of indices of the names in the federal census records. The Kansas State Historical Society has made a beginning of such an index for its early census enumerations, but it would have to be done for all of the states. For early years when numbers were relatively small such a project would not be prohibitive. If there were state enumerations between the federal recording dates, as in Kansas, that would make possible a check on the residence of each individual every five instead of every ten years. Without comparative studies, both as to time and area, it is impossible to evaluate in any quantitative and objective manner the process of the peopling of the United States and the changes in internal composition and structure through the years from the first pioneer settlement to the twentieth century.

The second aspect of the question is equally important. The center of interest of the studies described has been farm operators, wives, and families. But what was the behavior of other groups: town people, the professions, different types of business, the extractive industries, processors, marketing and distributive businesses, personal service businesses (barbers, blacksmiths, livery stables, garages, restaurants, real estate, and insurance), the general store, etc.? Were they more, or less, stable than farm operators? Preliminary investigations would indicate that the personal service businesses were far more unstable, probably the most unstable of all the professions. In the population turnover study of 1935, a comparison was made with a sample of college students. Their persistence over a period of six years, toward a college degree, provided a curve of the same conformation as the farm operator curve. Such graphs worked out comparatively are imperative to any real knowledge of historical development and change in population structure, and should be of outstanding importance to students of governmental policies, whether designed for over-all application to society, or to benefit particular groups. As suggested in 1935, the basic behavior pattern revealed in these farm population turnover studies is not peculiar to farm operators of Kansas, but seems to indicate "that the problem is primarily one of group behavior, apart from specifically assignable accidents of farm life"—a large percentage of losses during the early stages, with a gradual stabilization later.

# CHAPTER 18

# Agricultural Studies

[In this selection, James Malin summarizes his interdisciplinary research into the agricultural history of the grassland frontier. His synthesis of the related disciplines of history, geography, and ecology demonstrates the value of this approach in regional studies. Contrary to the prevailing wisdom that farms became even larger in the grassland region, Malin's detailed analysis of thousands of individual farms registered in the agricultural censuses showed that farm size fluctuated over time, depending on crop prices, climate, changes in communication and transport systems, mechanization, and availability of capital. Similarly, cropping patterns and the livestock mix changed over time, as pioneer farm operators tried to raise their "small, very small" cash incomes and improve the already high rate of return on the minimal capital invested in their businesses. In the long run, Malin suggests, grassland farmers learned the "stark realism of rural life," namely that "the hazards of weather on crops and prosperity were greater than the hazards of price."]

In studies of agriculture in the grassland the sampling method as described for population studies was extended and adapted for the purpose in hand, using the same communities. Because of this concentration of the present author's own research in the central portion of the grassland region, consideration of other portions is omitted except as to some statements of general matters. For the Prairie Peninsula of Illinois, or for the barrens of Kentucky, where Anglo-Americans first met the grassland problems, there have been no comprehensive studies of either population behavior or agricultural adaptation that deal explicitly with the grassland problem as such. The Illinois Centennial Commission history of that state (1920) did not meet the problem of the prairie, and the Bidwell and Falconer *History of Agriculture in the Northern United States, 160–1860* (1925) recognized it only in a general way. Poggi, *The Prairie Province* (1934) was a geographical study with a section on settlement which was inadequate as history. Studies by ecologists of the area were intensive and valuable. Even without new research, a competent synthesis of existing studies from all these related fields is much to be desired. Illinois was a leader in ecological, geographical, and historical studies in separate fields, but the several disciplines did not get together for cooperative synthesis that might have brought the data from all the sources to bear in an explicit and comprehensive presentation of the grassland problem and its impact upon Anglo-American behavior.

The problem of irrigation in the lowest-rainfall areas of the grassland and desert are likewise omitted from special consideration. Three aspects only of the problem are selected for emphasis: the importance of the synthesis of geographical, ecological, soil, and other scientific material with the historical; and the comparative study of the whole irrigation problem within the different areas of North America and among the other continents with similar problems. Sauer's type of approach from the standpoint of historical geography is particularly important. Comparative studies should reveal the differences, and limitations, in different parts of the world, and break down the provincialism that pervades so much of irrigation history. The final point is to keep the record straight relative to federal reclamation work under the Newlands Act of 1902, and its amendments, and the social myth built up by propaganda under that system. The work of irrigation was inaugurated and expanded in such haste as to bring a large number of the projects to a point of imminent collapse when they could not pay out, partly because of blunders, miscalculations, and incompetence, and partly because of a misunderstanding of the whole problem of American rural population behavior in its historical setting. The fact of governmental sponsorship and treasury support was no guarantee of success or of avoidance of large-scale hardship to the individual settlers. The relative failure of so many of these projects, as revealed during the 1920s, should have served as a warning of the high degree of failure in other government-sponsored settlement projects of the

1930s. The farm population studies reviewed in the preceding chapter point to a general principle, that in any group of people a large proportion (although variable in each sample group) will always fail to complete the plan, the largest losses appear near the outset, the rate of loss declining sharply after the initial test period and then tapering off to a relative stability among the surviving few. Each new increment added must in turn experience this selective process. This principle of group behavior was suggested in 1935, and further studies seem to confirm it.

As the advancing population reached Kansas in 1854, the problem of agriculture under the prairie environment was discussed. Missourians, and some Indians among the immigrant tribes from the East, had a limited experience prior to the opening of the territory. The recognition was quite general that the settlers were facing a new environment, one sufficiently different that modifications in crops and methods were accepted as inevitable (Malin, 1944b, chapters 1–3). The question was not whether changes were necessary, but what nature and extent of changes would be required. The long-term answer to that question was determined by the several factors of climate, topography, and soil. From east to west the moisture problem was most conspicuous. As the role of irrigation was negligible for the country as a whole, almost to the Rocky Mountains, the decreasing available moisture westward emphasized what came to be called dry-land farming as the settled area advanced toward the mountains.

Various traditions have become relatively stereotyped in dealing with the size of farms. The group of land reformers are disposed to adverse criticism of land policy on the ground that it did not fit conditions (President's Committee on Tenantry Report [1937], p. 5). Into this pattern is fitted the formula that the original land unit was too small, and that immediately upon patents being issued the process of consolidation into economical, larger units began. Statistical studies of farm size from the printed census figures are at best of limited value and often are positively misleading. First there was no uniform or adequate definition of what constituted a farm, and in pioneer days no definition could have been applied consistently. Students of the land problem should digest carefully the introductory explanations of the federal census, especially for 1870 and 1880. Furthermore, the very nature of mass statistics serves to conceal, rather than to reveal, actual changes and their significance. One kind of tendency may be cancelled by another. So long as there was unoccupied land held by the government or non-resident owners, it was used largely by the community as commons (Malin, 1942b, 1944b). Even if the pioneer had received larger acreages, under the terms of the governmental land policy, he seldom had the capital to finance adequately even the traditional quarter-section farm—the buildings, fences, machinery, horsepower, and manpower. Whether he could have marketed, profitably, large production is open to question. The early years were usually marked by the severest struggle to cultivate even small acreages.

Such limited discussion by resident farmers of the late nineteenth century as has been made a matter of record in the area of the present author's research leads mostly in one direction, emphasis on more efficient management of a smaller farm rather than enlargement of the unit (Malin, 1944b). This general trend, to which there were only occasional exceptions, is represented by a letter to the editor of the *Junction City* (Kansas) *Union,* February 20, 1862, in which the argument warned farmers against taking too much land, because of costs of taxes, improvements, breaking sod, fencing, building, and hiring help. The letter writer insisted that eighty acres was enough, and that excellence and profit in farming depended upon the operator doing his own work, with small expense; the income would be small, but sufficient, and the farmer would remain independent, and no outsiders would intrude upon his domestic circle.

This limitation to eighty acres was in part a sound argument from the standpoint of the small farmer's inability to finance adequately larger farms, even with the advantage of cheap or free land, and in part it illustrated the easterner's misconception, even when on the spot, of the size of farm necessary to support a family in the vicinity of the 97th meridian. In respect to the first point no adequate answer to financing has been forthcoming, and on the second point only experience with different types of farming could answer for any given time or place, and no answer on the matter of size could be final because of the changing conditions, especially those accompanying mechanization. Another factor in the farm-size problem was the element of speculation in land. The concept of "actual settler" or the permanent farm home was largely a myth as most owners of land, irrespective of whether they were resident or non-resident, bought land on the assumption that it would be resold soon at a profit (Malin, "Mobility and History," 1943). To a larger degree than any historian has yet been willing to admit, the much-discussed periods of agricultural prosperity and depression of history have been more accurately reflections of land prices rather than reflections of profits and losses on actual farm operations. It is probable that, over a period of years of fluctuating weather and prices, only the better managers made profits out of farm operations.

These matters become clear only when farms are studied individually at different times and in terms of acreages and yields for samples in the several farm-size groups.

The size of the farm possesses significance only in terms of utilization, and changes in use are reflected necessarily in size. New transportation facilities often change farm sizes, inducing such shifts as livestock raising to grain farming. The rise of cities provides new kinds of markets and induces dairying and truck farming; cannery contracts may determine the crops. A farm of ten to twenty-five acres may be a substantial size of intensive truck, fruit, poultry, or irrigation farm, but insufficient in size for grain or livestock. All such situations are lost in mass statistics printed in the federal census. Before statistical studies of farm-size can have any particular meaning, the data must be classified into groups of comparable kind, because only similar or substantially similar things can be compared statistically if results are to possess validity. In the selected samples used in the present author's studies, the history of each sample and its changing internal structure were studied to determine the kind of farm program prevailing and the nature of changes. Only under such known conditions do studies in farm-size possess much significance.

First, a sample community in eastern Kansas will illustrate several of the aspects of the problem under discussion (Tables 18.1–3). Kanwaka Township, Douglas County, Kansas, is an upland mixed farming community occupying the ridge between the historic towns of Lawrence and Lecompton. The tables and discussion present farm sizes, and crop and livestock programs over a period of eighty-five years (1855–1940).

When the state was first settled, the prevailing method of acquiring land from the public domain was the preemption system by which a settler might buy a quarter section, prior to the offering of the land at public auction, at the minimum price of $1.25 per acre. Under this land system the predominant size of farms was 160 acres with a few 80s. In 1860, 90 percent of all farms in Kanwaka Township were quarter sections.

Once the land was in private hands the readjustments in the size of farms were continuous. During the periods of rural depression the size decreased, or in other words, the number of farms of 160 acres or less increased. In prosperous times the smaller farms were consolidated in part into units of 160 acres or larger.

The period showing the greatest subdivision into small farms of less than a quarter section came in the years of depression immediately following the Civil War. In Kanwaka Township, in 1870, 25 percent of the farms were 40 acres, another 25 percent were 80 acres, and a third 25 percent were

**Table 18.1:** Size of Farms: Kanwaka Township, Douglas County, Kansas
(Figures in Percentage, Except as Indicated)

| Date | 1860 | 1865 | 1870 | 1875 | 1880 | 1885 | 1895 | 1905 | 1915 | 1920 | 1925 | 1930 | 1935 | 1940 |
|---|---|---|---|---|---|---|---|---|---|---|---|---|---|---|
| No. of farms | 79 | 100 | 109 | 143 | 152 | 125 | 159 | 168 | 138 | 149 | 169 | 154 | 176 | 162 |
| Size in acres | | | | | | | | | | | | | | |
| 3 | | | | | | | | | | | 1.18 | | 4.54 | 2.44 |
| 3–9 | | {6.4 | | {1.3 | | | 2.5 | 2.9 | 3.6 | 4.0 | 2.36 | {1.3 | 2.84 | 1.85 |
| 10–19 | | | | | 0.8 | | | | | | 0.59 | | 0.57 | 0.00 |
| 20–49 | | | 24.8 | 2.8 | 3.9 | 0.8 | 3.1 | 5.4 | 4.3 | 4.0 | 1.78 | 2.6 | 2.27 | 1.85 |
| 50–99 | 6.3 | 13.0 | 25.7 | 21.7 | 28.4 | 13.6 | 22.0 | 20.8 | 21.7 | 16.8 | 19.52 | 17.5 | 16.47 | 14.19 |
| 100–174 | 89.89 | 75.0 | 25.7 | 48.9 | 36.2 | 47.2 | 45.9 | 42.9 | 38.4 | 33.6 | 41.42 | 40.0 | 38.00 | 38.27 |
| 175–259 | 5 | | | | | | | | | | 18.93 | | 15.90 | 16.66 |
| | 3.9 | 12 | 17.4 | 25.9 | 28.3 | 36.8 | 24.5 | 26.8 | 29.0 | 37.6 | | 36.4 | | |
| 260–499 | 7 | | | | | | | | | | 11.83 | | 15.34 | 17.90 |
| 500–999 | | | | | | | 1.9 | 1.2 | 3.0 | 4.0 | 1.18 | 1.3 | 1.14 | 3.08 |
| | | | | | {1.9 | | | | | | | | | |
| 1,000–4,999 | | | | 0.7 | | 0.8 | | | | | 0.0 | | 0.0 | 0.0 |
| over 5,000 | | | | | | | | | | | 0.0 | | 0.0 | 0.0 |
| No data | | | | | | | | | | | 1.18 | | 2.84 | 3.70 |
| 160 or less | 96.2 | 88.0 | 82.6 | 73.4 | 69.8 | 62.4 | 73.5 | 72.0 | 68.0 | 58.4 | 66.85 | 61.4 | 64.69 | 58.60 |

Note: The difference in the total number of farms in this table and in the table giving numbers of farms is explained by the fact that for some years the data were missing on one or more farms. The percentages were figured, therefore, on the basis of the number of farms with specific data on the assumption that error would be less serious because the no-data farms were probably scattered randomly throughout the range of the census list. The problem was most serious for the years 1920 and 1930 and 1940 when no formal Kansas census was taken and agricultural statistical rolls had to be used for the present purpose.

quarter sections. There was an increasing number over 1865 of larger farms (half sections or three-quarters) but the proportion was small—only 17 percent of all farms.

In the boom period of the 1880s, the pendulum swung in the opposite direction, when in 1885 nearly two out of every five farms (37.6 percent) were approximately a half section or larger. Less than half were 160-acre farms. Forty-acre farms practically disappeared, and only a few 80s survived.

The depression of the 1890s broke up the big farms, restoring a moderate number of 80-acre and 40-acre operators, and it was not until 1920, as a result of the World War boom, that the large farms again came back in approximately the same proportion as in 1885. After 1920 there was no long-time trend in either direction, but short sharp swings of the

**Table 18.2**: Douglas County, Kanwaka Township
(Mixed Farming Upland)

| Date | 1860 | 1865 | 1870 | 1875 | 1880 | 1885 | 1895 | 1905 | 1915 | 1920 | 1925 | 1930 | 1935 | 1940 |
|---|---|---|---|---|---|---|---|---|---|---|---|---|---|---|
| No. of farms | 80 | 100 | 110 | 143 | 152 | 128 | 160 | 168 | 138 | 163 | 169 | 160 | 176 | 162 |
| Size in acres | | | | | | | | | | | | | | |
| 1–19 | 0 | 0 | 7 | 0 | 2 | 1 | 4 | 5 | 5 | 6 | 7 | 2 | 14 | 7 |
| 20–49 | 0 | 0 | 27 | 4 | 6 | 1 | 5 | 9 | 6 | 6 | 3 | 4 | 4 | 3 |
| 50–99 | 5 | 13 | 28 | 31 | 43 | 17 | 35 | 35 | 30 | 25 | 33 | 27 | 29 | 23 |
| 100–174 | 71 | 75 | 28 | 70 | 55 | 59 | 73 | 72 | 53 | 50 | 70 | 64 | 67 | 62 |
| 175–259 | 1 | 5 | 13 | 20 | 25 | 23 | 20 | 23 | 24 | 37 | 32 | 34 | 28 | 27 |
| 260–499 | 2 | 7 | 6 | 17 | 18 | 23 | 19 | 22 | 16 | 19 | 20 | 22 | 27 | 29 |
| 500–999 | | | | | 2 | | 3 | 2 | 4 | 6 | 2 | 2 | 2 | 5 |
| 1,000–4,999 | | | | 1 | 1 | 1 | | | | | | | | |
| No data | 1 | | 1 | | | 3 | 1 | | | 14 | 2 | 6 | 5 | 6 |

pendulum about every five years. In 1925 and 1935 the small farms multiplied, while in 1930 and 1940 the large farms appeared in increasing numbers. One exception must be made to this generalization, however, inasmuch as after 1925 the 80-acre farms declined continuously in numbers. From the standpoint of the political objective of preserving the traditional family-size farm, the statistics did not indicate any decisive success. As in earlier periods of history, economic and technological, rather than political factors, seem to control the size of farms. The larger the farm, and the more elaborate the equipment necessary to operate it, the more difficult it is for a single family to own.

During the early pioneer days it made little difference what size the farm might be as one man could care for only a limited number of acres of crops. The early census enumerations did not record the acreages in each crop, only the production. The census of 1860 reported on the crop of 1859 which was the most favorable crop raised in early Kansas history. The average production of corn per farm in Kanwaka Township that year was 600–700 bushels. With yields of 40 to 50 bushels per acre this meant that an average farm may have had 10 to 15 acres of corn, but a substantial number could have had only 2 to 5 acres. Nearly every farm produced white potatoes, some as few as 10 bushels, the highest was 300, but the average was 68 bushels. These were the two universal crops, corn and potatoes, but in addition to these about one-third of the farms produced a few bushels of oats, and a third of them some wheat, possibly from one to five acres in each case. Few farms raised both oats and wheat. Probably the total cultivated area of each farm did not exceed 15 to 20 acres. The year 1864, reported in the census of 1865, was not a good crop year, and army service had drained the country of labor, so farm production suffered. The average farm produced only 200–300 bushels of corn. By 1870, there was evidence of expansion of cultivated acreages somewhat in proportion to the size of the farm. Corn, potatoes, and oats being the standard crops, only a few farmers raised wheat, which was mostly of the spring variety. Among the more occasional crops, during the decade of the 1860s, were barley, rye, buckwheat, and sweet potatoes, but they were raised by only a few farmers and the acreages were small. Buckwheat was rather generally raised in 1859, but practically disappeared in later years.

In the census of 1875, for the crop year 1874, crop acreages were listed for the first time. Corn and potatoes were still the only crops raised by all farmers, but about two-thirds of the farms raised oats, and one of every six raised winter wheat.

The census of 1930, for the crop year 1929, showed only corn and

**Table 18.3:** Livestock: Kanwaka Township, Douglas County, Kansas (Averages for Farms with Each Type of Livestock)

| Date | 1860 | 1865 | 1870 | 1875 | 1880 | 1885 | 1895 | 1905 | 1915 | 1920 | 1925 | 1930 |
|---|---|---|---|---|---|---|---|---|---|---|---|---|
| Milk cows | | | | | | | | | | | | |
| 40 acres | | | 2.16 | 5.66 | 3.66 | 1.00* | 1.75 | 4.82 | 4.6 | 3.33 | 1.4 | 0 |
| 80 | 2.25 | 3.46 | 4.36 | 3.84 | 4.92 | 3.06 | 2.86 | 4.06 | 4.95 | 5.52 | 3.04 | 4.25 |
| 160 | 2.95 | 4.9 | 5.26 | 6.45 | 6.43 | 6.02 | 4.64 | 6.20 | 4.79 | 3.82 | 4.80 | 5.5 |
| 320+ | 5.66 | 8.75 | 9.9 | 7.22 | 8.8 | 782 | 6.05 | 8.5 | 6.38 | 4.0 | 5.4 | 8.62 |
| 500+ | | | | 15.00 | 8.00 | 20.00* | 4.66 | 14.00 | 5.25 | 5.75 | 6.0 | 14.00 |
| Other cattle | | | | | | | | | | | | |
| 40 acres | | | 5.66 | 6.0 | 8.15 | 0 | 1.00 | 15.4 | 5.75 | 3.33 | 8.33 | 5.5 |
| 80 | 5.66 | 3.53 | 5.69 | 7.61 | 8.45 | 3.37 | 2.5 | 5.11 | 14.04 | 6.95 | 6.5 | 6.8 |
| 160 | 5.44 | 8.6 | 10.48 | 13.64 | 15.3 | 8.32 | 11.36 | 7.94 | 11.90 | 5.4 | 12.4 | 13.91 |
| 320+ | 7.33 | 21.91 | 16.93 | 17.00 | 22.41 | 17.13 | 24.25 | 21.2 | 10.51 | 16.2 | 22.6 | 22.84 |
| 500+ | | | | 72.00 | 54.6 | 50.00 | 72.66 | 38.00 | 55.25 | 63.66 | 32.0 | 20.5 |
| Swine | | | | | | | | | | | | |
| 40 acres | | | 8.12 | 8.0 | 9.33 | 18.00 | 6.33 | 5.4 | 6.66 | 1.5 | 6.5 | 4.0 |
| 80 | 17.25 | 3.18 | 7.68 | 5.46 | 10.00 | 6.53 | 11.11 | 10.44 | 6.5 | 14.76 | 8.4 | 12.7 |
| 160 | 13.7 | 4.76 | 9.08 | 6.46 | 16.3 | 9.7 | 15.41 | 15.93 | 12.75 | 11.43 | 14.7 | 15.7 |
| 320+ | 11.66 | 6.73 | 17.11 | 8.74 | 21.95 | 19.13 | 24.18 | 23.27 | 14.4 | 9.5 | 24.1 | 22.87 |
| 500+ | | | | 2.00 | 36.00 | 100.00 | 41.66 | 17.00 | 9.25 | 9.25 | 32.0 | 29.00 |

*Only one farm is represented.

potatoes in the four 40-acre farms; corn and potatoes on practically every one of the twenty-seven 80-acre farms, with winter wheat on seven, oats on fifteen, and sorghum or kaffir corn on fourteen. There were sixty-four 160-acre farms with corn and potatoes as the universal crop combined with oats on forty-nine farms, sorghum or kaffir corn on thirty-five, and winter wheat on twenty-nine. The group of larger farms of 320–480 acres (2–3 quarters) numbered fifty-five, again with the corn-potato combination, and forty-two with winter wheat, forty-one with oats, and thirty-eight with sorghum or kaffir corn. Only two farms contained over 500 acres.

In respect to corn it is notable that the acreage devoted to that crop had reached the optimum suitable to each size of farm, the census of 1930 showing almost exactly the same average number of acres of corn, for each size-group of farms, as that of 1875. The average corn crop in both years for an 80-acre farm was 24 acres; for a 160-acre farm 37 acres, and for a half-section farm 48 acres in 1875, but only 43 acres in 1930. The oats crop had not been so definitely stabilized. In 1875 the average acreage in oats for the three sizes of farms was 5, 9, and 11 respectively, while the 1930 figures were 8.6, 10.4, and 13.5 acres. The wheat crop was much less stabilized, the acreages being 3, 13.6, and 8, in 1875, and 11, 22, and 31 in 1930. The potato acreage in 1875 ranged from one-half to two acres, while in 1930 the almost uniform report was one-quarter acre. The average total acreage devoted to the four principal crops combined in each size group had doubled approximately in the interval between 1875 and 1930.

In addition to these basic crops there had been a number of supplementary or experimental crops introduced from time to time, some of which soon dropped out, while others gained a permanent place in the crop program. The decade of the seventies is usually known as the period of the granger movement which grew out of a number of rural grievances, high railroad rates, monopoly, and low prices being most discussed. Other and possibly more serious difficulties grew out of a decade of erratic weather, drouth, heat, and winds, with attending dust storms and blowing soil, chinch bugs, and grasshoppers. The chinch bug menace became so serious during the decade of the seventies that every possible means of combating it was resorted to. As chinch bugs thrived especially in spring wheat, that crop was abandoned, and some farmers advocated discontinuing winter wheat. The problem of one or more substitute crops in eastern Kansas was made more insistent by overproduction on corn and its consequent low price. Such a substitute crop had to meet a number of tests, besides adaptability to climate and soil, especially a sure cash market, and small bulk and weight in proportion to value, in order to stand high transportation costs to market. Hemp, castor beans, and flax each received attention, especially flax. A St. Louis paint and linseed oil company offered to loan seed to eastern Kansas farmers, and the Kansas Pacific railroad carried on a publicity campaign to encourage experimentation. Some promoters went a step further, urging the building of mills in Kansas to crush flax seed, making the oil at home, thus promoting home industry, employment, home markets, and the saving of transportation costs. In consequence of such agitation, some flax was raised for a number of years, but it never attained an important or permanent place in the crop system. Some sweet sorghum had been raised for molasses as early as the territorial period, but the making of sugar from sweet sorghum attracted much attention during the eighties and nineties. As a sugar crop, sorghum was a failure, but it became a permanent part of the agricultural system as a forage or seed crop along with the non-saccharine varieties, kaffir in the nineties, and feterita and sedan grass after 1910, and more recently, atlas sargo, and other improved varieties.

Until the 1880s, the Kanwaka Township farmer depended primarily upon native grass for pasture and hay, but a few planted timothy, clover, and millet. In another ten years timothy was the dominant tame grass, supplemented by a little clover. By 1905 the field was divided among four rivals, timothy, clover, bluegrass, and alfalfa, but alfalfa was not generally grown until after 1905, when timothy dropped out for the most part. The latest of the newcomers were sweet clover and lespedesa, during the last fifteen years, 1925–1940. In spite of eighty-five years of agriculture in Douglas County, a substantial acreage of native grasses remained, and where given anything like a fair chance they survived in vigorous condition. The early settler began worrying about the grass problem very soon after settlement, predicting the early disappearance of native grasses for both pasture and hay. They were thinking, naturally, in terms of eastern forest clearings, not in terms of the western prairie-plains grass region, and they did not appreciate the vigor and recuperative power of Kansas bluestem and its associates.

Farm power in early Kansas was supplied by horses and oxen, and in 1860 the numbers were about equal in Kanwaka Township. By the close of the Civil War oxen were going out of use, rapidly, there being only one ox to six horses. By 1870 only a few oxen remained. Prior to 1905 there were only a few mules, and there was no general use of mules until about 1915. Prior to World War I this part of Kansas represented, quite literally, a man and horse power era. Any degree of mechanization came only in the very last years.

It is clear from the review of the crop program of the early years that Douglas County was a part of the corn belt, raising that crop almost to the exclusion of others. The only profitable way to market corn was in the form of livestock and their products. Sheep raising did not gain an important foothold during any period, so the livestock business centered around cattle and hogs. Although hog production fluctuated widely, there is little indication of an increase in the number of hogs per farm after the 1870s. The census statistics are not an altogether accurate indication, however, partly because of deficiencies in reporting, but partly also because more efficient feeding and the marketing of younger animals yielded a larger amount of pork from the same corn acreage. Not all farms, especially the small farms, had all three types of livestock, milk cows, beef-cattle, and hogs. The following averages apply only to such farms as had the particular class specified. If the averages were based ön the whole number of farms in the group, the figures would be much reduced.

Milk cows always occupied a substantial place in farm planning, such 80-acre farms as had cows having 3–5; the 160-acre farm 4–6, and the larger farms averaging about 6–10. After 1870, however, there was no permanent increase in average numbers of cows per farm. The increases in production were derived from better cows and more efficient management. In the beef-cattle division the numbers fluctuated inversely with the prosperity of field crops. During years of prolonged depression, such as the late 1870s, cattle increased. During the boom years of the mid-eighties, cattle declined. In 1880 the 160-acre farms reported an average of fifteen head of cattle per farm in addition to milk cows, but five years later the average had dropped to eight. During the depression of the nineties the average increased to eleven per 160-acre farm, declining again by 1905 to eight. Taking the last sixty years as a whole, however, there was no clear long-time trend in numbers in either direction. On the other hand, as in the case of hogs, there were substantial changes during the last years in the methods of feeding and in marketing younger animals which made comparisons for recent years uncertain. There is no record available, however, of feeders, either cattle or sheep, transient livestock, finished for market on Kanwaka corn.

Probably the most significant changes in the livestock picture during the last sixty years were the improvements in quality and emphasis on pure-bred or high-grade animals. During the 1880s William A. Harris built up his herd of Scotch Shorthorns, at Linwood, Kansas. Although his famous farm was just outside Douglas County, Harris was closely identified with Lawrence. He was one of the pioneers in the United States in developing the Scotch strain of Shorthorns, and was rated one of the nation's foremost breeders. During the same period the firm of Shockey and Gibb was among the foremost American importers of Hereford cattle, and gave Lawrence national publicity in that field. The depression of the nineties was disastrous to most of the breeders of fine stock. Although a number of fine herds of thoroughbred cattle were identified with the county later, probably none occupied so distinguished a position nationally as the Harris and Shockey cattle.

In days when the farmers were suffering from over-production of agricultural politicians, sensational statements often appeared on the subject of long-time depletion of soil fertility. As proof of the destruction of farm lands it is customary to cite instances of fabulous crop production in the early days compared with later yields. Much, if not most, of such propaganda should be discounted. There is good reason to doubt whether many of these reports of extraordinary yields are either reliable or representative. Early Kansans were real estate boomers, and because of the reputation of the state for drouth it was customary to exaggerate. Measurements of acres and of production were faulty—usually they were only rough guesses. Only small tracts of the best land were first opened up on each farm, and under favorable conditions they should have given high yields, higher than in later years when expansion of acreage under the plow could be accomplished only by cropping less fertile land. Of course, it should be emphasized that the definition of soil fertility is itself a debated question, and one of those that cannot be proven positively one way or the other. Neither can the question of productivity be settled, in part for the simple reason that there are no long-time comparative records that are adequate, and in part because production capacity depended so largely upon machinery and methods of culture. Without question, some land was abused, but on the other hand much land was more efficiently farmed as the years passed. It is not possible to strike a satisfying average for a whole county, and much less for a whole state. Modern machinery, especially power machinery, provided more efficient handling of land than was possible under a horse-power agriculture. Even if maximum yields per acre were not increased above those under more primitive methods, there were not so many failures. The greater stability insured higher average production over a period of years. The problem of soil fertility was not so much one of restoring past depletion as of guarding against losses from erosion and from the more intensive utilization which was being exacted of the land and which was becoming more intensive with the passing years.

Other samples have been presented elsewhere, for the early years of

Dickinson and Saline counties, between 97° and 98° (Malin, 1944b), and for parts of Edwards County, near 99° 30', fragments appear in separate articles (Malin, 1935a, 1935b, 1936, and 1940a). The reader must consult these publications for the details and the local setting. In those samples, the introduction and proving of hard winter wheat and the grain sorghums through the 1880s and the 1890s was reflected conspicuously in the nature of the farm program. Corn and livestock gave way to wheat and to the sorghums in their proportionate place even where actual corn acreages were not yet reduced. In Geary and Riley counties, just to the eastward of Dickinson County, the corn-hog-cattle combination persisted generally, with the addition of the sorghums and alfalfa, the transition line dividing corn and wheat being fairly sharply defined between the Bluestem Pastures region and the central hard winter wheat region. The hill and limestone rock topography entered into the sharpening of this transition, and to a lesser extent the soils, and farther west the outcrop of the Dakota sandstone strata.

Besides the Kanwaka Township, Douglas County, sample, tables are printed for five other samples, each representing a different type of farming area, or a different sub-area (Tables 18.4–8). The commercial corn-belt sample, Walnut Township, Brown County (Table 18.4), shows the clear predominance of the 80, 160, and 240-acre (3 eighties) farms until 1920 when, for the first time, there were more half-section farms than eighties, and thereafter the proportions remained fairly stable, with the quarter-section farm of historical tradition as the most numerous size, the 240-acre

Table 18.4: Brown County, Walnut Township (Commercial Corn-Belt County) Number of Farms in Each Size Group

| Date | 1860 | 1865 | 1870 | 1875 | 1880 | 1885 | 1895 | 1905 | 1915 | 1920 | 1925 | 1930 | 1935 | 1940 |
|---|---|---|---|---|---|---|---|---|---|---|---|---|---|---|
| No. of farms | 35 | 145 | 239 | 130* | 210 | 240 | 222 | 244 | 226 | 197 | 217 | 177* | 226 | 197 |
| 1–19 acres | 1 | 1 | 0 | 0 | 9 | 11 | 5 | 5 | 3 | 1 | 4 | 5 | 7 | 4 |
| 20–49 | 5 | 4 | 13 | 8 | 20 | 10 | 6 | 3 | 7 | 3 | 1 | 5 | 5 | 1 |
| 50–99 | 4 | 26 | 71 | 38 | 62 | 61 | 58 | 49 | 34 | 16 | 14 | 12 | 18 | 18 |
| 100–174 | 20 | 37 | 75 | 50 | 83 | 92 | 94 | 111 | 108 | 97 | 102 | 77 | 89 | 86 |
| 175–259 | 3 | 18 | 23 | 15 | 16 | 26 | 34 | 32 | 38 | 45 | 58 | 39 | 54 | 50 |
| 260–499 | 2 | 12 | 21 | 12 | 16 | 23 | 21 | 28 | 26 | 25 | 22 | 35 | 27 | 28 |
| 500–999 |  | 2 | 4 | 5 | 3 | 7 | 4 | 3 | 1 | 5 |  | 3 | 3 | 6 |
| 1,000–4,999 |  |  | 2 |  |  |  |  |  |  | 1 |  |  |  |  |
| No data |  | 45 | 30 | 2 | 1 | 20 |  | 13 | 9 | 4 | 16 | 1 | 23 | 4 |

*Evidently the census roll is incomplete for 1875 and 1930.

Table 18.5: Dickinson County, Buckeye Township (East Central Winter Wheat Region) Number of Farms in Each Size Group

| Date | 1860 (whole county) | 1865 (whole county) | 1870 (Grant Twp.) | 1875 (Buckeye Twp.) | 1880 | 1885 | 1895 | 1905 | 1915 | 1920 | 1925 | 1930 | 1935 | 1940 |
|---|---|---|---|---|---|---|---|---|---|---|---|---|---|---|
| No. of farms | 12* | 80* | 47* | 75 | 78 | 112 | 100 | 100 | 131 | 122 | 116 | 105 | 111 | 98 |
| 1–49 acres | 2 | | | 1 | | | | | 1 | 1 | 2 | 2 | 2 | 2 |
| 50–99 | | 6 | 8 | 33 | 30 | 37 | 19 | 18 | 21 | 17 | 12 | 14 | 12 | 11 |
| 100–174 | 7 | 45 | 13 | 31 | 31 | 43 | 47 | 53 | 59 | 70 | 48 | 52 | 40 | 35 |
| 175–259 | 2 | 4 | 7 | 5 | 11 | 11 | 12 | 10 | 15 | 18 | 24 | 18 | 24 | 19 |
| 260–499 | 3 | 7 | | 3 | 7 | 11 | 16 | 15 | 15 | 12 | 27 | 18 | 21 | 24 |
| 500–999 | | 1 | | 1 | 1 | 8 | 5 | 4 | 1 | 1 | 1 | 1 | 0 | 4 |
| 1,000–4,999 | 1 | | | | | 1 | | | | | | | 1 | 1 |
| No data | | | 19 | 1 | | 1 | 1 | | | 19 | 3 | 2 | | |

*The data for 1860 and 1865 are for the whole county; and those for 1870 are for Grant Township, which includes Buckeye. The data for 1875 and later are for Buckeye alone.

unit second in number, and the half-section third. The behavior pattern was substantially different from the Kanwaka sample in the mixed farming area. To the westward and southwestward of Douglas and Brown counties lies the Bluestem Pasture region. The nature and variety of farming, corn, sorghums, alfalfa, and some wheat, combined with the commercial summer pasture operations, produced so complicated a situation that statistical tables are an inadequate method of presentation. For large areas of upland, the pastures prevailed, while the broader river bottoms permitted farming operations of substantial proportions. Some reference has been made already to the manner in which the pasture practices interlocked with the southwestern range cattle industry, the corn belt, and grass-fat market. There are also stock farms devoted to the production of pure-bred cattle, hogs, horses, and sheep. Pending the completion of a full-scale historical treatment of the Bluestem Pastures, already in progress, the present author's introductory essay (Malin, 1942a) gives the best presentation of that region (see also, Doll, Kansas Experiment Station *Bulletin* 294, 1941).

Table 18.5 for Buckeye Township, Dickinson County, repeats part of the table in *Winter Wheat* (1944b), but gives the full chronological range 1860–1940. The quarter-section farm remained the largest size-group, with the next two large size-groups about equally represented in numbers. The list for 1940 indicated a slight break in the pattern, but only time can determine whether or not it was a change of trend. One degree westward on the

98th meridian, in the south central Kansas hard winter wheat belt, is Vinita Township, Kingman County (Table 18.6). The first census after settlement was 1880. By 1895 the half-section farms and the 80-acre farms were second and third in number to the 160-acre farms, which represented half of the whole number. The clear change of trend to the larger farm was not registered until the enumeration of 1905 (federal 1900 might indicate it, if available), but not until 1920 or forty years after the first settlement record did the half-section farm take the lead, 1930 indicating the extreme trend toward large units. The 1940 census again raised questions, the half and the quarter-section groups being equal.

On the 100th meridian, Highpoint Township, Ness County, offers much of interest, but the most of it cannot be read from the statistical table (18.7). Occupying an area particularly subject to uncertainties, livestock occupied an important part in its economy, and utilized non-resident-owned land during its early history. The reported size of farms often possessed little meaning even after 1905 when the census revealed a sharp shift to larger units. By 1920 more intensive settlement revealed even more clearly the fact that three-quarters to a full section-and-a-half farms were approximately the units that had actually been utilized irrespective of the way in which records were kept. From 1920 through 1940 there was little re-adjustment in size.

Wallace County (Table 18.8), lying against the Colorado line, the 102nd meridian, near the northwest corner of Kansas, was studied as a whole. It is typical of what is usually thought of as level grama-buffalo grass plains, with a soil fine-grained, heavy, dark, and windblown. It is that beautiful kind of

**Table 18.6:** Kingman County, Vinita Township (South Central Winter Wheat Region) Number of Farms in Each Size Group

| Date | 1880 | 1885 | 1895 | 1905 | 1915 | 1920 | 1925 | 1930 | 1935 | 1940 |
|---|---|---|---|---|---|---|---|---|---|---|
| No. of farms | 80 | 84 | 106 | 86 | 80 | 76 | 81 | 68 | | 71 |
| 1–49 acres | | | 1 | 4 | 0 | 2 | 0 | 0 | | 1 |
| 50–99 | 4 | 4 | 19 | 8 | 6 | 2 | | 3 | | 6 |
| 100–174 | 67 | 58 | 54 | 23 | 32 | 17 | 19 | 11 | | 24 |
| 175–259 | 1 | 5 | 10 | 19 | 8 | 13 | 12 | 10 | | 8 |
| 260–499 | 8 | 9 | 20 | 25 | 25 | 30 | 31 | 29 | | 24 |
| 500–999 | | | 1 | 1 | 6 | 6 | 10 | 9 | 11 | 7 |
| 1,000–4,999 | | | 1 | 1 | 1 | 1 | 1 | 1 | 1 | 1 |
| No data | | 6 | | | 2 | 1 | | 3 | | |

**Table 18.7**: Ness County, Highpoint Township (100° Winter Wheat–Livestock) Number of Farms in Each Size Group

| Date | 1880 | 1885 | 1895 | 1905 | 1915 | 1920 | 1925 | 1930 | 1935 | 1940 |
|---|---|---|---|---|---|---|---|---|---|---|
| No. of farms | 111 | 103 | 56 | 96 | 120 | 158 | 160 | 134 | 149 | 147 |
| 1–49 acres | | | 1 | 1 | 0 | 1 | 1 | 1 | 1 | 2 |
| 50–99 | | | 0 | 0 | 1 | 3 | 1 | 2 | 1 | 4 |
| 100–174 | 96 | 81 | 27 | 29 | 6 | 13 | 13 | 6 | 17 | 16 |
| 175–259 | 1 | 4 | 0 | 2 | 5 | 7 | 7 | 5 | 4 | 4 |
| 260–499 | 12 | 7 | 26 | 42 | 69 | 85 | 78 | 80 | 78 | 77 |
| 500–999 | 2 | 5 | 2 | 17 | 22 | 39 | 49 | 34 | 35 | 35 |
| 1,000–4,999 | | 3 | | 4 | 11 | 6 | 3 | 5 | 3 | 9 |
| No data | | 3 | | 1 | 6 | 4 | 8 | 1 | 10 | |

plains country that incites forest man to denounce it as the place where one can look farther and see less than any other place in the world. First settled near the end of the nineteenth century, the normal holdings were quarters and half-sections. The decade 1895–1905 worked a readjustment into larger holdings, and then the resettlement period 1905–1915 reverted partly to nominal quarter-section farms. By 1920 the emphasis was again on sizes of three quarters and up, continuing either the livestock tradition or yielding to wheat under the influence of mechanized farming. The trend to very large holdings represented in 1940 was probably abnormal, the figures in the last three enumerations being influenced by corporation farming and the intervention of the legislature to outlaw that form of business organization in agriculture.

Some conclusions should be clear from all these samples, especially the point that was made in the introduction of this discussion. In the early and middle years for all the samples, the possible income to the operator was small, very small, irrespective of prevailing prices of farm products, except for the few large farms. Few farms, even under favorable crop conditions, could have produced much to sell. Even survival requirements placed a heavy emphasis upon management, bare subsistence, and self-denial. Only the large farms, well managed in specialized agriculture, involved a cash income large enough that wealth could be accumulated out of farming operations, over a long period of years, as distinguished from value derived from enhancement in land prices resulting from the growth of settled communities. Men possessed with that sixth sense of business management often did make their fortunes out of both farming operations and buying and selling of land, but such was not the experience of the average small

Table 18.8: Wallace County, Size of Farms (West Line Wheat–Livestock Region)
Number of Farms in Each Size Group

| Date | 1895 | | 1905 | | 1915 | | 1920 | | 1925 | | 1930 | | 1935 | | 1940 | |
|---|---|---|---|---|---|---|---|---|---|---|---|---|---|---|---|---|
| | No. | % | No. | % | No. | % | No. | % | No. | % | No. | % | No. | % | No. | % |
| No. of farms | 360 | | 246 | | 314 | | 312 | | 270 | | 387 | | 475 | | 319 | |
| 0–19 acres | 0 | .0 | 0 | .0 | 0 | .0 | 2 | 1.2 | 0 | .0 | 3 | .75 | 2 | .0 | 1 | .0 |
| 20–49 | 3 | .83 | 1 | .40 | 2 | .63 | 2 | 1.2 | 2 | .5 | 1 | .25 | 4 | | 0 | |
| 50–99 | 6 | 1.67 | 2 | .81 | 6 | 2.0 | 3 | 1.8 | 4 | 1.0 | 2 | .6 | 4 | .6 | 2 | |
| 100–174 | 273 | 75.8 | 80 | 32.5 | 133 | 42.3 | 58 | 18.6 | 40 | 10.8 | 34 | 8.8 | 48 | 10.1 | 20 | 6.2 |
| 175–259 | 2 | .55 | 3 | 1.22 | 3 | 1.0 | 10 | 3.1 | 12 | 3.2 | 11 | 2.8 | 18 | 3.8 | 11 | 3.4 |
| 260–499 | 62 | 17.2 | 52 | 21.1 | 64 | 20.4 | 86 | 27.5 | 112 | 30.2 | 100 | 25.8 | 124 | 26.0 | 67 | 21.0 |
| 500–999 | 5 | 1.4 | 34 | 13.8 | 30 | 9.5 | 57 | 18.2 | 113 | 30.6 | 121 | 31.3 | 132 | 27.8 | 88 | 27.6 |
| 1,000–4,999 | 4 | 1.1 | 41 | 16.6 | 30 | 9.5 | 56 | 18.0 | 76 | 20.6 | 86 | 22.2 | 91 | 19.1 | 111 | 34.8 |
| 5,000+ | | | 17 | 6.8 | 6 | 2.0 | 10 | 3.1 | 5 | 1.3 | 10 | 2.5 | 6 | | 11 | 3.4 |
| No data | 5 | 1.4 | 16 | 6.5 | 40 | 12.7 | 28 | 9.0 | 6 | 1.5 | 19 | 5.0 | 47 | 10.0 | 8 | 2.5 |

Note: The large number of farms deficient in acreage data diminishes the meaning of the percentage figures. An important element of disturbance was the acquisition of a large acreage by farming corporations, which underwent forced liquidation when corporation farming was outlawed in 1933.

farmer. Periodic depressions, and especially the prolonged agricultural depression after 1920, bore down with particular weight upon American agriculture because they were periods of deflation of land values when the burden of financing agriculture fell exclusively upon the income from farm production. Nothing else could do more toward clarifying the whole farm problem, historical and contemporary, than to isolate successfully those two factors in their bearing upon the agricultural situation. As the present author has pointed out elsewhere (*Winter Wheat*, 1944), irrespective of how low an income was received during the early stages of agricultural development, on the basis of capital investment there were few, if any, productive industries that were expected to yield, and which did produce, so high a rate of return as agriculture. In fact, it is a mistake to treat early American agriculture, and especially pioneer agriculture, as a capitalistic enterprise in that sense, because the farmer's principal investment was labor, not capital. That fact, kept clearly in view, tends to clarify the farm problem as twentieth-century agriculture finds itself more and more in a position where it must operate for the first time on a cost accounting, strictly capitalistic, basis as any other productive industry, and must reduce its cost of production to a point where it can compete on the world's markets on a cost basis. Furthermore, the shift of farming operations to larger farm units coincided not only with mechanization, which came only with an effective low-cost mechanical power after World War I, but it coincided closely with the high level of farmer stabilization emphasized in the farm population turnover discussion. It is not intended that this statement is to be interpreted as a cause and effect relationship, merely that the two are closely associated chronologically and that all these independent variables interact together upon the whole rural scene.

The importance of the evils and abuses agitated by the historic farmer movements, and by agricultural politics (in the whole middleman chain of services) in relation to a possible rural prosperity, has been much exaggerated. They too must be reduced to perspective among the several independent variables, and even if all such alleged evils could have been fully remedied, they could not in themselves have made the farmer prosperous. As an example, an 80-acre Kanwaka Township farmer grew for his principal crop, on the average, 24 acres of corn, yielding 30 to 40 bushels per acre, or 720 to 960 bushels. If he sold half of it for cash and was "robbed" by the middlemen of 25 per cent of a supposed just price of 40 cents per bushel, the total loss would be $36.00 to $48.00 per year. Although those sums were appreciable in the economy of the last third of the nineteenth century, they should be a warning that such income differences on his leading crop would not explain adequately the difference between farm prosperity and depression. And such an approach to the problem of the farmer in his historical setting may contribute a better comprehension of how small the operations of the small farmer really were, and why a few dollars in money meant so much to him. In overall effect, the hazards of weather on crops and prosperity were greater than the hazards of price. To ponder agriculture in this perspective brings the historian face to face with the stark realism of rural life.

# CHAPTER 19

# Land Tenure, Operator Turnover, & Farm Organization

[The standard belief among agricultural historians was that farm renters were more likely than farm owners to be "rolling stones." Malin was the first to test persistence rates among these various farm tenure types. By linking individual farm operators in the 1920 and 1935 censuses, he discovered that operators who owned and also rented land were more stable than owners only, but that renters were the least stable. Malin concluded from this finding that tenancy did not destabilize communities; on the contrary, it was an economically rational means of lessening risk and increasing profits. This original research of the early 1940s on the subject of farm tenancy stimulated several full-scale midwestern studies, such as Allan G. Bogue's *Money at Interest* (1955) and Donald Winters's *Farmers without Farms* (1978).]

In an essay on agricultural policy under the title "Mobility and History" (*Agricultural History*, 1943), the present author discussed several aspects of the land problem and of the farm from the standpoint of business organization. A rethinking of the whole land tenure problem was advocated. Table 19.1 provides data on some aspects of that matter, using land tenure statistics drawn from twenty-three sample communities used in the other population and agricultural studies. The Kansas agricultural census of 1920 listed land tenure under three heads: owner, part owner and part renter (owner-renter), and renter. The procedure used in the original study of population turnover was applied to these three classes of operators, listed according to tenure, with a view to determining the behavior of each, 1920–1935. It is not possible to determine whether or not the operators occupied the same land throughout that period, only that they remained within the same census unit-area and were therefore still a part of the same community.

The results are tabulated in table 19.1. In twenty of the twenty-three samples the owner-renters were more stable in the community (not necessarily on the same piece of land) than other forms of tenure. In seven of the twenty samples, the stability of the owner-renter was approximately twenty or more points higher in the percentage scale than the closest other type of tenure. In another seven of the twenty samples, the stability of the owner-renter was about ten points higher than the closest other type. In another six samples, although higher, the differences between the owner-renter and the other forms of tenure were slight. In respect to the owner group in seventeen of the twenty-three samples, the owners were more stable than the renters. In twelve of this seventeen the owner persistence was substantially higher than the renter, but in the other five it was slight. Put in a different form, in only twelve cases, or about 50 percent of the whole twenty-three, was there a substantial difference. On the other hand, in three samples of the twenty-three, the renters were substantially more stable than the owners, in one, more stable than either owner or owner-renter. In only two samples was the owner more stable than the owner-renter. The second major conclusion, to supplement that at the head of this paragraph, is not that the owner was more stable than the renter, but the fact revealed by the statistics that the supposedly greater stability occurred in only about 50 percent of the cases and in even those it was slight. The real point is that there was little difference in respect to community stability as between owners and renters. Again, the distinction may be emphasized that it is persistence in the community, not on the same farm, that is being measured. No records exist that would determine exactly the land occupied for the period under consideration or for any earlier period. These conclusions do not change any facts, but they do modify the approach to the problem represented by those facts.

Statistics may show what happened, but they do not explain why. In the course of examination into the problem of an explanation, the situation was submitted to farmers, bankers, and grain men. In no case was anyone aware of the owner-renter form of tenure being adopted deliberately as a matter of considered policy, but in every instance the same explanation was

**Table 19.1:** Percentage of Farm Operators of 1920 Present in 1935 in the Same Community

| Township | County | Owner-Renter | Owner | Renter |
|---|---|---|---|---|
| Center | Doniphan | 76.1 | 54.7 | 53.0 |
| Eudora | Douglas | 54.5 | 51.1 | 32.7 |
| Kanwaka | Douglas | 61.2 | 54.9 | 27.5 |
| Valley | Linn | 43.4 | 40.4 | 15.3 |
| Walnut | Brown | 70.0 | 56.6 | 51.2 |
| Agnes City | Lyon | 68.4 | 59.5 | 29.7 |
| Pike | Lyon | 51.4 | 48.4 | 36.4 |
| Reading | Lyon | 73.5 | 51.6 | 29.0 |
| Macon | Harvey | 66.6 | 57.1 | 53.7 |
| Wayne | Edwards | 81.2 | 52.6 | 41.4 |
| Big Creek | Russell | 63.3 | 52.5 | 34.0 |
| Highpoint | Ness | 51.8 | 51.0 | 36.5 |
|  | Barber | 46.6 | 37.8 | 22.2 |
| Sinclair | Jewell | 58.8 | 53.4 | 37.2 |
|  | Hamilton (whole) | 37.5 | 32.2 | 16.3 |
|  | Wallace (whole) | 56.2 | 44.3 | 12.6 |
|  | Cheyenne (4 twps.) | 56.9 | 46.7 | 29.4 |

| Township | County | Owner-Renter | Renter | Owner |
|---|---|---|---|---|
| Vinita | Kingman | 70.8 | 51.4 | 23.5 |
| Center | Decatur | 70.5 | 47.0 | 37.5 |
| Grainfield | Gove | 71.4 | 32.2 | 23.8 |

| Township | County | Owner | Owner-Renter | Renter |
|---|---|---|---|---|
| Alexandria | Leavenworth | 60.2 | 57.0 | 40.8 |
| Long Island | Phillips | 45.0 | 34.6 | 23.2 |

| Township | County | Renter | Owner-Renter | Owner |
|---|---|---|---|---|
| Walnut | Saline | 46.8 | 45.8 | 32.5 |

given, along with illustrations drawn from the community known to the commentator. It offered a flexible method of expanding or contracting operations to suit conditions. Expansion was possible by renting such additional land as would make machinery units operate to capacity and reduce unit costs, without incurring debts for purchase of additional land, with its tax and interest burdens. When conditions did not seem to warrant large operations, the lease would not be renewed, the investment risks on the additional land being carried by the owner rather than the operating farmer. It was an object lesson in business organization for bringing together into one operating unit larger amounts of capital than one man could contribute, for dividing the risks among two or more persons, and for affording opportunity for the participants to enjoy a certain diversification of investment. It calls attention to one of the conspicuous aspects in which agriculture was deficient in comparison with city business organization, but illustrates how the practices of farm operators were evolving out of experience a sounder body of business practices. In conclusion there is one defect in the data that obscures the fullest analysis of the situation. The census data did not record the amount of land owned and rented, and therefore no conclusions are possible, whether or not there was a possible optimum ratio determinable as between the owned and the rented portions.

The "actual settler" concept and the "family size" farm are in large part social myths which were more closely associated with propaganda than with history. The idea of tenantry was branded with a social stigma. There is an increasing, though not yet a very substantial, tendency to recognize that tenantry is not necessarily a mark of pathology, but to some extent at least, it is a necessary adjustment to commercial agriculture in a machine age with high capital requirements. Tenantry became a form of rural business organization in which more than one person contributed the capital and shared the risks, and as such might serve as one of several sound and desirable methods of conducting a business (Malin, 1943). Ladd Haystead, agricultural editor of *Fortune* (1945c), presented excellent case studies of tenantry under certain circumstances as a positive advantage both individually and socially.

Salter (1943) presented an important monograph on a Wisconsin township settled in the 1850s and 1860s by a highly stable population. Much of the land was passed along within the membership of the resident families. When no heirs existed, or when one heir was unable to finance the purchase of the rights of other heirs, the land had to be sold out of the family. Tenantry and mortgages were essential factors in the succession of title, either within the family or when sold out of the family, and the better the land and improvements, the more necessary were these factors in the tenure problem.

As a matter of historical development, a part of the range livestock industry came to operate on essentially an owner-renter basis, the government becoming the landlord through the medium first of the forest reserve ranges (1905) and later of the public domain ranges. The stockman owned his home ranch and grazed his livestock during a regulated season under lease upon the public range. The Bluestem Pastures of Kansas, in private ownership, occupied a somewhat similar relation to the southwestern cattlemen. So much has verbalism and the stigma of a name confused thinking that men who denounced tenantry and pledged themselves to the preservation of the family-size farm, at the same time demanded the Taylor Grazing Act and the extension of the leased grazing system of the forest reserves to the whole of the public lands—an owner-tenant system.

Along with the re-thinking on land tenure in terms of business organization is the associated problem of farm management. The present author emphasized management in his *Winter Wheat* (1944b), and Renne (1945), in reviewing the book took issue, emphasizing group action and area diversification rather than management of the individual farm. The point that Renne overlooked was that in either case the issue was management, and that he was only arguing for a particular kind of management. Again, Haystead has presented something of the management side in his *Meet the Farmers* (1944) and in *Fortune* (Haystead, 1945a, 1945b, 1945c)—not community planning, but planning for the individual farms under the direction of professional farm-managerial service. The family-size farm myth assumed tacitly that all farmers were endowed equally with managerial ability, an assumption long abandoned in connection with the industrial city factory worker. There were several possible methods of achieving division of labor in agriculture as in industry, and a number of adjustments were in evidence, but only a beginning had been made in exploring the extent and efficiencies of available alternatives.

# Selected Bibliography
# of the Works
# of James C. Malin

James C. Malin published eighteen books—two posthumously—and more than eighty articles during his long career. He also directed ninety-seven masters theses and seven doctoral dissertations at the University of Kansas. This selected bibliography lists (in alphabetical order) all of Malin's books, and the articles that pertain to his ecological interpretation of history. For a complete bibliography, readers are referred to "Appendix A—Publications of James C. Malin" in *Essays in American History in Honor of James C. Malin,* edited by Burton J. Williams (Lawrence, Kans.: Coronado Press, 1973), pp. 239–50. All the privately printed books are now marketed by Coronado Press.

## Books

*A Concern about Humanity: Notes on Reform, 1872–1912 at the National and Kansas Levels of Thought.* Lawrence, Kans.: Author, 1964.

*Confounded Rot about Napoleon: Reflections upon Science and Technology, Nationalism, World Depression of the Eighteen-Nineties and Afterwards.* Lawrence, Kans.: Author, 1961.

*The Contriving Brain and the Skillful Hand in the United States.* Lawrence, Kans.: Author, 1955.

*Doctors, Devils, and the Women: Fort Scott, Kansas, 1870–1890.* Lawrence, Kans.: Author, 1975.

*Essays on Historiography.* Lawrence, Kans.: Author, 1946.

*Grassland Historical Studies: Natural Resources Utilization in a Background of Science and Technology.* Vol. 1, *Geology and Geography.* Lawrence, Kans.: Author, 1950.

*The Grassland of North America: Prolegomena to Its History.* Lawrence, Kans.: Author, 1947. Reprints, with addenda and postscript. Gloucester, Mass.: Peter Smith, 1967.

*H. H. Sargent and Eugene F. Ware on Napoleon.* Lawrence, Kans.: Author, 1980.

*Indian Policy and Westward Expansion.* Bulletin of the University of Kansas, Humanistic Studies, vol. 2, no. 3, 1921.

*An Interpretation of Recent American History.* New York, London: Century Company, 1926.

*Ironquill—Paint Creek Essays.* Lawrence, Kans.: Coronado Press, 1972.

*John Brown and the Legend of Fifty-Six.* Philadelphia: American Philosophical Society, 1942. Reprint. Lawrence, Kans.: Coronado Press, 1961.

*The Nebraska Question, 1852–1854.* Lawrence, Kans.: Author, 1954.

*On the Nature of History: Essays about History and Dissidence.* Lawrence, Kans.: Author, 1954.

*Power and Change in Society.* Lawrence, Kans.: Coronado Press, 1981.

*The United States after the World War.* New York: Ginn & Co., 1930.

*The United States, 1865–1917: An Interpretation.* Bulletin of the University of Kansas, Humanistic Studies, vol. 3, no. 2, 1924.

*Winter Wheat in the Golden Belt of Kansas: A Study in Adaptation to Subhumid Geographical Environment.* Lawrence, Kans.: University of Kansas Press, 1944. Reprint. New York, Octagon Books, 1973.

Articles

"The Adaptation of the Agricultural System to Sub-humid Environment: Illustrated by the Activities of the Wayne Township Farmers' Club of Edwards County, Kansas, *1886–1893.*" *Agricultural History* 10, no. 3 (July 1936): 118–41.

"The Agricultural Regionalism of the Trans-Mississippi West as Delineated by Cyrus Thomas." *Agricultural History* 21 (1947): 208–17.

"Beginnings of Winter Wheat Production in Upper Kansas and Lower Smoky Hill River Valleys: A Study in Adaptation to Geographical Environment." *Kansas Historical Quarterly* 10 (1941): 227–59.

"Dust Storms, 1850–1900." *Kansas Historical Quarterly* 14 (1946): 129, 144, 265–96, 391, 413.

"Ecology and History." *Scientific Monthly* 70 (May 1950): 295–98.

"The Evolution of a Rural Community (Wayne Township, Edwards County, Kansas)," *Lewis* (Kansas) *Press,* 1, 8, 15, 22, 29 June and 6 July, 1933.

"The Grassland of North America: Its Occupance and the Challenge of Continuous Reappraisals." In *Man's Role in Changing the Face of the Earth*, edited by William L. Thomas, Jr., pp. 350–66. Chicago: University of Chicago Press, 1956.

"Grassland, 'Treeless' and 'Subhumid': A Discussion of Some Problems of the Terminology of Geography." *Geographical Review* 37 (1947): 241–50.

"The Historian and the Individual." In *Essays on Individuality*, edited by Felix Morley, pp. 146–67. Philadelphia: University of Pennsylvania Press, 1958.

"An Introduction to the History of the Bluestem-Pasture Region of Kansas: A Study in Adaptation to Geographical Environment." *Kansas Historical Quarterly* 11 (1942): 3–28.

"J. A. Walker's 'Early History of Edwards County': Introduction." *Kansas Historical Quarterly,* 9 (1940): 259–84.

"Kansas: Some Reflections on Culture Inheritance and Originality." *Journal of the Central Mississippi Valley American Studies Association* 2 (Fall 1961): 3–19.

"The Kinsley Boom of the Late Eighties." *Kansas Historical Quarterly* 4 (February and May 1935): 23–49, 164–87.

"Local Historical Studies and Population Problems." In *The Cultural Approach to History,* edited by Caroline Ware, pp. 300–307. New York: Columbia University Press, 1940.

"The Lower Missouri Valley." In *The North American Midwest: A Regional Geography,* edited by John H. Garland, pp. 218–28. New York: John Wiley and Sons, Inc., 1955.

"Man, the State of Nature, and Climax: As Illustrated by Some Problems of the North American Grassland." *Scientific Monthly* 74 (1952): 29–37.

"Mobility and History: Reflections on the Agricultural Policies of the United States in Relation to a Mechanized World." *Agricultural History* 17 (October 1943): 177–91.

"On the Nature of Local History." *Wisconsin Magazine of History* 40 (1957): 227–39.

"The Soft Winter Wheat Boom and the Agricultural Development of the Upper Kansas River Valley," parts 1–3. *Kansas Historical Quarterly* 11 (1942): 379–98; 12 (1943): 58–91; 12 (1943): 156–89.

"Soil, Animal, and Plant Relations of the Grassland, Historically Reconsidered." *Scientific Monthly* (1953): 207–20.

"Space and History: Reflections on the Closed-Space Doctrines of Turner and Mackinder and the Challenge of Those Ideas by the Air Age." *Agricultural History* 18 (April 1944): 65–74; (July 1944): 107–26.

"The Turnover of Farm Population in Kansas." *Kansas Historical Quarterly* 4 (1935): 339–72.

"Wheat, Geology, and 'Professor' Foster." *Transactions of Kansas Academy of Science* 59 (1956): 240–48.

# References

Abert, Lt. J. W. 1845. *Journal of Lt. J. W. Abert from Bent's Fort to St. Louis.* S. Ex. Doc. 438, 29th Cong., 1st sess., Pub. Doc. 477.

Adams, C. C. 1902a. "Postglacial Origin and Migrations of the Life of the Northeastern United States." *Journal of Geography* 1:303–10, 352–57.

———. 1902b. "The Southeastern United States as a Center of Geographical Distribution of Flora and Fauna." *Biological Bulletin* 3:115–31.

Aiton, A. S. 1939. "Coronado's Muster Roll." *American Historical Review* 44:556–70.

Ball, E. D. 1937. "Problem of the Range Grasshopper." *Journal of Economic Entomology* 30:904–10.

Barnes, Lela, ed. 1936. "Journal of Isaac McCoy for the Exploring Expedition of 1830." *Kansas Historical Quarterly* 5:339–77.

Beilman, A. P., and L. G. Brenner. 1951. "The Recent Intrusion of Forests in the Ozarks." *Annals of the Missouri Botanical Gardens* 38:261–82.

Bennett, H. H. 1939. *Soil Conservation.* New York.

Bidwell, P. W., and J. I. Falconer. 1925. *History of Agriculture in the Northern United States, 1620–1860.* Carnegie Institution Publication no. 358. Washington, D.C.

Borchert, John R. 1950. "The Climate of the Central North American Grassland." *Annals of the Association of North American Geographers* 40: 1–39.

Boynton, C. B., and T. B. Mason. 1855. *Journey through Kansas.* . . . Cincinnati.

Bridgman, P. W. 1927. *The Logic of Modern Physics.* New York.

Briggs, H. E. 1940. *Frontiers of the Northwest: A History of the Upper Missouri Valley.* New York.

Burlingame, M. G. 1942. *The Montana Frontier.* Helena, Mont.

Carpenter, J. R. 1936. "Concepts and Criteria for the Recognition of Communities." *Journal of Ecology* 24: 285–89.

———. 1939. "The Biome." In *Plant and Animal Communities,* edited by Theodore Just, pp. 75–91. Notre Dame, Ind.

———. 1940. "The Grassland Biome." *Ecological Monographs* 10: 617–84.

Carter, G. F. 1956. "Man in America: A Criticism of Scientific Thought." *Scientific Monthly* 73: 297–307.

Clements, F. E. 1905. *Research Methods in Ecology.* Lincoln, Neb.

———. 1907. *Plant Physiology and Ecology.* New York.

———. 1916a. *Plant Succession: An Analysis of the Development of Vegetation.* Carnegie Institution Publication no. 242. Washington, D.C.

———. 1916b. "Development and Structure of the Biome." *Abstracts of the Ecological Society of America.*

———. 1920. *Plant Indicators: The Relation of Plant Communities to Process and Practice.* Carnegie Institution Publication no. 290. Washington, D.C.

———. 1924. *The Phytometer Method in Ecology: The Plant and Community as Instruments.* Carnegie Institution Publication no. 356. Washington, D.C.

———. 1928. *Plant Succession and Indicators.* New York.

———. 1934. "The Relict Method in Dynamic Ecology." *Journal of Ecology* 22: 39–68.

———. 1936. "The Nature and Structure of the Climax." *Journal of Ecology* 24: 252–84.

———. 1938. "Climatic Cycles and Human Population in the Great Plains." *Scientific Monthly* 47: 193–210.

———. 1943. Reports on Ecological Investigations, 1914–1941. In *Yearbook of the Carnegie Institution,* no. 42. Washington, D.C.

Clements, F. E., and R. W. Chaney. 1936. *Environment and Life in the Great Plains.* Carnegie Institution Supplemental Publication, no. 24. Washington, D.C.

———. 1938. *Climatic Cycles and Human Populations in the Great Plains.* Carnegie Institution Supplemental Publication, no. 43. Washington, D.C.

Clements, F. E., and E. S. Clements. 1933. "Climate and Climax." In *Yearbook of the Carnegie Institution,* no. 32, pp. 203–5. Washington, D.C.

———. 1937. "Climate, Climax, and Succession." In *Yearbook of the Carnegie Institution,* no. 36, pp. 224–26. Washington, D.C.

———. 1938. "Climax, Succession, and Conservation." In *Yearbook of the Carnegie Institution,* no. 37, pp. 233–35. Washington, D.C.

———. 1940. "Climate, Climax, and Conservation." In *Yearbook of the Carnegie Institution,* no. 39, pp. 169–75. Washington, D.C.

_____ ."Climate, Climax, and Conservation." In *Yearbook of the Carnegie Institution,* no. 40, pp. 176–82. Washington, D.C.

Clements, F. E., and V. E. Shelford. 1927. *Concepts and Objectives in Bioecology. Yearbook of the Carnegie Institution,* no. 26. Washington, D.C.

_____ . 1939. *Bio-ecology.* New York.

Coues, Elliott, ed. 1893. *History of the Expedition under the Command of Lewis and Clark, to the Sources of the Missouri River. . . .* New York.

_____ , ed. 1895. *The Expedition of Zebulon Montgomery Pike, to Headwaters of the Mississippi River, through Louisiana Territory and in New Spain, during the Years 1805–6–7. . . .* New York.

Cowles, H. C. 1899. "The Ecological Relations of the Vegetation on the Sand Dunes of Lake Michigan." *Botanical Gazette* 27:95–391.

_____ . 1901a. "The Physiographic Ecology of Chicago and Vicinity. . . ." *Botanical Gazette* 31:73–108, 145–82.

_____ . 1901b. *The Plant Societies of Chicago and Vicinity.* Chicago.

_____ . 1911a. *Chicago Textbook of Botany.*

_____ . 1911b. "The Causes of Vegetative Cycles." *Botanical Gazette* 51:161–83. Reprint. *Annals of the Association of American Geographers* 1 (1912): 1–20.

_____ . 1928. "Persistence of Prairies." *Ecology* 9:380–82.

Cross, Major O. 1849. *A Report in the Form of a Journal, to the Quartermaster General of the March of the Regiment of Mounted Riflemen to Oregon, from May 10 to October 5, 1849.* S. Ex. Doc. 1, 32d Cong., 2d sess., Pub. Doc. 587.

Crowe, P. R. 1933. "An Analysis of Rainfall Probability." *Scottish Geographical Magazine* 49:73–91.

_____ . 1936. "The Rainfall Regime of the Western Plains." *Geographical Review* 26:463–84.

Dana, R. H., Jr. 1840. *Two Years before the Mast.* New York.

Danhof, C. H. 1944. "The Fencing Problem in the Eighteen Fifties." *Agricultural History* 18:168–86.

Dick, E. 1937. *The Sod-House Frontier, 1854–1890.* New York.

Doll, R. J. 1941. *Planning the Farm Business in the Bluestem Belt of Kansas.* Kansas Agricultural Experiment Station Bulletin no. 294.

Edwards, A. D. 1939. *Influence of Drought and Depression on a Rural Community: A Case Study in Haskell County, Kansas.* Farm Security Administration Social Science Research Report no. 7. Washington, D.C.

Elias, M. K., ed. 1945. "Symposium on Loess, 1944." *American Journal of Science* 243:225–303.

Emory, Brig. Gen. W. H. 1846. *Notes of a Military Reconnaissance from Fort Leavenworth, in Missouri, to San Diego, in California, Including Part of the Arkansas, Del Norte, and Gila Rivers, 1846, 1847.* H. Ex. Doc. 41, 30th Cong., 1st sess., Pub. Doc. 517.

Featherstonhaugh, G. W. 1835. *Geological Report of an Examination Made in 1834 of the Elevated Country between the Missouri and the Red Rivers.* H. Ex. Doc. 151, 23d Cong., 2d. sess., Pub. Doc. 274.

Febvre, L. P. W. 1925. *A Geographical Introduction to History.* New York.

Formosov, A. N. 1928. "Mammalia in the Steppe Biocensse." *Ecology* 9:449–60.

Frémont, J. C. 1843. *Report of the Exploring Expedition to the Rocky Mountains in the Year 1842.* S. Ex. Doc. 243, 27th Cong., 3d sess., Pub. Doc. 427.

————. 1845. *Report of the Exploring Expedition to Oregon and North California in the Years 1843–44.* S. Ex. Doc. 174, 28th Cong., 2d sess., Pub. Doc. 461.

Gilpin, W. 1857. "Physical Geography of Our Continent." *National Intelligencer*, 13, 15, 22 October, and 3 December.

————. 1860. *The Central Gold Regions: The Grain, Pastoral, and Gold Regions of North America.* Philadelphia and St. Louis.

————. 1870. *Notes on Colorado And Its Inscription in Physical Geography of the North American Continent.* London.

————. 1873. *The Mission of the North American People, Geographical, Social, and Political.* Philadelphia.

————. 1890. *The Cosmopolitan Railway, Compacting and Fusing together All the World's Continents.* San Francisco.

Gleason, H. A. 1909. "Some Unsolved Problems of the Prairies." *Bulletin of the Torrey Botanical Club* 36:265–71.

————. 1910. "The Vegetation of the Inland Deposits of Illinois." *Bulletin of the Illinois State Laboratory of Natural History* 9:23–174.

————. 1917. "The Structure and Development of the Plant Association." *Bulletin of the Illinois State Laboratory of Natural History* 44:463–81.

————. 1922a. "The Vegetational History of the Middle West." *Annals of the Association of American Geographers* 12:39–83.

————. 1922b. "On the Relation between Species and Area." *Ecology* 3:158–62.

————. 1925. "Species and Area." *Ecology* 6:66–74.

————. 1926. "The Individualistic Concept of the Plant Association." *Bulletin of the Torrey Botanical Club* 53:7–26.

————. 1927. "Further Views on the Succession Concept." *Ecology* 8:299–326.

————. 1939. "The Individualistic Concept of the Plant Association." In *Plant and Animal Communities,* edited by Theodore Just, pp. 92–108. Notre Dame, Ind.

Gleason, H. A., and F. C. Gates. 1912. "A Comparison of the Rates of Evaporation in Certain Associations in Central Illinois." *Botanical Gazette* 53:478–91.

Goodrich, C., et al. 1936. *Migration and Economic Opportunity.* Philadelphia.

Gordon, C. 1884. *Report on Cattle, Sheep, Swine. . . . Tenth Census of the United States (1880)*, vol. 3.

Grinnell, J. 1923. "The Burrowing Rodents of California as Agents in Soil Formation." *Journal of Mammalogy* 4:137–49.

———. 1935. "Review of the Recent Mammal Fauna of California." *University of California Publications in Zoology* 40:71–234.

Hafen, L. R., and C. C. Rister. 1941. *Western America.* New York.

Haley, J. E. E. 1936. *Charles Goodnight, Cowman and Plainsman.* Boston and New York.

Hall, E. R. 1930a. *Control of Predatory Animals.* Hearing before the Committee on Agriculture, House of Representatives, 61st Cong., 2d sess., on H.R. 9599, by Mr. Leavitt, April 29, 30, and May 1, 1930; Serial O, E. R. Hall testimony, pp. 56–66.

———. 1930b. "Predatory Mammal Destruction." *Journal of Mammalogy* 2:362–72.

Hallsted, A. L., and O. R. Mathews. 1936. "Soil Moisture and Winter Wheat, with Suggestions on Abandonment." *Kansas Agricultural Station Bulletin* no. 273.

Haven, C. T., and F. A. Belden. 1940. *A History of the Colt Revolver and the Other Arms Made by Colt's Patent Fire Arms Manufacturing Company, 1836–1940.* New York.

Hayden, F. V. 1863. "On the Geological and Natural History of the Upper Missouri [Expedition of 1857]." *Transactions of the American Philosophical Society* 12, chap. 12.

Hayes, W. P. 1927. "Prairie Insects." *Ecology* 8:238–50.

Haystead, L. 1944. *Meet the Farmers.* New York.

———. 1945a. " 'Faulknerizing' Soil." *Fortune,* January 1945, pp. 170, 172, 175.

———. 1945b. "Centralizing Might Save Family Farm." *Fortune,* May 1945, pp. 158, 160.

———. 1945c. Not All Tenants Are Jeeter Lester." *Fortune,* December 1945, pp. 190, 192.

Hayter, E. W. 1939. "Barbed Wire Fencing—A Prairie Invention: Its Rise and Influence in the Western States." *Agricultural History* 13:189–207.

———. "The Western Farmers and the Drivewell Patent." *Agricultural History* 16:16–28.

Hilgard, E. W. 1860. *Report on the Geology and Agriculture of the State of Mississippi.* Jackson, Miss.

———. 1878. "The Agriculture and Soils of California." *USDA Report,* pp. 476–507.

———. 1884. "Report on Cotton Production in the United States. . . ." In *Tenth Census of the United States (1880),* vols. 5, 6, Pub. Doc. serial nos. 2129–52. Washington, D.C.

———. 1892. "A Report on the Relation of Soil to Climate." *USDA Weather Bureau Bulletin* 3:59.

———. 1896. "Steppes, Deserts, and Alkali Lands." *Popular Science Monthly* 48:602–16.

_____. 1898. "Some Physical and Chemical Peculiarities of Arid Soils." *Proceedings of the Society for the Promotion of Agricultural Science,* pp. 70–76.

_____. 1902. "The Causes of the Development of Ancient Civilization in Arid Countries." *North American Review* 175:309–15.

_____. 1904. "Soil Management." *Science* 20:605–8.

_____. 1906a. "Some Peculiarities of Rock Weathering and Soil Formation in the Arid and Humid Regions." *American Journal of Science,* 4th ser., 171, no. 21:261–69.

_____. 1906b. *Soils: Their Formation, Properties, Composition, and Relations to Climate and Plant Growth in the Humid and Arid Regions.* New York.

Illinois Centennial Commission. 1918–20. *Centennial History of Illinois.* 6 vols. Springfield, Ill.

Johnson, W. D. 1899. "The High Plains and Their Utilization." *Twenty-first Annual Report of the U.S. Geological Survey,* part 4 (1899–1900) pp. 609–741; *Twenty-second Annual Report of the U.S. Geological Survey,* part 4 (1900–1901), (1902), pp. 635–69. Washington, D.C.

_____. 1901. "The High Plains and Their Utilization." In *Twenty-first Annual Report, United States Geological Survey,* part 4, *Hydrology,* pp. 601–768. Washington, D.C.

_____. 1902. "The High Plains and Their Utilization," 631–669 in *Twenty-second Annual Report, United States Geological Survey,* Part 4, *Hydrology.* Washington, D.C.

Jones, S. B. 1932. "Classification of North American Climates." *Economic Geography* 8:205–8.

Kearney, T. H., and H. L. Shantz. 1911. "The Water Economy of Dry Land Crops." *USDA Yearbook,* pp. 351–61.

Kendall, H. M. 1935. "Notes on Climatic Boundaries in the Eastern United States." *Geographical Review* 25:117–24.

Lackey, E. E. 1937. "Annual-Variability Rainfall Maps of the Great Plains." *Geographical Review* 27:665–70.

Larson, F. 1940. "The Role of Bison in Maintaining the Short Grass Plains." *Ecology* 21:113–21.

Mackinder, Sir H. J. 1902. *Britain and the British Seas.* London. Reprint. New York, 1914.

_____. 1904. "The Geographical Pivot of History." *Geographical Journal* 23:421–44.

_____. "Man-Power as a Measure of National and Imperial Strength." *National Review* 45:136–43.

_____. 1919. *Democratic Ideals and Reality.* Reprint. New York. 1942.

_____. 1931. "The Human Habitat." *Scottish Geographical Magazine* 47:321–35.

_____. 1943. "The Round World and the Winning of the Peace." *Foreign Affairs* 21:595–605.

Mahan, Alfred T. 1890a. *The Influence of Sea Power upon History, 1660–1783*. Boston.

———. 1890b. "The United States Looking Outward." *Atlantic Monthly* 66:816–24. Reprint. In *The Interest of America in Sea Power, Present and Future*, pp. 3–27. Boston, 1897.

———. 1895. "The Future in Relation to American Naval Power." *Harper's Magazine* 91:767–75. Reprint. In *The Interest of America in Sea Power, Present and Future*, pp. 137–72. Boston, 1897.

———. 1897. "A Twentieth-Century Outlook." *Harper's Magazine* 95:521–33. Reprint. In *The Interest of America in Sea Power, Present and Future*, pp. 217–68. Boston, 1897.

Malin, J. C. 1921. *Indian Policy and Westward Expansion*. University of Kansas Humanistic Studies, no. 2.

———. 1935a. "The Kinsley Boom of the Late Eighties." *Kansas Historical Quarterly* 4:23–49, 164–87.

———. 1935b. "The Turnover of Farm Population in Kansas." *Kansas Historical Quarterly* 4:339–72.

———. 1936. "Adaptation of the Agricultural System to Subhumid Environment: Illustrated by the Activities of the Wayne Township Farmers' Club of Edwards County, Kansas, 1886–1893." *Agricultural History* 10:118–41.

———. 1940a. "J. A. Walker's Early History of Edwards County." *Kansas Historical Quarterly* 9:259–84.

———. 1940b. "Agricultural Adaptation to the Plains." In *Dictionary of American History*, 1:22–24. New York.

———. 1940c. "Bluestem Pastures." In *Dictionary of American Agriculture*, 1:205–6. New York.

———. 1940d. "Dry-Farming." *American Agriculture*, 2:171. New York.

———. 1940e. "Local Historical Studies and Population Problems." In *The Cultural Approach to History*, edited by Caroline Ware, pp. 300–7. New York.

———. 1942a. "An Introduction to the History of the Bluestem-Pasture Region of Kansas." *Kansas Historical Quarterly* 11:3–28.

———. 1942b. *John Brown and the Legend of Fifty-Six*. Philadelphia.

———. 1943. "Mobility and History: Reflections on Agricultural Policies of the United States in Relation to a Mechanized World." *Agricultural History* 17:177–91.

———. 1944a. "Space and History: Reflections on the Closed-Space Doctrines of Turner and Mackinder and the Challenge of Those Ideas by the Air Age." *Agricultural History* 18:65–74, 107–26.

———. 1944b. *Winter Wheat in the Golden Belt of Kansas*. Lawrence: University of Kansas Press.

———. 1946. "Dust Storms, 1850–1900." *Kansas Historical Quarterly* 14:129–44, 265–96, 391–413.

————. 1947. "Grassland, 'Treeless,' and 'Subhumid.'" *Geographical Review* 37:241–50.

Marbut, C. F. 1922. "Soil Classification Report." *Annual Report of the American Association of Soil Survey Workers* 2:24–33.

————. 1923. "Soils of the Great Plains." *Annals of the Association of American Geographers* 13:41–66.

————. 1927, trans. *The Great Soil Groups of the World and Their Development,* by K. D. Glinka. Ann Arbor, Mich.

————. 1928. "A Scheme for Soil Classification." *Proceedings of the International Congress of Soil Science* 4:1–31.

————. 1936. "Soils of the United States (July 1935), part III." In *Atlas of American Agriculture.*

Marcy, R. B. 1849. *Report of Exploration and Survey of Route from Fort Smith, Arkansas, to Santa Fe, Made in 1849.* H. Ex. Doc. 45, 31st Cong., 1st sess., Pub. Doc. 577.

Marcy, Capt. R. B. 1852. *Explorations of the Red River of Louisiana in the Year 185. . . .* S. Ex. Doc. 54, 32d Cong., 2d, sess., Pub. Doc. 666.

————. 1854. *Message of the President to the United States Communicating . . . a Copy of the Report and Maps of Captain Marcy of His Explorations of the Big Wichita and the Headwaters of the Brazos Rivers, 1854.* S. Ex. Doc. 60, 34th Cong., 1st sess., Pub. Doc. 821.

Maximov, N. A. 1929. *The Plant in Relation to Water: A Study of the Physiological Basis of Drought Resistance.* London.

————. 1931. "The Physiological Significance of the Xeromorphic Structure of Plants." *Journal of Ecology* 19:273–83.

————. 1938. *Plant Physiology.* New York.

Merrill, G. P. 1924. *The First Hundred Years of American Geology.* New Haven, Conn.

Meyerhoff, H. A. 1936. "Floods and Dust Storms." *Science* 83:622.

Nicollet, I. N. 1840. *Report Intended to Illustrate a Map of the Hydrographical Basin of the Upper Mississippi. . . .* S. Ex. Doc. 237, 26th Cong., 2d sess., Pub. Doc. 380.

Oliphant, J. O. 1932a. "Winter Losses of Cattle in the Oregon Country, 1847–1890." *Washington Historical Quarterly* 23:3–17.

————. 1932b. "The Cattle Trade from the Northwest of Montana." *Agricultural History* 6:69–83.

————. 1946. "The Eastward Movement of Cattle from the Oregon Country." *Agricultural History* 20:19–43.

Osgood, E. S. 1929. *The Day of the Cattleman.* Minneapolis, Minn.

Park, R. E. 1915. "The City: Suggestions for the Investigation of Human Behavior in City Environment." *American Journal of Sociology* 20:577–612.

————. 1929. "Urbanization as Measured by Newspaper Circulation." *American Journal of Sociology* 35:60–79.

————. 1936. "Human Ecology." *American Journal of Sociology* 42:1–15.

————. 1939a. "Symbiosis and Socialization: A Frame of Reference for the Study of Society." *American Journal of Sociology* 45:1–25.

————. 1939b. *An Outline for the Principles of Sociology.* New York.

Paxson, F. L. 1930. *When the West Is Gone.* New York.

Person, H. S. 1936. *Little Waters: A Study of Headwater Streams and Other Little Waters: Their Use and Relations to the Land.* Washington, D.C.

Peterson, E. T. 1942. *Forward to the Land.* Norman, Okla.

Poggi, E. M. 1934. *The Prairie Province of Illinois: A Study of Human Adjustment to the Natural Environment.* Urbana, Ill.

Powell, J. W. 1878. *Report on the Lands of the Arid Region of the United States, with a More Detailed Account of the Lands of Utah.* Washington: Government Printing Office.

————. 1890. "Institutions for the Arid Lands." *Century* 18:111–16.

————. 1895. *Physiographic Regions of the United States.* New York.

————. 1896. *The Physiography of the United States.* New York.

President's Committee. 1937. *Report on Farm Tenancy.* Washington,. D.C.

Raup, H. M. 1941. "Botanical Problems in Boreal America." *Botanical Review* 7:147–247.

Renne, R. R. 1945. Review of *Winter Wheat in the Golden Belt of Kansas,* by James C. Malin. *Journal of Land and Public Utility Economics* 21:84–86.

Richardson, A. D. 1867. *Beyond the Mississippi from the Great River to the Great Ocean, Life and Adventure on the Prairies, Mountains, and Pacific Coast, . . . 1857–1867.* Hartford, Conn.

Richardson, R. N. 1943. *Texas, the Lone Star State.* New York.

Robinson, Charles. 1959. "Letters to the Editor." *Lawrence* (Kans.) *Herald of Freedom,* 7 May.

Rodgers, A. D., III. 1942. *John Torrey: A Story of North American Botany.* Princeton, N.J.

Rockefeller Foundation. 1942a. *Proceedings, Conference on the Great Plains Area, April 17–18, 1942, New York City, under the Auspices of the Rockefeller Foundation.* New York. Mimeographed.

————. 1942b. *Conference on the Northern Plains, June 25–27, 1942, Lincoln, Nebraska.* Transcript of discussions held under the auspices of the Rockefeller Foundation. New York. Mimeographed.

Russell, R. J. 1926. "Climates of California." *University of California Publications in Geography* 2:73–84.

————. 1931. "Dry Climates of the United States, I: Climatic Map." *University of California Publications in Geography* 5:1–41.

————. 1932. "Dry Climates of the United States, II: Frequency of Dry and Desert Years, 1901–1920." *University of California Publications in Geography* 5:245–74.

————. 1934. "Climate Years." *Geographical Review* 24: 92–103.

———. 1941. *Climatic Change Through the Ages. USDA Yearbook.*

———. 1945. "Climates of Texas." *Annals of the Association of American Geographers* 35: 37–52.

Salter, L. A., Jr. 1943a. "Farm Prosperity and Agricultural Policy. *Journal of Political Economy* 51:13–22.

———. 1943b. *Land Tenure in Process: A Study of Farm Ownership and Tenancy in a Lafayette County (Wisconsin) Township. Research Bulletin of the Wisconsin Agricultural Experiment Station* no. 146.

Sauer, C. O. 1916. "Geography of the Upper Illinois Valley and History of Development." *Illinois State Geological Survey.*

———. 1927. "Recent Developments in Cultural Geography." In *Recent Developments in the Social Sciences,* edited by E. C. Hayes, chap. 4. Philadelphia.

———. 1941. "Foreword to Historical Geography." *Annals of the Association of American Geographers* 31:1–24.

———. 1944. "A Geographic Sketch of Early Man in America." *Geographical Review* 34:528–73.

Sears, P. B. 1935. *Deserts on the March.* Norman, Okla.

———. 1936. "Floods and Dust Storms." *Science* 83:9.

Seltzer, F. M. 1940. "Archeological Perspective in the Northern Mississippi Valley." *Smithsonian Miscellaneous Collection* 100:253–90.

Shaler, N. S. 1883. "Improvement of the Native Pasture-Lands of the Far West." *Science* 1:186–87.

———. 1884a. "Physiography of North America." In *Narrative and Critical History of North America,* ed. Justin Winsor, vol. 4, chap. 1, introduction.

———. 1884b. *A First Book of Geology.* Boston.

———. 1886. *Kentucky: A Pioneer Commonwealth.* Boston.

———. 1888a. "Introduction to Richard A. F. Penrose, Jr., Nature and Origin of Deposits of Phosphate of Lime." *U. S. Geological Survey Bulletin* 46.

———. 1888b. "Animal Agency in Soil Working." *Popular Science Monthly* 32:484–87.

———. 1889a. "Chance or Design." *Andover Review,* pp. 1–17.

———. 1889b. *Aspects of the Earth: A Popular Account of Some Familiar Geological Phenomena.* New York.

———. 1891a. *The Story of Our Continent.* Boston.

———. 1891b. *Nature and Man in America.* New York.

———. 1892. "The Origin and Nature of Soils." *Twelfth Report of U. S. Geological Survey,* part 1, pp. 219–345.

Shannon, F. A. 1940. *An Appraisal of Walter Prescott Webb's "The Great Plains: A Study in Institutions and Environment."* Critiques of Research in the Social Sciences 3. Social Science Research Council, New York.

———. 1945. *The Farmers' Last Frontier, 1865–1900.* New York.

Shantz, H. L. 1911. "Natural Vegetation as an Indicator of the Capabilities of Land for Crop Production in the Great Plains Region." *USDA Bureau of Plant Industry Bulletin* 201:1–100.

———. 1923. "The Natural Vegetation of the Great Plains Region." *Annals of the Association of American Geographers* 13:81–108.

———. 1927. "Drought Resistance and Soil Moisture." *Ecology* 8:145–57.

———. 1938. "Plants as Soil Indicators." *USDA Yearbook,* pp. 835–60.

———. 1940. "The Relation of Plant Ecology to Human Welfare." *Ecological Monographs* 10:311–42.

———. 1945. "Frederic Edward Clements." *Ecology* 26:317–19.

Shelford, V. E. 1940. "Deciduous Forest Man in the Grassland of North America." *Proceedings of the Eighth American Scientific Congress,* vol. 9, *History and Government,* Washington, D.C.

———. 1944. "Deciduous Forest Man and the Grassland Fauna." *Science* 100:135–40, 160–62.

Shreve, F. 1910. "The Rate of Establishment of Giant Cactus." *Plant World* 13:235–40.

———. 1911. "Establishment Behavior of the Palo Verde." *Plant World* 14:289–96.

———. 1929. "Changes in Desert Vegetation." *Ecology* 10:364–73.

———. 1934a. "Rainfall, Runoff, and Soil Moisture under Desert Conditions." *Annals of the Association of American Geographers* 24:131–56.

———. 1934b. "Problems of the Desert." *Scientific Monthly* 38:195–209.

———. 1934c. "Vegetation of the Northwestern Coast of Mexico." *Torrey Botanical Club Bulletin* 61:373–80.

———. 1936. "Plant Life of the Sonoran Desert." *Scientific Monthly* 42:195–213.

———. 1937. "Lowland Vegetation of Sinaloa." *Torrey Botanical Club Bulletin* 64:605–13.

———. 1942. "The Desert Vegetation of North America." *Botanical Review* 8:195–246.

Shreve, F., and A. Hinckley. 1937. "Thirty Years of Change in Desert Vegetation." *Ecology* 18:463–78.

Simpson, Lt. J. H. 1849a. *Report and Map [4 maps] of the Route from Fort Smith, Arkansas, to Santa Fe, New Mexico, 1849.* S. Ex. Doc. 12, 31st Cong., 1st sess., Pub. Doc. 554.

———. 1849b. *Report of Exploration and Survey of Route from Fort Smith, Arkansas, to Santa Fe, New Mexico, Made in 1849.* H. Ex. Doc. 45, 31st Cong., 1st sess., Pub. Doc 577.

Smith, W. O. 1943. *The Sharps Rifle: Its History, Development, and Operation.* New York.

Steward, J. H. 1940. "Native Cultures of the Intermontane (Great Basin) Area." *Smithsonian Miscellaneous Collection* 100:445–502.

Strong, Josiah. 1885. *Our Country: Its Possible Future and Its Present Crisis.* New York: Baker and Taylor Co.

———. 1900. *Expansion under New World Conditions.*

Strong, W. D. 1940. "From History to Prehistory in the Northern Great Plains." *Smithsonian Miscellaneous Collection* 100:353–94.

Sumner, F. B. 1925. "Some Biological Problems of Our Southwestern Deserts." *Ecology* 6:352–71.

Swallow, G. 1866. *Preliminary Report of the Geological Survey of Kansas.* Lawrence, Kans.

Tanner, A. M. 1892, 1893. "Communications on Barbed Wire Patents." *Scientific American* 67:313, 68:283.

Thornthwaite, C. W. 1931. "The Climates of North America according to a New Classification. *Geographical Review* 21:633–55.

———. 1933. "The Climates of the Earth." *Geographical Review* 23:433–40.

———. 1934. *Internal Migration in the United States.* Philadelphia.

———. 1940. "Atmospheric Moisture in Relation to Ecological Problems." *Ecology* 21:17–28.

———. 1941. *Atlas of Climatic Types in the United States, 1900–1930.* USDA Miscellaneous Publications, no. 421.

Torrey, J. 1953. *Plantae Frémontianae.* Smithsonian Institution Publication no. 46.

Towne, C. W., and E. N. Wentworth. 1945. *Shepherd's Empire.* Norman, Okla.

Transeau, E. N. 1903. "On the Geographical Distribution and Ecological Relations of the Bog-Plant Societies of Northern North America." *Botanical Gazette* 36:401–20.

———. 1905. "Forest Centers of Eastern America." *American Naturalist* 39:875–89.

———. 1908. "The Relation of Plant Societies to Evaporation." *Botanical Gazette* 45:217–31.

———. 1909. "The Point of View in Vegetation Problems Involving Climate." *Plant World* 12:102–4.

———. 1929. "Progress in the Survey of the Vegetational Types of the North Central States." *Annals of the Association of American Geographers* 20:45.

———. 1930. "Precipitation Types of the Prairies and Forested Regions of the Central States." *Annals of the Association of American Geographers* 20:44–45.

———. 1935. "The Prairie Peninsula." *Ecology* 16:423–37.

Turner, F. J. 1893. "The Significance of the Frontier in American History." In *The Frontier in American History,* edited by F. J. Turner, pp. 1–38. New York, 1920.

———. 1932. "The Significance of the Section in American History." In *The Significance of Sections in American History,* edited by F. J. Turner. New York.

USDA *Yearbook.* 1938. *Soils and Men.*

USDA *Yearbook.* 1941. *Climate and Man.*

Van Royan, W. 1937. "Prehistoric Droughts in the Central Great Plains." *Geographical Review* 27:637–50.

Vestal, A. G. 1913a. "An Associational Study of Illinois Sand Prairie." *Bulletin of the Illinois State Laboratory of Natural History* 10:1–96.

———. 1913b. "Local Distribution of Grasshoppers in Relation to Plant Associations." *Biological Bulletin* 25:141–80.

———. 1931. "Strategic Habitats and Communities in Illinois." *Transactions of the Illinois Academy of Science* 24:80–85.

Warren, G. K. 1859. "Preliminary Report of Explorations in Nebraska and Dakota." *American Journal of Science* 77:378–80.

Warren, L. 1926. *Lincoln's Parentage and Childhood.* New York.

Weaver, J. E., and F. W. Albertson. 1936. "Effects of the Great Drought on the Prairies of Iowa, Nebraska, and Kansas." *Ecology* 17:567–639.

———. 1939. "Major Changes in Grassland as a Result of Continued Drought." *Botanical Gazette* 100:576–91.

———. 1940a. "Deterioration of Midwestern Ranges." *Ecology* 21:216–36.

———. 1940b. "Deterioration of Grassland from Stability to Denudation with Decrease in Soil Moisture." *Botanical Gazette* 101:598–624.

———. 1943. "Resurvey of Grasses, Forbs, and Underground Plant Parts at the End of the Great Drought." *Ecological Monographs* 13:63–117.

———. 1944. "Nature and Degree of Recovery of Grassland from the Great Drought of 1933 to 1940." *Ecological Monographs* 14:393–479.

Weaver, J. E., and W. E. Bruner. 1927. *Root Development of Vegetable Crops.* New York.

———. 1945. "A Seven-Year Quantitative Study of Succession in the Grassland." *Ecological Monographs* 15:297–319.

Weaver, J. E., and F. E. Clements. 1929. *Plant Ecology.* 1st ed. New York.

———. 1938. *Plant Ecology.* 2d ed. New York.

Weaver, J. E., and J. W. Crest. 1924. "Direct Measurement of Water-Loss from Vegetation without Disturbing the Normal Structure of the Soil." *Ecology* 5:153–70.

Weaver, J. E., and R. W. Darland. 1944. "Grassland Patterns in 1940." *Ecology* 25:202–15.

Weaver, J. E., and T. J. Fitzpatrick. 1932. "Ecology and Relative Importance of the Dominants of Tall-Grass Prairie." *Botanical Gazette* 93:113–50.

———. 1934. "The Prairie." *Ecological Monographs* 4:109–295.

Webb, W. P. 1931. *The Great Plains.* Boston.

Wedel, W. R. 1940. "Culture Sequence in the Central Great Plains." *Smithsonian Miscellaneous Collection* 100:291–352.

———. 1941. "Environment and Native Subsistence Economies in the Central Great Plains." *Smithsonian Miscellaneous Collection* 101:1–29.

_____. 1947. "Prehistory and Environment in the Central Great Plains." *Transactions of the Kansas Academy of Science* 50:1–18.

Wentworth, E. N. 1942. "Eastward Sheep Drives from California and Oregon." *Mississippi Valley Historical Review* 28:507–38.

Whittlesey, D. 1935. "The Impress of Effective Central Authority upon Landscape." *Annals of the Association of American Geographers* 25:85–97.

_____. 1936. "Major Agricultural Regions of the Earth." *Annals of the Association of American Geographers* 26:199–240. The bibliographies incorporated into this monograph are invaluable.

_____. 1939. *The Earth and the State: A Study of Political Geography.* New York. Reprint. 1944.

_____. 1945. "The Horizon of Geography." *Annals of the Association of American Geographers* 35:1–36.

Wislizenus, Dr. F. 1912. *A Journey to the Rocky Mountains in the Year 1839.* St. Louis.

_____. 1848. *Memoir of a Tour to Northern Mexico . . . , with a Scientific Appendix and Three Maps.* S. Misc. Doc. 26, 30th Cong., 1st sess., Pub. Doc. 511.

# Acknowledgments

The editor wishes to thank the following persons, publishers, and organizations for permission to reprint the following copyrighted material.

"The Grassland of North America: Its Occupance and the Challenge of Continuous Reappraisals," reprinted from *Man's Role in Changing the Face of the Earth,* W. L. Thomas, Editor, copyright 1956 by the University of Chicago Press, by permission of the Wenner-Gren Foundation for Anthropological Research, Inc., New York, and the University of Chicago Press.

"Grassland, 'Treeless,' and 'Subhumid': A Discussion of Some Problems of the Terminology of Geography," reprinted from *Geographical Review,* vol. 37 (1947), by permission of the American Geographical Society.

"Factors in Grassland Equilibrium," "Webb and Regionalism," "On the Nature of the History of Geographical Area, with Special Reference to the Western United States," "Methodology for History of Social Change: Population Studies," "Agricultural Studies," and "Land Tenure, Operator Turnover, and Farm Organization," reprinted from *The Grassland of North America: Prolegomena to Its History, with Addenda and Postscript* (1967), by permission of Pearl E. Malin.

"Space and History: Reflections on the Closed-Space Doctrines of Turner and Mackinder," reprinted from *Agricultural History,* vol. 18 (1947); and "The Adaptation of the Agricultural System to Subhumid Environment: Illustrated by the Activities of the Wayne Township Farmers' Club of Edwards County,. Kansas,

1886–1893," reprinted from *Agricultural History,* vol. 10 (1936), by permission of the Agricultural History Society and Pearl E. Malin.

"Ecology and History," reprinted from *Scientific Monthly* 70 (May 1950): 295–98; and "Man, the State of Nature, and Climax: As Illustrated by Some Problems of the North American Grassland," reprinted from *Scientific Monthly* 73 (January 1952): 29–37, by permission of the American Association for the Advancement of Science.

"An Introduction to the History of the Bluestem-Pasture Region of Kansas: A Study in Adaptation to Geographical Environment," reprinted from the *Kansas Historical Quarterly,* vol. 11 (1942); "The Turnover of Farm Population in Kansas," reprinted from the *Kansas Historical Quarterly,* vol. 4 (1935); and "Introduction to J. A. Walker's Early History of Edwards County," reprinted from the *Kansas Historical Quarterly,* vol. 9 (1940), by permission of the Kansas State Historical Society.

"Rural Life and Subhumid Environment during the Decade of the Seventies: 'The Clean Shirt and Good Living,'" reprinted by permission from James C. Malin, *Winter Wheat in the Golden Belt of Kansas: A Study in Adaptation to Subhumid Geographical Environment,* copyright 1944 by the University Press of Kansas.

"The Lower Missouri Valley," reprinted from *The North American Midwest: A Regional Geography,* edited by John H. Garland (1955), by permission of John Wiley & Sons, Inc.

"Kansas: Some Reflections on Culture Inheritance and Originality," reprinted from *The Journal of the Central Mississippi Valley American Studies Association (American Studies),* Fall 1961, pages 3–19, © Midcontinent American Studies Association, 1983.

"Local Historical Studies and Population Problems," reprinted from *The Cultural Approach to History,* edited by Caroline F. Ware (1940), by permission of Columbia University Press.

# Index